MAGDALENA ABAKANOWICZ

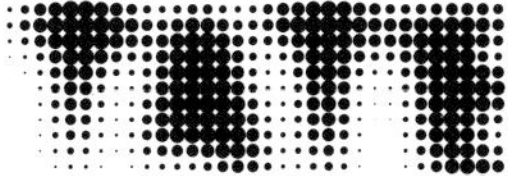

Edited by Ann Coxon and Mary Jane Jacob

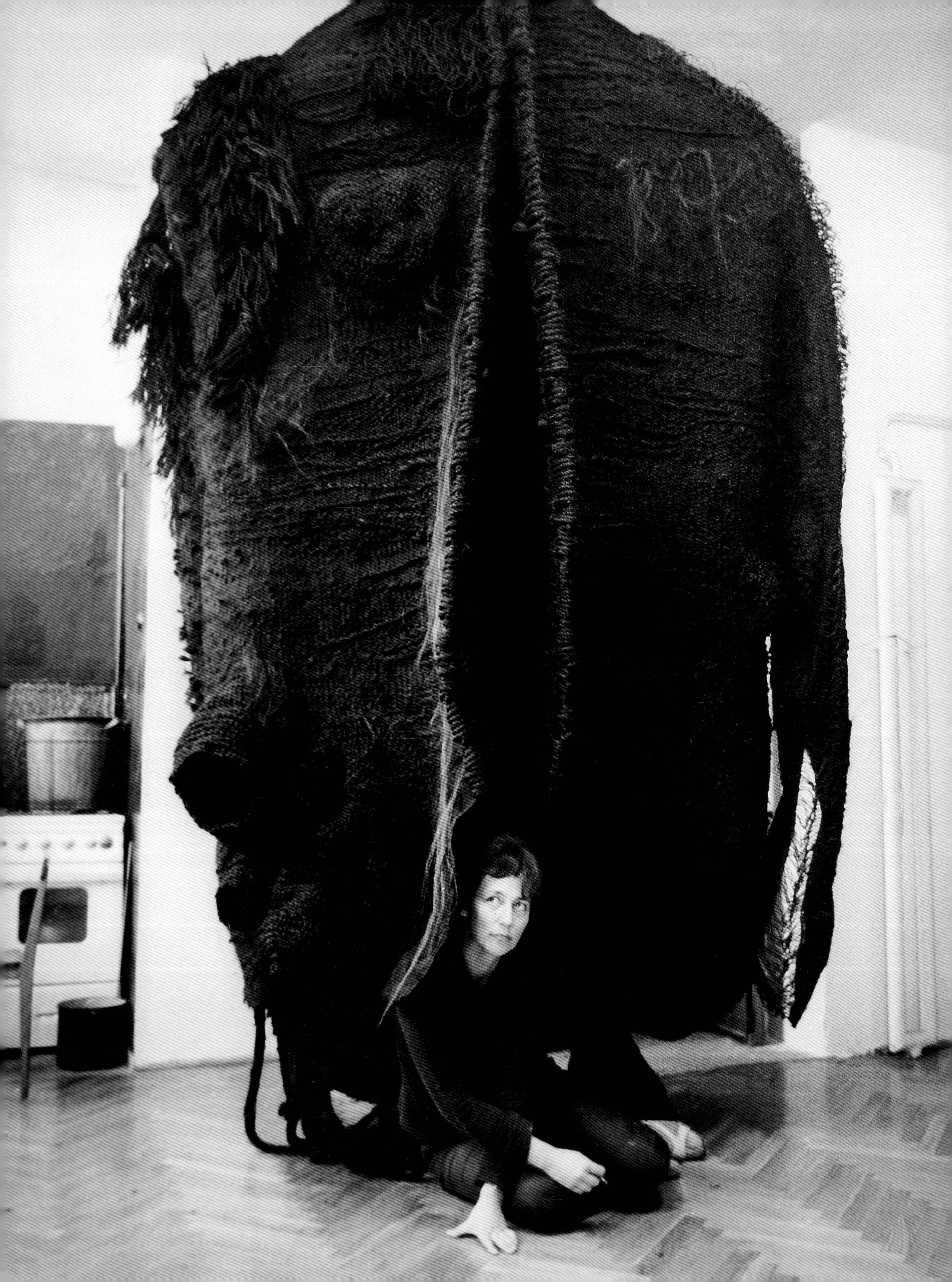

CONTENTS

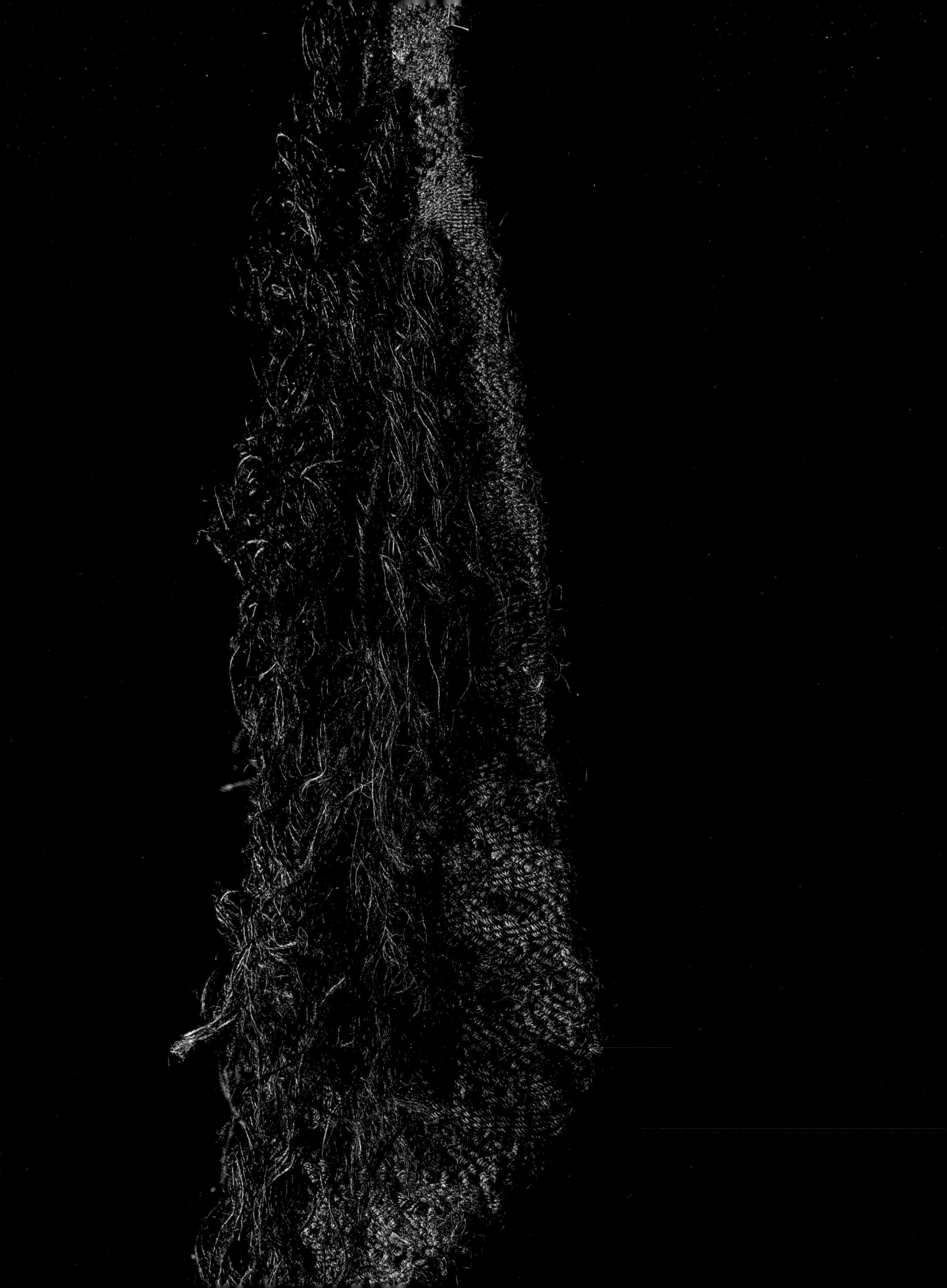

FOREWORD

There are few artists whose career includes a distinct body of work so significant in scale and ambition; so radical in effect; and so rich in meaning that it provides fertile ground for the presentation of a large-scale and focused exhibition enabling new perspectives on both their work and its place within broader histories of art. Fifty years after their creation, the re-examination of Magdalena Abakanowicz's *Abakans* seems both necessary and urgent.

Deriving their name from the artist's own family name, the *Abakans* astounded and confused critics when they were first presented in the late 1960s. What exactly are these curious woven forms that seem to defy categorisation as either sculpture or tapestry; as art or craft? Much of the existing literature about Abakanowicz paints the picture of a lone pioneer, a unique figure battling against harsh personal and political circumstances to give voice and shape to a set of inner beliefs. While this characterisation is grounded in certain truths, it limits our understanding of her significance within and contribution to twentieth-century art history.

Each of our institutions supported the artist at different stages of her career and was instrumental in locating her practice within the broader art histories of the late twentieth century. Abakanowicz made her name at the 1st International Tapestry Biennial in Lausanne in 1962, and she was at the forefront of the New Tapestry or Fiber Art movement, as it later became known in the US. With the support of Pierre and Alice Pauli, she exhibited widely throughout the 1960s and 1970s, holding a landmark monographic exhibition at Henie Onstad Art Centre, Norway, in 1977. By this time her work had expanded in ambition and she saw her installations as 'environments', combining trailing ropes and other found elements alongside her woven forms.

When a small number of key works by Abakanowicz came into Tate's collection in 2009, *Abakan Red* 1969 and *Abakan Orange* 1971 were shown within a suite of galleries exploring parallel developments from the US and Western Europe. These two *Abakans* were – perhaps for the first time – seen alongside works by Bruce Nauman, Louise Bourgeois and others associated with North American post-minimalism; as well as works by arte povera or process artists such as Jannis Kounellis, Marisa Merz and Robert Morris.

Abakan Red had already been included in the exhibition *WACK: Art and the Feminist Revolution* which toured in the US in 2007–8. In that context, the monumental, woven, labial forms became emblematic of the feminist struggle to create a bold and unapologetic artistic language reflecting and encompassing what it meant to be both a woman and an artist. But Abakanowicz did not identify as a feminist, preferring to speak of what was fundamentally human and universal. Since its showing at Tate Modern, *Abakan Red* has been lent to international exhibitions as far afield as Hangzhou, China, and as close as Aubusson, France. In all of these contexts, the work has caught the attention of diverse publics, as well as younger generations of artists and curators who no longer feel bound by the restrictive definitions of art and craft or sculpture and textile that troubled their predecessors. It seems that we are now able, finally, to look at the *Abakans* with clear vision, to encounter them 'in person', unencumbered by the heavy baggage of artistic hierarchies or geopolitical divisions.

We have been extremely fortunate in benefitting from the curatorial intelligence, energy and experience of Mary Jane Jacob, who has shaped the exhibition and this accompanying publication. She has worked closely alongside Ann Coxon, Curator at Tate Modern, who brings to the project her own interest in textile-based practice of the period.

We are enormously grateful to the Abakanowicz Arts and Culture Charitable Foundation for its generous support towards this exhibition, without which it would not have been possible. We would also like to extend our gratitude to the Magdalena Abakanowicz Exhibition Supporters Circle, including the Polish Cultural Institute in London, and Tate International Council, Tate Patrons and Tate Members.

The exhibition has also been made possible by the provision of insurance through the Government Indemnity Scheme, and we thank HM Government for providing this, and the Department for Digital, Culture, Media and Sport and Arts Council England for arranging the indemnity.

Finally, we express our generous thanks to the Fundacja Marty Magdaleny Abakanowicz Kosmowskiej i Jana Kosmowskiego in Warsaw.

Frances Morris, Director, Tate Modern

Giselle Eberhard Cotton, Director, Fondation Toms Pauli, and Bernard Fibicher, Director, Musée cantonal des Beaux-Arts de Lausanne/Plateforme 10

Tone Hansen, Director, Henie Onstad Art Centre

ACKNOWLEDGEMENTS

So much has changed since we began to discuss the possibility of creating a large-scale, touring exhibition focusing on the remarkable career of Magdalena Abakanowicz. The exhibition was due to open at Tate Modern on the ninetieth anniversary of Abakanowicz's birth in June 2020, yet a global pandemic meant inevitable delay. The extra time has allowed for greater reflection and richer conversations around the artist's work during a period of intense social, political and environmental pressure and transformation. Though her *Abakans* were created behind the 'Iron Curtain', Abakanowicz saw herself as an international artist. Her chief concerns resonate not only with the radical ideas of the late 1960s (the period in which they were made), but also with many of the global issues we are facing today. When resources were limited, Abakanowicz made her artistic statement using materials available to her: plant and animal fibres. Her woven forms and environments still confront us with their material and metaphorical possibilities and remind us that we are all 'fibrous structures' belonging to larger eco-systems, and subject to biological evolution as well as the man-made catastrophes of war and political oppression. We hope that in bringing together this 'forest' of *Abakans*, this exhibition will both inspire and delight.

We hold in our hearts and minds those who are no longer with us to celebrate the exhibition's completion. We would like to dedicate this publication to Dr Achim Borchardt-Hume, our former Director of Exhibitions and Programme, who guided the exhibition process in the early stages of its development and who believed that exhibitions should tell a number of stories. His wisdom and professionalism will continue to inspire us for years to come. We also remember Alice Pauli, Abakanowicz's lifelong friend and supporter.

The exhibition would not, of course, have been possible without the guidance and support of the Fundacja Marty Magdaleny Abakanowicz Kosmowskiej i Jana Kosmowskiego in Warsaw. We are extremely grateful to the Board, notably Magdalena Grabowska and Tomasz Piątkowski for their cooperation and loans to the exhibition, as well as the artist's long-time assistant Stefanią Zgudką for her insight, as they continue their dedication to the artist's legacy.

We are also most grateful to the National Museum in Wrocław, Poland, for generously lending a number of works to the exhibition. As told here by the Head of the Four Domes Pavilion Iwona Dorota Bigos, a trusted friendship between the artist and former director Mariusz Hermansdorfer led to the museum's acquisition of some fifty works dating from 1967 to 2008. In addition, the exhibition has benefitted greatly from the support of the following museums, institutions and individuals who have kindly loaned works: The Andrzej Wawrzyniak Asia and Pacific Museum in Warsaw, Poland; Art collection of the city of Biel-Bienne, Switzerland; ASOM Collection; Central Museum of Textiles in Łódź; Collection of Cezary Lisowski, Design Archives Foundation; Collection Stedelijk Museum Amsterdam; Fondation Toms Pauli, Lausanne; Grażyna Kulczyk Collection; Harkey Family Collection, Dallas, Texas; Henie Onstad Collection; Marlborough Gallery, New York; Musée des beaux-arts, La Chaux-de-Fonds; Museum of the Central Pomerania in Słupsk; Muzeum Sztuki, Łódź; Nationalmuseum, Stockholm; National Museum in Poznań; Röhsska museet, Göteborg; WFO (Wytwórnia Filmów Oświatowych); and all those who wish to remain anonymous.

The exhibition opens at Tate Modern before touring to the Fondation Toms Pauli at the Musée cantonal des Beaux-Arts de Lausanne/Plateforme 10, Lausanne, and Henie Onstad Art Centre, Høvikodden. It is fitting that the artist's work from this period should be an exhibition in the town in which she made her name at the prestigious International Tapestry Biennial in Lausanne, and under the visionary leadership of Pierre and Alice Pauli, and also, in Norway at a museum in which she presented one of her most important solo exhibitions in the 1970s. The collection of the Fondation Toms Pauli offers the chance for its curator Magali Junet to look deeply at the artist's works on paper, some of which are included in this exhibition, in addition to some of the collection's sculptural works. We are extremely thankful to Giselle Eberhard Cotton, Director of the Fondation Toms Pauli, and to Bernard Fibicher, Director of the Musée cantonal des Beaux-Arts/Platforme 10. At Henie Onstad, we are grateful to Tone Hansen, Director, and Caroline Ugelstad, Chief Curator, for their enthusiasm to present the exhibition in Høvikodden, where Abakanowicz showed her works in 1977 (as outlined in Ugelstad's contributing text).

In addition to those acknowledged above, this book brings together a range of voices shedding new light on various aspects of Abakanowicz's life and work beyond the possibilities of the exhibition. We extend our gratitude to the following authors for their illuminating perspectives: Dina Akhmadeeva, Michał Jachuła, Marta Kowalewska, Clare Lilley, Magdalena Moskalewicz and Gabi Scardi. In addition to her perceptive text, we wish to thank Dina Akhmadeeva, Assistant Curator, International Art, for her input throughout all stages of the exhibition planning process, as well as Exhibition Assistants Beatriz Garcia-Velasco and Emma Jones for their invaluable support, and Curatorial interns Anastasia Pineschi and Anastasia Kolomiets for their excellent assistance.

The exhibition occasioned a thorough review of the literature on the artist which was skilfully undertaken by Jenny Dally (Curatorial Assistant, Painting and Sculpture at the San Francisco Museum of Modern Art) when a graduate student at the School of the Art Institute of Chicago. Her authoritative study is not only comprehensive, but has already proven to offer insights with potential for future scholarship, as reflected in her contribution of a chronology of the artist's life and career.

In addition we would like to thank the following: Runa Boger, Marjan Boot, Jolanta Gola, Zuzanna Grzeszek, Janis Jeffries, Narelle Jubelin, Patricia Leighton, Russell Lewis, Walter Osika, Jasia Reichardt, Merete Røstad, Jan Suffczyński and Anne Wilson. We are also deeply indebted to Norbert Piwowarczyk, who brilliantly captured the essence of the *Abakans* through his beautiful photography.

The experience of a great number of colleagues navigated the exhibition towards realisation. We must express our immense gratitude to them all. In particular, Frances Morris, Director, Rachel Kent, Head of Programme, and Neil Casey, Head of Business and Operations, championed the exhibition, giving astute advice particularly during the unprecedented challenges of the global pandemic. Carol Burnier Magno deftly oversaw the transport of works with great care. The exhibition's design came together through the vision of Phil Monk, Senior Design and Production Manager, and its production and installation was capably overseen by Richard Install. For their work on this accompanying publication, we are grateful to the tireless efforts of Emma Poulter, Senior Editor at Tate Publishing, Emma O'Neill, for her picture research, and Bill Jones and Elizabeth Stanton for its production. The book's elegant design is thanks to the skilful work of Astrid Stavro, Sara Martin and Alessandro Molent.

Ann Coxon and Mary Jane Jacob
Curators

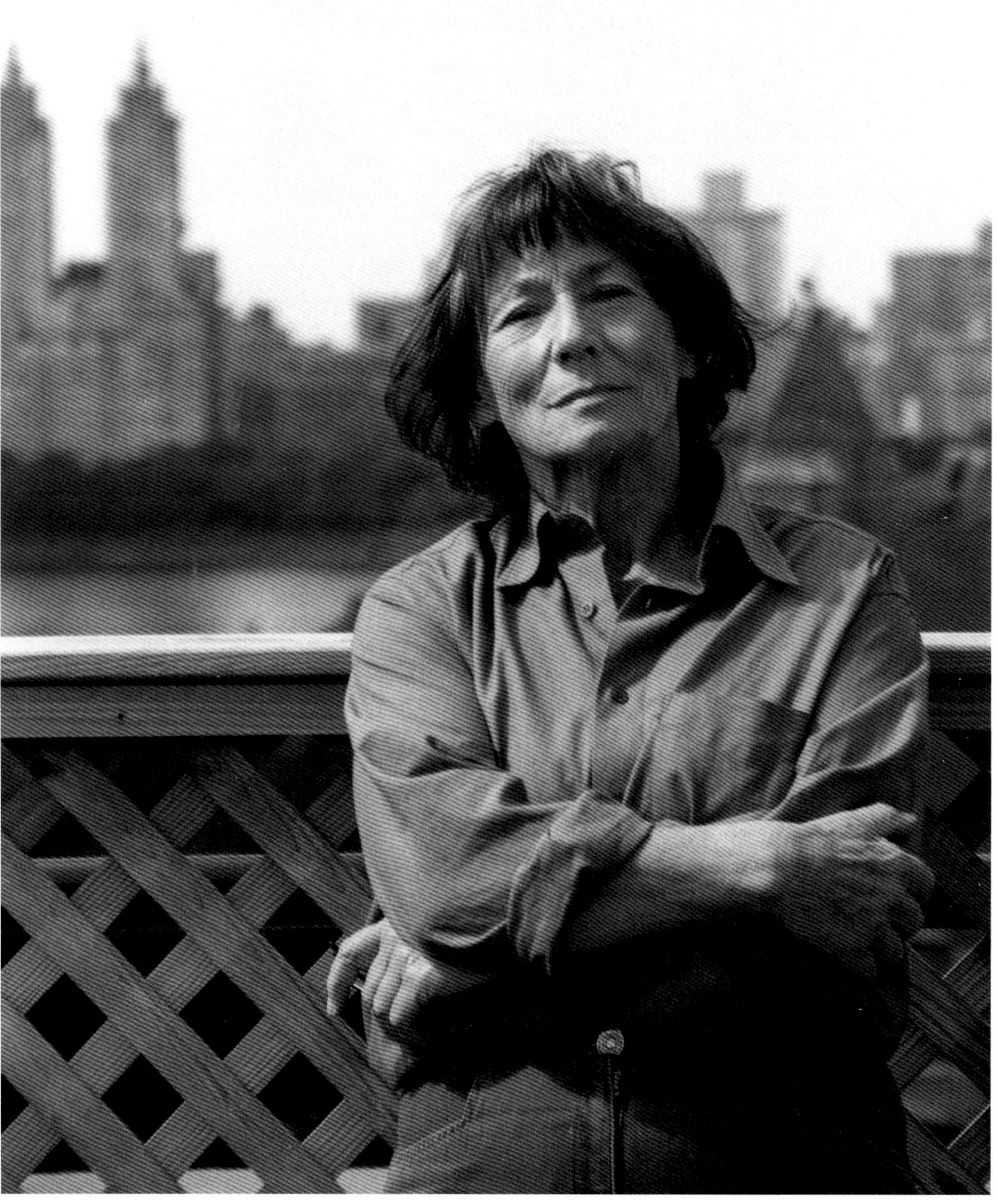

MARY JANE JACOB

THE ARTIST THE PERSON

Magdalena Abakanowicz always put great stock in words: speaking seven languages to connect with others in their own tongue, valuing the tradition of letter writing, and expressing her ideas and feelings as precisely as she could. Here are some of the artist's words, which go some way towards characterising her exceptional nature.

Family

Abakanowicz kept her family history close, wearing her father's signet ring all her adult life and safeguarding what remained of her mother's jewellery from another era. Once she had a proper home of her own, she sought to incorporate aspects of the atmosphere in which she grew up.

She adopted students and others, offering motherly guidance:

> *You have to create such conditions which can be the basis, the trampoline for overcoming the chaos of everyday ... I am dreaming – but in the face of the intellectual disorder of our existence, one has to recall very, very old prescriptions for life, to look back at how our grandparents managed to do this. Your difficulties are transitional, temporary, and in fact very creative (tension and pains generate unusual energy). I am sure that in a few years you will overcome the unfavorable circumstances. But you have to realize to what you are aiming at and to defend this with the same energy as you defend the truth in art ... My dear, forgive me for all my advice for life which sound like instructions. Once my mother told me 'you have to get married', and she repeated this to me so long that I finally did so. I do not regret that she pressed me so strongly.*[1]

She looked at how those to whom she became close constructed their lives, as she consciously built hers and made her own family.

> *I think of you and try to imagine your life which is so unusual. In your office room I suddenly felt*

Opening page: The artist, c.1999.

Below: The artist's studio, 1981.

Opposite: The artist in her study, 1981.

embraced by children – some very small – smiling faces of family and friends – tiny, intimate photos around you. I imagine that they must constitute your tribe, justify everyday efforts and they are those to whom you listen and who listen to you in this very private, confidential way. I have taken the atmosphere of your study along with me. [2]

It has been said that Abakanowicz shirked motherhood by those somehow oblivious to the fact that she lived at a time when women could not 'have it all'. But a family can also be two people, and she spoke of the daily communion that happens over morning coffee. She longed for normality in spite of socialist controls and as a woman (unlike most male counterparts) she played that balancing game, even finding it brought stability to her life:

I like this household activity because there is a definite result when I cook potatoes. In my studio, never. It's very relaxing. [3]

She always proved insightful about human nature.

I am fascinated and amazed by your thoughts about the baby. Please don't forget that what will come is, like we all, a 'mistake of nature', something deprived of the order animals have in their mind, a mixture of twisted instincts unknown to you, and a mixture of intellect of generations of you both ... Life taught me how much childhood is decisive for the whole life. [4]

In the end art populated her world. As her husband, Jan Kosmowski, remarked: 'We're married twenty-six years and from the start I have lived with these hanging forms [*Abakans*], call them garments, columns, the shapes are not important. I don't try to imagine what they could be. I feel well with them. They're my children, a part of my life.' [5]

Growth

To make art is to bring something new into being, and of the making process she said:

I feel there is something growing in my whole body. I work with it for a long time until I feel that I must separate myself from it. Then I begin to bring it into reality. My whole body grows ugly when I bring this imagined object out of me. I have to concentrate myself completely, completely, on my feeling to bring it out. I have to be absolutely alone. This is not a problem for the brain alone; it has something to do with the whole biological rhythm. Some artists find it hard to endure this suffering. It is like standing on a rock in a very unsure position wondering, will I fall? Creating is a very painful process. When it begins to be easy, it is no longer creation. [6]

To her, art was a living thing, and she created a lived practice. She said her work was:

like a diary of my life, with all its disappointments and longings. Working with it, I integrate myself into the whole cycle of existence. Creativity is not a profession; it is a way of existing. [7]

And she sought to probe the mystery of the organic world as she queried every scientific mind she encountered to find out more, because for her nature held the power. It was nature's regeneration and mutations that served as endless inspiration.

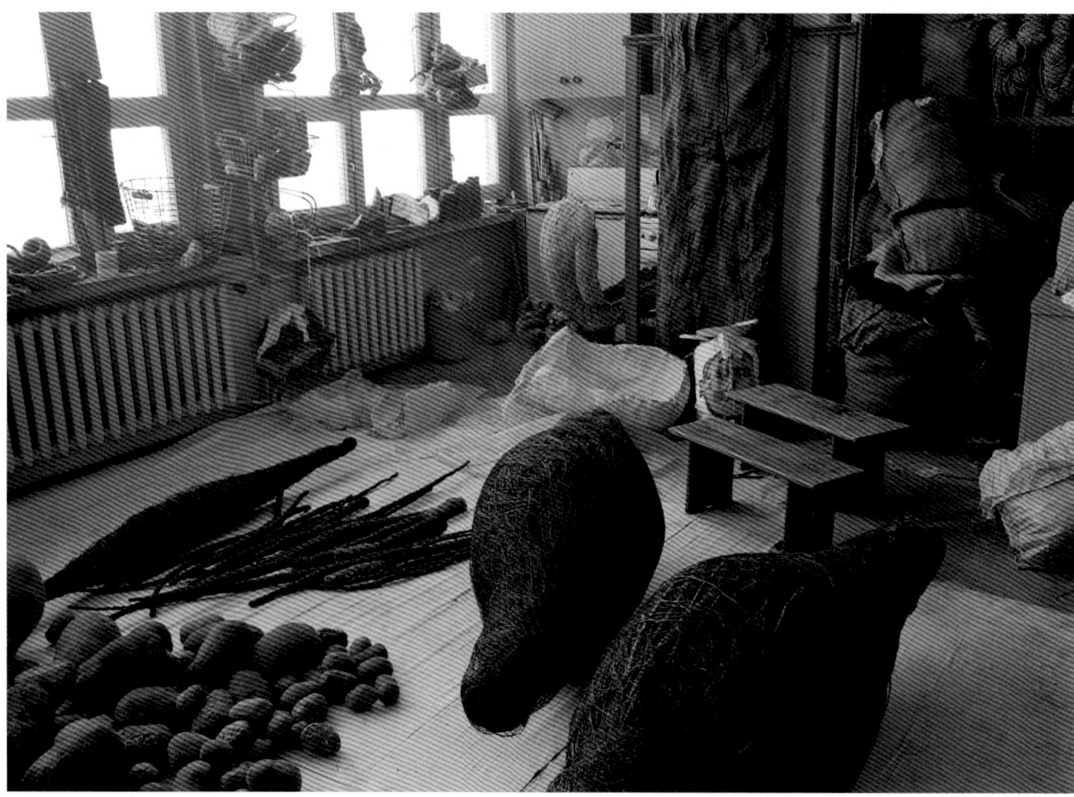

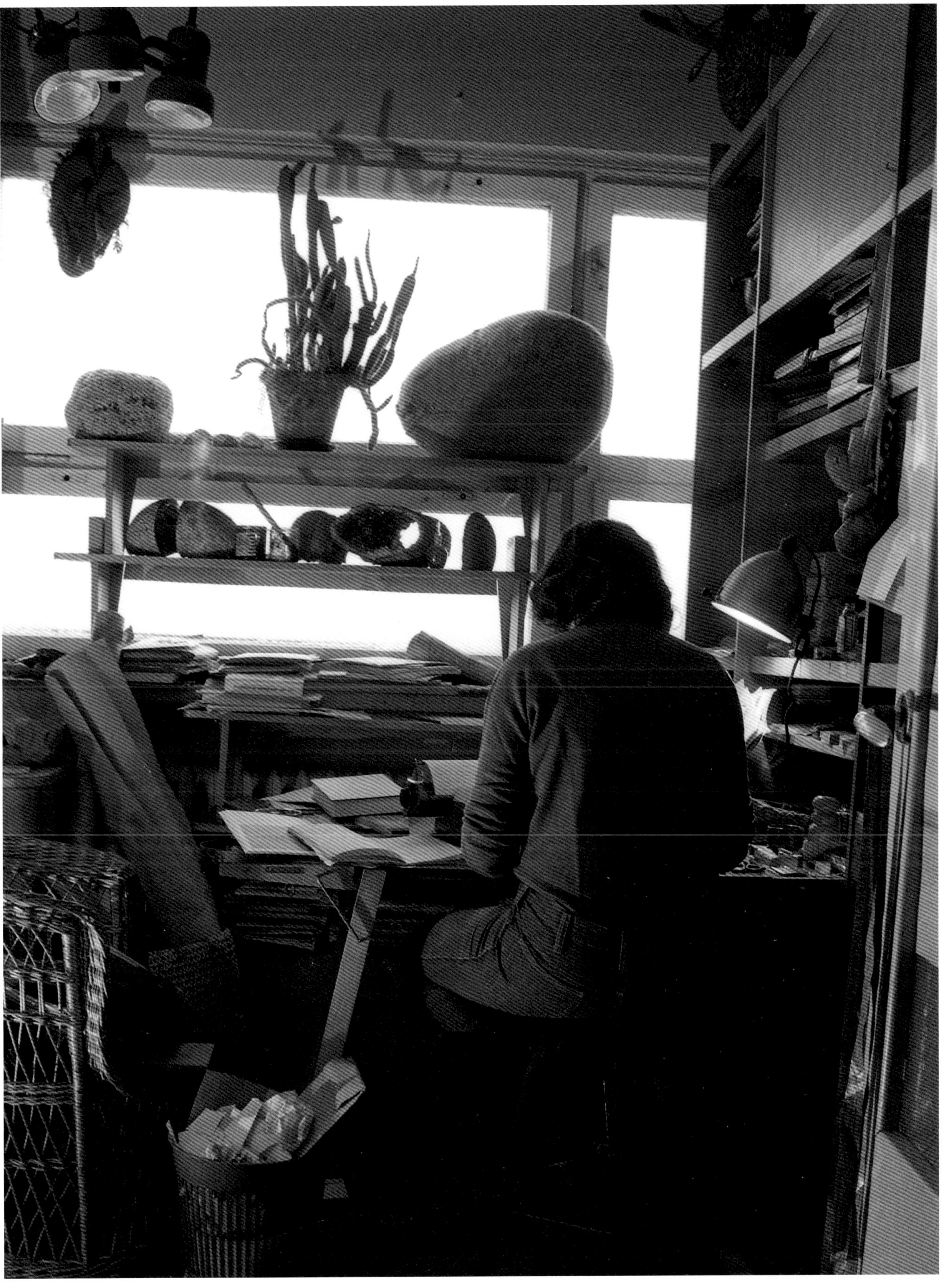

Below: The artist in her studio, 1991.

In her poem, 'Grain of Sand', she wrote:

I immerse in the crowd like a grain of sand in the friable sands.
I am fading among the anonymity of glances, movements, smells, in the common absorption of air, in the common pulsation of juices under the skin.
I become a cell of this boundless organism of the crowd like others already integrated and deprived of expression.
Similar in our bone structure, in the construction of our brain, in sensitivity of our skin we are prone to emotions.
Through hate and love, we stimulate each other. Destroying each other, we regenerate.[8]

Strength

Abakanowicz could swim the length of a lake and back. She could carry materials that would take two men. Her powerful hands needed to move every fibre and shape every aspect of the casting process. In the gallery she was formidable; she commanded space and made art happen. She had to claim her right to create 'spaces to contemplate', 'spaces to experience', at a time when there was no word for installation art.

From the outset, the intensity of her activities, marked by the phenomenal pace of shows, was stunning. Her ambition was propelled by a need to explore, participate and be in the world. Meanwhile in the business of art, she was relentless: maintaining a vast number of international correspondences, without staff and during challenging times. Yet with each letter that gained traction, she moved deeper into human contact and forged friendships:

The fact that you have written to me made me very happy. It is terribly important in this overcrowded and overpopulated reality to keep together. The distances do not matter.

She encouraged others to come to Poland despite their need for visas:

I am a good cook and my husband prepares an excellent vodka.[9]

But for the most part it was she who had to make the journey. Thus, she travelled almost continuously, but in so doing also found:

Every trip to the so-called capitalistic world could involve a nervous breakdown, a catastrophe, or an adventure. The permission to go could be suddenly refused. Sometimes even if I applied several months in advance, I would only receive my passport two hours before my flight. Standing with my suitcase in the police passport office, my hands were shaking, my brain seemed to stop. There was no thinking; instead, a kind of pain like a toothache, like a gastric ulcer, like a muscle cramp. Finally, sitting in the airplane, I was again a victor in this competition. A victor and a victim. The price I paid for winning was high. The competition was based on what I had to defend: my existence as an artist, my desperate need to communicate with people through my

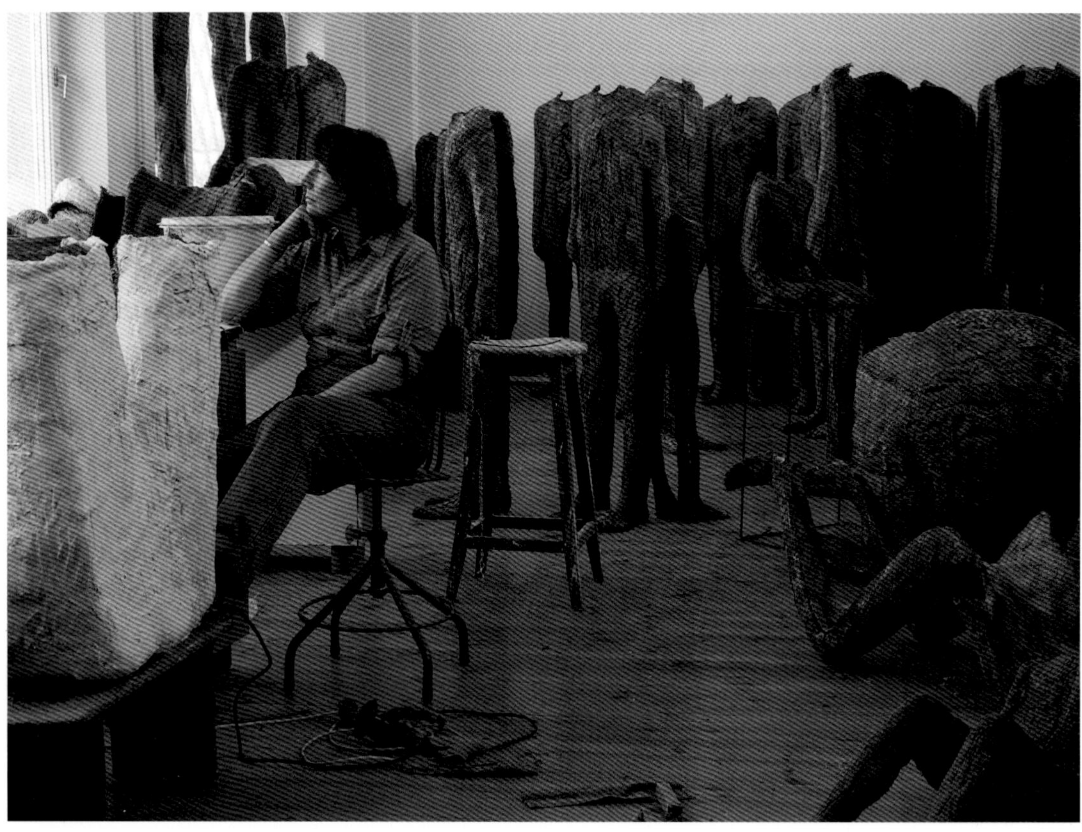

art, my identity as a citizen of the world, and the identity of my country belonging to the world of culture. This may sound banal, but at that time it was true. There was only one existence.[10]

Energy

Abakanowicz's animism met the shamanism of Joseph Beuys (1921–86), at the edge of belief and mythmaking, at a time when the feminist world was looking for its art world heroes. She had her heroes too:

I admire [Georgia O'Keeffe] for the radiant energy embodied in her work and for her very personal vision. She had the courage to show the analogy between sexual organs of mammals and forms of plants, flowers, snail shells – forms used by animated nature and also the analogy between flesh, muscles, and mountains, or landscapes.

I think she is unique in observing the limitations of forms used on this planet, maybe in the whole solar system – as the landscape of Mars is so similar to our deserts. Her paintings are like small windows through which one looks at enormous, monumental forms, real but bewitched.[11]

When Barbara Rose and the artist agreed, women 'are much stronger than men', the art historian added, 'men don't believe it, and so they are always waiting for you to fall down. And when you don't fall down they get very upset; this is the thing that makes them the most crazy.' Yet the artist replied:

[Men] worked for us the whole history along; now they are dying and we stay. This is just horrible. They live much shorter than we. Look at the buses with old women ... The men are all gone ... When I hear the word 'female' or 'women' I am immediately allergic.[12]

That leads to ghettoizing and can be very dangerous. For Louise Nevelson and Nancy Graves it's the quality of their work that counts, not their sex.[13]

Every situation has advantages and disadvantages. Men have advantages and disadvantages and we have in a different way. So, what is the struggle about? I don't know. To be better than we are? Or not to do what nature wants us to do?[14]

Empathy

Abakanowicz admired the diversity of America. Its romantic immigrant story seemed an ideal from the perspective of the ethnic wars in the 1990s.

I am always fascinated by your country and the fact that an incredible mixture of nations produces an incredible energy.[15]

During the making of her monumental public work, *Negev*, in Jerusalem, she felt a sense of hope that a world of tolerance was possible.

Later, in Jerusalem, while preparing to stand the stone disks upright, I worked with Bedouins, Kurds, Israelis, and Arabs. A peaceful atmosphere, surrounded constantly by the same nostalgic music from small portable radios and drinking strong, black, very sweet tea prepared by Bedouins.[16]

But she was deflated as the fall of communism ushered in capitalist values and revealed, yet again, man's basest instincts and cruelties. She recognised that differences unite us, but similarities can separate, reminding us that sharing race or geography can lead to nationalism. So she was as vigilant in her warning of our destruction of each other as she was the human disregard for the planet.

Her universalism and humanism may have seemed old-fashioned in an art world of postcolonial identity politics, her belief in art as a universal language outdated.

I am still deeply interested in mankind and our problems and I think this is the most stimulating factor for my creative work ... I appreciate the opportunity to learn so much about life, conflicts, pressures, and hopes all around the planet.

Poetics

For her, poetics offered a path for the future.

In the unconscious of contemporary man mythology is still buoyant. It belongs to a higher spiritual plane than his conscious life. The most superficial being is crowded with symbols and the most logical person lives through images. Symbols never disappear from the field of reality, they can change their guise, but their role remains unchanged ...

To have imagination and to be aware of it is to benefit from possessing an inner richness and a spontaneous and endless flood of image[s].

It means to see the world in its entirety, since the point of the images is to show all that which escapes conceptualisation.[17]

From Okakura Kakuzō's *Book of Tea*, a work she felt was important to everybody, she quoted:

The seeker for perfection must discover in his own life the reflection of the inner light.[18]

Finally, Abakanowicz was a seeker. She left us with art by which we can continue our own journey.

ARTIST'S WRITINGS

The following selection of writings by Abakanowicz span the years 1969–94 and provide insight into her motivations and thoughts. They are complemented by photographs of the Polish and Sardinian landscape from her archive which hint at sources of inspiration.

ON FIBER

I see fiber as the basic element constructing the organic world on our planet, as the greatest mystery of our environment. It is from fiber that all the living organisms are built, the tissue of plants, leaves and ourselves.

Our nerves, our genetic code, the canals of our veins, our muscles.

We are fibrous structures. Our heart is surrounded by the coronary plexus, the plexus of most vital threads.

Handling fiber we handle mystery. A dry leaf has a net reminiscent of a dry mummy.

What can become of fiber guided by the artist's hand and by his intuition?

What is fabric? We weave it, sew it. We shape it into forms.

When the biology of our body breaks down, the skin has to be cut so as to give access to the inside. Later it has to be sewn, like fabric.

Fabric is our covering and our attire. Made with our hands, it is a record of our souls.

My raw material is vegetable fiber, in its natural form or twined into fabric or ropes. I like working with it and feeling it. It is sensitive. It has a past of its own.

My works grow to a leisurely rhythm, like creations of nature. They are organic like creations of nature. And like creations of nature, they will eventually turn into earth.

They are born from the effort of my fingers, wrists and muscles. Only in this way can I pass on to them my energy and my secrets. Only in this way can I learn their secrets.

The number of possible manual activities is determined by the construction of my body, by the rhythm of my breath, by the circulation of blood. It is a good thing to know the limits of this rhythm.

The capacity of a day is different for thoughts, different for decisions, different for physical movement. One has to accept it.

The threads I weave make up homogeneous fabric, the expression of which depends on the tension or the relaxation of my nerves. On the inner circulation of the juices under my skin.

Forms result from everyday emotions, like a diary. They are the product and the record of my time, with its experiences, disappointments, longings and fears.

My forms change as time goes by like my face.

They were a protest against the weaving conventions. A need to guide people into a world different from that of a noisy street and brutal technique. They were a cry of despair in the face of the ailments of civilization.

They are, like sweat, a symptom of my existence.[1]

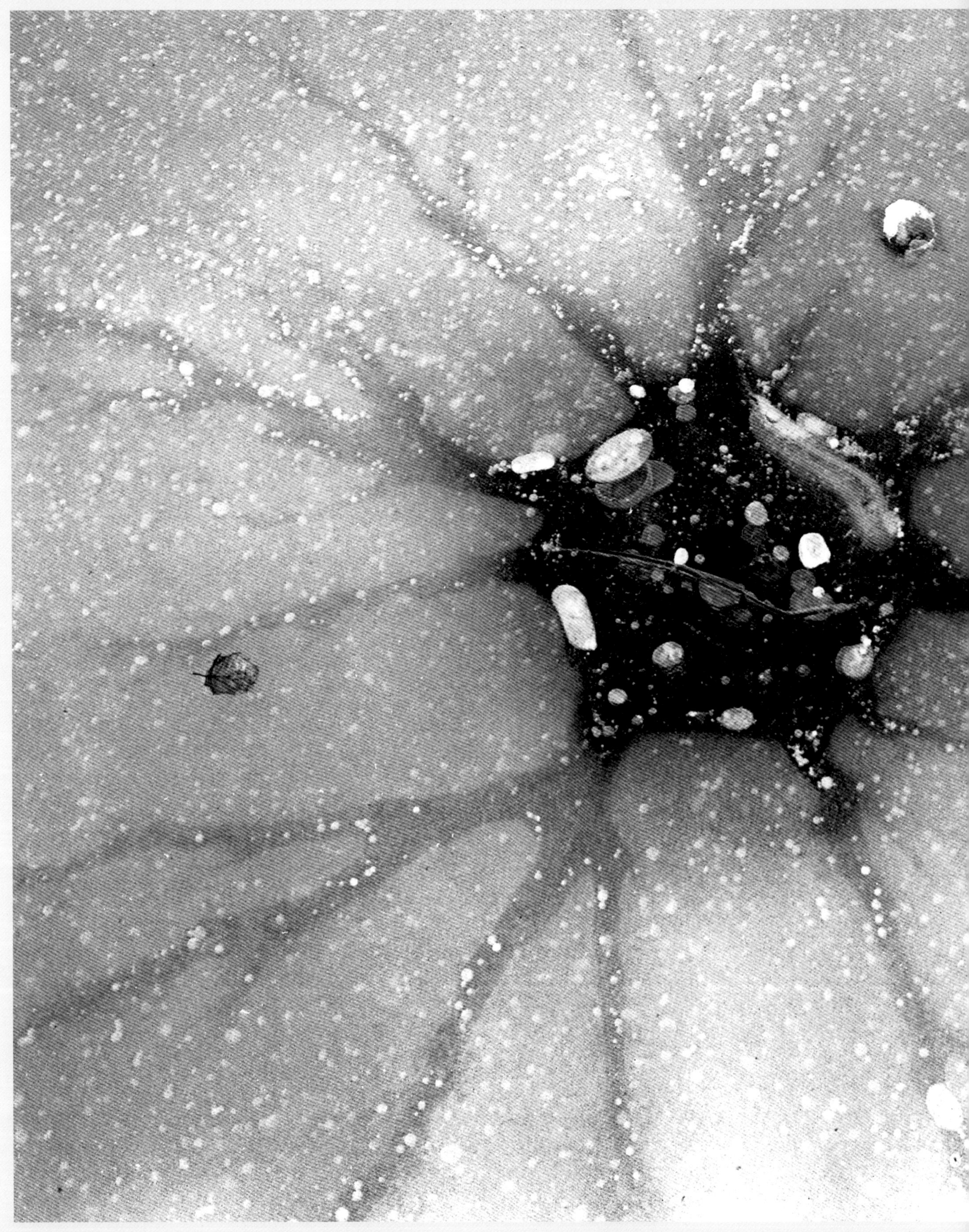

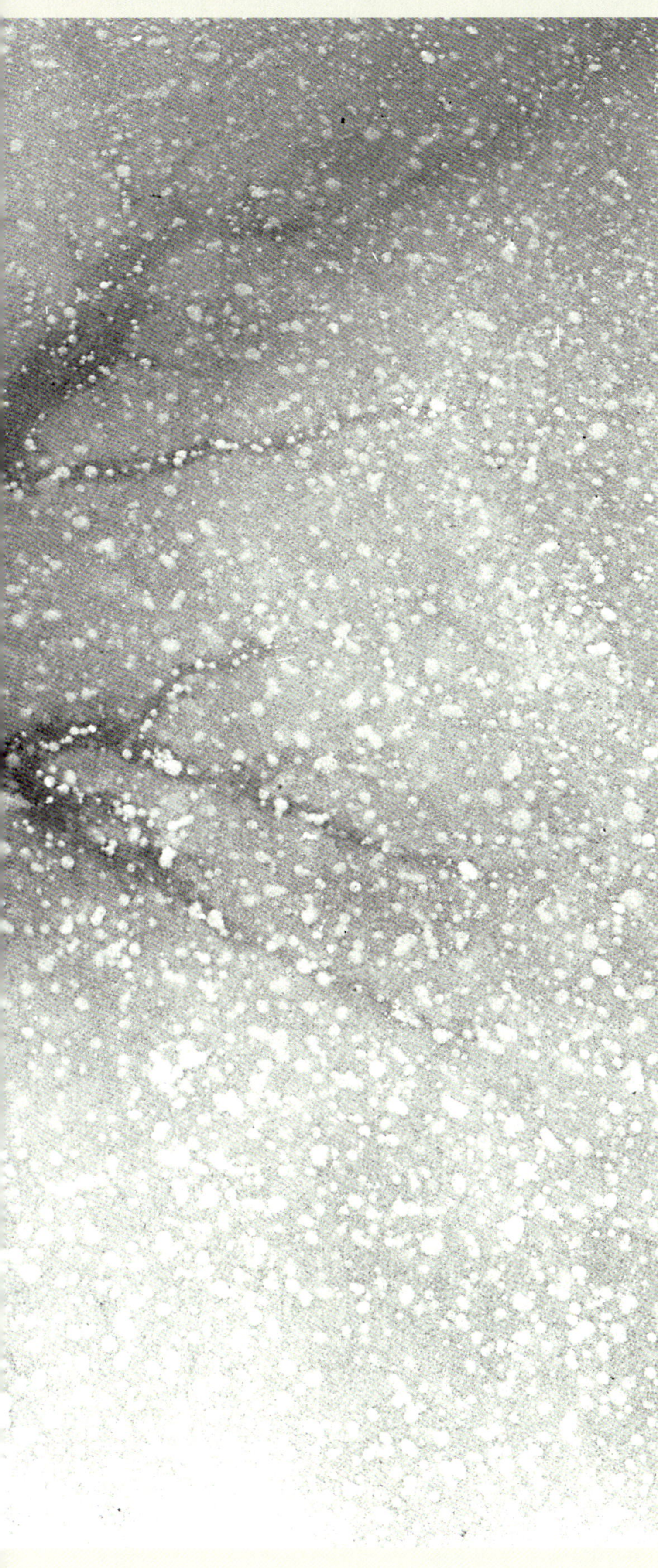

ON MATERIALITY

I like neither rules nor instructions, these enemies of imagination. I make use of the technique of weaving by adapting it to my own ideas. My art has always been a protest against what I have met with in weaving. I started to use rope, horsehair, metal, and fur because I needed these materials to give my vision expression. It mattered little that they were part of the tradition in this field. Moreover tapestry, with its decorative function, has never interested me. I simply became extremely interested in all that could be done by weaving. How one forms the surface reliefs, how the mobile markings of the horsehair will be put into place, and finally how this constructed surface can swell and burst showing a glimpse of mysterious depths through the cracks.

In 1966 I completed my first woven forms, which are independent of the walls and which existed in space. In creating them I do not want to relate to either tapestry or sculpture. At the most it is the total obliteration of the utilitarian function of tapestry which enraptures me. My particular aim is to create possibilities for complete communion with the object of which the structure is fleshy and soft. Through cracks and openings, I try to get the onlooker to penetrate into the deepest corners of the composition. I am interested in the scale of tensions which intervene between the woven form, rich and fleshy, and the surroundings.

Each time I reject my own experience, I consider it as a success. There are all too many fascinating problems for one to confine oneself to a single one. Repetition is contrary to the laws of the intellect in its progress onward, contrary to imagination.[2]

ON MAKING

I like it that working on my form with my hands I exert control over its every detail. The movements of my hands correspond to the natural rhythm of my body, to my breath.

This rhythm determines the number of the logical activities which can be performed from morning until evening, from my morning until my evening. I never work at night.

The growth and the establishment of my form is slow, just as biological processes. All the time they are controlled by the imagination which the hands convey to reality with all the effort and awkward movements of a living creature.

It is good to know one's own rhythm, the limits which it determines of perception and response to stimuli.[3]

ON SPACE

An *Abakan* is an independent entity, but it is also one of the elements by which we can conceive of space. Other matters, too, contribute to our conception of space: trees, parks, buildings, and roads of course, but also the means by which space is experienced, such as television, which shows thousands of aspects of that space on its screen. All these are elements which make us aware of the scale that is being employed, which determines how involved we are with one another, or how detached, and which influence our behavior.

How is the space we live in?

What is the space between Warsaw and London? The line between two abstract points on a map? The space you hurtle through in an airplane? The space that can be experienced somewhat more rationally when traveled in a train or a car? The space by day or by night? Or perhaps the space that is seen through an intermediary? The space that impresses us on the TV, or that hardly appeals to our imagination any more on the telephone?

I am looking for my own space.

I am constructing it from the tensions emerging between the forms I arrange – and the light.

I insert this space into the existing one getting my own sector.

I lead the people into it.[4]

ON ABAKANS

The *Abakans* were a kind of bridge between me and the outside world. I could surround myself with them; I could create an atmosphere in which I somehow felt safe because they were my world; they were something between figurative and natural, like animals, like figures, while abstract, like geometric forms, but never to be definitively described. They were terribly important not only for me but because they are different from everything.

It was absolutely a conscious decision that for an object [such] as an *Abakan* I must construct the materials from which I will make it. Like our skin is constructed, I wanted to make this skin for the created object. I wanted to be fully responsible. They have nothing to do with weaving, as such, because I used it only to build a skin for the created object. The making of skin allowed me to be absolutely responsible for everything in this object. Really creating, like God, from the very beginning, everything that is inside, outside, what is the body of it. I am making the body.[5]

Many of the *Abakans*, and deriving from them *Garments*, are first of all interior-shelter-garments. You can enter them. They surround you tightly. You become a part of a body.

They have, among others, to do with desire of protection, of identity, of home that could move with you, being one with you like your skin. Our first shelter-garment is our mother's belly – [it] not only protects but also carries the responsibility for us.

Next is our skin – in some cases it remains our only shelter-protection-identity (Australian aborigines, etc.).

Your dress, garment, can become shelter when you are homeless.

I experienced this during a short period of my life (war, revolution). Then your imagination and invention makes astonishing discoveries, transforming very little into meaningful property.

Another experience was when as a student I used to spend free time in forests without a tent and equipment. I slept inside heaps of dry leaves or hay. I experienced the feeling of being part of something that is of the same origin as me.[6]

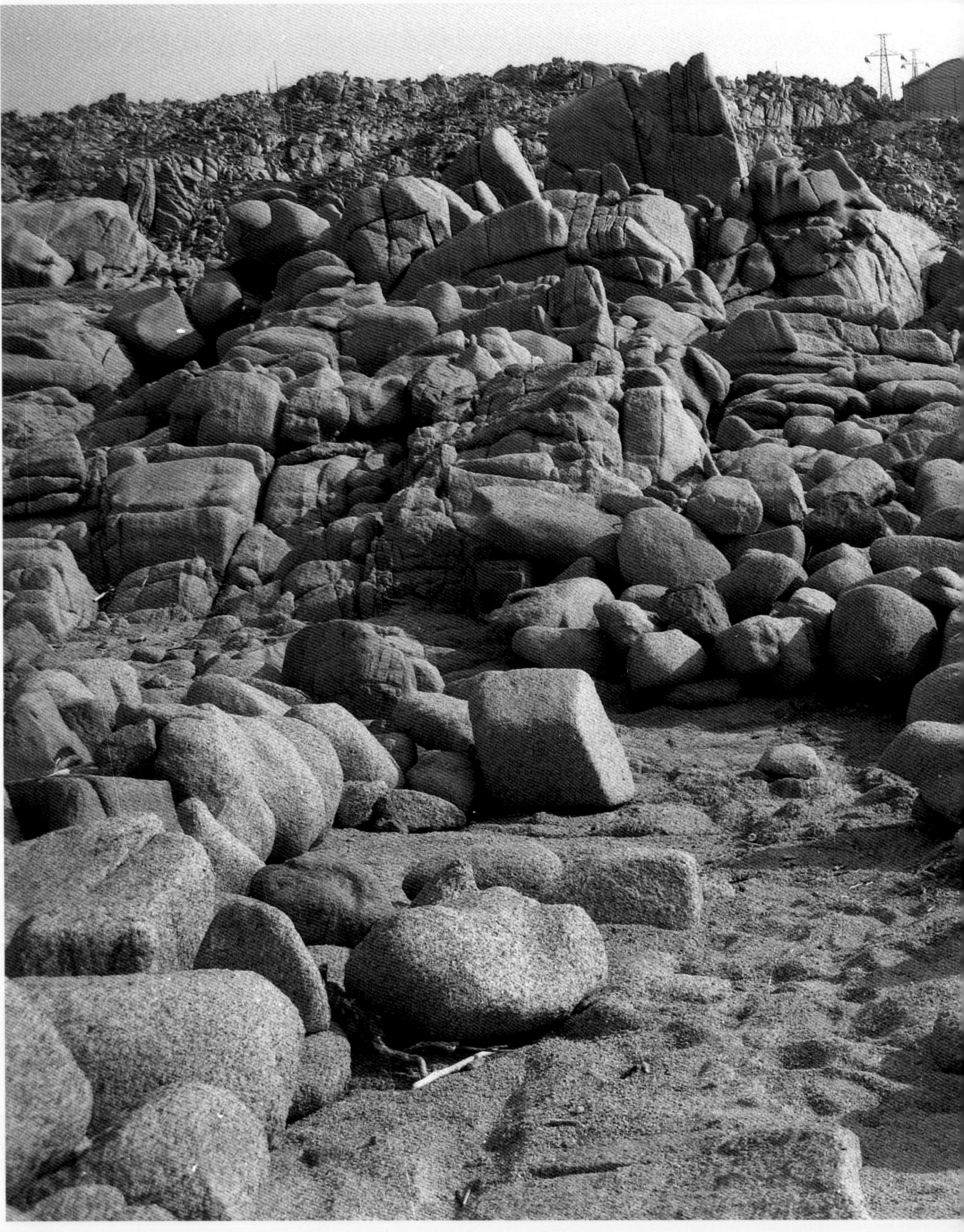

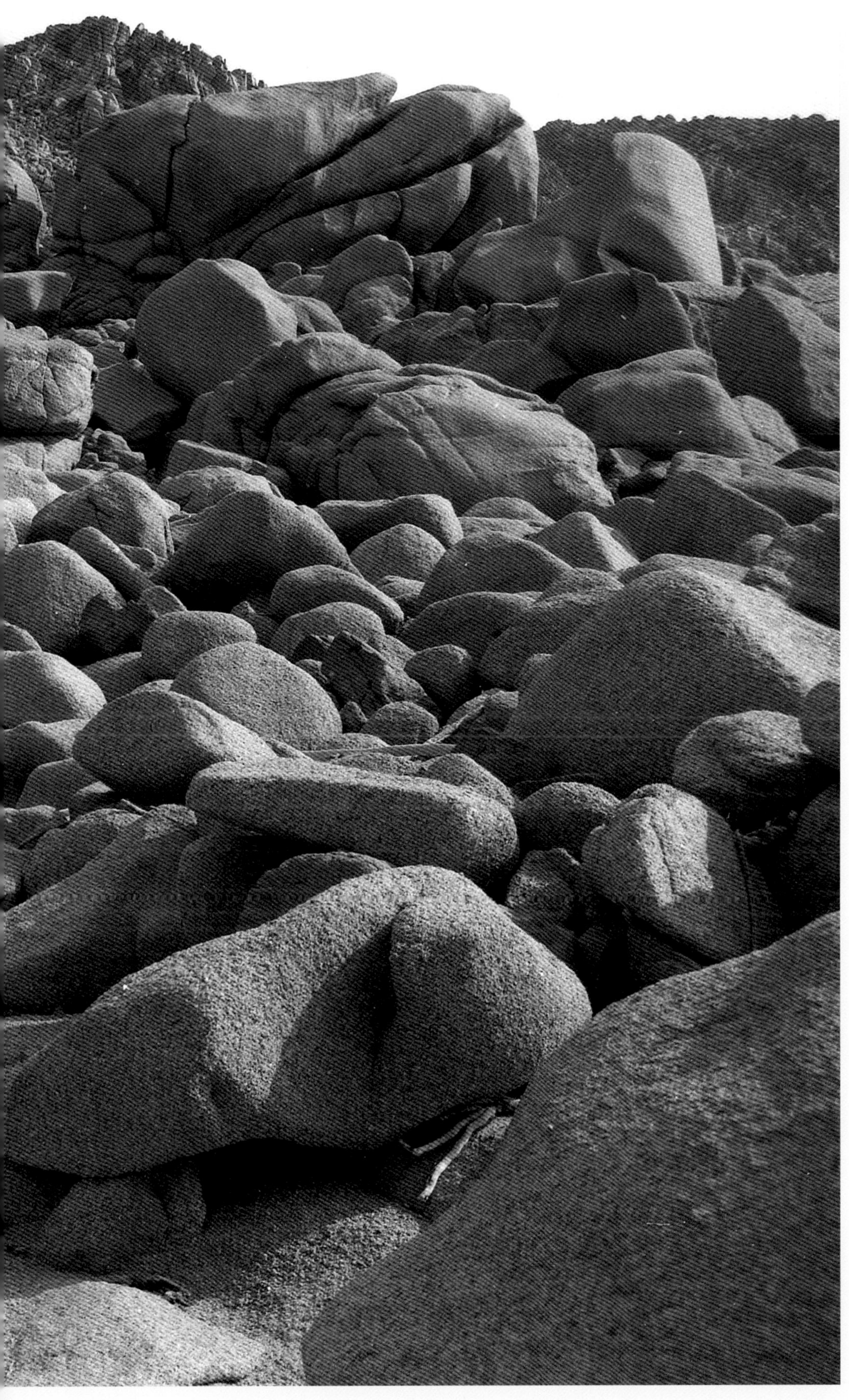

ON SOFT

Once upon a Time

I was a small child, crouching over a swampy pond, watching tadpoles. Enormous, soon to become frogs, they swarmed around the bank. Through the thin membrane covering their distended bellies, the tangle of intestines was clearly visible. Heavy with the process of transformation, sluggish, they provoked one to reach for them. Pulled out onto shore with a stick, touched carelessly, the swollen bellies burst. The contents leaked out in a confusion of knots. Soon they were beset by flies. I sat there, my heart beating fast, shaken by what had happened. The destruction of soft life and the boundless mystery of the content of softness. It was just the same as confronting a broken stem with sap flowing out, provoked by an inexplicable inner process, a force only apparently understood. The never fully explored mystery of the interior, soft and perishable.

Many years later, that which was soft with a complex tissue became the material of my work. It gives me a feeling of closeness to and affinity with the world that I do not wish to explore other than by touching, feeling, and connecting with that part of myself which lies deepest.

Becoming

Between myself and the material with which I create, no tool intervenes. I select it with my hands. I shape it with my hands. My hands transmit my energy to it. In translating idea into form, they always pass on to it something that eludes conceptualization. They reveal the unconscious.

Interior

The shapes that I build are soft. They conceal within themselves the reasons for the softness. They conceal everything that I leave to the imagination. Neither through the eye nor the fingertips nor palm that informs the brain can this be explained. The inside has the same importance as the outer shell. Each time shaped as a consequence of the interior, or exterior as a consequence of the inside. Only together do they form a whole. The invisible interior which can only be guessed at is as important as when it opens for everyone, allowing physical penetration.

Meditation

To make something more durable than myself would add to the imperishable rubbish heaps of human ambitions, crowding the environment. If my thoughts and my imaginings, just as I, will turn to earth, so will the forms that I create, and this is good. There is so little room.

Coexistence

My forms are like successive layers of skin that I shed to mark the stages along my road. In each case they belong to me as intimately as I belong to them, so that we cannot be apart. I watch over their existence. Soft, they contain within an infinite quantity of possible shapes from which I choose only one as the right, meaningful form.

In exhibition rooms I create spaces for them in which they radiate the energy I have imbued them with. They exist together with me, dependent on me, I dependent on them. Coexisting, we continually create each other. Veiling my face, they are my face. Without me – like scattered parts of the body separated from the trunk – they are meaningless.

Confession

Impermanence is a necessity of all that lives. It is a truth contained in a soft organism. How to give vent to this innate defeat of life other than by turning a lasting thought into perishable material? Thought – a monument. Thought – a defense against disappearance. Timeless thought. A perverse product of the soft tissue that will disintegrate, that one day will cease to connect. Expressed in material whose durability is related to the matter from which it came, it begins to really live – mortally.

Contact

I touch and find out the temperature. I learn about roughness and smoothness of things. Is the object dry or moist? Moist from warmth or from cold? Pulsating or still? Yielding to the finger or protected by its surface? What is it really like? Not having touched, I do not know.

Embryology

Carried for a long time in the imagination, shapes ripen. When out of pent-up tension, they have to be discharged, I become one with the object created. My body grows ugly, exhausted by bringing forth an image. My body gets rid of something that had been a part of it, from the imagination to the skin. The effort of discharge makes it hideous. In my belly life was never conceived. My hands shape forms, seeking confirmation of each individual specimen in quantity. As in a flock subordinating the individual, as in the profusion of leaves produced by a tree.

Reminiscence

But, at the very beginning, when I started to weave and to use soft material, it was from a need to protest. From a wish to question all the rules and habits connected with this material. Soft is comfortable and useful. It is obedient, wrapping our body. It deadens the sound of footsteps. It covers walls, decoratively and warmly. It is easy on the eyes.

It is practical. Accompanying our civilization from its very beginnings, it has its roles, a definable range of tasks governed by our needs and habits. It has its own system of classifications. That is why I found the struggle with these acquired habits so fascinating. That is why it has been so fascinating to reveal and disclose the organic quality of fabric, of softness. To show the qualities overlooked through the blindness of habits. The autonomous qualities. To show all that this material could be as a liberated carrier of its own organic nature. And later, the showing of objects which contradict the former functions of this material, broadening man's awareness of the matter which surrounds him, the objects which surround him, the world which surrounds him.

Softness

I touch my body. It still obeys me. It fulfills orders efficiently, without resistance. The muscles move wisely. When needed, they raise my hand, move my fingers. When needed, I lower and raise my eyelids. I move my tongue. Under the skin the flesh is precisely shaped. Springy. Everywhere, in the wholly enclosed, porous skin-covering – pulsation. All uniformly heated, saturated with moisture, with thick red juice, white mucus, jellylike secretion. All stretched on bones. Inside them – canals, intertwined with nets and threads, soft and fragile. Hot, greasy. It belongs to me. It is me. It causes me to be.[7]

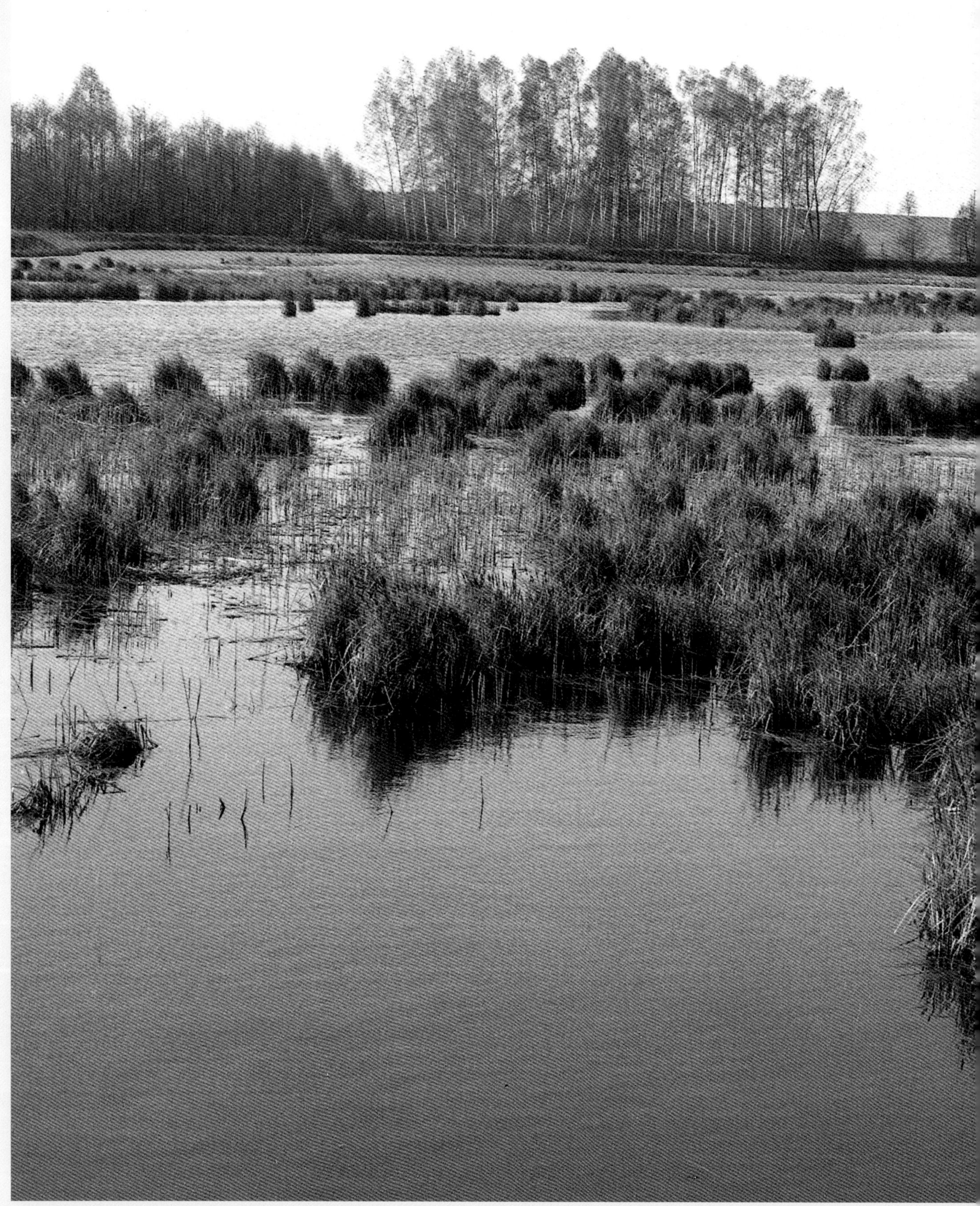

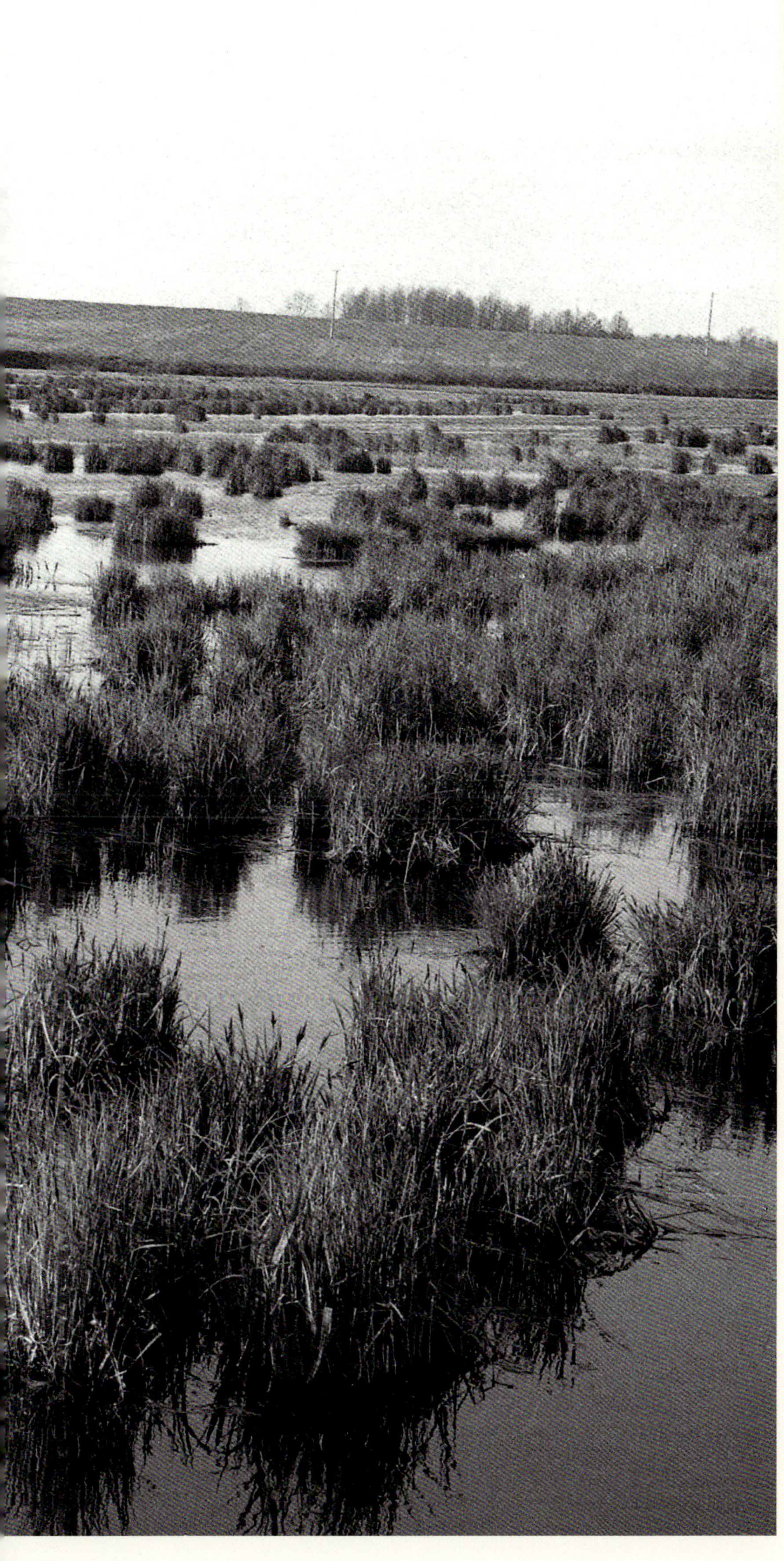

ON HISTORY

I wanted to tell you that art is the most harmless activity of mankind, but I suddenly recalled that art was often used for propaganda purposes by totalitarian systems.

I wanted to tell you also about the extraordinary sensitivity of an artist, but I recalled that Hitler was a painter and Stalin used to write sonnets.

Art will remain the most astonishing activity of mankind born out of struggle between wisdom and madness, between dream and reality in our mind.

Each scientific discovery opens doors behind which we are confronted with new closed doors.

Art does not solve problems but makes us aware of their existence. It opens our eyes to see and our brain to imagine.

To have imagination and to be aware of it means to benefit from possessing an inner richness and a spontaneous and endless flood of images. It means to see the world in its entirety, since the point of the images is to show all that which escapes conceptualization.[8]

ON POLAND

When I speak about the dependence of art on the development of society, there is also the landscape, how people live on it, build their houses. The way the landscape behaves, looks. For instance, the lack of color in Polish landscape, the enormous importance of gray everywhere. I have a very strong feeling of scale in which I move in a comfortable way or in which I am lost. I absolutely belong to a certain area of this planet.

This is my fate. I belong also to a language, also to a history which makes the mentality of people in such a way. And I belong terribly to what one can call Polish landscape in an incredible way. I know every blade of grass in my country, every cloud in the sky, every tree, every little creature that goes there, that walks, that flies, that moves. My experiences with people at home are strong. This means something, and I feel extremely comfortable in a complete discomfort in Poland and very uncomfortable in a great comfort in other places.[9]

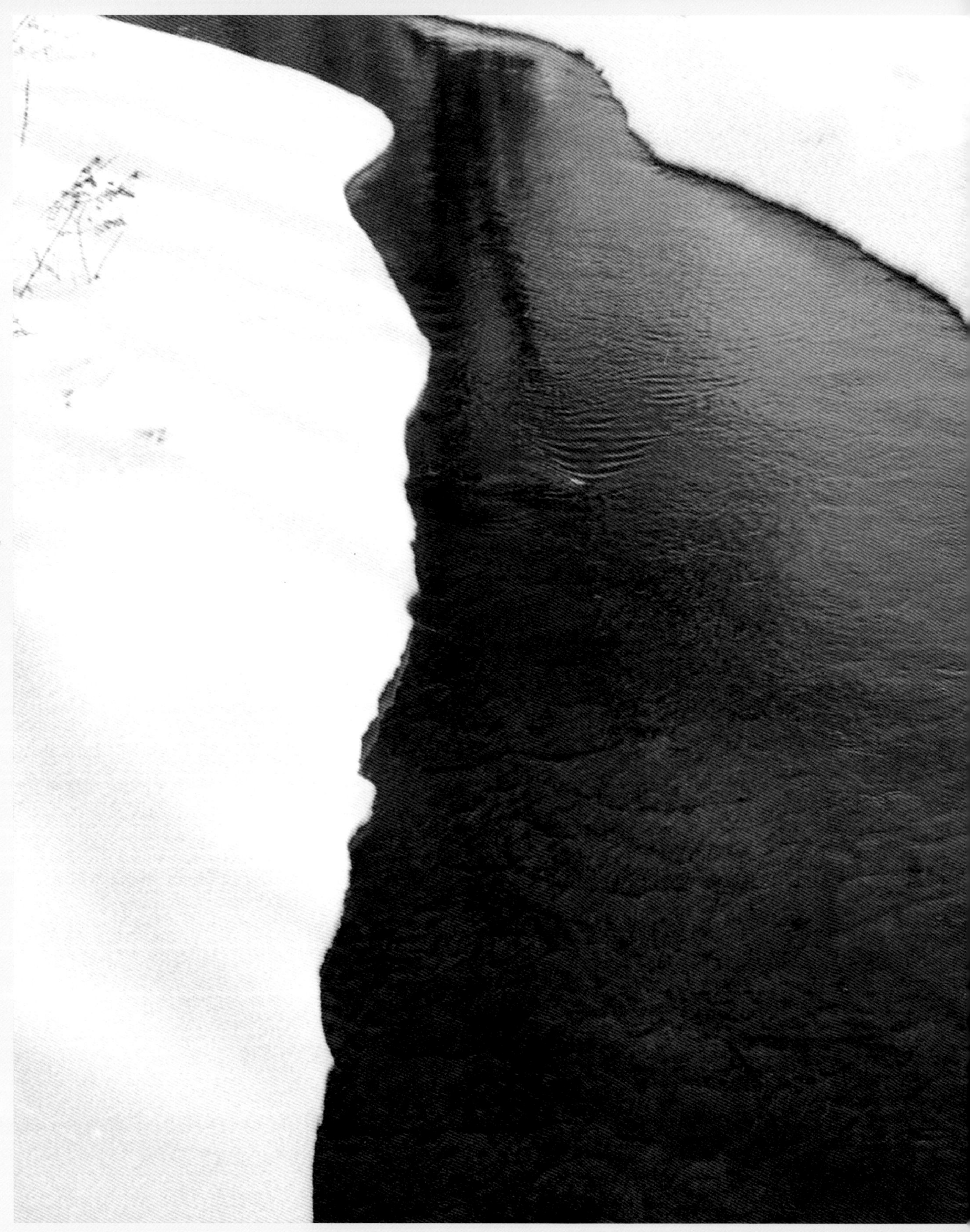

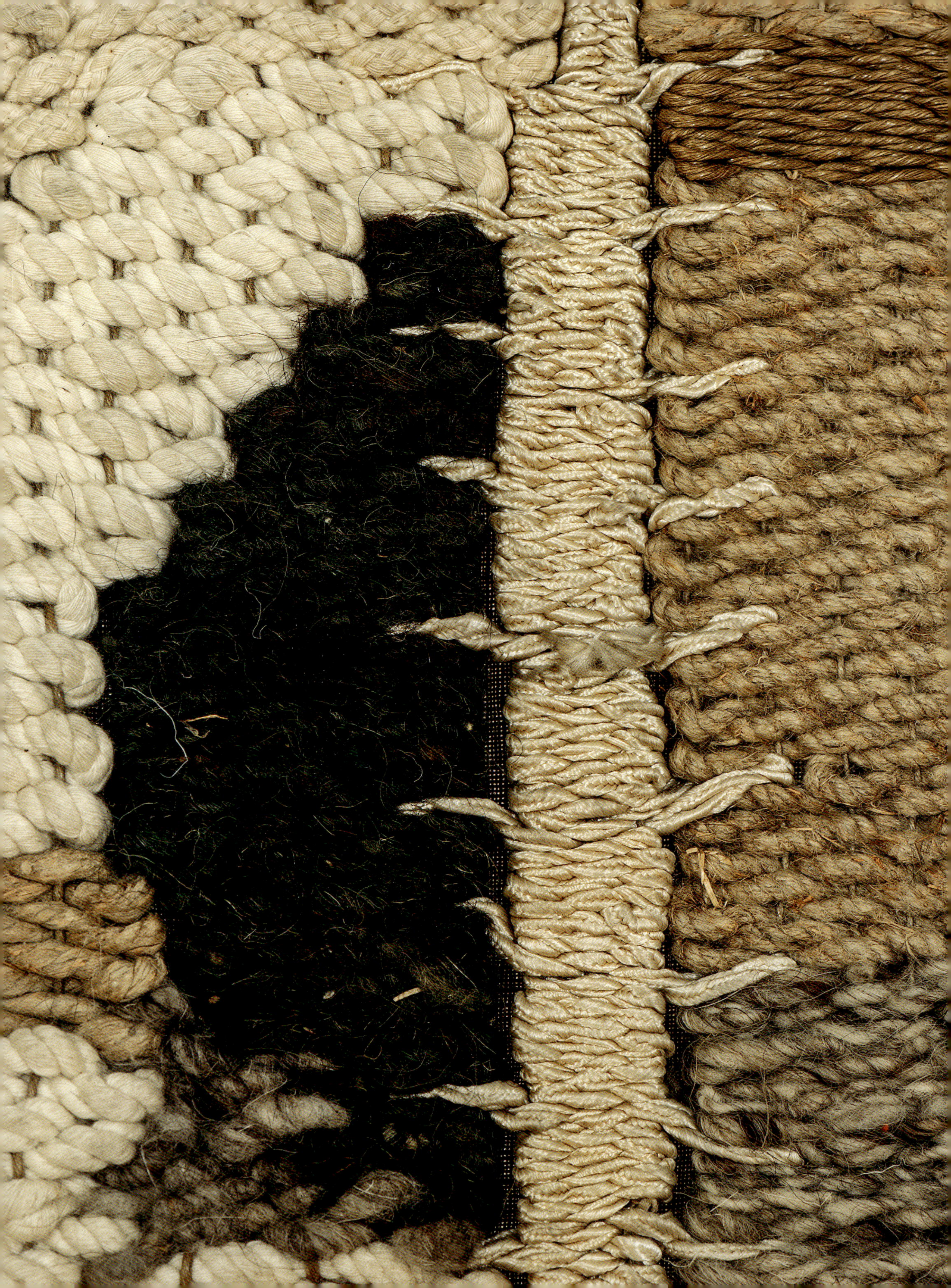

MAGDALENA MOSKALEWICZ

KNOTS
ABAKANOWICZ AND THE POLISH ART SCENE IN THE 1960S

A woman is seen walking through the desert, moving along the sand dunes, her figure small in the distance. The accompanying music, a sequence of electronic sounds, is suggestive of outer space, or some otherwise unworldly soundscape, and produces a feeling of alienation. The woman is Magdalena Abakanowicz and this is the opening scene of the 1970 documentary film *Abakany*, by Stanisław Brzozowski (1878–1911) and Kazimierz Mucha (1923–2006), with music composed by Bogusław Schaeffer (1929–2019). Soon after, the film transitions into a more typical narrative: the artist is shown skilfully weaving on a vertical loom, wandering through her studio immersed in thought, and installing her large, demanding *Abakans* in a gallery space – all the while an off-screen male voice explains the recent transformations in the 'century-old art of tapestry' and Abakanowicz's immense contribution to its advancement. But the experimental music continues throughout, and the sensation of estrangement remains with the viewer. The thirteen-minute film ends with more images of the desert, this time with the *Abakans* seemingly levitating in space. At one point, the weavings are carried into the scene by a group of half-naked men evocative of ancient Egyptian slaves or other archetypal peoples from a distant era. At another, the solitary framing of an individual *Abakan* is reminiscent of surrealist compositions by René Magritte (1898–1967). (For more on the film *Abakany*, see pp.152–9.)

There are two extraordinary things about this film. One is how the surrealist-like images, the experimental music, and the straightforward, almost educational, voiceover all contribute to the general bizarreness of the film.[1] The 'desert' scenes were shot among the sand dunes by the Polish resort of Łeba on the Baltic, but nothing gives away that location, or the seaside character of the landscape. The *Abakans* are presented in an empty space devoid of either geographical specificity or cultural locality. They are shown as autonomous creatures (at one point, a bundle of threads is shown trembling and convulsing as if it were a living organism) created by a unique and solitary individual (Abakanowicz alone walking through the desert or leaning against a blank, white wall). All the while the voiceover explains that the artist has multiple continuators around the world, but it mentions no collaborators or predecessors: 'There is just the material, the studio, the anxiety of creation,' the voice says, as we see the artist moving pensively around her studio. 'There is just the sense of solitude and the understanding, that one needs to search on one's own, that no one will pass you the answer.'[2]

The second extraordinary thing is how this visionary directing, in a way, foretold the erasure of artistic context that Abakanowicz's oeuvre sustained in the 1970s, 1980s and later. The film inadvertently constructed what would become one of the most detrimental clichés for the understanding of the artist's practice internationally: that of an individual creative mind independent of time and space.

Contrary to this message and multiple other narratives – including her own – that have since posited Abakanowicz to be a singular, uninfluenced artistic genius, this essay seeks to argue that both *Abakany* and the artist's other revolutionary works would be impossible outside the context of the art scene that emerged after 1955 in socialist Poland. Abakanowicz's conception of space, her understanding of the medium of weaving, together with its place among other art disciplines, and the terminology she used to describe her changing work can all be traced back to her training, her collaborations and her friendships in 1960s Poland. This essay seeks to determine the individual threads that tie Abakanowicz's oeuvre back to the Warsaw and the greater Polish art scene, and to identify those multiple knots where her investigations had been entangled with those of her Polish peers. This is not to claim any traditionally conceived 'influence' that would diminish the originality of Abakanowicz's own vision, or lessen the importance for her development of the international textile world that she had become a part of as early as 1962.[3] Rather, it is to ground the first fifteen years of Abakanowicz's work – after her graduation in 1954 from the Academy of Plastic Arts in Warsaw – within the art discourse that was a part of her everyday as a Warsaw-based artist and also (from 1965) a Poznań art school professor.

Abakanowicz's practice emerged from the cross-media experimentation taken up enthusiastically by many Polish painters, sculptors and weavers during the post-Stalinist Thaw from about 1955 to 1960, a period known as *nowoczesność* (literally: modernity). Her work matured among the tensions between the autonomy of form and the social context of display that characterised modernism's twilight moment. Abakanowicz's work captured and embodied these tensions to become almost a signifier of Poland's high modernism. The importance of this local ground is often overlooked in accounts of her practice – partly as a result of the ghettoisation of textile art, and because of the self-mythologisation of Abakanowicz herself, partly due to the antipathy of the local scene she experienced later,[4] and certainly because of the limited amount of knowledge that exists about artistic life beyond the Iron Curtain.

The tremendous task of deconstructing the mythology around Abakanowicz was undertaken by Joanna Inglot in her 2004 book *The Figurative Sculpture of Magdalena Abakanowicz: Bodies, Environments and Myths*.[5] In the absence of virtually any English-language literature on Polish postwar art at the time, Inglot focused on the basic reconstruction of historical facts, establishing the general cultural background for Abakanowicz's education and practice and shedding light on the artist's figurative sculpture. This essay is, in a sense, a continuation of Inglot's work: it provides a deeper analysis of the artistic discourses and dominant conceptual frameworks that influenced Abakanowicz in the pre-figurative period of the 1960s, while also considering contemporaneous reception of her work. It concentrates on the artist's textiles and their development into *Abakans* beyond the impact of her weaving teachers and peers in the context of the two foundational traditions for *nowoczesność*: on the one hand, Poland's postwar modernism, *art informel*, painting grounded in the French tradition of postwar abstraction, and on the other, neo-constructivism, claiming they form the double root of Abakanowicz's artistic practice.[6]

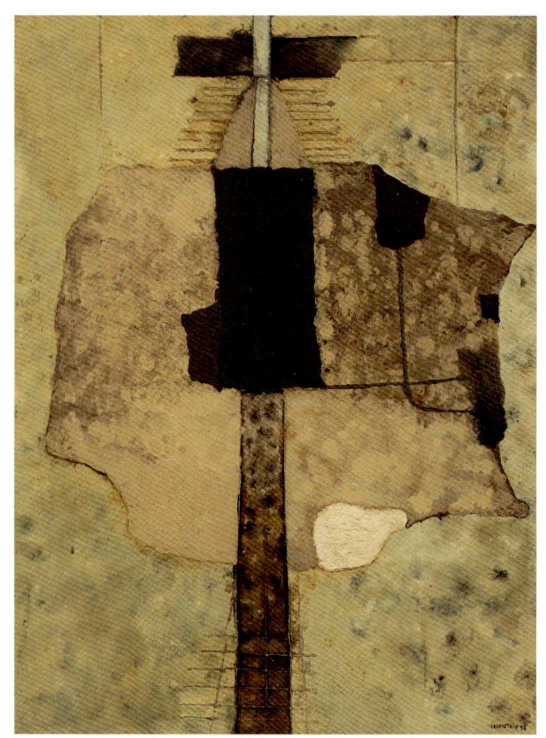

Opening page: *Textural Composition White* (detail) 1961–2
Sisal and cotton
164 × 106. See p.44

Below: Jan Lebenstein
Axial figure 1958
Oil paint on canvas
99 × 74

Opposite: *Composition* 1960
Oil paint on canvas
100.5 × 82

Matter

Abakanowicz's first solo exhibition took place in 1960 at the Galeria Kordegarda in Warsaw, run by the Ministry of Art and Culture. To the artist's disbelief, the exhibition was temporarily closed down by the authorities, in one of a series of decisions that came to mark the end of the post-Stalinist Thaw in the People's Republic of Poland.[7] As evidenced by this first individual presentation, the artist had skilfully absorbed the lesson of Thaw abstraction: the gouaches and oils on cardboard displayed at Kordegarda, filled with abstract, biomorphic forms in dark ochres, resembled many of the paintings presented at *III Exhibition of Modern Art* held at Zachęta Centralne Biuro Wystaw Artystycznych (Zachęta CBWA) in Warsaw in 1959, a major overview of new artistic production.[8]

In the few years of the Thaw, Polish artists developed a unique version of *informel* painting, which focused more on its material, rather than its gestural aspect. One of the leaders of this new direction, Tadeusz Kantor (1915–90), outlined the conception in his 1957 manifesto 'Abstraction is dead – long live abstraction', inspired by his 1955 trip to Paris. In the text, he hailed formless abstraction to be the epitome of modernity, a 'manifestation of life' contrary to geometric abstraction, which he saw as an equivalent of pedantic, scholastic life. 'Matter – element and fury, continuity and infiniteness, thickness and slowness, continuity and fickleness, lightness and transience,' wrote the artist, characterising the new aesthetics in a highly poetic language. 'Matter [that is] red-hot, exploding, fluorescing, filled with light, lifeless and quiet. Coagulation, in which we discover all traces of life. Lack of any construction, only persistence and structure.'[9] Kantor described the new work of art as an autonomous creation emergent through the artist's physical struggle with the matter. The artwork thus became – in a similar sense to that promoted in the United States by the critic Harold Rosenberg – a continuation of life.

Based on Kantor's unprecedented approach to painting, the influential art historian and critic Mieczysław Porębski authored what became possibly the most original conception of Polish *informel.*[10] He proposed the term 'structuralism', since the ideal work maintained for him the perfect balance ('structure') between three crucial elements: illusion, which had dominated in realism; form, which had dominated in the avant-garde; and matter, which had dominated in colourism – a popular Polish version of post-impressionism. Structural painting was, according to Porębski, an existentialist attempt grounded in the struggle with matter, a struggle that is the expression of the general concerns of human existence. Matter painting (as it would be called) 'attempts to discover the lost proportions between reality, action, and aspiration'.[11] As such, it is never complete; its form

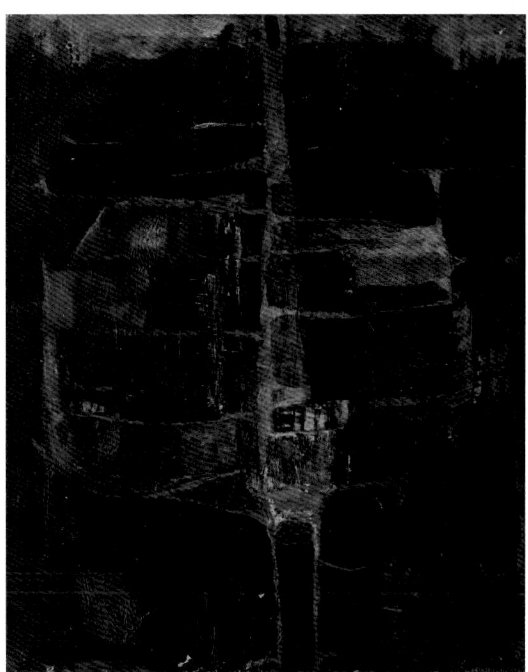

not stable; it is a process, since matter needs to be harnessed and tamed every time anew.

By the early 1960s, paintings made in Poland were characterised by thick impasto surfaces and executed in monochromatic, often brownish tones, as developed from the more organic and colourful compositions of biomorphic forms that had been popular a few years earlier. Artists often mixed paint with sand or other materials to achieve a paste-like structure, which allowed them to almost sculpt on the surface. Such were the paintings of Jan Lebenstein, awarded the Grand Prix at the 1st Paris Biennial, in 1959 (opposite), as well as Aleksander Kobzdej, who received the acquisition prize at the 5th São Paulo Biennial the same year (see p.40).

Though her medium was different, Abakanowicz's work underwent the same transformation: from more decorative organic abstractions painted on lightweight textiles in the mid 1950s to 1960 (also shown at Kordegarda), to weavings with thick knots and bulky textures already in evidence by 1961. The artist took the thick, dark impastos of matter painting and translated them into weft and warp. The uneven surfaces with multiple protrusions that characterise Abakanowicz's weavings since 1961 may have been at odds with the current French textile techniques – as was proven by the heated reactions they received at the 1st International Tapestry Biennial in Lausanne in 1962 – but they were at home on the Polish art scene. Abakanowicz's strong opposition to the French tradition of sleek *tapisserie*, whereby works were first designed by an artist as a cartoon and then executed by a craftsperson, together with her insistence on engaging with her material at every stage of the process, and her inclusion of found materials in her weavings, all stemmed from the matter-oriented Polish *informel*.

Construction

There is a paradox within Abakanowicz's practice which can only be recognised when seen in the context of the Polish art developments of the early to mid 1960s: for all the *informel*-like biomorphism and materiality, Abakanowicz's work is deeply indebted to constructivist thinking, and specifically to the local, neo-constructive reworkings of the interwar tradition.

Abakanowicz transformed the joyful and colourful organic forms of her painted textiles under the influence of artists Henryk Stażewski (1894–1988) and Maria Ewa Łunkiewicz-Rogoyska (1895–1967). Both were over a generation older and provided the young Abakanowicz with friendship and mentorship. Stażewski who, together with Władysław Strzemiński (1893–1952) and Katarzyna Kobro (1898–1951), constituted the core of the interwar constructivist movement in Poland, and who was then connected to both the French and the Dutch circles of abstract art, served in socialist Poland as a messenger of the legacy of the early avant-garde. Together with the poet and art critic Julian Przyboś, Stażewski was seminal for the rebirth of geometric abstraction tendencies (top right) when enthusiasm for gestural and matter-oriented painting began to wane.

While the two traditions were originally very different, *art informel* began to move towards constructivism in Polish art of the mid 1960s when many painters that previously identified as matter-oriented or gestural, began to create works grounded in the more rational visual language of geometry. Examples of this tendency can be found among painters from Wrocław of Abakanowicz's generation. The thick, almost monochromatic matter paintings (right) of Jerzy Rosołowicz (1928–82) from the late 1950s continued the visual poetics of Strzemiński's unism that focused on resolving any visual tensions in the image through the complete union of forms with the picture plane. However, his organic, bulging shapes created with impastos slowly smoothed out and solidified, and gave way around 1965 to more organised structures with distinct colours, ultimately turning into vividly coloured grids. This new work was visually closer to the compositions of Victor Vasarely (1906–97) than Jean Fautrier (1898–1964). Rosołowicz's Wrocław-peer Jerzy Chwałczyk (1924–2018) similarly departed from solemn, ochre-coloured compositions, incorporating stones, bones and other organic matter in the early 1960s, to op-art-style experiments with light and shadow by the end of the decade.

It may seem contradictory that Abakanowicz's works had nothing to do with the political radicality of the early constructivist attitudes, but the postwar Polish neo-constructivism was already entirely

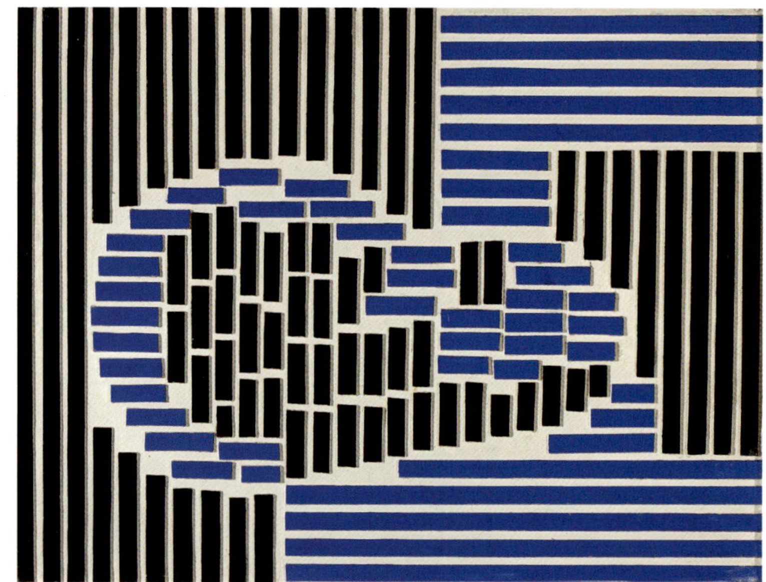

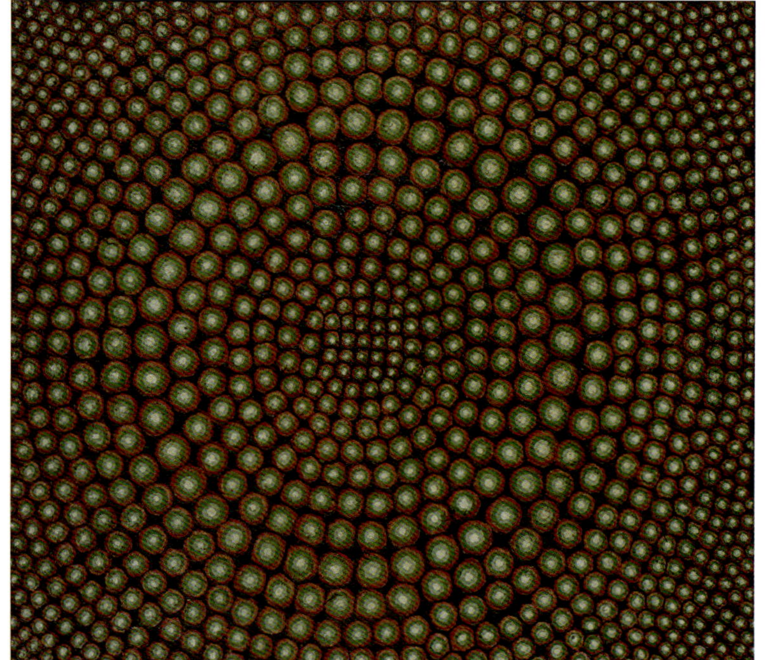

devoid of the political zeal and the social engagement present in the early avant-gardes. The character of Thaw modernism was anchored in the avoidance of openly political topics (beyond those dictated by official state commissions). Remaining within the narrow spectrum of addressing only artistic problems was a guarantee for continuing the semi-freedom of expression and relative cultural openness of the Polish communist authorities, who accepted abstraction and formalist experiments – unlike the governments running other Soviet satellite countries.[12]

Abakanowicz had met Stażewski and Łunkiewicz-Rogoyska in 1957, and this connection influenced how she began to think about the composition and organisation of her painted textiles, coming to consider them 'too flamboyant and lacking in structure'.[13] The artist Roman Owidzki (1912–2009), who was a part of that social group, admitted later, 'we made her loathe those beautiful flowers!'[14] The comparison of Abakanowicz's gouaches painted on textile in 1955–7, such as the *Green Composition* 1956–7 (p.42) with works such as *Composition* 1960 (p.33) (both shown at Kordegarda), reveal an increasingly stricter organisational principle in the later works. A kind of loose grid starts underlying the compositions that – while still operating with non-geometric, organic shapes – possess symmetry and have clearly delineated vertical and horizontal divisions. In other words, they acquire a sense of visual rhythm. The same characteristics are true of the artist's weavings from the early 1960s, including *Textural Composition White* 1961–2 (pp.30 and 44) and the *Composition of White Forms* included at the Lausanne Biennial in 1962.

In 1964, Abakanowicz even created a work based on a Stażewski drawing, creating an unusual piece that stood out from the other wall hangings she made around that time. *Composition 32 (After a drawing by Stażewski)* (right) was woven in parallel lines of white and black comprised within several multi-sided shapes. The black-and-white pattern was grounded in the visual formula that Stażewski had developed for his abstract paintings in the late 1920s and now used again for his drawings. Since his early post-cubist, and later mature constructivist experiments, contrast was Stażewski's foundational principle for the visual organisation of his canvases.[15] Since the late 1950s, he increasingly applied this principle to his experiments with space in a series of abstract reliefs built from plywood, and later metal. A similar linear motif in white and black lines appears in 1963 as an element in Abakanowicz's work, in *Le reliefs noir II* and *Tapisserie 21 brune* (p.45). The latter was made for production by the Cooperative-State Central Agency for Folk and Art Industry, known as Cepelia, from the artist's finely composed collage (pp.46–7), and both were shown at her solo exhibition in 1963 at the Galeria Sztuki Nowoczesnej, 'Krzywe Koło', Warsaw. (Her interest in defined shapes demonstrated in this composition can also be seen in her weaving, *Sun* of the same year, pp.48–9).

A close review of Abakanowicz's weavings from around 1962 to 1965 reveals that the artist took from Stażewski not only the notion of contrasting colour values, but the very idea of contrast as an organising principle. This is evident in *Study of Textures I* and *II* 1964 (p.36). Almost identical, the weavings each consist of three kidney-shaped forms somewhat similar to the ovals from *Composition 32*, but the opposition of black and white is not internal to these shapes (as was the case with the thin-lined pattern), it is between figure and ground, executed in dark brown-black and light beige. Yet, for all the intensity of the contrast, the colour composition is not the most striking element of the piece, for it is here that Abakanowicz used horsehair for one of the first times. Attaching the hair so that it would drop loosely from the surface of the weaving, the artist achieved yet another type of contrast: that of texture and structure, emphasising her material's tactile qualities. The year 1964 was the beginning of this practice, which was to become a highly animated and important element in her work.

This and other examples from 1964–5 demonstrate how taking the idea of contrast and translating it to the medium of textiles allowed Abakanowicz to experiment with the visual and haptic power of juxtaposing textures, as well as thicknesses of the weave. She began exploring the potential of having a smooth, flat knot sit close by a multi-knot bulge: the perceptual strength of allowing a set of threads to hang loosely along the textile's surface, while the other threads, woven tightly and methodically constituted the fabric behind it. And finally, these investigations allowed Abakanowicz to discover, soon after, the ultimate contrast that any surface can allow – that of an opening.

Opposite top: Henryk Stażewski *Relief Composition* 1961
Oil paint on fibreboard
46 × 61

Opposite bottom: Jerzy Rosołowicz *Neutrons-Image IV (Neutrony-Obraz IV)* 1964–5
Oil paint and mixed media on canvas
54 × 63

Below: *Composition 32 (After a drawing by Stażewski)* 1964
Wool 75 × 100

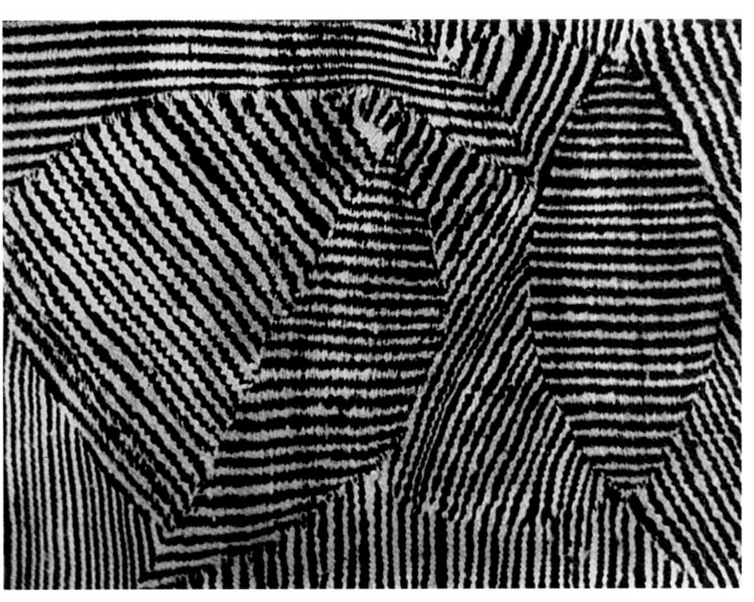

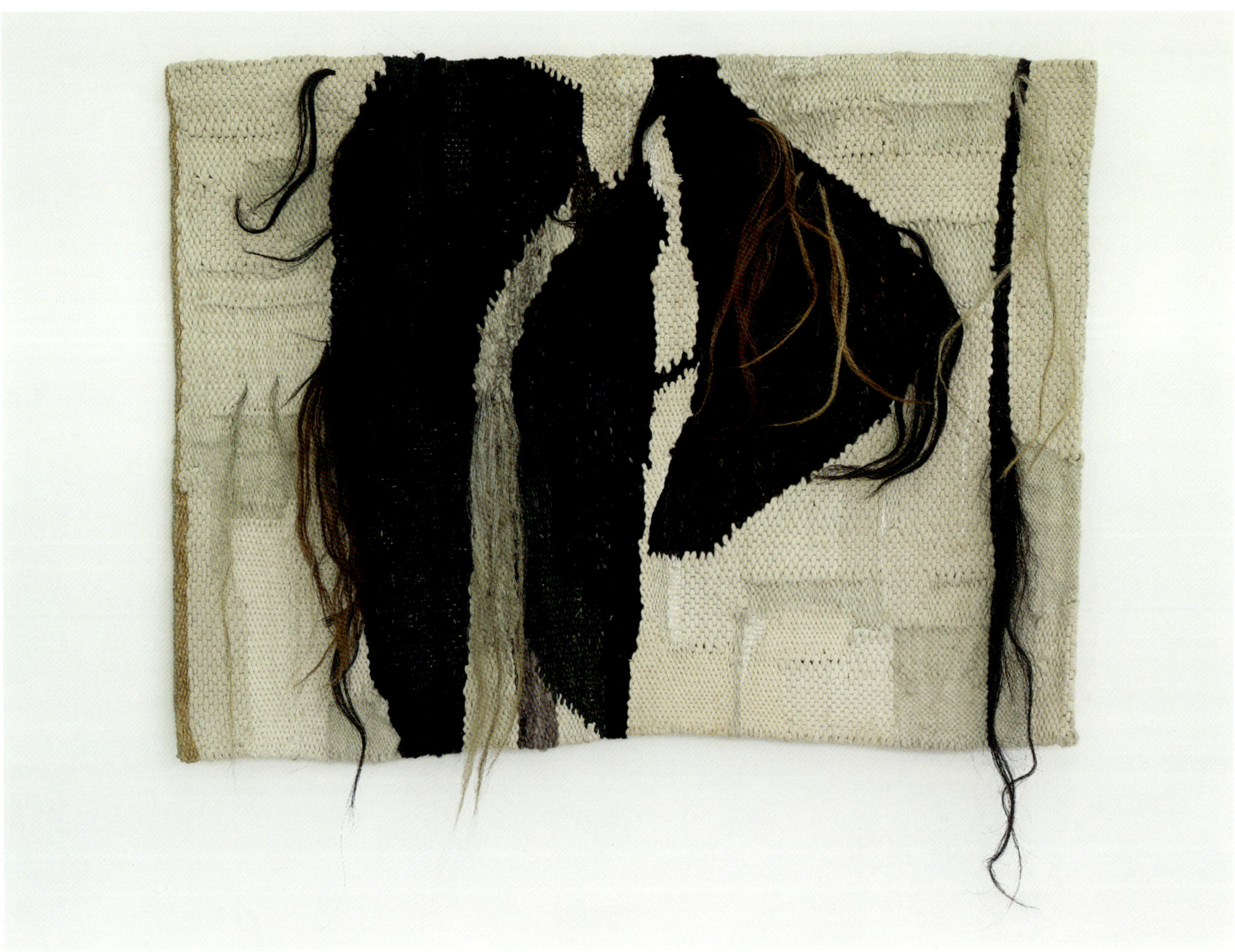

Above: *Study of Textures II* 1964
Sisal, cotton cord, horsehair and wool
100 × 145

Opposite: *Design for tapestry 'Teresa'* 1963
Gouache on papers on paper 39 × 55

Borders

The reviewers of Abakanowicz's 1965 exhibition of *Gobelins* (tapestry) at Zachęta CBWA, Warsaw, universally agreed on two things: that the fourteen works exhibited were beautiful and impressive ('what a beauty!' exclaimed one),[16] and that they were not Gobelins at all. 'It would be difficult to find a more vivid example of the vanishing of the borders separating the disciplines of contemporary art than Magdalena Abakanowicz's Gobelins', wrote the critic of Warsaw's paper *Stolica*.[17] 'None of the existing names applies ideally to what is coming out from the artist's hands,' decided the author of the weekly lifestyle magazine *Zwierciadło*, providing three reasons as to why Abakanowicz's artworks could not be considered Gobelins: because the artist not only designed them, but also executed the works herself; because her techniques extended far beyond conventional tapestry techniques; and finally, because the effects of her process transgressed traditional weaving.[18] This article was titled simply 'Abakany' and, in the body of the text, the author directly suggested using this new name for Abakanowicz's creations.

The magazine had already attempted to introduce this term a year earlier[19] and, in fact, the term *Abakans*sprang up in many recorded conversations surrounding the 1965 show that included multiple large-scale wall hangings titled with women's names: *Helena* (pp.50–1), *Teresa* (opposite), and *Kleopatra* 1964, as well as *Composition 32 (After a drawing by Stażewski)* and *Study of Textures II* discussed earlier. All of these pieces still hung flat against the wall.[20]

The issue of nomenclature preoccupied Polish critics for the full decade, starting with Abakanowicz's 1960 exhibition at Kordegarda,[21] during her 1963 show at the Galeria Sztuki Nowoczesnej 'Krzywe Koło',[22] and the 1965 display at Zachęta CBWA, all the way up until her 1967 presentation at Galeria Współczesna KMPiK 'Ruch'.[23] If there had been no name for the pieces created by Abakanowicz in the 1960s, it was because in conceiving and producing these works the artist had broken free from the confines of traditionally regarded art disciplines (Polish critics did not use the term 'medium' but spoke about 'artistic disciplines'). There were also strict divisions between what was considered to be utilitarian, applied art, labelled as 'design', and the autonomous art forms considered 'fine art'. When the critic Ignacy Witz, in his otherwise enthusiastic review of the Zachęta CBWA exhibition, decided that, 'The show of Magdalena Abakanowicz became, if one puts aside the utilitarian substance of these works, truly an important art event,'[24] his rather patronising tone towards the weavings' utility only revealed the separation that had existed between 'applied' and 'fine' art.

Abakanowicz's success in breaking through this confinement was lauded by the critic Hanna Ptaszkowska, who believed the most striking mark of the artist's recent progress had been specifically this move from utility to autonomy. Debating the status of the new objects, Ptaszkowska concluded that 'the exhibition of Abakanowicz suggests three alternatives: textile? painting? or works of an irrelevant affiliation realised in a material?'[25] Ptaszkowska decided the answer was the last of the three, stating that 'the composition came alive' only after Abakanowicz 'touched the material and allowed its genre-specific characteristics to shine'. By stating that Abakanowicz had 'revolutionised the methods used in textile', Ptaszkowska acknowledged what had been common knowledge since the 1962 biennial in Lausanne, but – interestingly – she also claimed that 'the originating power of this revolution was the marriage with modern painting.'[26]

Other critics reached similar conclusions: 'They are, in fact, painterly works – just made without the use of brushes and paint,' decided Aleksy Czerwiński about the early *Abakans*.[27] 'Just like in a good painting', explained Elżbieta Żmudzka in *Zwierciadło*, 'here also an important role is played by colour, composition, texture, the saturation of every single centimetre, and the internal tensions that decide whether a visual artwork attracts attention, stimulates reflection, provides an experience.' Witz also praised 'the authentic sense of colour, temperament and dynamics of the compositional structures, boldness in using an often-conventional material, and beyond everything – links to the ideals of truly contemporary painting.'[28]

In the Zachęta CBWA exhibition catalogue, Wiesław Borowski shared similar medium-related observations: Abakanowicz had 'unearthed the essence of contemporary textile', in order to move past it.[29] The echoes of the typically modernist quest for medium specificity, and its later expansion, are evident here. According to Borowski, Abakanowicz's work contributed to 'the radical transformation taking place in artistic practice today, where the definition of Gobelin cannot hold, just as the encyclopedic definition of painting has stopped to hold a long time ago.' For Borowski, Abakanowicz's was the most experimental practice possible now – and akin to many of her peers.

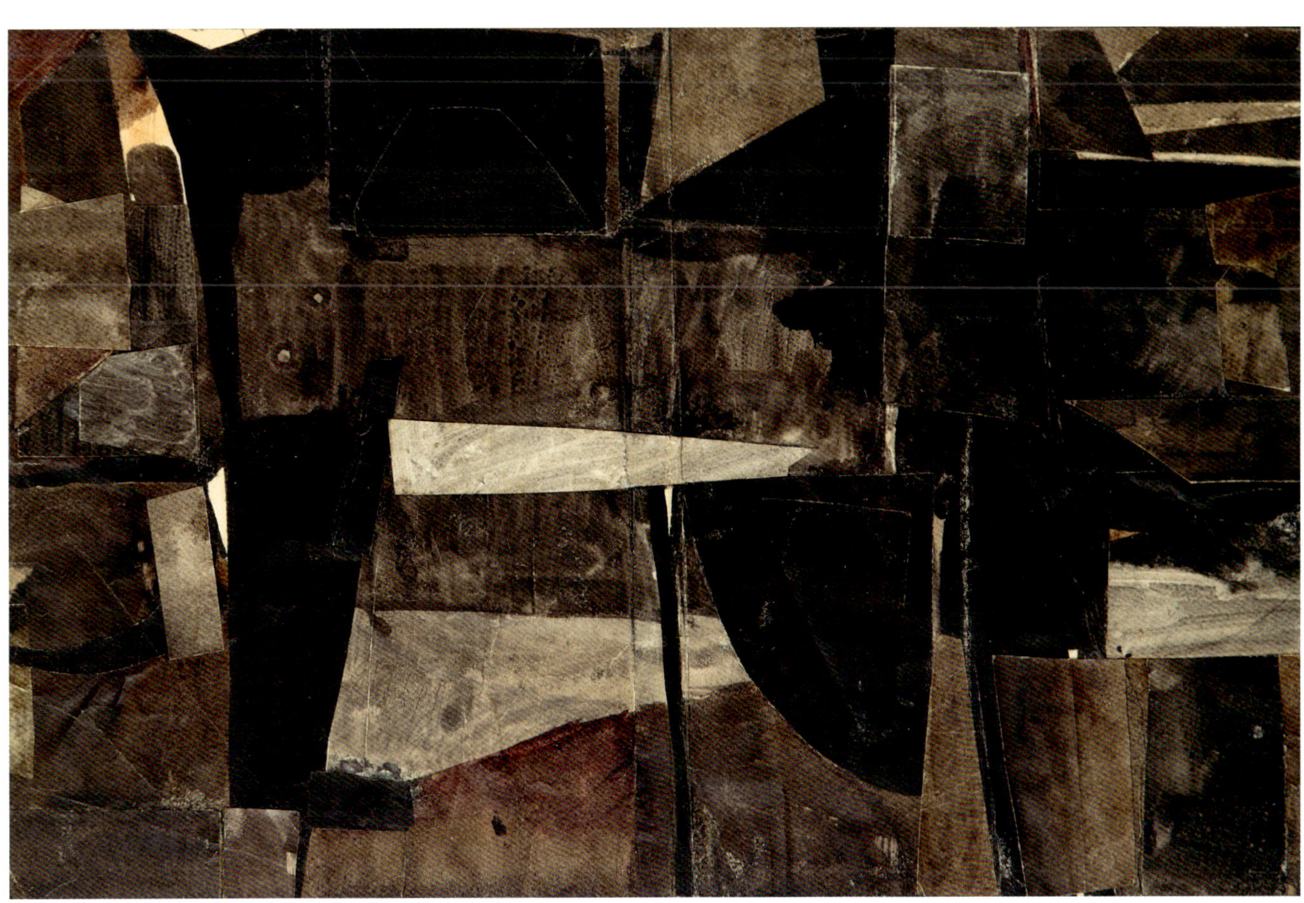

Yet, Ptaszkowka's affirmation of the artist's experiments was partial still in 1965. 'The process, in which textiles started becoming autonomous, has not yet reached the totality [of her work].' The critic noticed that the composition of the weavings recalled painted pictures and deemed the Gobelins' dependence on painting as not-so-positive. Ptaszkowska observed 'the light of Rembrandt', flickering between the loosely hanging ponytails; shiny patches of white that reminded her of touches made by a painter's brush. The critic found both 'somewhat disappointing'. Her hope and goal for Abakanowicz's woven works was clearly to become the non-textile and non-painting – that third category ('work of irrelevant affiliation') listed in her initial question about disciplines. In a sense, with that disappointment, Ptaszkowska predicted the direction that Abakanowicz's tapestries, already in the process of becoming the full-blown *Abakans*, would take within the next few years.

The critic's disappointment, as it happens, says a lot not only about Abakanowicz's work, but also about Ptaszkowska's own thinking at the time. In the following year, 1966, she co-founded, together with Borowski and the critic Mariusz Tchorek, Galeria Foksal, a seminal spot for the neo-avant-garde art of the late 1960s and 1970s. (Henryk Stażewski would be an important inspiration and mentor for these younger critics – as would be Tadeusz Kantor, regardless of the divergent traditions from which these artists came). The gallery would often present projects evading clear-cut discipline/medium affiliations. This is not to say that Ptaszkowska simply incorporated Abakanowicz's new works into her own, already pre-existing theoretical framework. Quite the contrary: there seems to be a dialectical relationship between Ptaszkowska's thinking (as expressed in her writing) and Abakanowicz's thinking (as expressed in her making). The artist's experiments with weaving only confirmed the critic's earlier intuitions and prognosis regarding future developments of modern art. In the linearity of her understanding of artistic processes, Ptaszkowska was a typically modernist critic, just as Abakanowicz was – at least at the time – a very modernist artist. In the end, both women were deeply embedded in the post-Thaw, neo-constructivist, anti-purity of medium zeitgeist of the Polish art scene around 1965.

Forms

A collective revival of constructivist thinking in Poland took place in July and August 1965 in Elbląg. Conceived by the local artist Gerard Kwiatkowski (1930–2015) in collaboration with Warsaw artist and organiser Marian Bogusz, the Ist Biennial of Spatial Forms commissioned artists to create three-dimensional works for the city's public spaces under the auspices of state patronage. More than forty artists worked collaboratively with employees of the Elbląg steel plant to create pieces from metal – intentionally called 'spatial forms' rather than simply 'sculptures' – and erect them throughout the city. Recalling the thinking of Władysław Strzemiński, the organisers emphasised the role of the artist in constructing or composing living spaces in the same way one composes a painting, as well as the need for egalitarian access to art.[30]

Abakanowicz recalled Bogusz was drunk when he invited her to participate in the biennial.[31] There may well have been some truth behind this – everyone in the Polish art world drank like a fish – but the implication that the decision was made impulsively, not so much. Bogusz had organised Abakanowicz's 1963 exhibition at the Galeria Sztuki Nowoczesnej 'Krzywe Koło', which he ran in Warsaw's Old Town and where she first presented her new weavings in Poland after the success in Lausanne. But even without this prior connection, the almost ecstatic reception of her exhibition at Zachęta CBWA in March 1965 – only four months before the Elbląg event – would have warranted such an invitation.[32]

The tall untitled work created by Abakanowicz for the biennial in Elbląg is reminiscent of a tree: a lofty trunk extends both upwards and outwards through multiple smaller cylindrical protrusions. In a sense, this piece forecasts the artist's arboreal architecture designed twenty-five years later and the series of bronze *Hand-like Trees* in the early 1990s (p.172). However, the Elbląg tree is hollow. Made of sheet metal through folding, instead of cast, this spatial form is entirely devoid of volume. The piece does not occupy space as much as it directs it. Rather than through volume, the work operates via a series of flat, folded barriers that only partially enclose the space and let it flow. The central, trunk-like form directs the space upwards, while the branch-like protrusions guide it towards the outside, integrating this non-invasive form with the environment, as if visualising the forces that were already there. The piece serves as a conduit of space.

This is not a work made by a sculptor. The form feels tentative and fragile, as if rolled up from a piece of cardboard: an enlarged paper model that one can imagine the artist nimbly folding in her hands. But then, Abakanowicz wasn't a sculptor in 1965. There is no paradox here, since the majority of the biennial's participants were educated as painters. Elbląg gave its artists the opportunity to expand beyond the constraints of their medium, to advance their spatial thinking.

For many, the Biennial of Spatial Forms crowned media experimentation emergent with Thaw modernism a decade earlier. For Abakanowicz, it marked a culmination as well as a breaking point. On the one hand, the tree-like form was directly connected to her early work: the sculpture had its small-scale predecessor in the no-longer-extant *Relief III* 1958, a small piece of wood encrusted with

Below: *Untitled* 1965
Steel 700 × 250 × 220
Elbląg, Poland

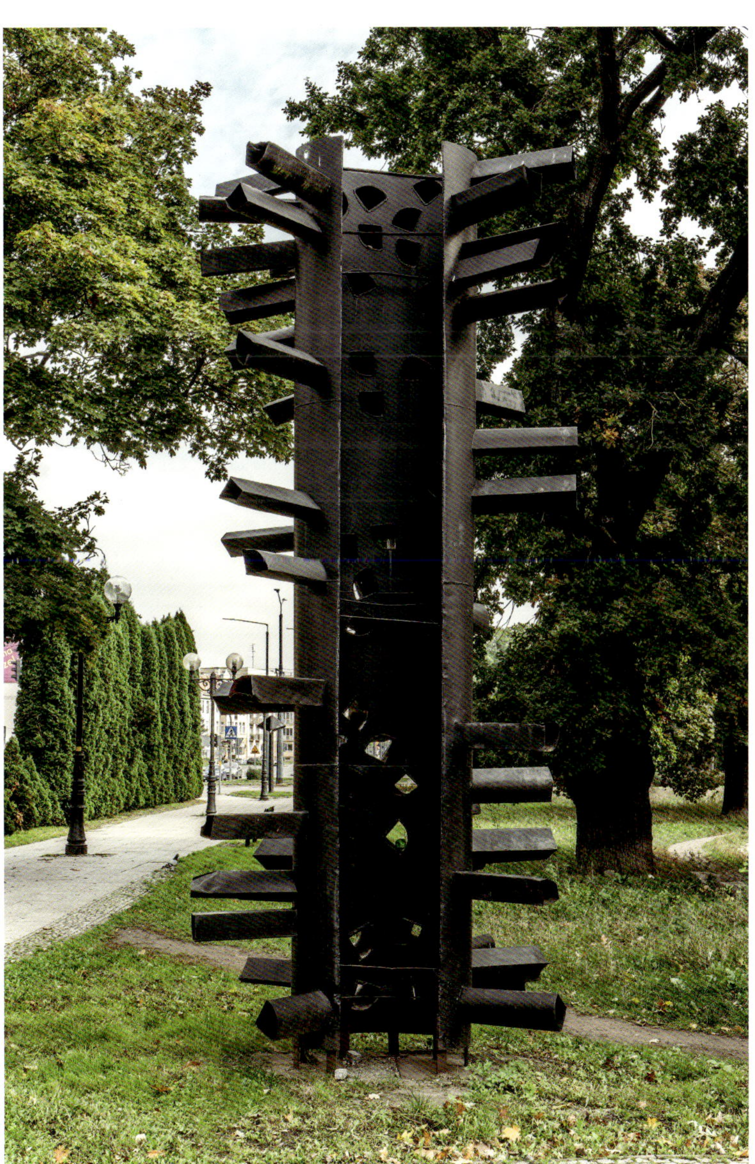

protruding bits of cork. On the other, the Elbląg sculpture led Abakanowicz to rethink the construction and spatiality of her weavings, resulting in her giving up the orderly, rectangular format of her previous works and shifting her focus on to the centre.[33] In a sense, the inside of that sculpture, how it organised and directed space, enabled Abakanowicz to abandon the perpendicular logic of warp and weft. The space flowing through the metal trunk did not have a clear beginning and end in the same way that a thread – inevitably destined to linearity – always does.

Later, Abakanowicz wrote: 'The *Abakans* were my escape from categories in art; they could not be classified. Larger than me, they were safe like the hollow trunk of the old willow.'[34]

Space

Black 1966 (pp.56–7) as well as *Assemblage noir* 1966 (pp.58–61) both include a central, oval shape partially covered with strands of hair and a heavily worked central core of folded textile, with vertical flaps running vertically through the middle. Coloured differently to the surrounding tapestry, these ovoid, vaginal forms look as though they are detachable from the rest of the composition: *Black* has small openings at the top and bottom, with warp thread lines visible. Such detachment already takes place in *Assemblage noir*, the work itself a sectionalised ovoid. The formal leaps taken in these works, can be seen as predictions for what was to happen with the *Abakans* in late 1967 and early 1968, when the artist decided to separate works fully from the wall. The word 'assemblage' in the title suggests a composition of various materials and hints, too, at the difference between the organic, autonomous oval piece and the rectangular frame, which had previously constituted a unified whole.

Calling her work *assemblage* may have been Abakanowicz's response to Janusz Bogucki, who proposed that term in the exhibition catalogue accompanying her 1967 show at Galeria Współczesna KMPiK 'Ruch', Warsaw: 'It is actually not weaving, but painting, tempestuous and expressive, whose weight comes from a magnificent control of material bearing such an archetypal beauty and poise', Bogucki repeated the now-common observation, then added that the artist's new works should be 'counted among the category called montage or assemblage'.[35] Współczesna is where Abakanowicz first presented a series of weavings made after the 1965 Zachęta CBWA exhibition and Elbląg, many of which were composed of openings, slits and thick, rope-like cords protruding outwards from the body of the piece (e.g. *White* 1966), as well as shapes that increasingly broke away from a rectangle, such as the ones discussed above. Detachment from the wall was just one step away.

The transition that took place in Abakanowicz's practice in late 1967 also finds its equivalents in other Polish artists' attempts to expand their respective media. Around the same time, Aleksander Kobzdej

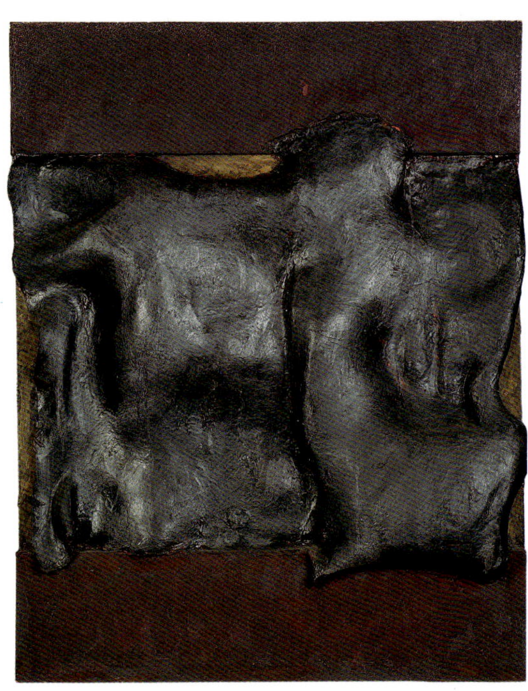

Left: Aleksander Kobzdej *Two Spaces (black) no.3* 1970
From the series *Hors Cadre*
Oil paint, glue and mixed media 99.5 × 80

Opposite: Stanisław Zamecznik's model for the Polish Pavilion at the International Fair in Barcelona 1959.

transformed his *informel* paintings into three-dimensional works constructed from modelling compound, akin to a loosely hanging, curved cloth. Reflecting on the process of transformation and becoming, his series *Crevices* and *Hors Cadre* (left) were – much like Abakanowicz's changing weavings – destined towards physical space.

The year 1967 was also when the Polish art scene discovered and embraced *environments* (pronounced the French way). At Galeria Foksal, Zbigniew Gostomski (1932–2017), known for his black-and-white paintings titled *Optical Objects*, put together a spatial arrangement from plywood, foam and light reflectors, creating a total space with dim lighting and an uneven floor. His *environment* allowed the viewers to lose themselves in the spatial maze and reflect on the entirety of the bodily sensations the project provided. At the III 'Złote Grono' symposium and exhibition in Zielona Góra the same year, Henryk Morel and Piotr Perepłyś constructed a *Space for Multisensory Perception*, an environment (the term 'installation' was not yet in use) put together from cloth, rubber and tow that encouraged phenomenological experience from viewers-turned-participants. It constituted a part of the exhibition *Space and Expression* where artists were prompted to each organise a selected gallery space, rather than simply install their individual artworks.[36] Considering the spatial conditions of display, together with the viewer's body, was a part of late modernism's emerging vocabulary.

Most important for Abakanowicz's spatial awareness was her friendship with Stanisław Zamecznik (1909–71), an innovative designer and stage designer. The two artists were simultaneously hired at the State Higher School of Plastic Arts in Poznań in 1965, sharing the train commute as well as meetings in the Saska Kępa neighbourhood of Warsaw, where they both lived.[37] Zamecznik had developed original thinking about the construction of space in the 1940s, which he used for transforming existing museum and gallery standards in the decades which followed. He elevated interior design to the level of high art, akin to that of modern architecture, constructing sophisticated spatial arrangements that were able to create new meanings between displayed objects. His installations, including the extraordinary room dedicated to coal at the *Exhibition of Regained Territories* in Wrocław in 1948 that Abakanowicz visited as a high school student, 'affected the viewer's emotions to an unprecedented degree'.[38]

In the late 1950s, Zamecznik developed an installation model grounded in the use of rounded, free-standing walls built from bent plywood. It was used, among others, at the Polish Pavilion at the 27th International Fair in Barcelona in 1959 (opposite). The fundamental element of this model was 'the biologism of the folding walls that have the ability to morph continuously, that is: to create oneself in constant interaction with the environment', as the art historian

Marta Leśniakowska explained, '[the biologism] operating with a fluid line that runs accordingly to the rhythm of a living organism'.[39] The body of the viewer was given a deliberate consideration within this structure – it completed the installation.

This bodily rhythm was later repeated in Abakanowicz's free-hanging *Abakans* – always carefully arranged by the artist herself – since they not so much filled, as actively held, space and welcomed the viewers' touch. Abakanowicz contemplated the physical body of the beholder as she allowed her *Abakans* to acquire their own, independent-of-the-wall bodies, providing them with the autonomy of separate creatures. Compared to the wall-bound weavings, the free-hanging *Abakans* lose the authority and the safety provided by the stable support of the gallery wall. They are on their own. It is this vulnerability, as much as the organic quality of the wavy and fluctuating material, that is reminiscent of a body.

'An *Abakan* is an independent entity, but it is also one of the elements by which we can conceive of space', wrote the artist in 1971, staying true to Zamecznik's thinking.[40] 'I am interested in the scale of tensions that arises between the various shapes which I place in space'.[41] It was specifically the realm of environment that allowed Abakanowicz to express herself as not only a fibre artist, but also as a contemporary artist.[42] The spatial consciousness that allowed this development was deeply embedded in all the experimentation that Abakanowicz witnessed and in which she participated in Poland. The three-dimensional *Abakans* – with their spatial orientation, their inviting tactility, the relationships they formed with each other, as well as the bodies of their viewers – were deeply rooted in the Polish art scene around 1967.

Coda: The Body

To the artist, her *Abakans* clearly had vaginal connotations: 'Their bodies sometimes opened to reveal a hairy interior, similar to interiors where one does not gaze with ease,' she wrote.[43] Abakanowicz also used the metaphors of flowers or seashells. For all the connections between the artist and her contemporaries, it is necessary to note that almost none of those associations were picked up by Polish criticism at the time. Unlike the American feminist interpretations that saw in the soft bodies of *Abakans* a direct reference to female genitalia, the vertical flaps signifying women's labia,[44] Polish critics shied away from such erotic connotations – be it for the puritanism of public discourse in socialist Poland or the authors' obsession with only formalist criticism. Their preoccupation was with the *Abakans*' ontological status rather than any metaphorical meanings.

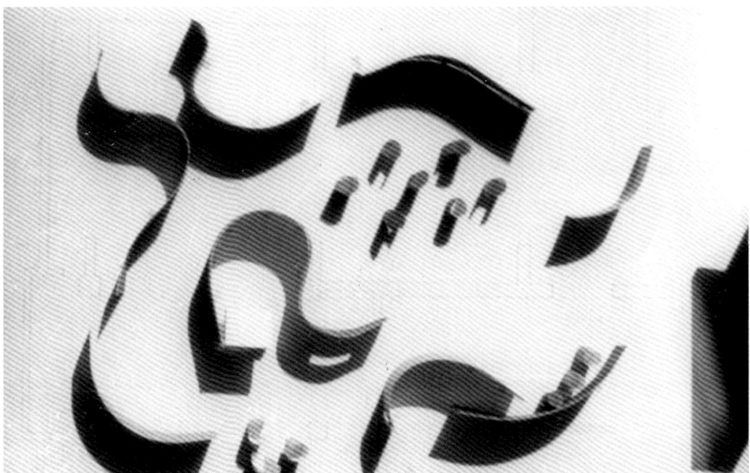

All the while it is only apparent in the Polish language, which recognises male, female and neutral forms of nouns and adjectives, that the artist's weavings were always female – even when the titles were descriptive of colours, such as white and black in the case of *Textural Composition White (Kompozycja fakturowa biała)* 1961–2 and *Black (Czarna)* already mentioned, as well as *Black and White (Czarno-biała)* of 1965 (pp.54–5).

Abakanowicz also directly assigned women's names to her weavings in the early to mid 1960s: *Ana, Teresa, Desdemona* and more. When she dropped that convention in favour of naming her weavings with adjectives – not uncommon among the existentialist matter paintings – she still used their female form. This was the case for works presented at Galeria Współczesna KMPiK 'Ruch', such as: *The Cracked One* (*Popękana*) and *The Separated One* (*Rozchylona*). These adjectives all describe qualities of a female body. And so, when Abakanowicz detached the oval, vaginal shapes from the rest of her weavings, leaving behind the framing rectangle, it was not only a formalist gesture of spatial awakening: in detaching from the constraints of the painting's frame, she was also liberating her work – and herself – from the phallic order of modernism.

Anna Markowska compellingly argued that it was the critics' refusal to understand her weavings as radical soft sculpture that had Abakanowicz move away from the tender bodies of the *Abakans* into much more masculinist and more literal, figurative form in the 1970s.[45] Because of the lack of an appropriate intellectual framework for grasping the true, bodily radicality of *Abakans* in 1960s Poland, critics failed to notice that Abakanowicz had created an 'interactive, mobile space full of erotic connotations, whose intimacy in the public space dramatically obliterated the borders between the public and the private.'[46] Polish critics, oblivious to their suggestive corporal associations, or maybe unable to accept their subversive character, saw *Abakans* as only formally new and strange – the same way Brzozowski pictured them in his *Abakany* film.

Green Composition
1956–7
Gouache on cotton
canvas
205 × 135

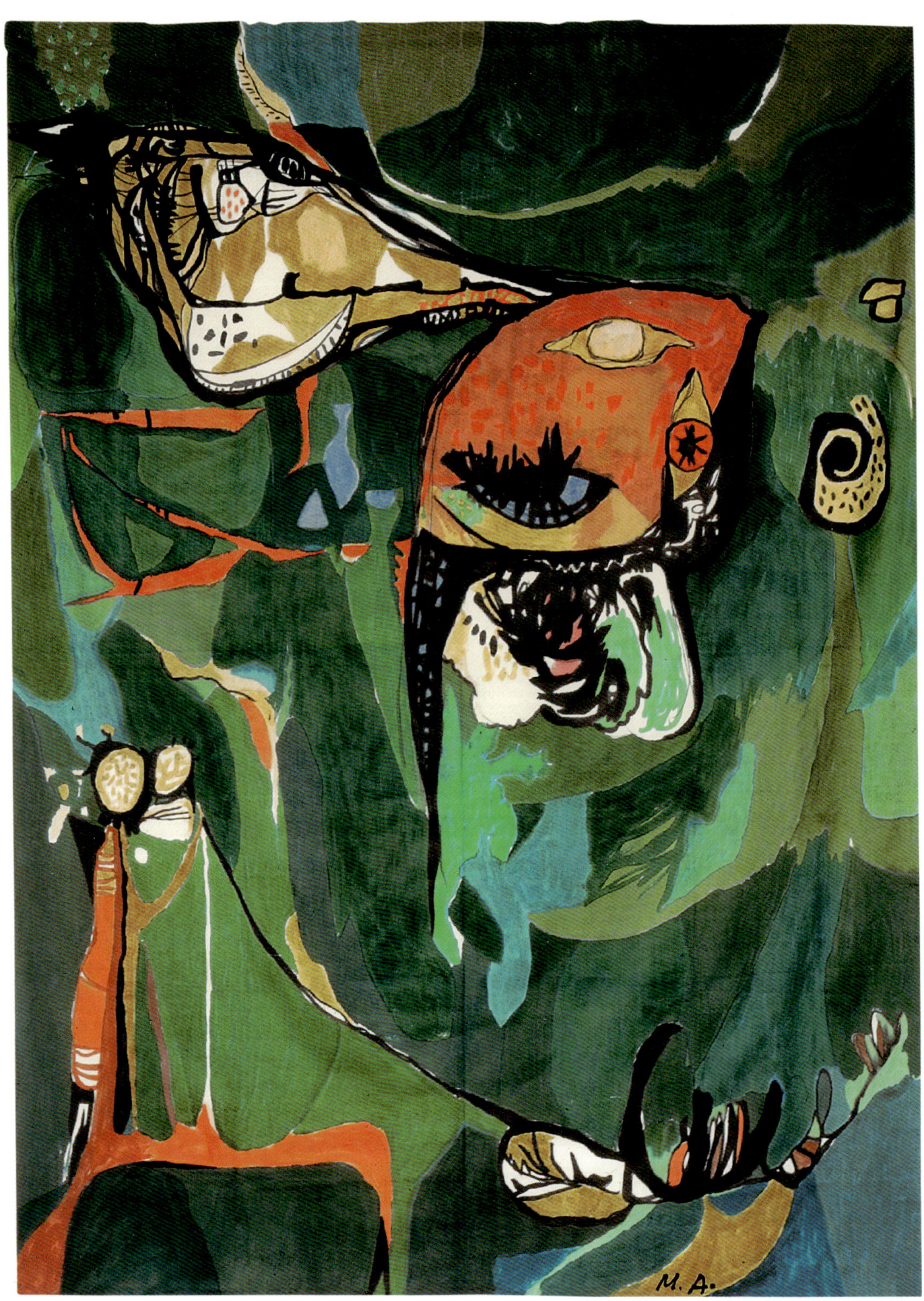

***Composition* 1960**
Gouache on linen
280 × 140

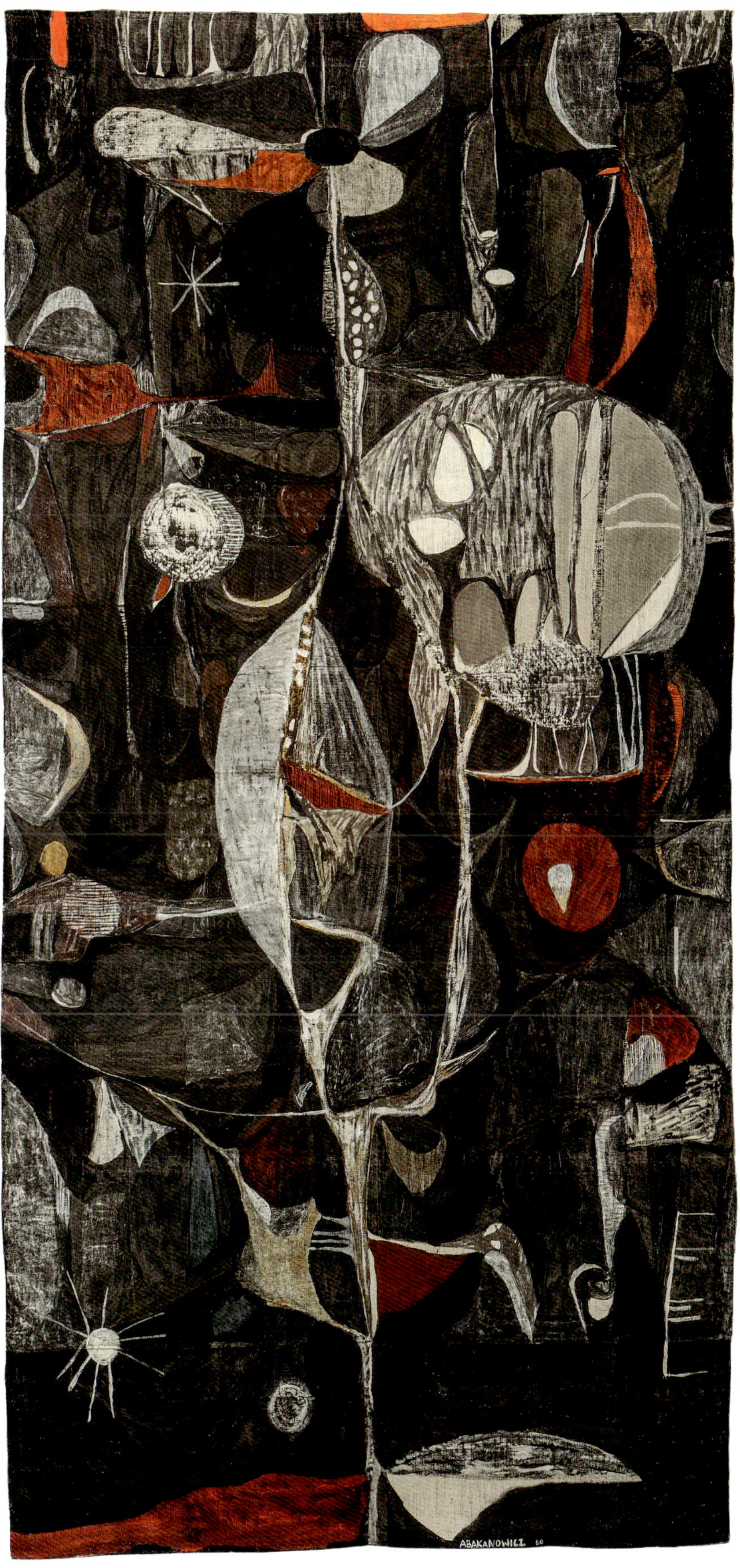

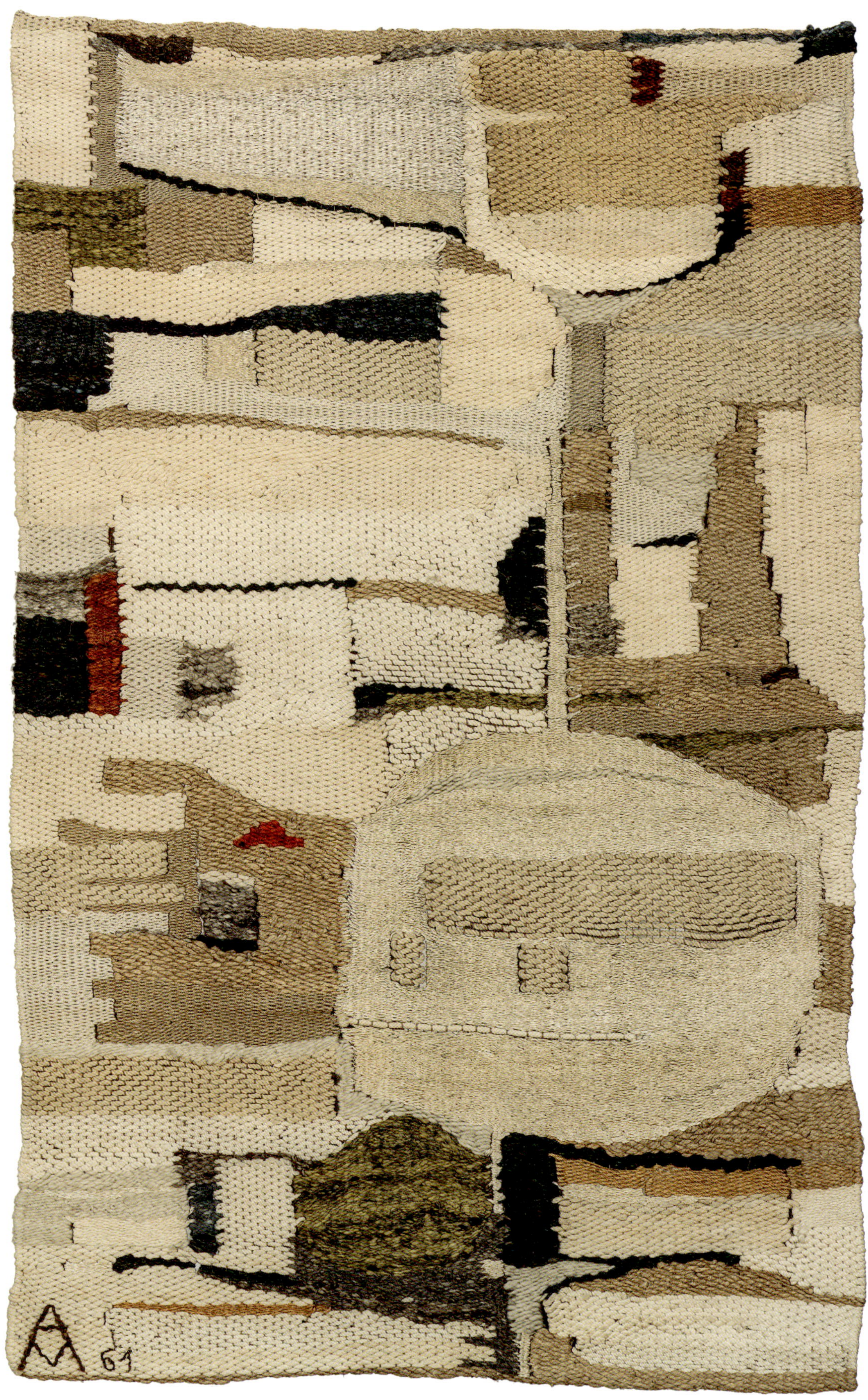
61

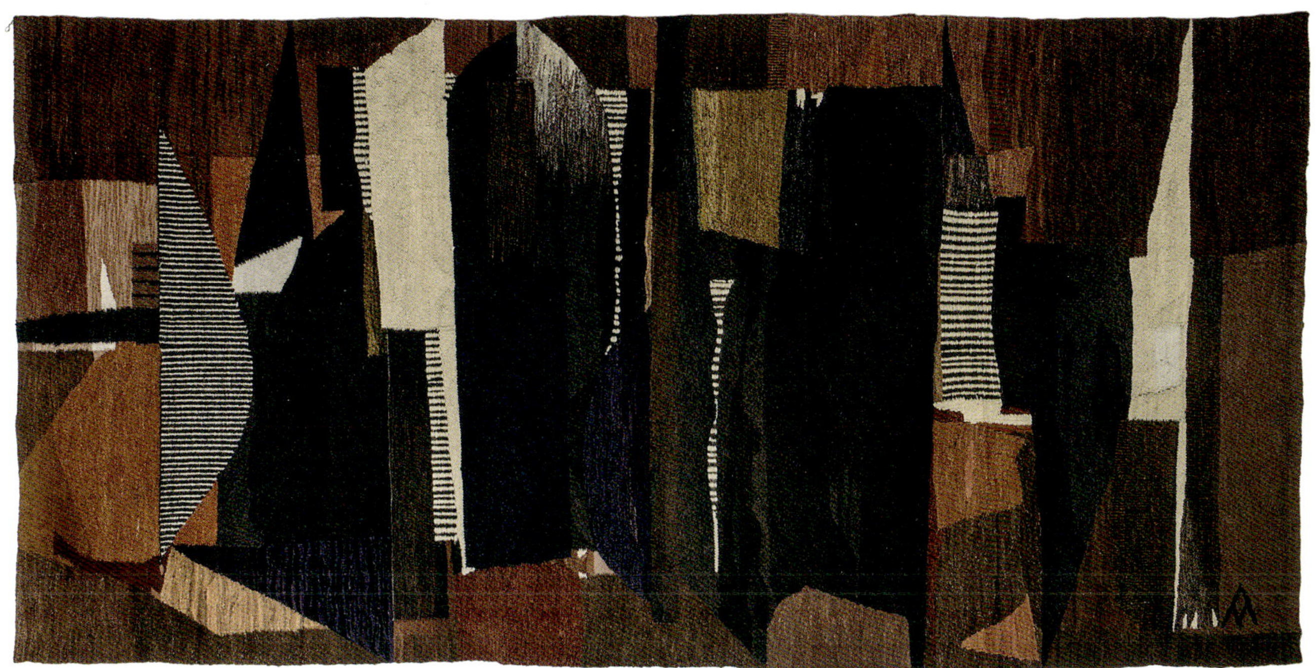

Tapisserie 21 brune
1963
Wool
150 × 295

Textural Composition
***White* 1961–2**
Sisal and cotton
164 × 106

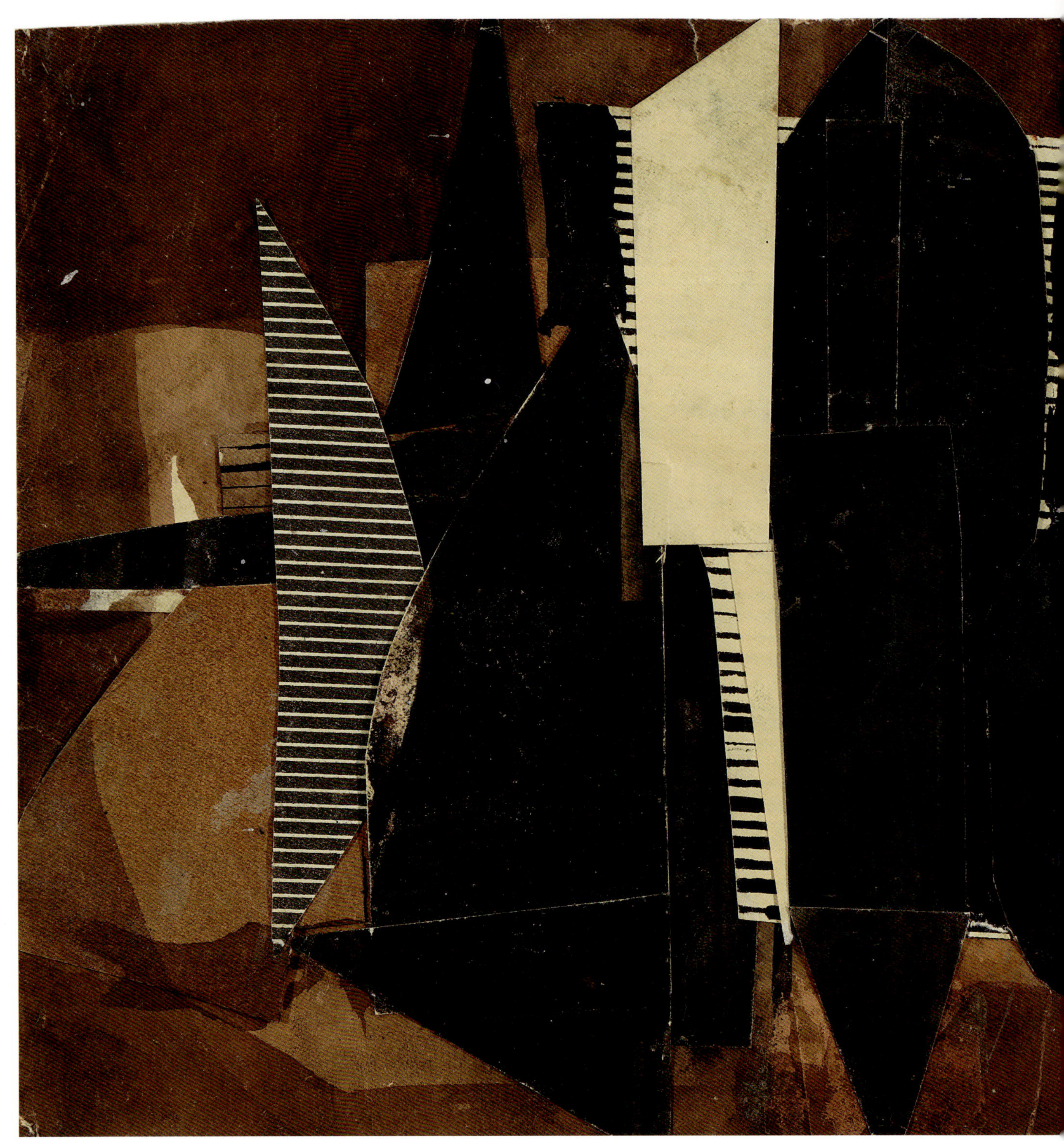

***Design for 'Tapisserie 21 brune'* 1963**
Ink and gouache on papers on paper
19 × 39.5

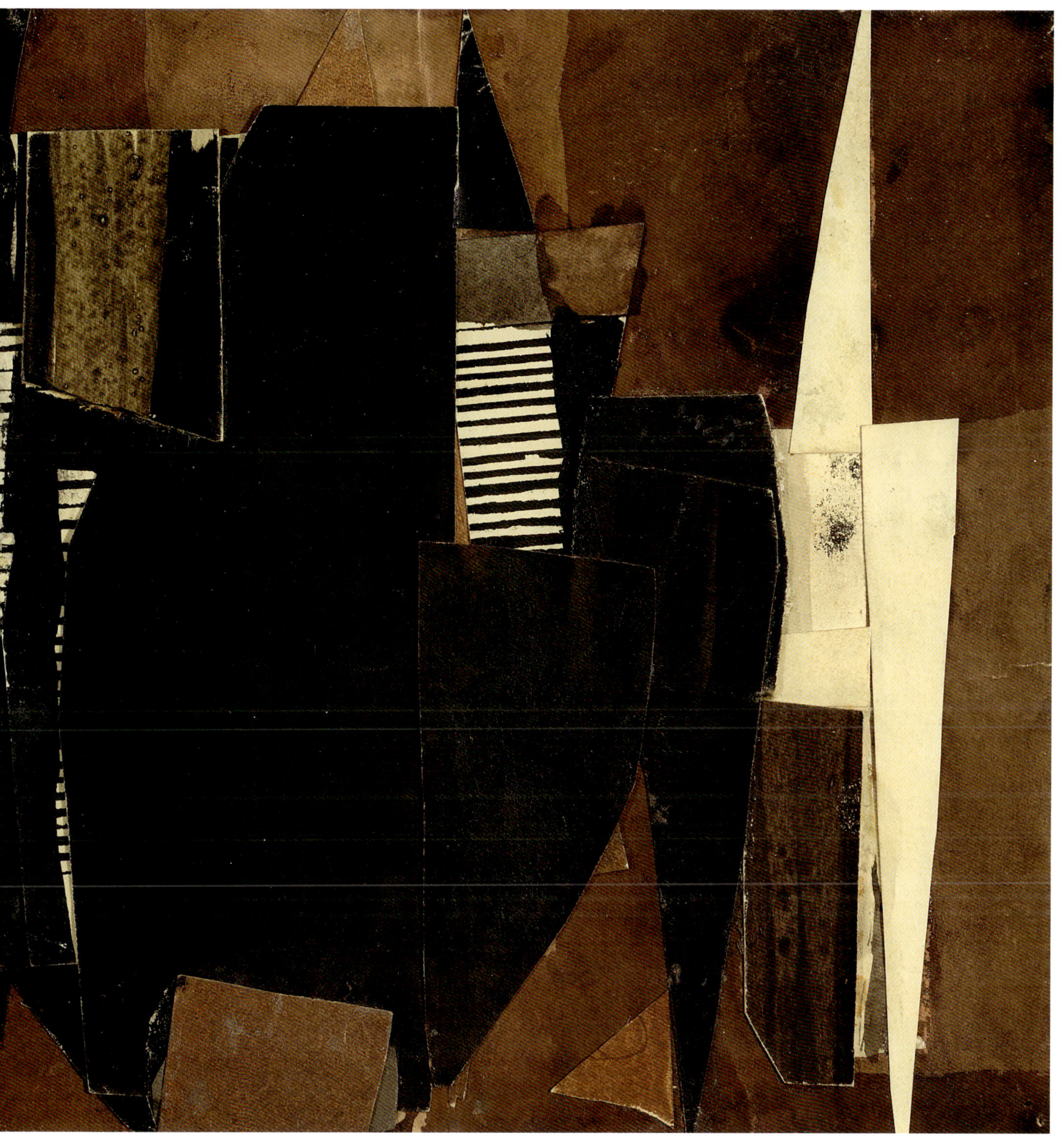

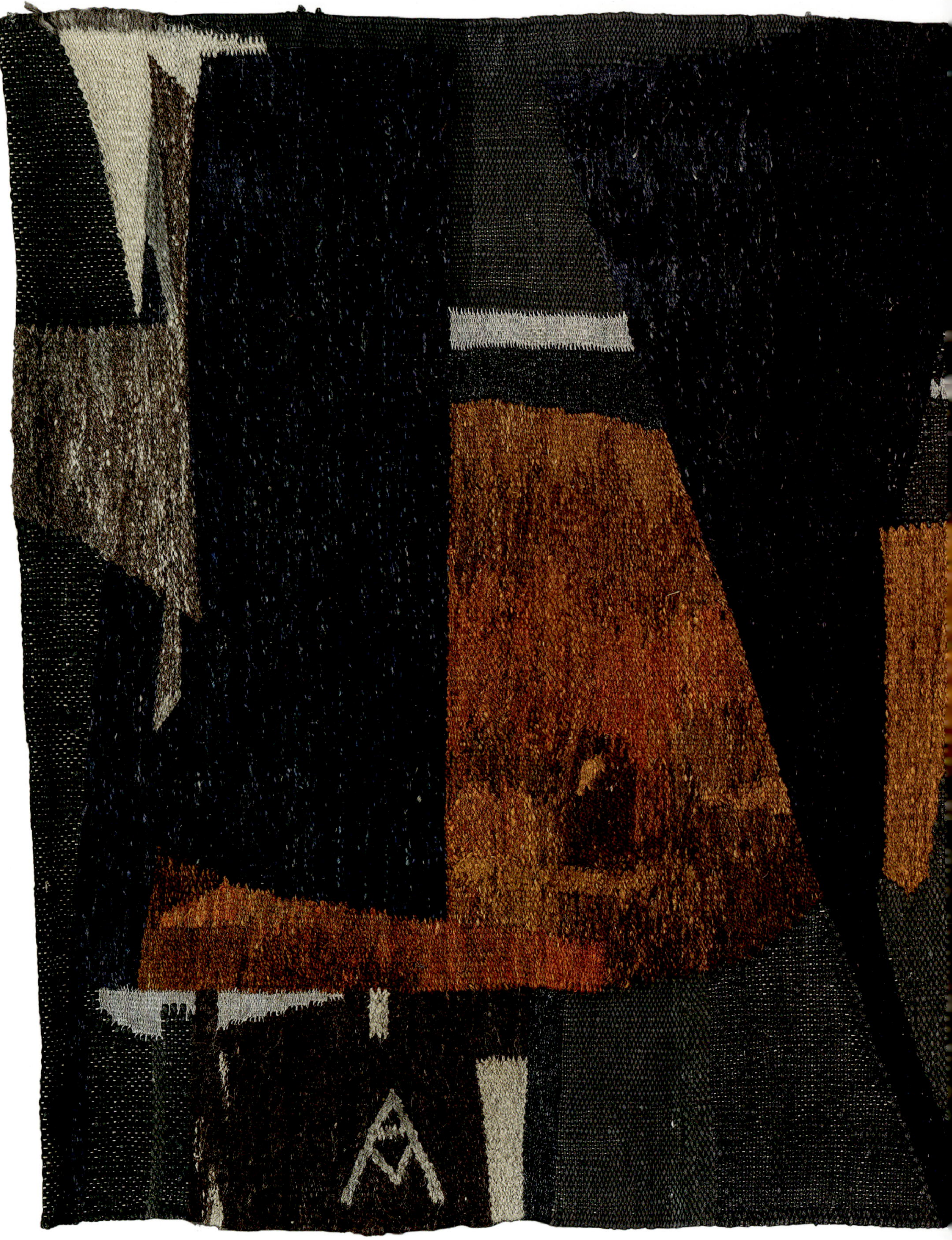

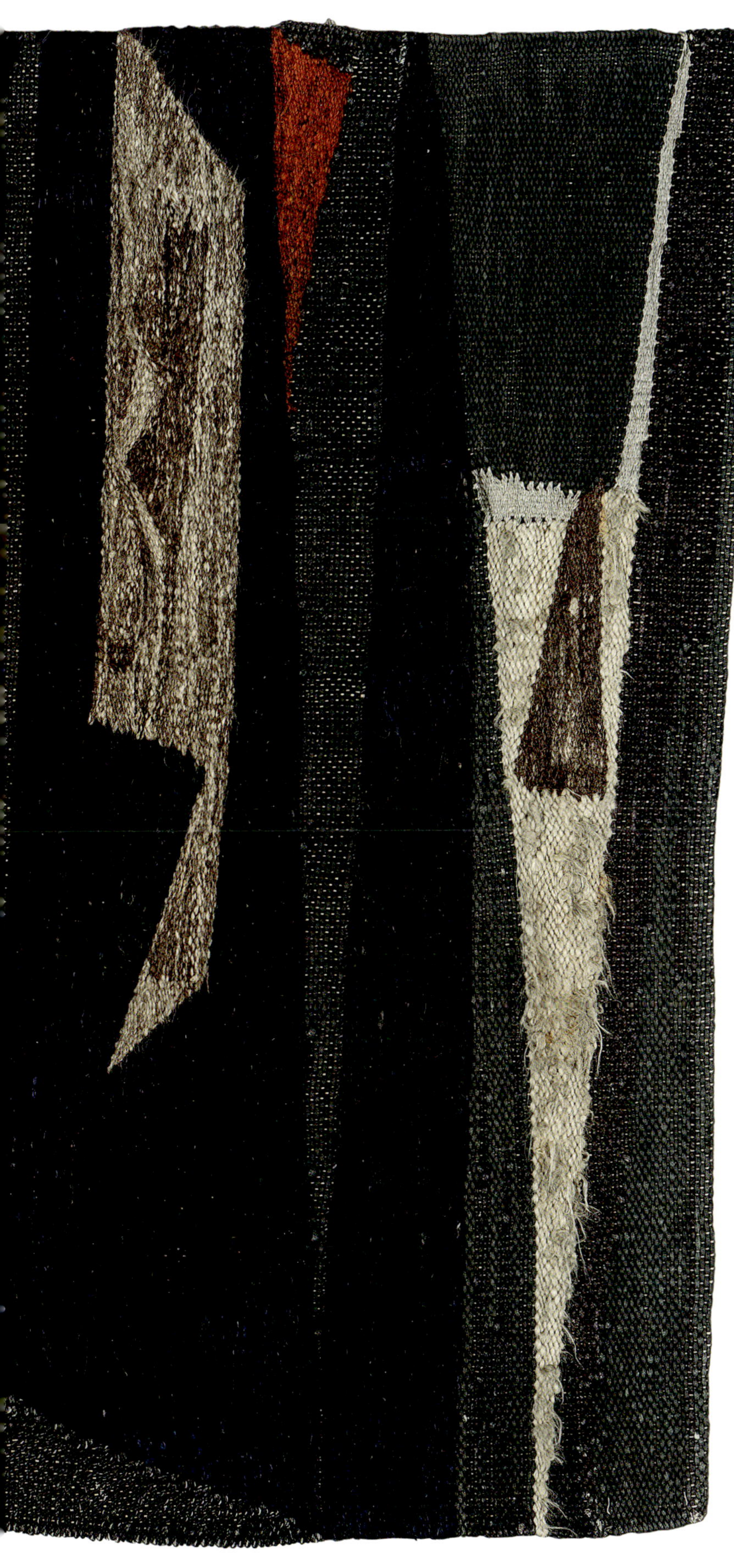

***Sun* 1963**
Wool, cotton and artificial silk
152 × 211

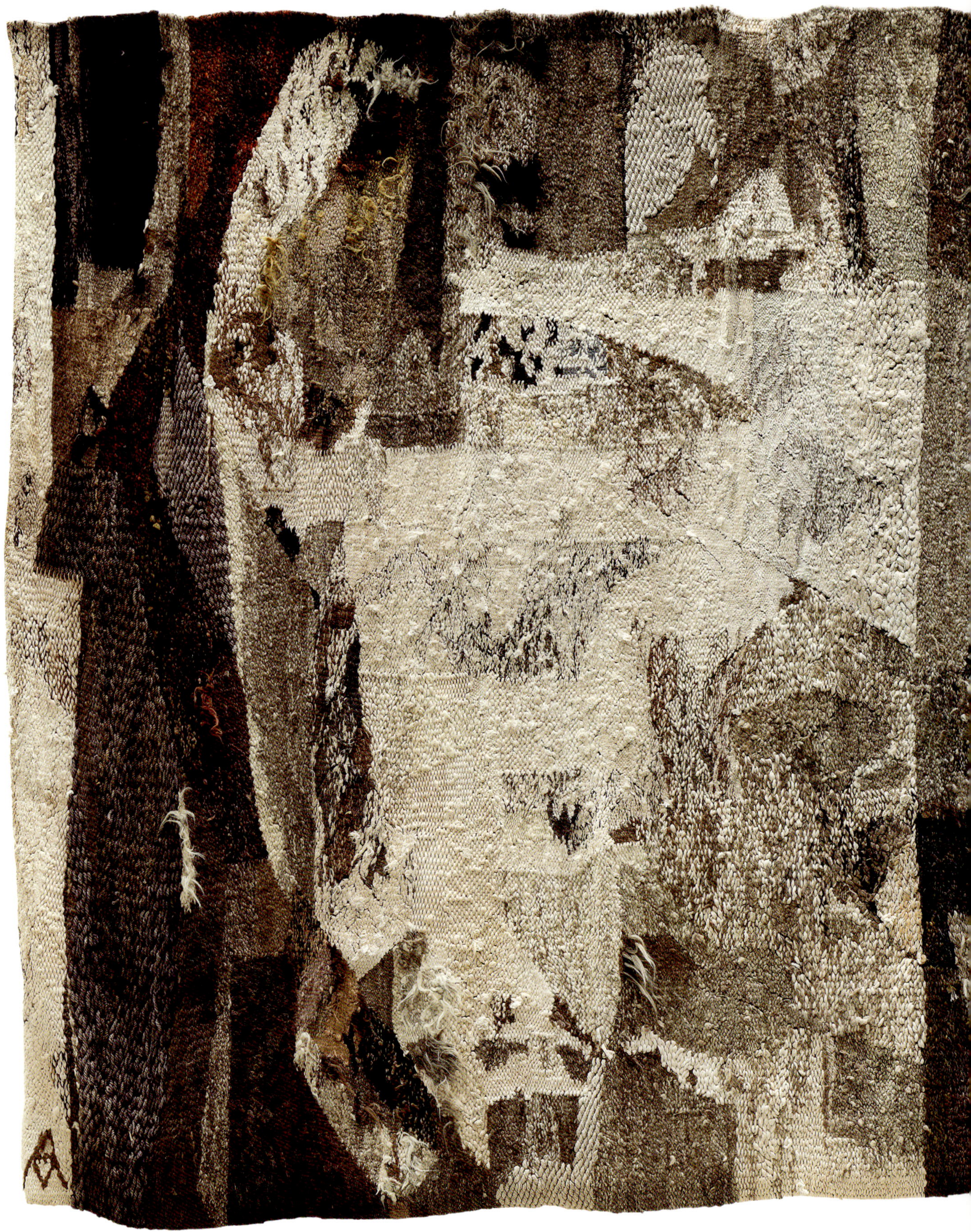

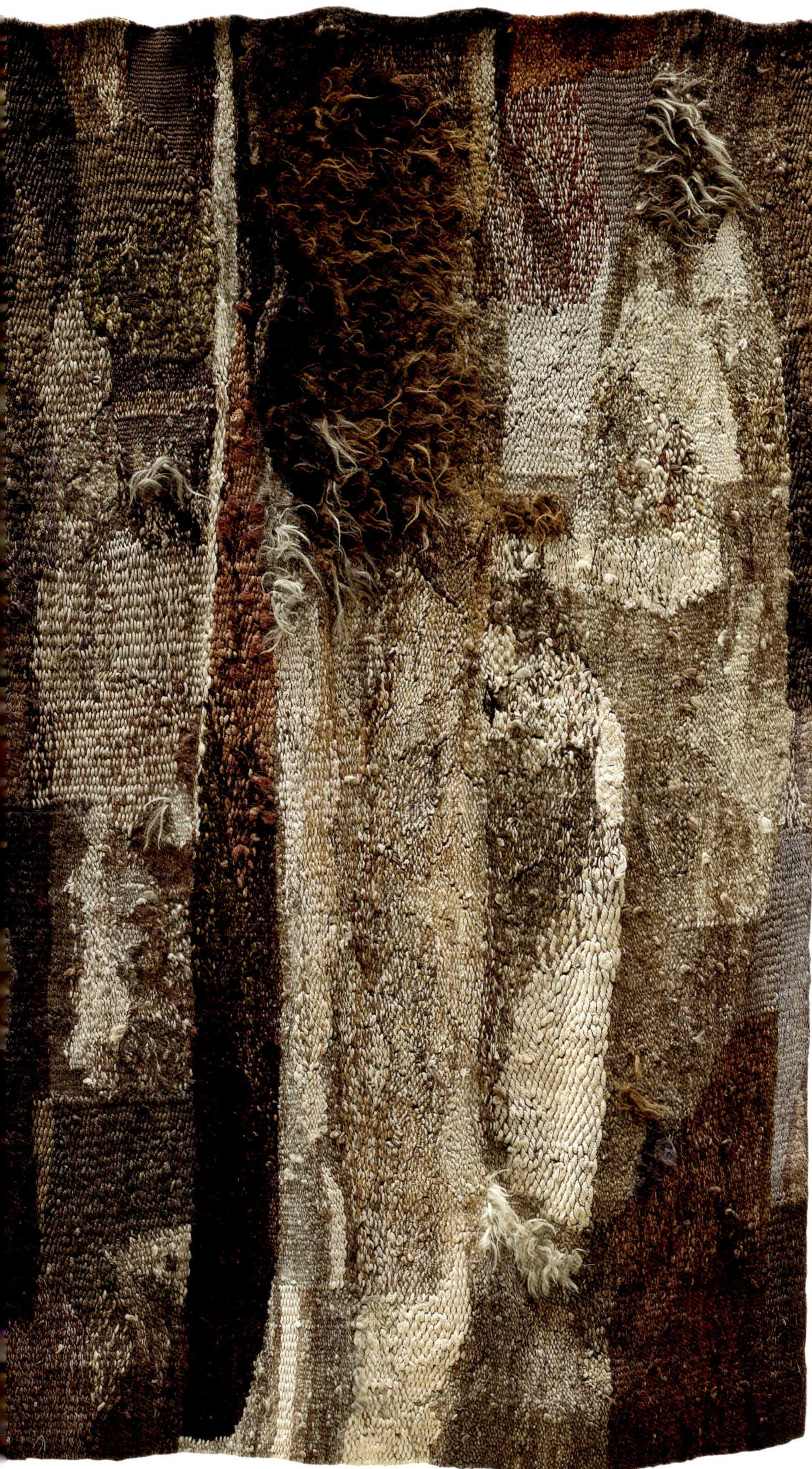

Helena **1964–5**
Wool, cotton, sisal
and horsehair
300 × 480

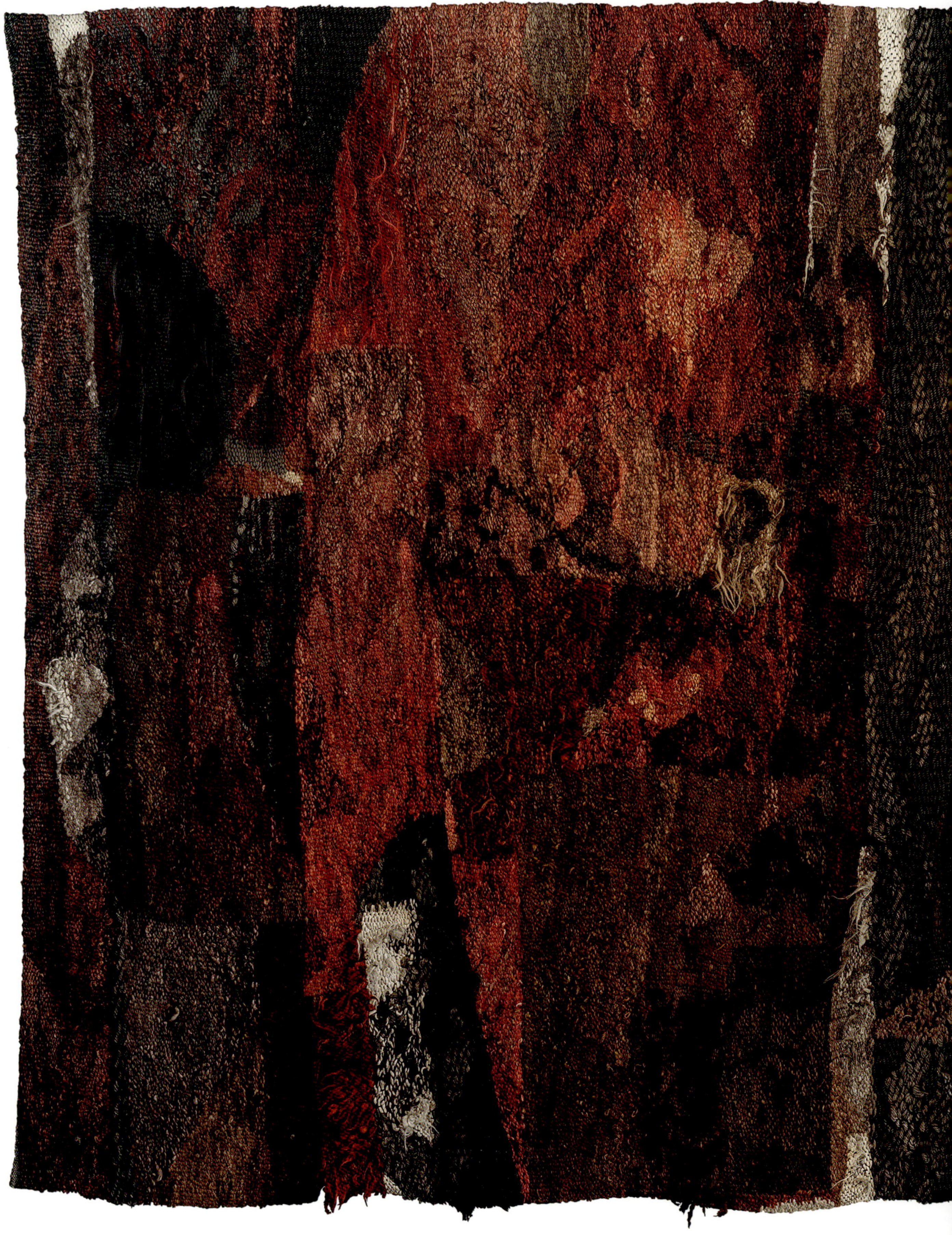

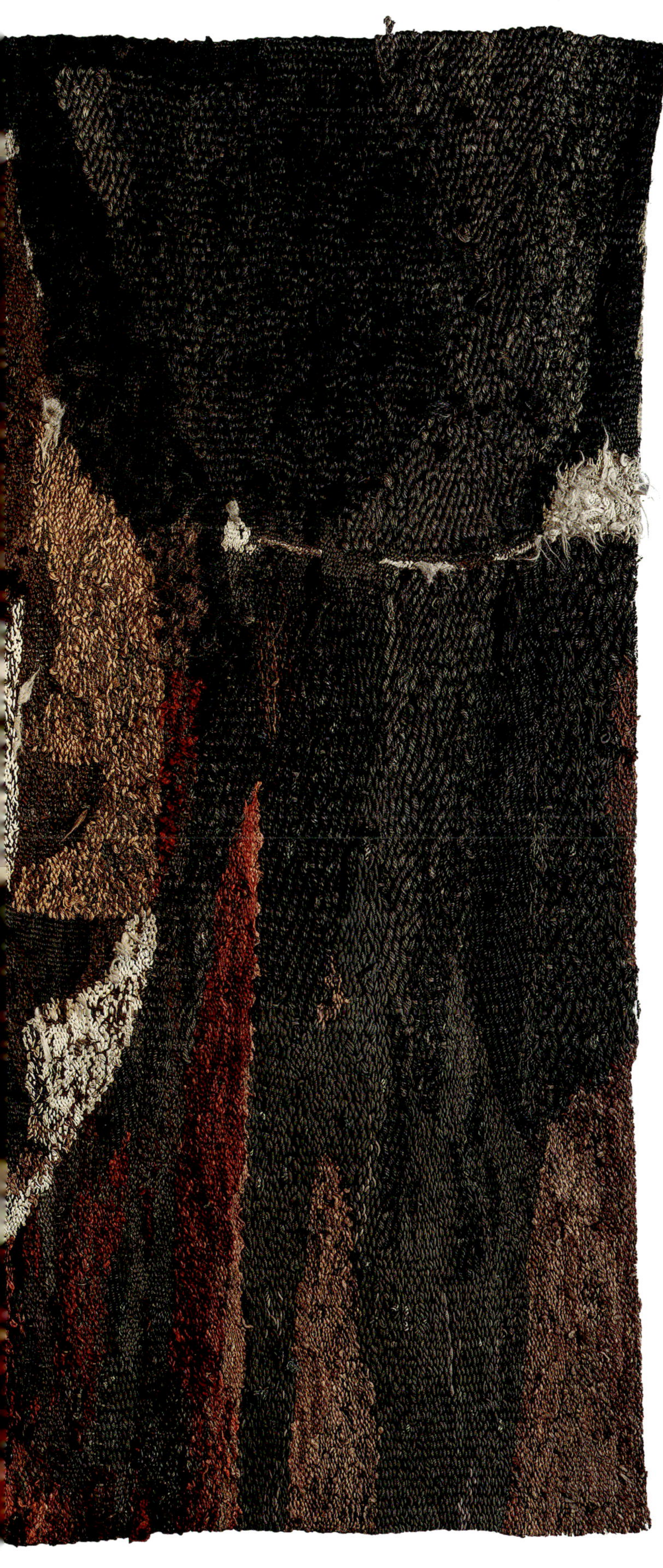

***Desdemona* 1965**
Wool, fleece, sisal, cotton, artificial silk and horsehair
300 × 410

Black and White **1965**
Hemp, horsehair, sisal
and wool
118 × 294

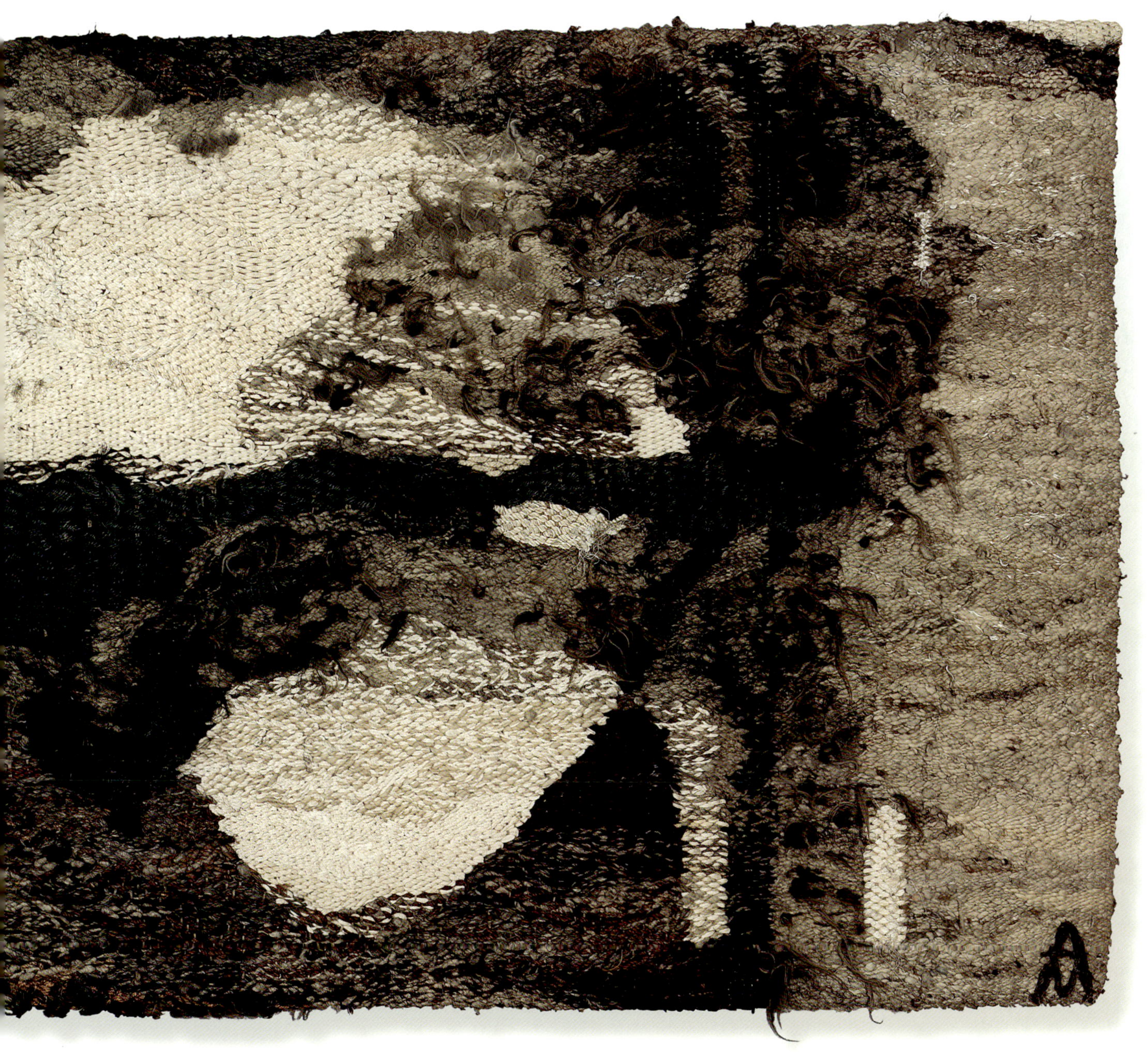

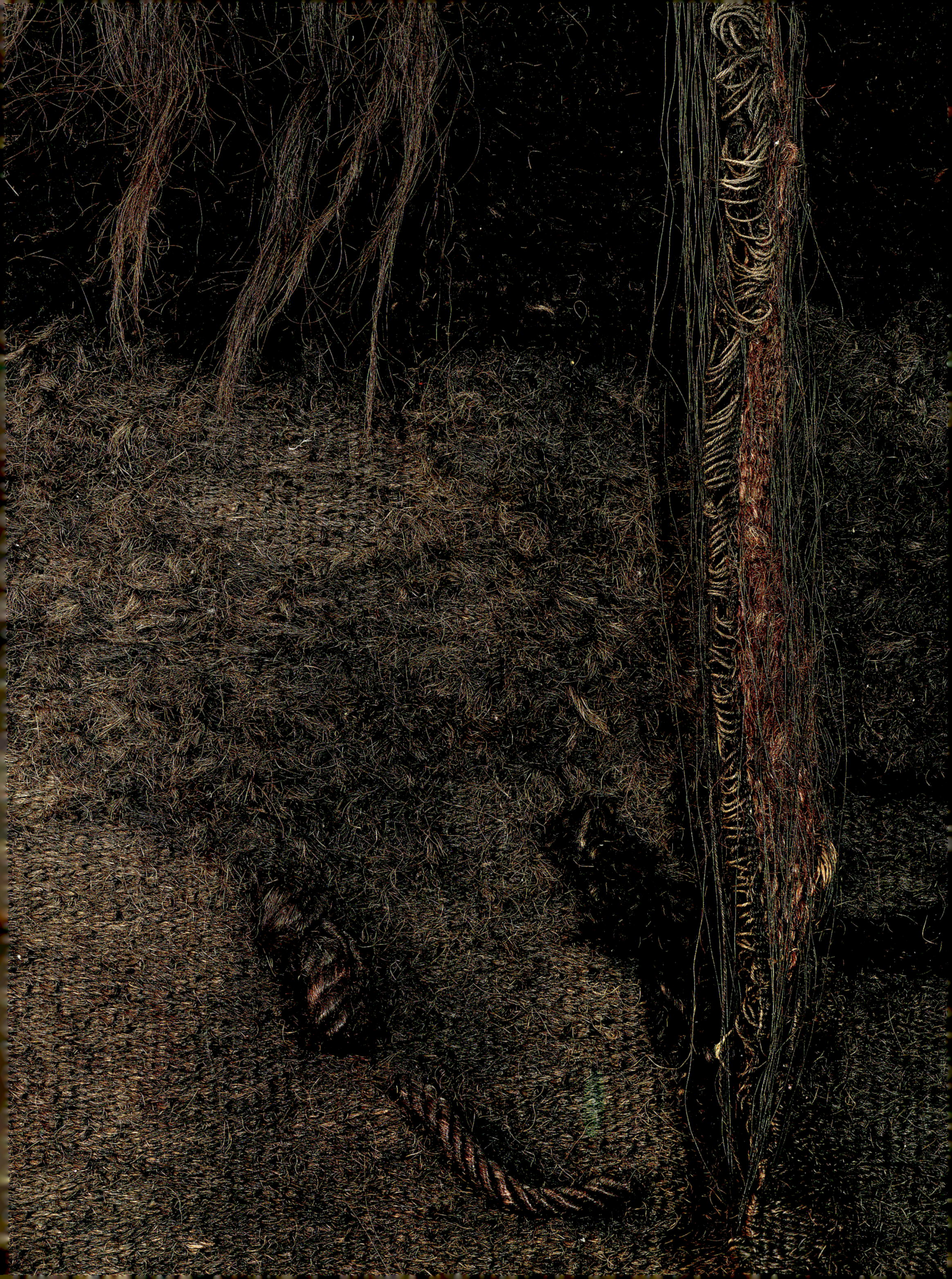

Black **1966**
Sisal, rope and horsehair
300 × 156

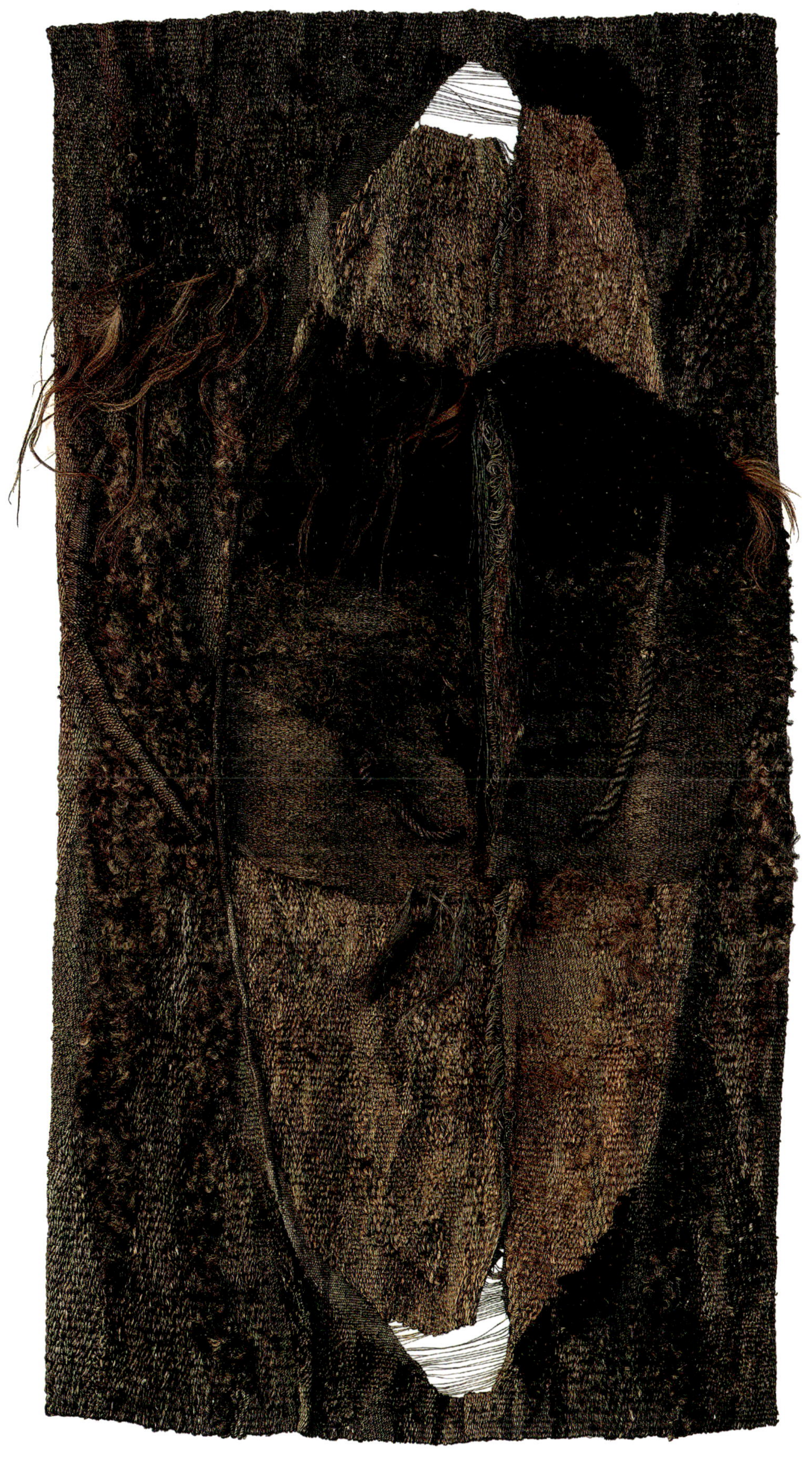

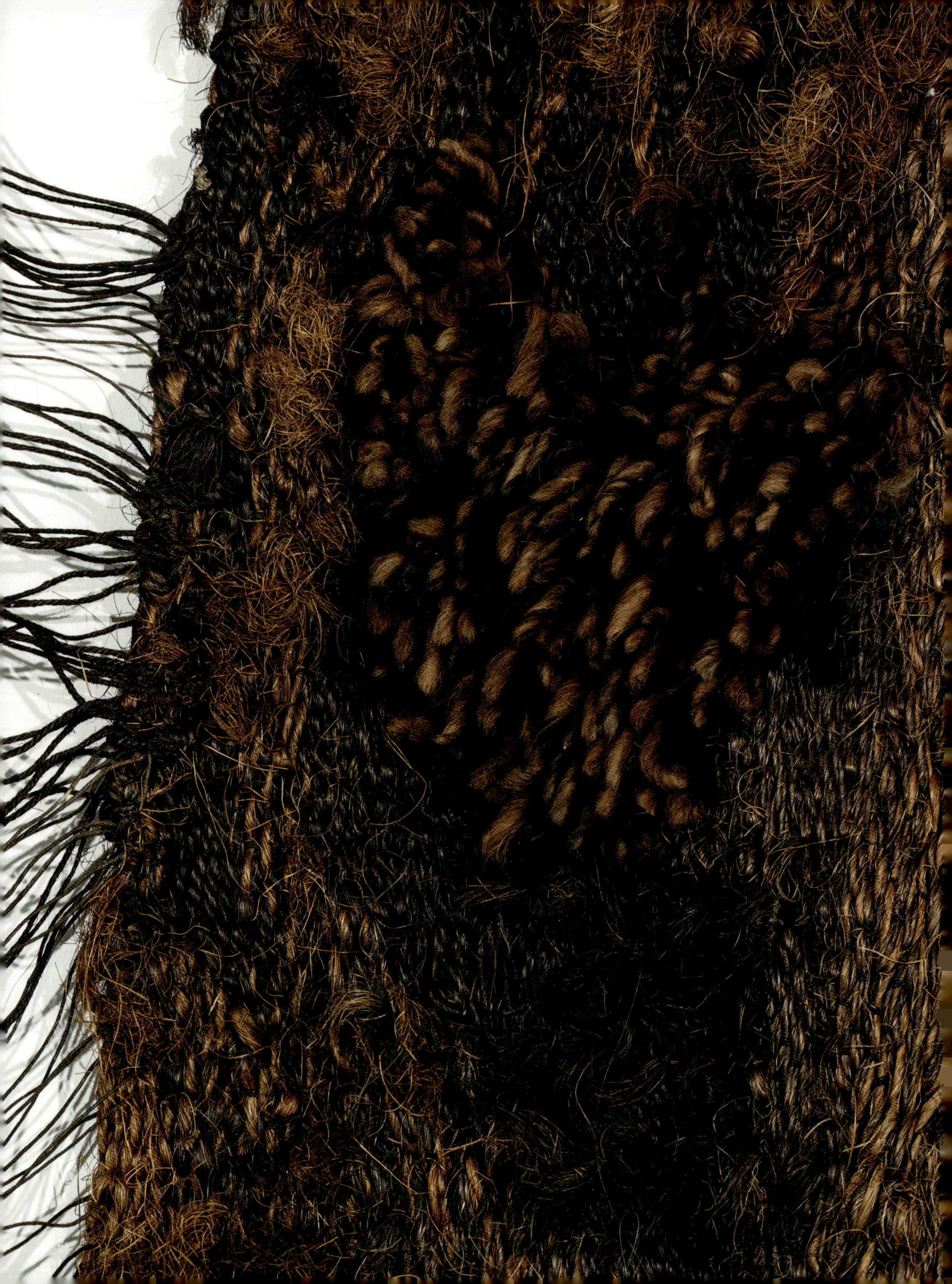

***Assemblage noir* 1966**
Sisal, wool, hemp and horsehair
300 × 220

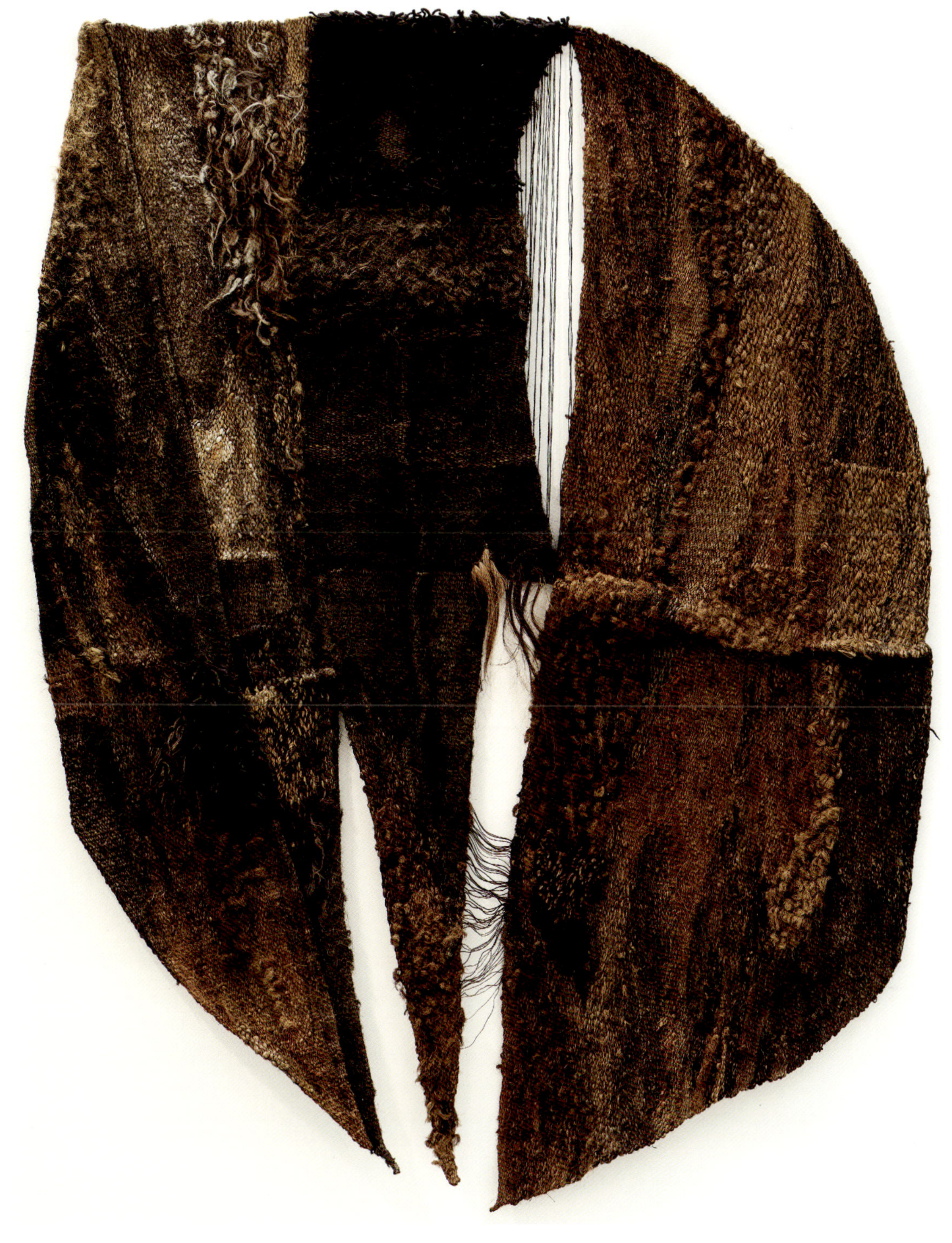

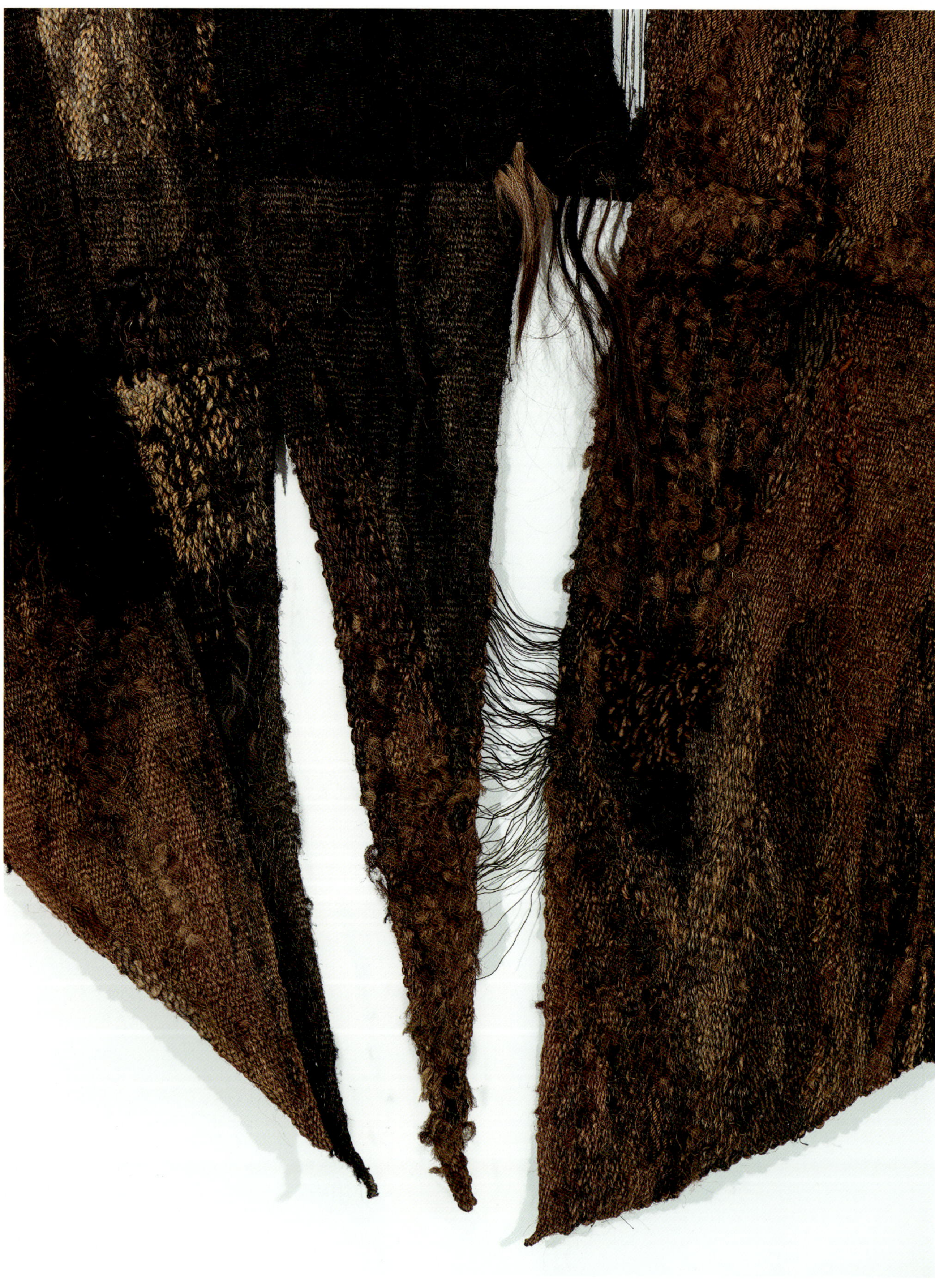

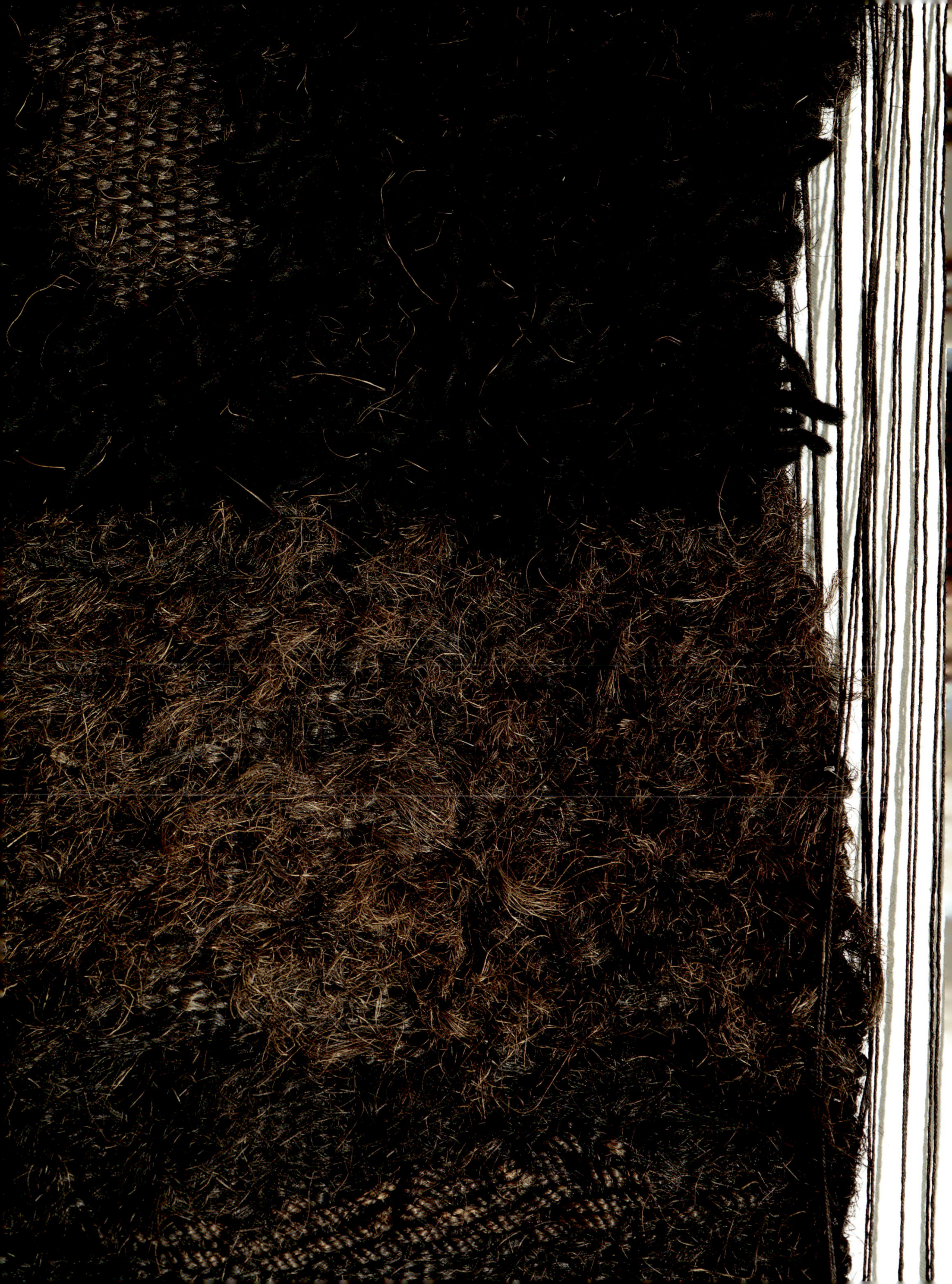

***Diptère* 1967**
Hemp, sisal and horsehair
270 × 260

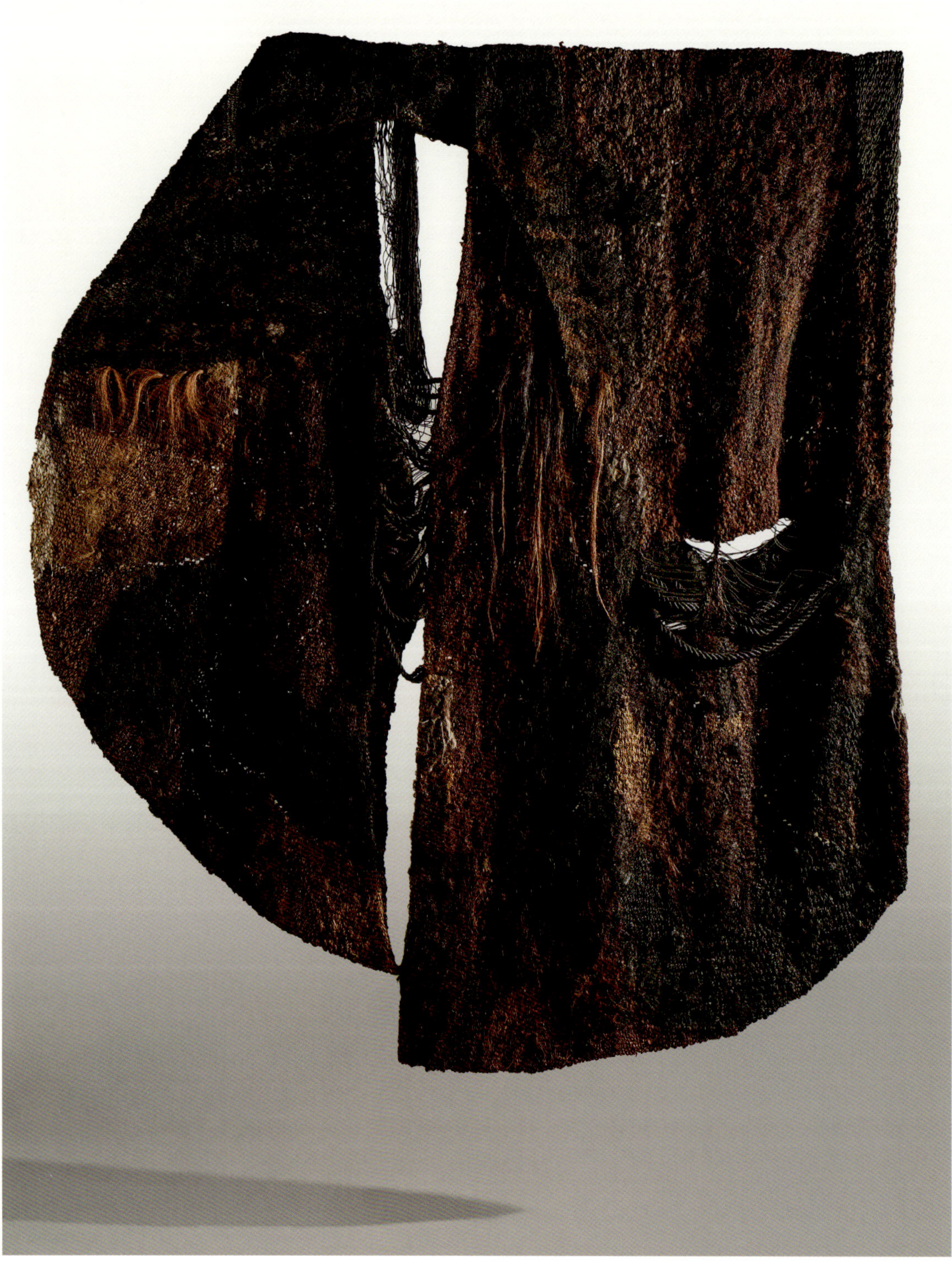

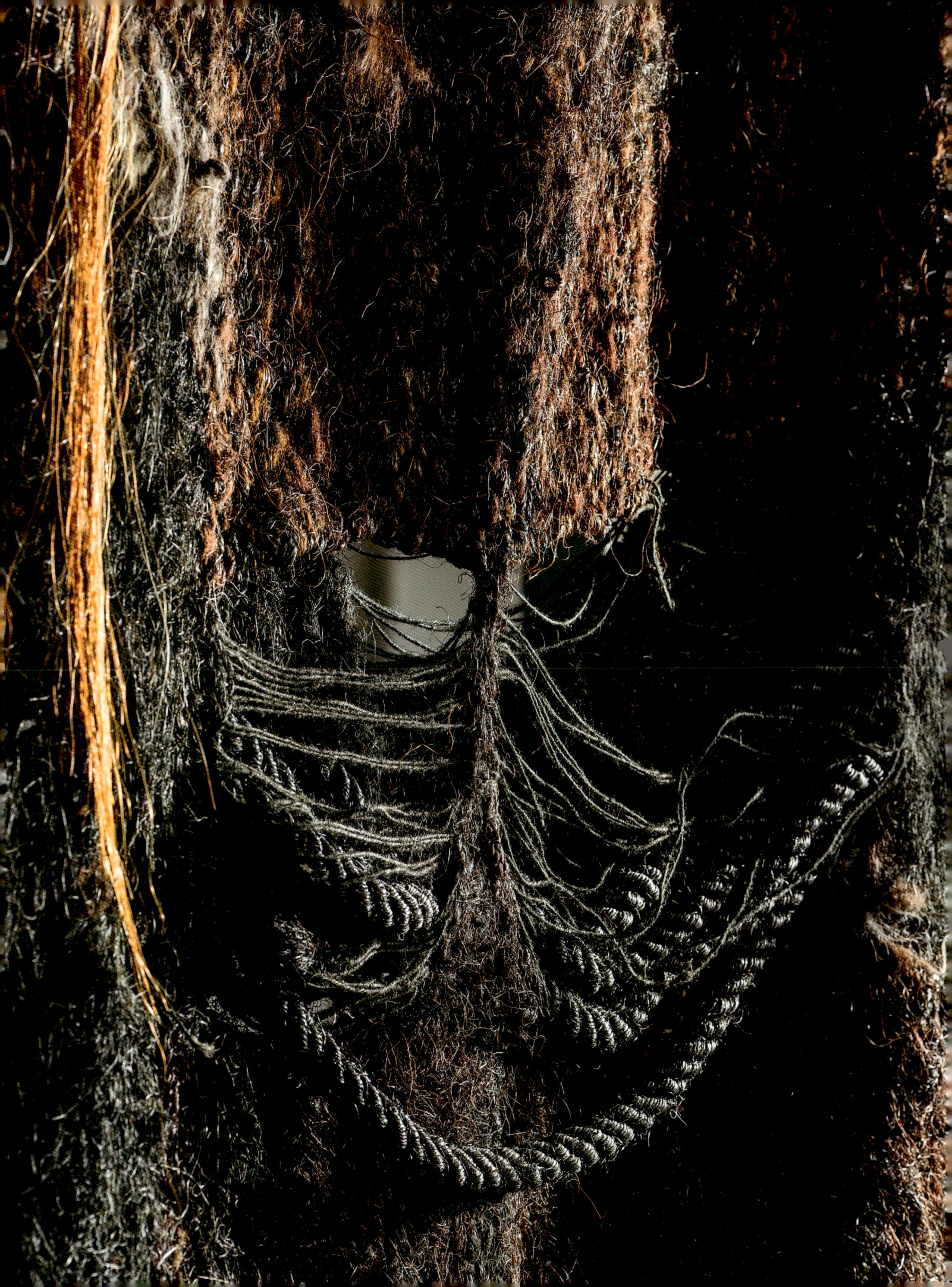

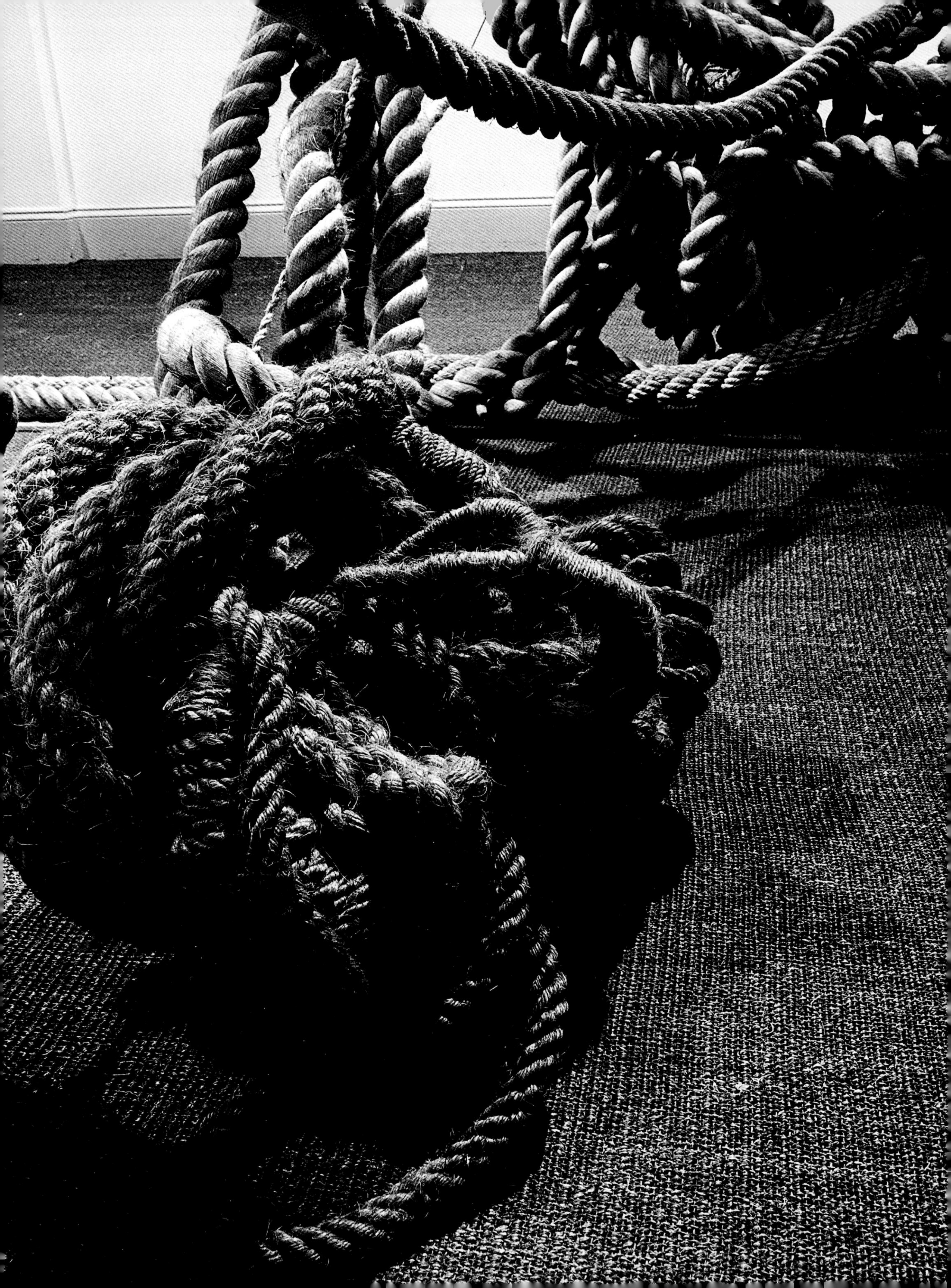

ANN COXON

EVERY TANGLE OF THREAD AND ROPE
ABAKANOWICZ'S ORGANIC ENVIRONMENTS

Creating, I am using woven materials and strings.
These components allow me to construct different forms.
I like the surface I make of threads, every square inch differs from the other, as in the creations of nature.
I want man to penetrate the inside of my forms.
For I want him to have the very intimate contact with them, the same contact you could have with your clothes, animal skins or grass.
I am interested in constructing an environment for man from my forms.
I am interested in the scale of tensions that arises between the various shapes which I place in space.
I am interested in the feeling of man confronted by the woven object.
I am interested in the motion and waving of the woven surfaces.
I am interested in every tangle of thread and rope and every possibility of transformation.
I am interested in the path of a single thread.
I am not interested in the practical usefulness of my work.[1]

Misunderstandings about the status and nature of her practice and how it could be situated within the broader fields of 'Fiber Art' and/or fine art may have motivated Magdalena Abakanowicz to write the above statement, which was printed in the catalogue for her solo exhibition at the Pasadena Art Museum, California, in 1971. She considered the 'personally mounted environment' in Pasadena to be one of her most important exhibitions at the time.[2] Photographs show that she had given over one gallery space to the installation of a large rope, which swept across the centre of the space and coiled up onto a metal-framed bed (p.71). Adjacent gallery spaces presented several 'situations' where large, hanging woven pieces were clustered together to create a total composition.

Dramatic spot-lighting heightened the tension between the looming, organic forms. The photographs are unable to describe the earthy smell Abakanowicz's woven pieces still emit. Created only two years after the success of her *Abakan Red* (pp.124–9) at the 4th International Tapestry Biennial in Lausanne, the environment in Pasadena, with its 'found' elements, was a radical departure from the large, but hand-woven, compositions and forms for which she had made her name.

In the decade from 1966 to 1977 Abakanowicz travelled extensively, installing her work in seventeen solo international presentations, as well as many group exhibitions. In letters and documents from this period she underlines the necessity of her presence during the installation of the work, stressing to curators and exhibition organisers that she sees her exhibitions as environments created from the placement of woven forms, trailing ropes and other objects in a given space. Abakanowicz was rare in her ability to navigate and cross the institutional divides between what has been crudely classed as craft (tapestry, fibre, weaving) and art (sculpture, environment, installation). This ability was most evident in the period in which she made and presented the *Abakans*. As she stated,

> *I built organic environments of many meanings using my* Abakans, *sometimes totally transformed into one large object and entanglements of ropes dividing spaces. These were my very first 'spaces to contemplate, to experience.' ... Nobody would listen except fiber artists, who were saying, 'She is opening the door of our ghetto' ... I balanced between categories. I was simultaneously the Great Lady of Tapestry and the sculptor.* [3]

The fact that Abakanowicz was able to launch her artistic career from underneath the weighty cloaks of an oppressive political regime and the highly specialist and traditional field of tapestry-weaving is well documented territory. What is less widely recognised is that Abakanowicz occupied a position both 'inside' and 'outside' of those seemingly impenetrable socio-political and art historical situations. Through the presentation of her ambitious environments on the world stage of contemporary art exhibition-making in the 1970s, she made a bold move, repositioning her practice as 'art' and rejecting the limitations imposed by both her national identity and the international movement most widely known as Fiber Art through which she had begun to make her name.[4] Her environments from this period could be categorised as pioneering forms of installation, a possibility I will explore later. Tracing a path through the early years of Abakanowicz's career and the opportunities that became available to her, it is evident that the trajectory of her work (from woven objects on the wall, to free-hanging forms in space and then full-scale environments) and her particular use of found materials reflects her awareness of and movement within concurrent developments in international contemporary art practice. Taking Abakanowicz's Pasadena exhibition statement as a point of departure, and exploring the organic environments from this most radical period of her career, we can unravel the meaning of her work and reconsider her contribution to the expanded field of twentieth-century sculpture and installation.

Opening page: Installation view, *Magdalena Abakanowicz: Textile Sculpture, Textile Environment*, Södertälje Konsthall, Sweden, 1970.

The Woven Object

Early influences on Abakanowicz give some indication as to why she might later have been able to envisage weaving as a practice greatly expanded in form, method and space. As a student at the State Higher School of Fine Arts in Sopot she took a trip to Wrocław to see the *Exhibition of Regained Territories* – an exhibition triumphantly declaring the social, economic and cultural benefits of Poland's acquisition of former German territories in the West. The young Abakanowicz was impressed by the large-scale installations created by Polish artists such as Henryk Stażewski (1894–1988) and Stanisław Zamecznik (1909–71). She also encountered for the first time artists using non-traditional materials. In Sopot she became engaged with textile design in a school which encouraged the flexible use of media. This attitude stayed with her despite her move to the more restrictive environment of the Academy of Plastic Arts in Warsaw which came under scrutiny at a time when socialist realism was declared the only acceptable form of art and literature. Abakanowicz entered the Department of Painting that at that time incorporated textiles. There she was taught by the weaver Eleonora Plutyńska (1886–1969) about traditional methods of hand-weaving and became one of a group of students influenced by Plutyńska who were later credited for their innovations in textile art. She was also inspired by the teaching of Jerzy Sołtan (1913–2005), Professor of Architecture and Industrial Design, who promoted an 'integrationalist' model of art and design, and whose department became an escape from those more strictly adhering to the dogmas of socialist realism.

In 1960, Abakanowicz was invited to work in the weaving studio of Maria Łaszkiewicz (1891–1981), a renowned weaver with an interest in the three-dimensional effects of fibrous materials. Here she was able to use the modest basement space Łaszkiewicz made available to others under the grand name of Atelier Expérimental de l'Union des Artistes Polonais. The tapestry designer Mieczysław Szymański (1903–90) also shaped her development. His interest in using materials such as sisal, hemp, paper, plastic and wire was influential on the group of textile artists who created a stir at the 1st International Tapestry Biennial in 1962, among them Magdalena Abakanowicz. The biennial was founded that year by French artist Jean Lurçat (1892–1966) and Swiss curator Pierre Pauli, its mission to promote the postwar revival of tapestry. Though the majority of artists exhibiting were from

Western Europe, Abakanowicz was one of five artists from Poland included in the 1962 biennial whose works collectively stole the show. Radically departing from the traditional forms of tapestry produced in the renowned workshops of France and Belgium, the contributions from Eastern Europe were more concerned with the materiality of fibres, their abstract compositions growing organically from the hand of the artist, rather than being copied by skilled workers from a pictorial cartoon. In breaking free of the traditional relationship between the artist who creates a painting or design and the weaver who crafts a faithful copy, the Polish weavers were rejecting the inherited hierarchy of art and craft.

Abakanowicz's *Composition of White Forms* 1962 dominated a room in the Musée cantonal des Beaux-Arts in Lausanne where it reached almost from floor to ceiling. Maria Łaskieweicz provided work space and encouragement to the young textile artists lining up to make use of her basement studio and Abakanowicz had woven this piece on her loom. Restricted as she was by the width of the loom in setting up her warp, Abakanowicz wove a six-metre length in order to answer the size requirements of the biennial. The resulting composition is an abstract study of form and texture that hints at the direction she would follow in the coming years.

By 1967, Abakanowicz's compositions had come off the wall and out into three-dimensional space. Arguably her boldest presentation was at the 4th International Tapestry Biennial in 1969 when works were no longer bound by the rules to be wall-mounted and the undulating forms and unapologetic protuberance of *Abakan Red* confronted visitors from its position as a suspended, sculptural centrepiece. By this time the biennial had become a showcase for international artists associated with the emerging Fiber Art movement. Standout works by Elsi Giauque (1900–89) and Françoise Grossen (b.1943) from Switzerland, Jagoda Buić from Croatia (b.1930) and Peter and Ritzi Jacobi from Romania/Germany (b.1935 and 1941 respectively) were among those included. Abakanowicz had found her international peers, but it was the gallerist Alice Pauli (wife of Pierre) who would introduce the artist to the international network of museum directors, curators and collectors who converged in Lausanne. Abakanowicz was represented by the Galerie Alice Pauli, holding her first solo exhibition there in 1967. Pauli worked hard to promote the artists in her fold. As well as painters such as Sam Francis (1923–94), Pierre Soulages, Antoni Tàpies (1923–2012) and Maria Helena Vieira da Silva (1908–92), she supported the work of Abakanowicz and Buić, two stars of the tapestry biennial, and showed their woven pieces in dialogue in her gallery exhibitions.

Inspired by visits to Lausanne and the concurrent emergence of Fiber Art in the US in the mid to late 1960s, Mildred Constantine, a curator in the Department of Architecture and Design at the Museum of Modern Art (MoMA), New York, teamed up with the eminent textile designer Jack Lenor Larsen (1927–2020) to present the exhibition *Wall Hangings*, which toured to eleven cities beginning in 1968 before it was presented at MoMA in 1969. Constantine persuaded superiors and colleagues at MoMA to allow the show to occupy the special exhibition galleries instead of being presented in those reserved for her department, making a significant statement about what she and Larsen later termed 'Art Fabric'. Yet despite the curators' ambitions to present the selected works as serious forms of contemporary art practice, *Wall Hangings* was not entirely successful. In an interview for *Craft Horizons* magazine (the only review to reach a broad international readership), sculptor Louise Bourgeois (1911–2010) drew the disparaging conclusion that: 'The pieces in the show rarely liberate themselves from decoration.'[5] Abakanowicz was represented in the exhibition by her *Abakan 27* 1967 and *Yellow Abakan* 1967–8, which was later accessioned to MoMA's collection, under the care of the Department of Architecture and Design. Images of the exhibition's installation show that the work was hung against the wall in an alcove (p.68), though it might have softened Bourgeois's critical voice and provoked more serious consideration as textile sculpture if it had been hung in space as the artist intended. While the historic presentation and reception of *Yellow Abakan* at MoMA failed to free Abakanowicz's work from the categories of design or wall-hanging, significant exhibitions on the west coast of North America and in Europe arguably went further in exploring the ambitions of emerging textile-based practice at the time.

Already in January of 1969 the exhibition *Perspectives in Textile* (p.69) had opened at the Stedelijk Museum, Amsterdam. Abakanowicz was one of ten artists chosen to present large-scale textile structures, making a powerful statement about developments in international practice. Here the works were given ample space. Abakanowicz and Buić were each represented in a monographic room, and both artists chose to show a selection of their woven forms hanging freely in space. A further exhibition surveying the momentum of international Fiber Art, *Deliberate Entanglements* opened at the University of California, Los Angeles, in November 1971. The exhibition aimed to: 'assess as art the recent conceptual, formal, and structural developments in fabric forms. However related to tapestry in scale and prominence, these new forms command their own presence.'[6]

A week-long seminar was held at several venues in Los Angeles and among others, Abakanowicz, Buić and Sheila Hicks (b.1934) took part. By this time, the three leading figures of the Fiber Art movement knew each other well. In 1968, Buić even designed a coiling, architectural, woven environment in which works by Abakanowicz, Hicks and two others could

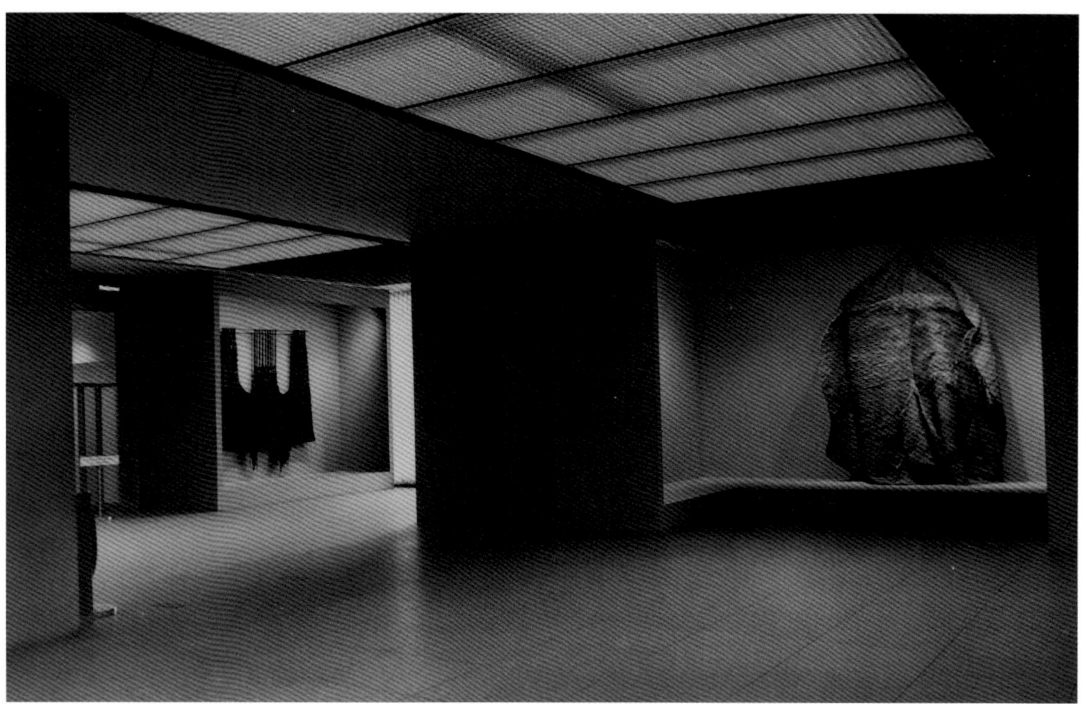

Above: *Yellow Abakan* 1967–8 Sisal 315 × 304.8 × 152.4. Installation view, *Wall Hangings*, Museum of Modern Art, New York, 1969.

be shown together.[7] Yet Abakanowicz's frustrations at being contained within the fold of so-called Fiber Art soon became apparent. As much as it afforded her opportunities to exhibit and network internationally, and despite the efforts of curators such as Mildred Constantine and Bernard Kester, Fiber Art and the artists associated with it were not entirely embraced by either the respected institutions of modern and contemporary art or the art market. In her analysis of North American Fiber Art and the struggle for legitimacy in the 1960s and 1970s, Elissa Auther has argued that in seeking to distinguish their practice from craft and/or applied design, artists associated with the movement stressed the autonomy of their textile works at a time when other developments in the art world saw artists employing everyday materials in order to question that very autonomy:

> *artists associated with Process or postminimalist art of the 1960s and 1970s, such as Robert Morris and Eva Hesse, found forms of fiber such as rope or felt attractive for the ordinariness and other 'non-art' attributes – the very attributes fiber artists struggled to dismiss. Indeed, to the extent that they embraced fiber's everyday utility, Process or postminimalist artists worked at cross-purposes with fiber artists, undermining the latter's belief in art's autonomy, preciousness and durability.*[8]

Auther is correct in her observations about the lack of parity between artists who chose to work with fibre (among other media) in a self-referential refusal of the maker's hand and of autonomy as necessary criteria for art; and those who trained in weaving and therefore needed to prove that their hand-work could even be considered as art, beyond the crafting of objects for everyday use. Close consideration of Abakanowicz's work of the period would suggest, however, that she was not entirely concerned with autonomy, preciousness or durability. Several of the *Abakans* were adapted according to the space in which they were shown. They were stretched, flayed, manipulated and hung to fit the context. In the early 1970s, Abakanowicz went one step further, using the opportunities afforded by the presentation of her work in international museums and galleries to expand her practice beyond the woven objects that were so successful in the context of the Lausanne biennials and the exhibitions of Fiber Art, and to incorporate everyday and found materials in the creation of ambitious temporary environments, both within and beyond the gallery. In combining her woven, hand-made forms with found objects, Abakanowicz was able to operate as both fibre artist and artist and to create a new form of expression.

Thread and Rope

It was Mieczysław Szymański who encouraged Abakanowicz to use sisal in her weaving. Though other materials were available to her, she was drawn to the properties of the organic plant-derived fibre, which would hold dyes well and was strong and thick enough to create three-dimensional weaves. Because of its inherent strength and pliability, sisal is also the fibre most commonly used to create industrial-strength rope. From the mid 1960s, in pieces such as *Black* 1966 (pp.56–7), and *Diptère* 1967 (pp.62–3), twisted, rope-like cords project from the woven surface of the object like intestines spilling from an animal carcass. In 1969, rope began to emerge from the *Abakans*, hanging beneath the woven forms and trailing onto the floor. Soon rope became a major component of the artist's environments and situations, linking forms and providing paths for the viewer through space.

Rope was used widely and significantly in the 1960s and 1970s by artists associated with both Fiber Art and process-based, postminimalist, or 'povera' practices – from Françoise Grossen (b.1943), Jackie Winsor (b.1941) and Mariyo Yagi (b.1948) to Eva Hesse (1936–70), Robert Morris (1931–2018), Barry Flanagan (1941–2009) and Pino Pascali (1935–68). Though the materials, and sometimes even the techniques used to manipulate them, were the same (with artists employing processes of coiling, draping, trailing, knotting, repetition and wrapping), the exhibiting contexts were often very different. The American artist Alice Adams (b.1930) was the only person to have work included in both Lucy Lippard's now iconic exhibition *Eccentric Abstraction* at the Fischbach Gallery in New York in 1966 and in the *Woven Forms* exhibition that so inspired Mildred Constantine when it was held in New York City's Museum of Contemporary Crafts in 1963. Both *Eccentric Abstraction* and *String and Rope*, at the Sidney Janis Gallery, New York, in 1969 sought to show avant-garde tendencies in contemporary sculpture. Rope was trailed through spaces, off plinths and onto the floor. In an oft-quoted passage, Lippard explains that while such works clearly provoked visceral reactions, they were to be understood as studies in process and materiality, not as metaphoric or metonymic body parts: 'In eccentric abstraction, evocative qualities and specific organic associations are kept at a subliminal level … Ideally a bag remains a bag and does not become a uterus, a tube is a tube and not a phallic symbol.'[9]

When Abakanowicz came to use rope not just as a material to pull apart and weave into new forms, but as a giant thread to lead the viewer through and around the spaces into which she inserted her woven forms, it was surely the most appropriate material for an artist who wished to build upon the successes of her textile practice, but also to elevate her critical reception in the eyes of those in the contemporary art world who mattered to her. Both organic and industrial, humble and heroic, found and made, Abakanowicz's ropes (which she often encased in cloth) bound together her many concerns and grounded them in the locations in which she was invited to exhibit her work. However, unlike the artists championed by Lucy Lippard and the Sidney Janis Gallery, Abakanowicz was deeply interested in the symbolic and metaphoric possibilities of her materials and forms. In 1976, she explained:

> *The rope is to me like a petrified organism, like a muscle devoid of activity. Moving it, changing its position and arrangement, touching it, I can learn its secrets and the multitude of its meanings. I create forms out of it, I divide space with it. Rope is to me the condensation of the problem of thread, the thread composed of many fibers whose number nobody tries to establish. Transported from one place to another it grows old. It carries its own story within itself, it contributes this to its surroundings. I used it in urban landscapes where it became an echo of the banished organic world … I sense its strength, which is carried by all intertwined elements, such as those in a tree, human hand, or a bird's wing.*[10]

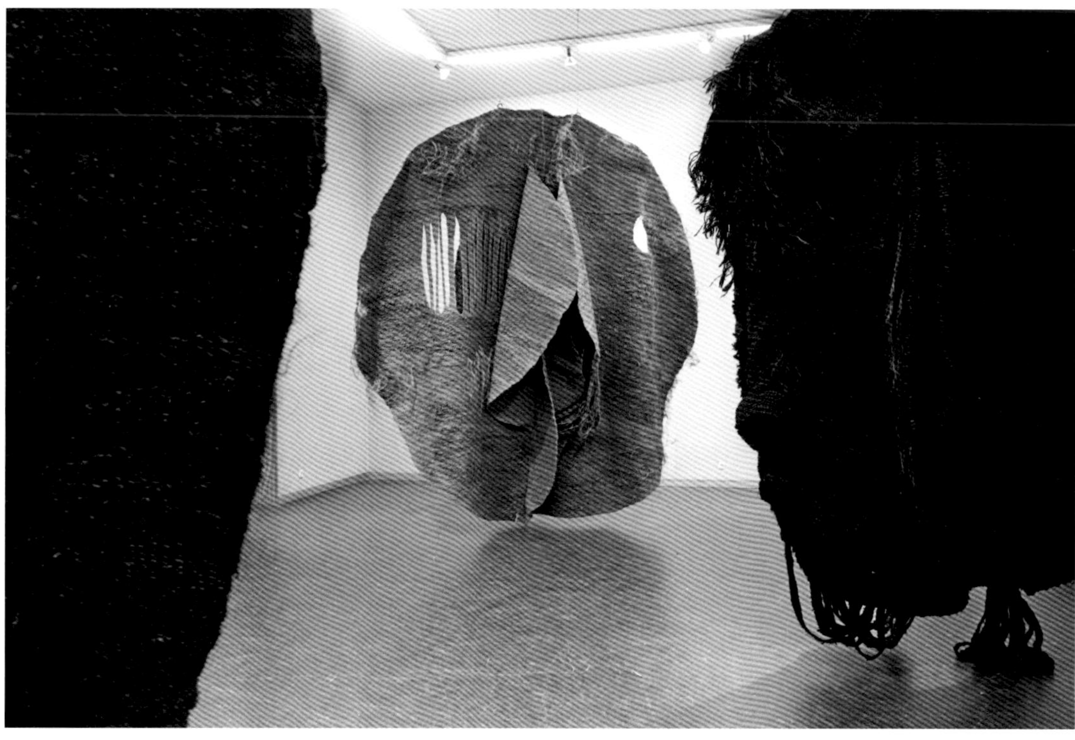

Below: *Abakan Orange* 1968 (centre) Sisal 360 × 360 × 45. Also featured: *Abakan Round* 1967–8 (left) and *Black Garment* 1968 (right). Installation view, *Perspectives in Textile*, Stedelijk Museum, Amsterdam, 1969.

Opposite: *Rope: Penetrations, Location in Space* 1971. Installation view, *The Fabric Forms of Magdalena Abakanowicz*, Pasadena Art Museum, California (now Norton Simon Museum of Art).

Her exhibition at the Pasadena Art Museum, California, in 1971, curated by Kester, was successful in bringing her work to the attention of the artistic community on the American West Coast. Judy Chicago (b.1939) and Miriam Schapiro (1923–2015) had started their Feminist Art Program at the California Institute of Arts that year, and there is no doubt that the *Abakans* impressed groups of young women artists who were looking to reclaim fibre as a feminist medium, and who read the *Abakans* as bold statements of female power and sexuality with their labial folds and dark, vaginal spaces.[11] Yet the use of a large sweeping length of rope and a metal-framed bed in the Pasadena exhibition show that Abakanowicz was by this time moving away from the production of the *Abakans* and was using found objects to stage dramatic encounters for the viewer. She referred to her exhibitions in Pasadena and at the Södertälje Konsthall, Sweden, in 1970 as 'environments' composed of different 'situations' yet intended to be seen as a single composition – a single work. The artist described her environment in Sweden as follows:

> *In a hall, the empty room is divided by ropes running on the floor and under the ceiling in several predetermined directions. Each rope, after a certain period of free run, is transformed into a knot. The spectator observes this phenomenon in its static state – no transformation is in process. However, the movement can be started again and be stopped only after the free run of the rope is completely enmeshed. The division of the room is thus eliminated and in its place there is a single object – the environment – formed by all the ropes interlaced.*[12]

Abakanowicz identified her solo show at Södertälje as the first of a series of exhibitions she staged in various European cities. In a further statement from 1970 she outlines her desire to create three types of situations: environments of multiple *Abakans* and woven pieces; single objects to be observed from all sides; and spaces divided by ropes that trail, sweep and coil with the possibility of transformation.[13] Further solo exhibitions in 1971 at the Galeria Współczesna KMPiK 'Ruch', Warsaw, and in 1972 at the Kunstverein für die Rheinlande und Westfalen, Düsseldorf, in Germany, enabled her to continue her presentation of experimental and innovative environments and to incorporate found objects. Images of the exhibition in Düsseldorf, for example, show that she had brought several shop mannequins, which she covered with back-dyed burlap, into dialogue with the hanging *Abakans*. Certainly, she saw her presentations as uniquely and specifically created at each exhibition site. Correspondence from this period reveals that she did not see her woven structures as autonomous objects, but as parts of a pliable, site-responsive environment which only she could create in a given space with the right amount of time and support. In November 1972 Abakanowicz wrote to Dr Robert Brenn, Exhibition Officer at the Scottish Arts Council, explaining:

> *During the last three years I have been showing my works only in the form of personally mounted environments. In these types of exhibitions, which I had in Nationalmuseum, Stockholm, Pasadena Art Museum and Düsseldorf Kunsthalle I have used a lot of ropes, out of which I am improvising compositions in given spaces. In any case I am getting the ropes from the centers inviting me. It is very important to me that my creations are being shown and understood in a proper way.*[14]

In the summer of that year Abakanowicz had used rope as a thread to connect the exhibition space of the Richard Demarco Gallery in Edinburgh to the city's St Mary's Cathedral as part of Atelier '72, organised and presented by the gallery for the Edinburgh International Festival. Rare colour photographs of the intervention show that a vivid red rope exited from the first floor window in the gallery where it originated, occupying the floor space alongside a hanging woven structure (p.72). The rope then trailed along the streets and up onto the façade of the cathedral. A further rope emerged from an upper storey window and rose up to the roof of the Melville Crescent building, home to the Demarco Gallery, and continued through parts of the city. Abakanowicz later wrote,

> *In Edinburgh I threaded the rope through the gallery building, as if sewing ... That penetration of the city of Edinburgh by the rope, its linking of the gallery and the cathedral, was noted, commented upon by critics and artists. Next year* [1974]*, the Royal College of Art in London granted me an honorary doctorate ... my promoter spoke of the Edinburgh rope that had 'traversed all categories in art.'*[15]

The exhibition was organised by the Demarco Gallery in collaboration with Ryszard Stanisławski, director of the Muzeum Sztuki in Łódź. An important figure in the establishment of an international art scene in Edinburgh, Richard Demarco made his first trip to Poland in 1968 and soon became a strong supporter of contemporary art practice from Eastern Europe. In a telling handwritten letter to Abakanowicz dated 18 January 1974, Demarco asserted her importance as an artist: 'As far as the art of tapestry weaving is concerned you are for me without equal in the world because you are a sculptor – an artist beyond craft.'[16]

Abakanowicz also made an intervention with rope in the city environment of Bordeaux in 1973. As she recalled, 'The city's great Baroque fountains stood dry so the rope came out of their openings like a frozen cascade.'[17] In the UK, two further opportunities to present solo exhibitions came very quickly on the heels of the Edinburgh project. Abakanowicz was invited to show her work at the Arnolfini Gallery, Bristol, in 1973 (p.73), and at the Whitechapel Gallery, London, in 1975 on the invitation of Jasia Reichardt – a fellow Pole who was director of the gallery at the time. Bristol's history as a major port and centre of rope-making for the shipping industry could not have been more fitting as a site for Abakanowicz to present

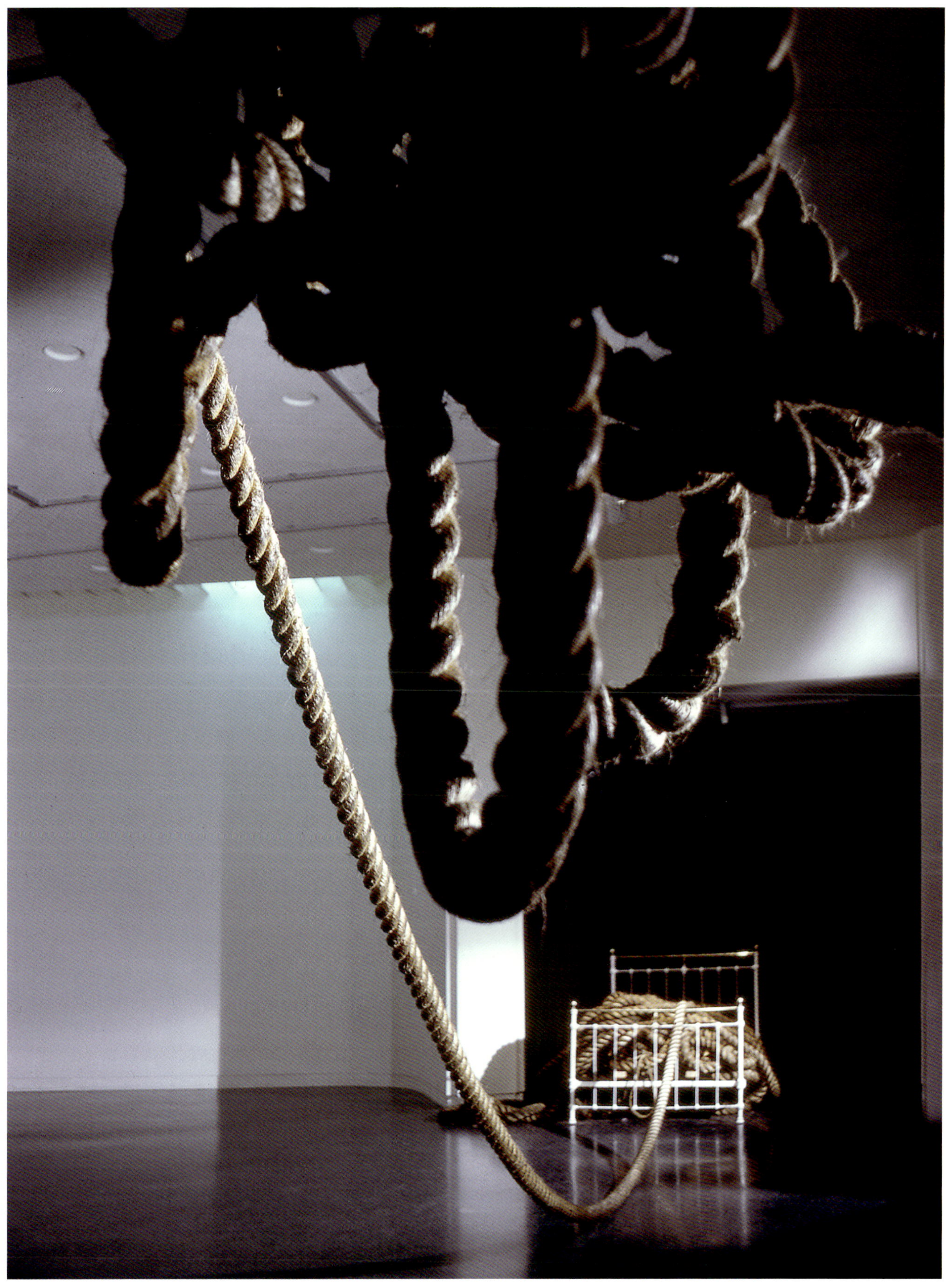

Below: *Red Rope* 1972. Installation view, Atelier '72, Edinburgh International Festival, Scotland.

her work. Photographs of the exhibition show that the artist used the ships' large hawsers, covering them with black sacking to hide the joins and hanging them from the rafter, or draping them on the rough stone-tiled floors of the space.

On multiple occasions Abakanowicz commissioned specific photographers to record her temporary exhibition environments. The resulting high-contrast black-and-white images show that she favoured dramatic spot-lighting with shadows cast upon the walls and floor. The directional, raking light drew attention to the texture of her woven pieces, while adding a sense of theatricality and mystery to the looming forms.

Every Possibility of Transformation

In the introduction to her book *Installation Art: A Critical History*, Claire Bishop defines installation art as a term 'that loosely refers to the type of art into which the viewer physically enters, and which is often described as "theatrical", "immersive" or "experiential" ... installation art presupposed an embodied viewer whose senses of touch, smell and sound are as heightened as their sense of vision. This insistence on the literal presence of the viewer is arguably the key characteristic of installation art.'[18]

Abakanowicz's original intention was for people to move around, between and within her pieces. She was interested in the organic properties of the materials she used and their ability to create atmosphere or provoke emotion – the 'feeling of man confronted by the woven object'.[19] In works such as *Black Forms* 1970–8 and the three-part *Abakan Brown* 1969–78 she began to create relationships between her woven forms in singular 'situations' made up of multiple parts. As in her exhibition environments of the early 1970s, she set a path towards a form of installation art in which the artist creates a dialogue between the work and the viewer in a given space. The artist was photographed on multiple occasions touching and entering her *Abakans* – especially those with a cylindrical structure. Though we can no longer enter, we can imagine the experience of standing inside the dark, coiling woven mass as one might enter and stand inside an ancient, hollowed-out tree trunk. The artist saw her *Abakans* as hanging, moving, living works to be experienced, not static sculptures to be looked at. She wanted others to experience her works with their pungent smell and heavy threads. To penetrate the forms, then to stare up and out at the small chinks of light that pierce the black tapestry from the outside, like stars in the night sky. When Abakanowicz spoke of the 'feeling of man confronted by the woven object' and 'every possibility of transformation', she was interested in more than the formal and material concerns of the US-based postminimalist or process artists. When in 1982 she wrote in her autobiographical essay *Portrait x 20* of her memories of growing up in rural Poland, of myth and folklore, about the spirits of the forest and the awe this inspired in her young imagination, Abakanowicz separated herself yet further from the cerebral practices of the late 1960s and early 1970s in which fibre and rope were found materials to be claimed and placed by the artist, signifying nothing beyond themselves. Through this revealing text she led the reader to understand that hers was a practice rooted in the ambition to transport the individual through the environments she created to another world entirely.

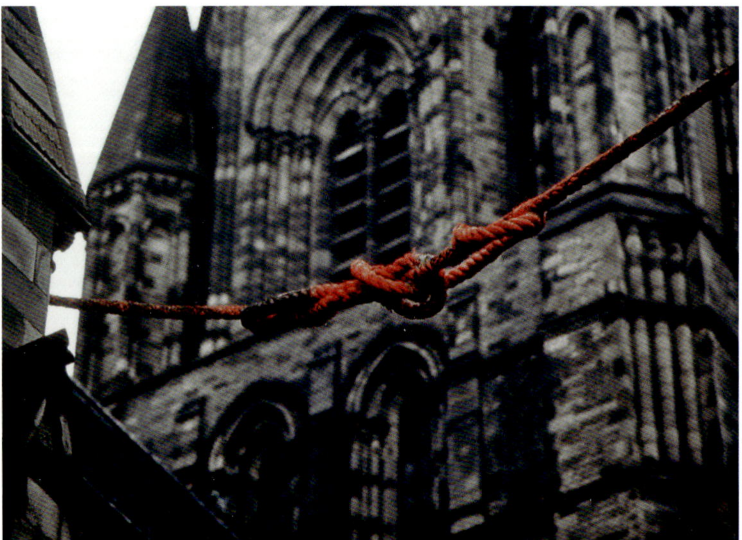

As a logical extension of her interest in creating environments specifically at and for the site of her exhibitions, Abakanowicz also began to create public artworks in the early 1970s in response to a number of commissions. In addition to the rope pieces she installed on the streets of Edinburgh and Bordeaux, she created two particularly significant environments for public interior spaces. In 1971, she was commissioned to create a textile environment for the Huddinge Hospital, near Stockholm in central Sweden (p.74). The environment was created specifically for an open public area of the hospital. Abakanowicz thought through every detail, covering the floor in carpet and painting the wall in the correct shade of brown. Several woven elements hung from floor to ceiling, their black and brown-red colours and crescent-shaped or oval forms creating silhouettes echoing those found in early flat weavings. In her proposal for the *Black-Brown Environment*, which she typed out in English and accompanied with sketches, she explains that the dark colours create a 'cosy and relaxed atmosphere'. Abakanowicz was shocked to learn that the hospital intended to re-locate the work a few years later. In 1976, they wrote to her to ask if she would assist in its relocation. Her response makes her disappointment plain: 'I was very surprised and sorry to hear that you have taken down my environment, without telling me in advance ... An environment of mine could never be reconstructed

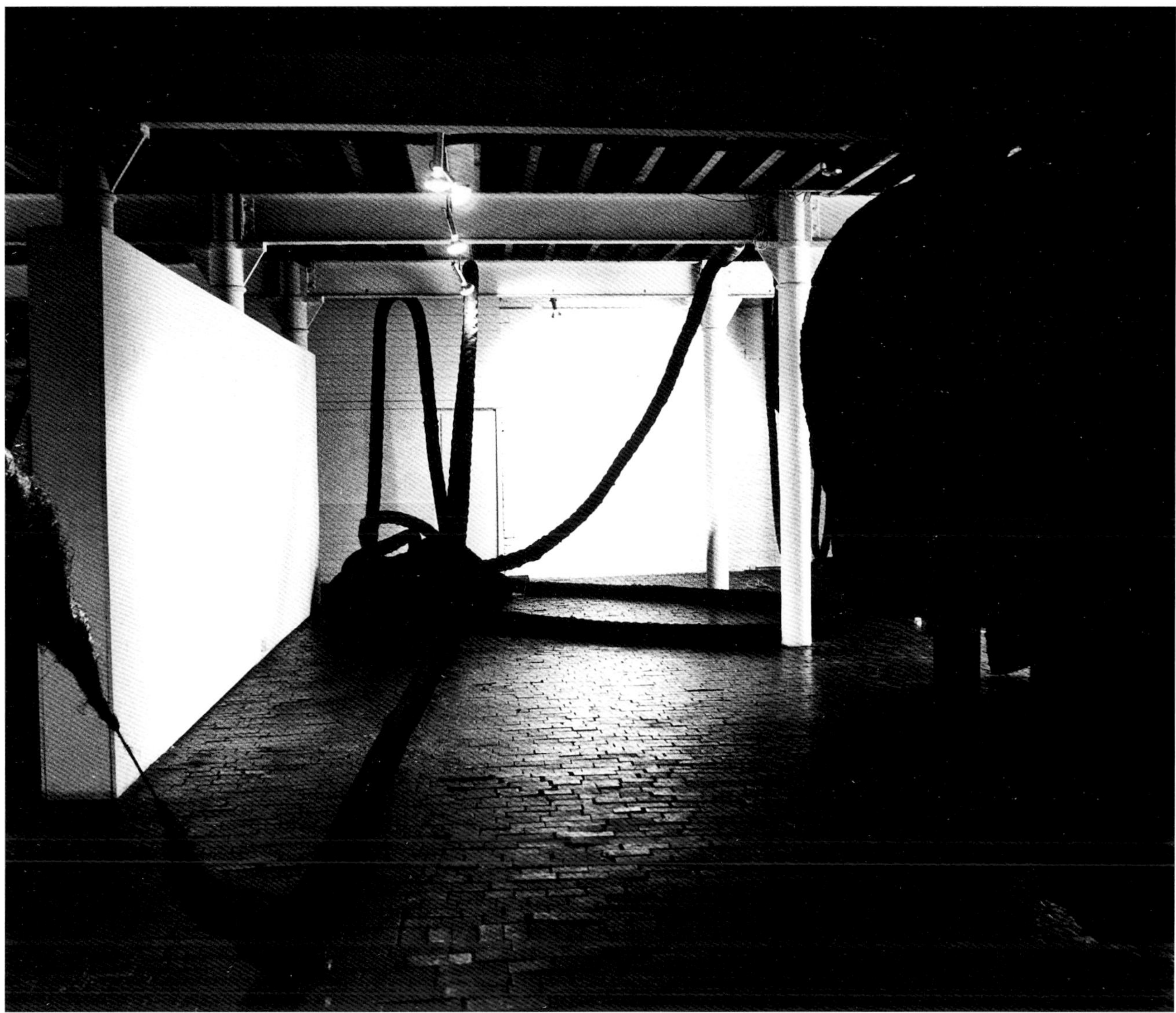

Above: *Rope Structures* 1973. Installation view, Arnolfini Gallery, Bristol, England, 1973.

again in another space – as you propose it – but only by myself.'[20]

Though site-specificity was not yet a widely used term and the commissioning of contemporary works for public spaces through governmental agencies was a practice still in its infancy, Abakanowicz clearly felt that her environments were specific to the contexts for which they were created and could not be transported to another site. Her struggle to express this is clear. Considering the development of site-specificity in contemporary art and in particular the ways in which Fiber Art was at the forefront of such developments in public and commercial spaces, art historian T'ai Smith has stated: 'another story needs to be told, one that begins not with sculpture but with tapestry, an art form whose identity historically depended on an intimate relationship with the interior spaces of architectural constructions.'[21]

Bois le Duc 1970–1 – the largest indoor work Abakanowicz ever created – still dominates the auditorium space of the North Brabant government building in 's-Hertogenbosch, the Netherlands (pp.75–7). The monumental environment stands at seven metres high and twenty-two metres wide. In a factory space in Utrecht the artist worked with assistants, employing scaffolding and an enormous temporary loom construction to complete the work. Though ambitious in scale, environmental, and site-specific, *Bois le Duc* is arguably also the most tapestry-like piece the artist created in the 1970s – its architectural aspect; its relationship to the room for which it was made; and its naturally sound-proofing and insulating qualities reflecting certain characteristics of historic tapestry. While installation art is often seen as the contemporary offspring of theatre, Abakanowicz's environments assert a parallel development in which installation emerges from the relationship between architecture and tapestry. Though Abakanowicz's giant tapestry/environment is not pictorial, it should not be forgotten that

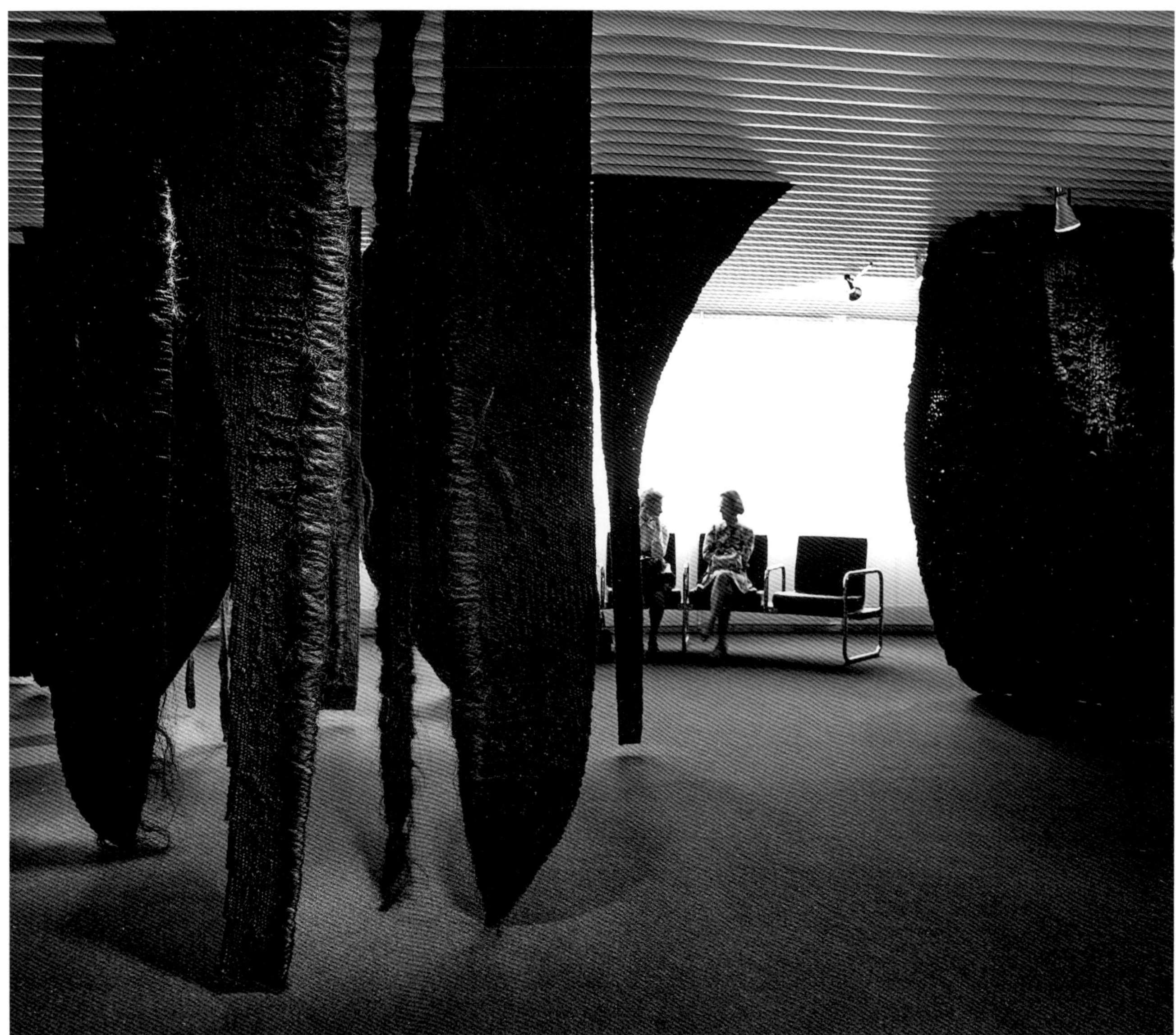

Above: *Black-Brown Environment* 1971. Installation view, Huddinge Hospital, Sweden.

the theatrical creation of scenes was not the only purpose of the ancient medium, which tied practical, environmental considerations with the symbolic and pictorial; form with function. *Bois le Duc* – the name of the area in which the work is installed – translates literally as 'Forest of the Duke'. Standing two metres away from the wall, the monumental weaving with its characteristically earthy tones and areas of varied, complex texture certainly evokes a forest-like environment, suggestive of depth and mystery. It is easy to imagine that one could push through this dense wall and emerge, Narnia-like, into another land entirely. Perhaps this is what Abakanowicz meant by 'every possibility of transformation'. Interested in more than the inherent properties of the materials themselves, her ambition was surely to transport the viewer beyond the limitations of the spaces in which she lived and worked, to open up the possibilities of memory and imagination.

In departing from traditional forms of tapestry weaving, taking her works off the wall and out into three-dimensional space in the late 1960s and early 1970s, Abakanowicz was asserting the continued importance of fibre and its possibilities as a radical and contemporary form of art, and suggesting that meaning could be carried by the material itself and through our encounter with it. She was neither in the business of creating decorative pictures in wool, nor of making objects that signify nothing beyond their own materiality and process of making. The nineteenth-century architect and art historian Gottfried Semper underlined the historic function of woven fabrics and tapestry as 'conspicuous spatial dividers' and 'textile walls'. Reflecting upon this history in his essay 'Reflections on Fabric and Meaning: The Tapestry and the Loincloth', philosopher and art critic Arthur Danto has explored the importance of clothing and cloth within contemporary art installation:

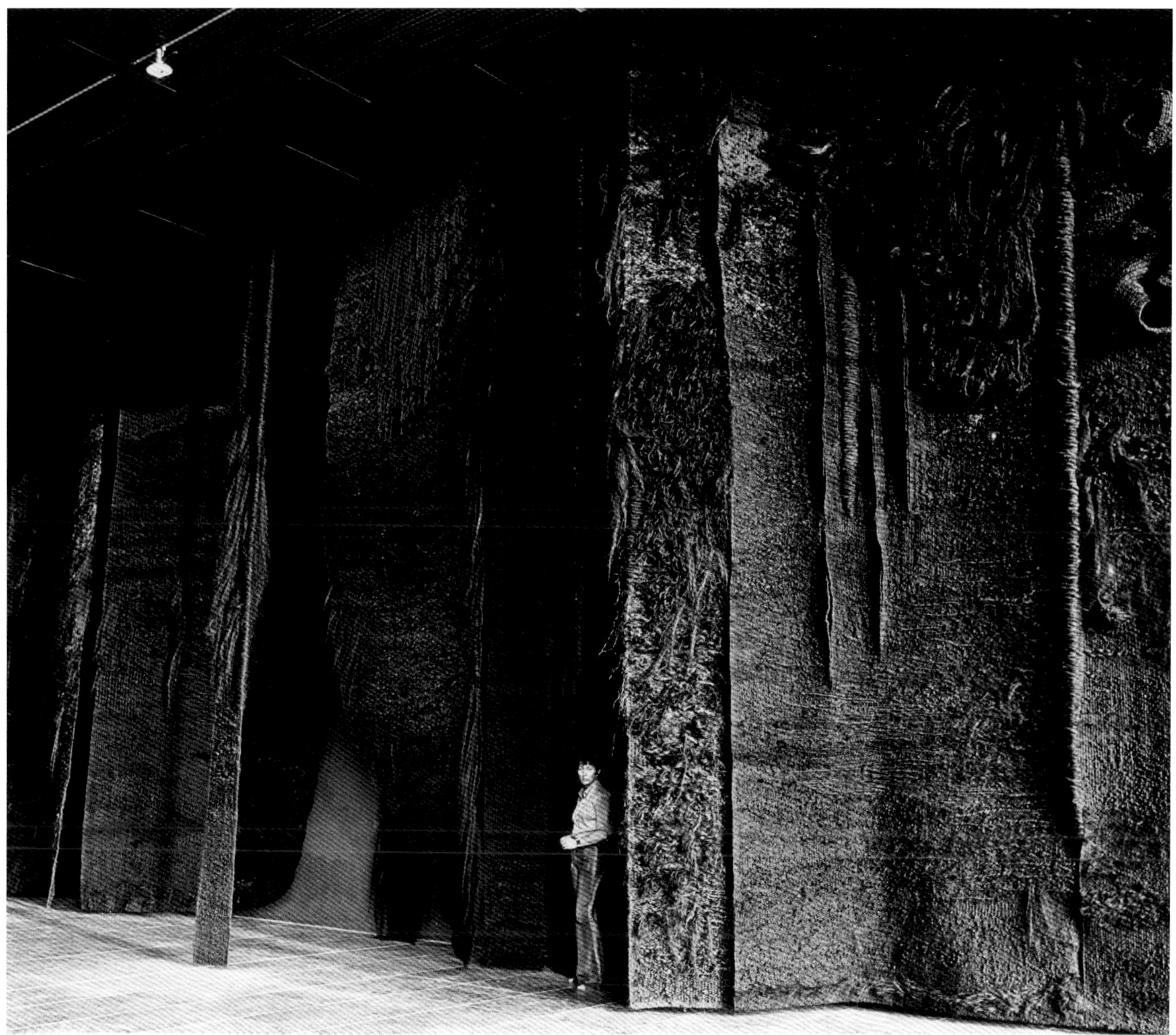

Above and overleaf: *Bois le Duc* 1970–1 Sisal, wool, rope and horsehair 720 × 2200 × 200. Installation view, Provinciehuis 's Hertogenbosch, the Netherlands. Above: The artist is shown in front of the work.

> *Fabric ... is not merely a medium, as it was in Raphael's tapestries. It is in its own right a source of meaning, such as [Gandhi's] loincloth was perceived symbolically to possess in India's struggle for political independence and economic autonomy. Fabric carries such meanings because of the way it fits into forms of life that are lived by very ordinary people in contexts typically remote from those of high or fine art, to which the tapestry now belongs.*[22]

As Danto points out, tapestry (and its revived form as celebrated in the biennials of Lausanne) now belongs to the contexts of high and fine art. It is encountered in museums and galleries, as well as in living environments. Against this backdrop, Abakanowicz managed to weave a radical form of tapestry from humble materials and to present it architecturally in the gallery and in public space so as to bring a contemporary relevance and necessity to the medium. It was through the creation of her environments that Abakanowicz found a way to express herself as both weaver and artist. In moving towards the emerging medium of installation, she was able to complicate our understanding of and received ideas about thread and rope, tapestry and sculpture. Though the artist ultimately moved away from woven forms to explore the burlap and more recognisable sculptural materials (such as bronze, plaster and steel) and develop expressive forms in other media, her work from the late 1960s and early 1970s remains revolutionary as a statement on the possibilities of combining handmade forms with found, industrially produced objects to create situations in space. With every tangle of thread and rope, Abakanowicz's organic environments reject the received categories of art and craft, tapestry and sculpture, vision and touch, spectacle and experience in place of an art that draws upon all of these aspects to take us to new possibilities of transformation.

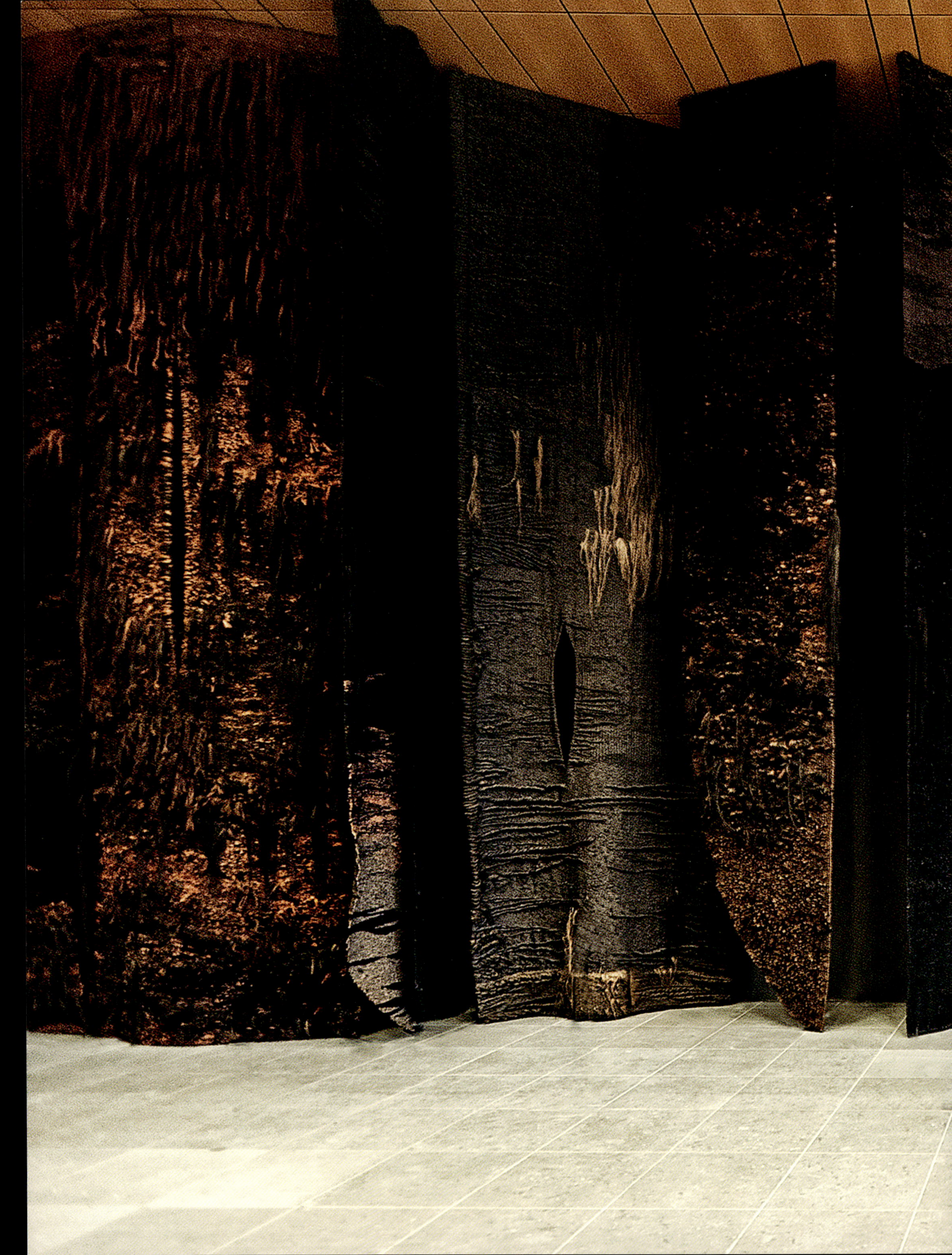

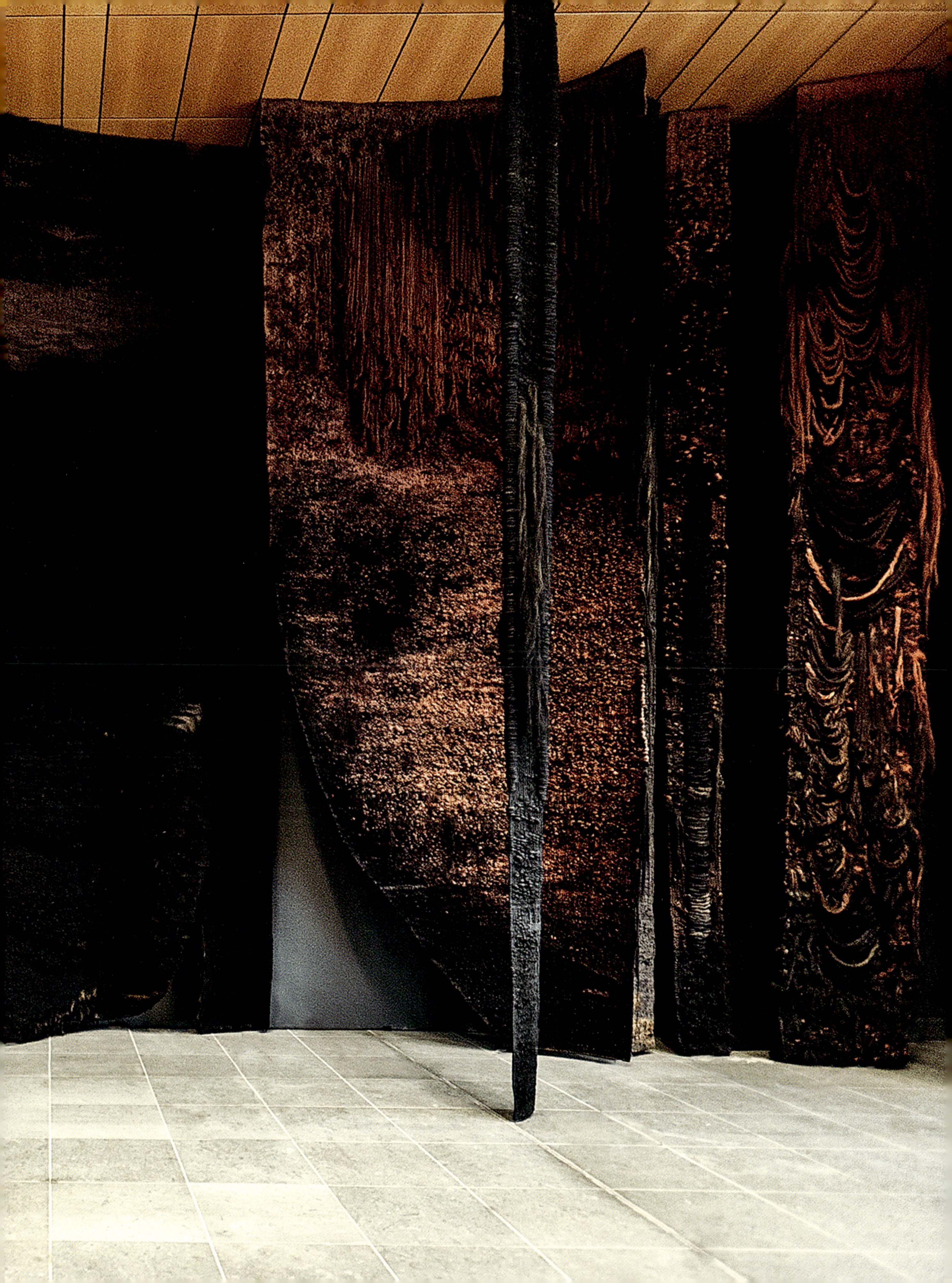

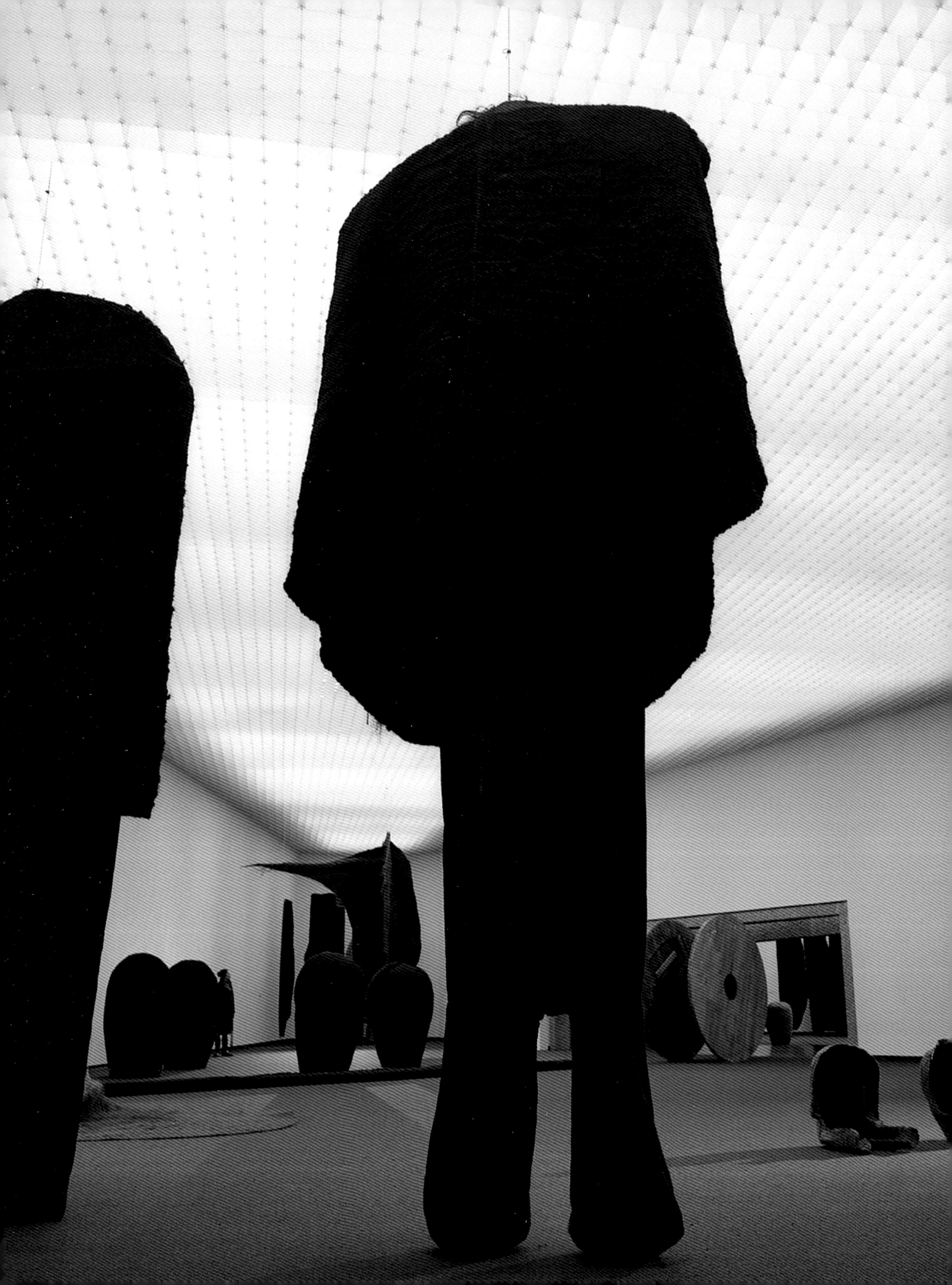

GABI SCARDI

ART AS SPATIAL DRAMATURGY: POLISH AND ITALIAN POVERA

For Magdalena Abakanowicz, art is an experience and that experience, in her hands, takes on a theatrical nature. In the most direct way it is performative, immersive – an experience that happens in space. Her *Abakans* and *Garments* become actors, imbued with life and a presence of their own. Yet beyond spatiality and the dramatic dimension of her practice, her work speaks on a profound level. In this, it resonates deeply with both the radical work of Polish theatre directors and Italian visual artists of the 1960s and 1970s. Like Abakanowicz, these creatives were greatly influenced by the postwar situation and the changing cultural climate that ensued. The palpable nature of their work and its raw expression was derived from a need to give perceptible form to the phantoms of recent history, most notably the callousness of mankind, its destructive force, and the resulting disintegration of human heritage. Considering Abakanowicz's work in this context, her sense of materiality, evocative of animism and history, as well as ritual and repair, reveals just how strongly connected she was to the times. This is evident not just in a shared sociopolitical position in response to great human tragedy, but also in her use of 'poor' materials and new processes of making.

From 1970, Abakanowicz's exhibitions are troubling. Arranged solely by the artist at a time when this practice was rare and unnamed, she gathered dark, animalesque and sculptural masses to form environments of great expressive power. In these total works of art she interpreted space as a stage:

> *I began to use my three-dimensional forms in a different manner: I would transform their original shape and group them differently in different exhibition spaces. Among the many things that prompted me to do that was my intention to show the changeability inherent to every soft object. This changeability is its life; hard objects do not have it ...*

Looking back, I no longer see these shows as completely abstract; I see them as acts or challenges. As a kind of ceremony, if silent and static. The viewer is 'introduced' to a sphere of sensations, 'confronted' with objects that await him inside. I infuse it with myself for many long days beforehand. The pieces are like actors to whom I assign roles. They participate in a ritual that first 'comes to life' – when I work on it – and then emanates the energy it has absorbed – when it interacts with the viewer. Both of those stages are very important to me.[1]

At its essence, Abakanowicz's art is metaphorical. It traces the eternal conflict between human beings and the primordial forces of nature, in spaces suggestive of forests, caves or symbolic and psychic mazes. These themes originate not only from her innate and deeply-sensed participation in the natural world, but also from life under the totalitarian regimes that governed Poland during much of the twentieth century. Thus, her work expresses both a personal attitude and a collective response to the context in which she lived: it is a form of protest to any sort of limitation, categorisation or ideological imposition.[2] Regardless of the shape or scale of her works, she consistently engaged space to create dramatic, immersive experiences in which the individual is consumed within a world at once protective and threatening.

In the 1970 film *Abakany* (see also pp.152–9), Abakanowicz first makes explicit the performative character of her art. She stages a selection of *Abakans* and ropes stretched out on wooden armatures as if they were animal hides ready for tanning. Amid a primordial soundtrack, she brings them to life in a lunar-like landscape – a *terra incognita* – where wandering becomes a ceremonial experience. As 'actors' in the film, her *Abakans* and ropes play an active role, and this is common to all her work. For this reason, modes of installation are always essential for Abakanowicz: they allow her works to become active agents of and vehicles for unprecedented perceptions and mental projections.

Theatre, Poverty and Ritual

While parallels have been drawn between Abakanowicz and her fibre contemporaries internationally, her art also connects at its essence with Polish avant-garde theatre of the 1960s and 1970s. In particular, it speaks to the work of radical innovators Jerzy Grotowski (1933–99), Tadeusz Kantor (1915–90) and Józef Szajna (1922–2008). These directors were responding to a common experience – a shared trauma – and, like Abakanowicz, were so doing by rethinking spatial relationships in the pursuit of intensity, exploring ancestral and ritual aspects through pronounced materiality.

Immediately after the war, in the decades of the first communist regime, poverty became a central theme for all these theatre directors. They alluded to the trauma of occupation and war, the myths and ideals that collapse under an imposed regime, and an overall historical dimension of individual and collective loss. Grotowski used the name *teatr ubogi* ('poor theatre') in his text *Towards a Poor Theatre.*[3] He advocated absolute rigour to strip things down as much as possible in order to concentrate

Opening page: *Black Garment Rounded* 1973 (left) and *Black Garment with Sacks* 1971. Installation view, *Magdalena Abakanowicz: Organic Structures* at Henie Onstad Kunstsenter, Høvikodden, Norway, 1977.

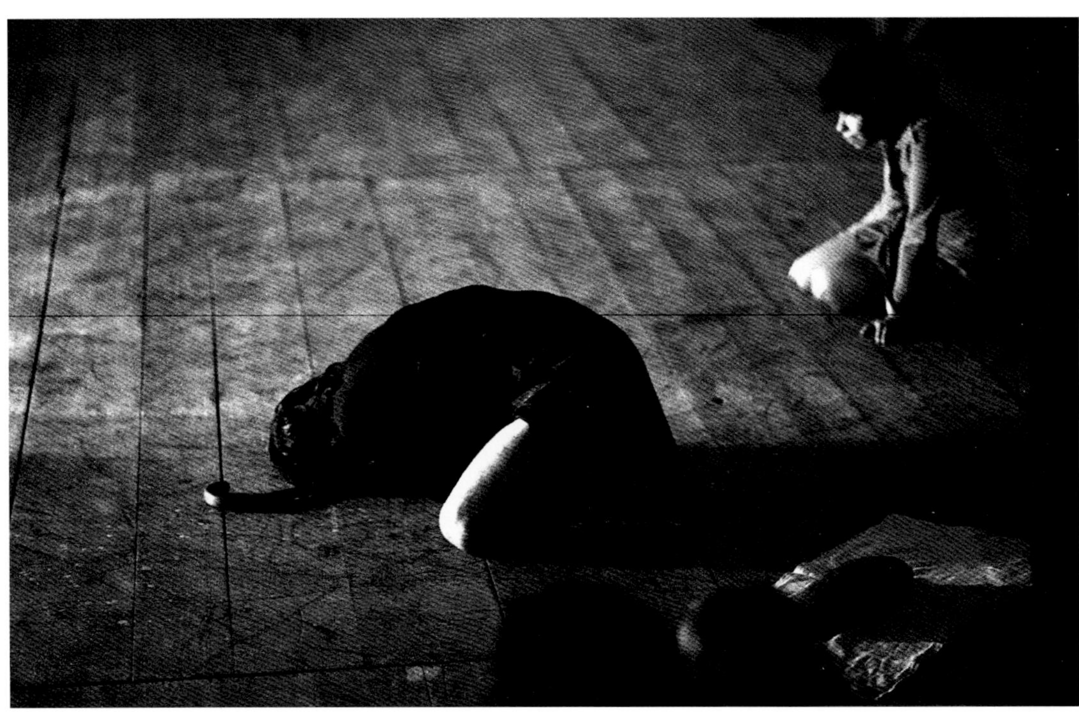

Below: Photograph of the official premiere of *Apocalypsis cum figuris* in Wrocław, Poland, 11 February 1969. Adapted and directed by Jerzy Grotowski; co-directed by Ryszard Cieślak.

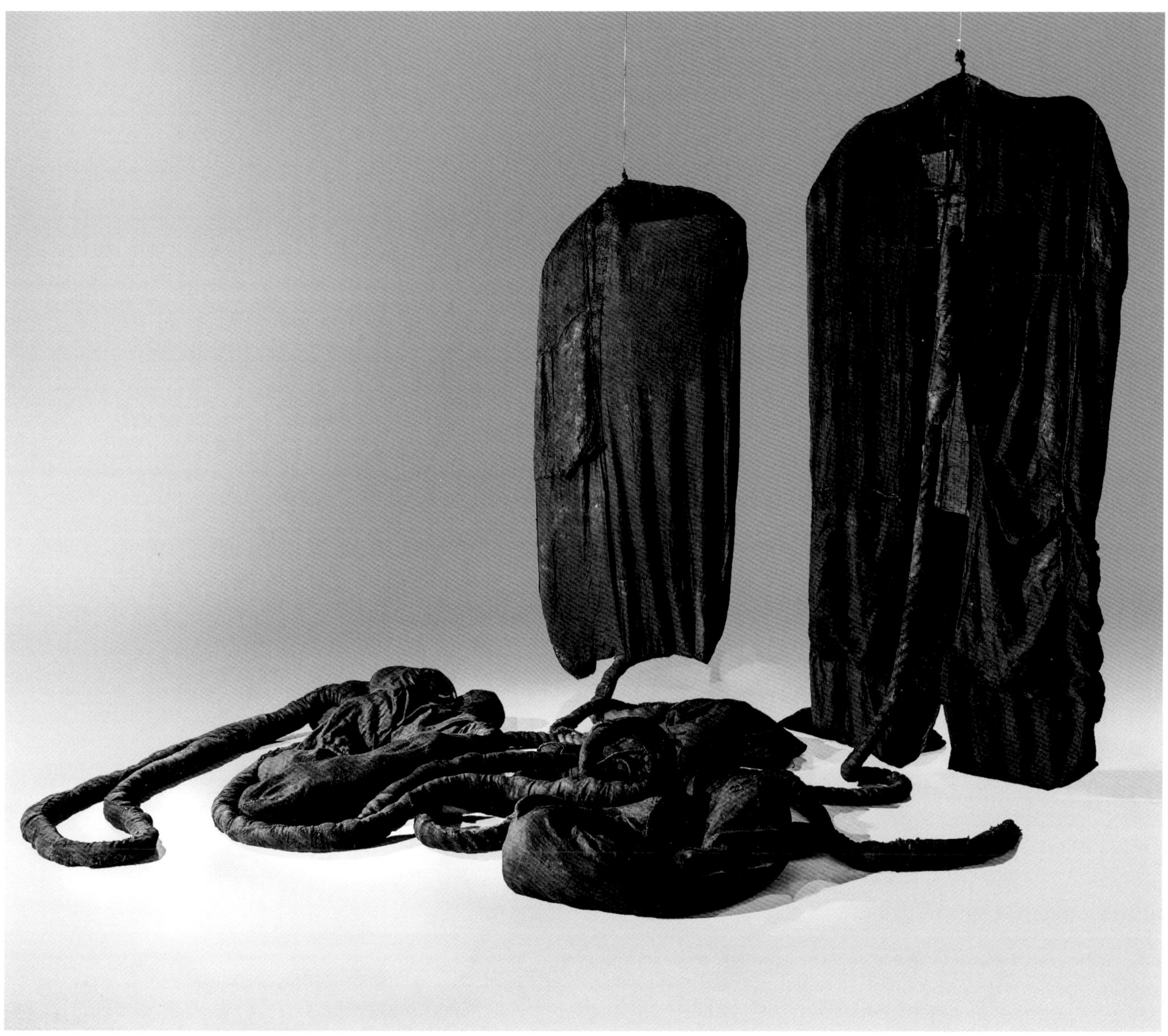

Above: *Set of Black Organic Forms* 1974
Rope, canvas and sisal
Dimensions variable

specifically on the actor-spectator relationship. Grotowski's theatre is oriented towards an expression of ulteriority and spiritual elements. Works such as *Acropolis*, centred on the concentration camp, and *The Constant Prince*, with its references to martyrdom, among other themes, deeply and directly link to the director's interest in living rituals. He discarded all fixed patterns to make room for a flow of interior impulses, which were then structured with formal precision. Accessing this truth within the actor's body allowed the public – or witnesses as he called them – to achieve an absoluteness of perception, a kind of revelation. With an aspiration akin to Grotowski, Abakanowicz's work seeks to embody the primal force of origin that resides within the body. This is present from the outset in the large, powerful and disturbing *Abakans*. These complex, organic micro-universes formulate an unpredictable compositional balance: gaps and cracks, cavities and orifices, outcroppings and protuberances expand in space while also at times projecting fibrous bundles suggestive of nervous and arterial systems. Everything about them speaks of connections between a restless inside and the outside, while the intentionally raw materials imply a rejection of finitude, giving them a sort of totemic force.

Kantor also formulated the concept of the 'poor object' – a degraded object that 'ends up showing its true value at the threshold of the dustbin: rags, scraps, papers, mouldy books'. [4] It is precisely the 'object deprived of its functions, of its reason for being, which through that "poverty" becomes capable of taking on the function of a work of art'. [5] Kantor's theatre replaced the traditional narrative fabric with a collage of surreal scenes arising from humanity in ruins. In the performances by his experimental theatre company called Cricot 2, that he had founded in Kraków in 1955, in particular in his *Theatre of*

Death, and including *The Dead Class* and *Wielopole Wielopole*, he demonstrates a need to give form to both the crude reality of life and transcendence lurking inside.[6] This is also alluded to in many of Abakanowicz's works, such as her *Abakans* and *Garments* – dark compositions of monumental, indefinite, overlapping woven forms, whose exterior as well as interior spaces are offered to the viewer. Later, in her painful *War Games* series, gigantic logs are cut with scars, marked by burns, and wrapped in rags or metal cladding to simultaneously evoke artillery pieces and mutilated bodies. Endowed with names, these portrait-like pieces suggest the reality of physical violence, while uniquely extending the vocabulary to represent war's extreme effects. To come to terms with the imposing physical presence of these works is to come to terms with the tragic dimension of history.

Szajna was both a theatre director and visual artist who survived Auschwitz and Buchenwald. As with Grotowski and Kantor, his allusion to the extreme experience of the death camps is of central importance. In his *Plastic Theatre*, dummies and masks emit inarticulate groans to convey the horrors of the camps, putting the emphasis on scenic elements rather than words. In his saturated, visionary and often grotesque theatre, Szajna used jumbles of objects, scraps and junk to express the horror of an inhuman experience and the devastation and rubble left behind by war. For example, in his installation *Reminiscences* for the Polish Pavilion at the Venice Biennale in 1970, he evoked the reality of the deportees and of the concentration camps: a reality torn apart in which the concept of poverty bonds with a sense of the inevitability of death.

Ten years later in the same pavilion, Abakanowicz represented simultaneous points of life and death through *Wheel and Rope, Embryology* and *Backs*. *Wheel and Rope* (seen in the background on p.78 and pp.178 and 180) metaphorises the adaptable thread of life that is seemingly always about to snap despite its tenacity. *Embryology* (pp.174 and 176–7) embodies the wholeness of existence within an ensemble of nuclei, dramatic chrysalises, fossilised wombs, or scarred embryonic cocoons. Their all-too fragile skin, torn by lacerations and marked by stitching, leaves a glimpse of tangled innards, of an exposed and tormented life. In this work of great poetic force and dramatic existential depth, there is a coexistence of generative potential amid fragility and regression. All these pieces are painful reminders of the vulnerability that accompanies us in every stage of existence, from the prenatal phase till its end. The *Backs* series posits anonymised representations of the human being: sitting figures, gathered in groups, turned away from the beholder, and bent as though subject to an invisible weight. While not fixed in meaning, the *Backs* are nonetheless inescapably tied to the same moment in history Szajna sought to capture.

The animism and symbolism in Abakanowicz's work adds to its theatrical presence. Responding to the crushing brutality of historical events and the depersonalisation of an oppressive regime, she relies on what is unique, singular, inalienable and, therefore, not subject to infiltration by an ideological language. On the one hand, this centres on the corporeal, its energy and irrepressible sexual potential. On the other, it embodies the remote echoes of ancestral ceremony shared by all human beings. Evoking this sense of ritual as well as the sense of magic that she felt in the forest as a child, Abakanowicz's immersive installations have the potential to transmit a shamanistic energy: 'In exhibition rooms I create spaces for them in which they radiate the energy I have imbued them with. They exist together with me, dependent on me, I dependent on them ... Without me – like scattered parts of the body separated from the trunk – they are meaningless.'[7]

Ancestral energy and mystery are also prevalent themes in Grotowski's theatrical form. With an interest in liturgical traditions, he described his works as 'theatrical magic' that aimed to 'enable the reconstruction, the restitution of that 'primitive ritual unity'.[8] In terms of spatial composition, this meant 'eliminating the conception of stage and seating as separate places, and making the performance of the actor a stimulus to plunge the spectator into the action'.[9] For Abakanowicz, an innate interest in the cathartic and primal sources of the earth's energy is revealed in its alliances to other cultures. Her anthropological interests were nourished by her voyages to Australia and Papua New Guinea in 1976, then to Celebes (now Sulawesi), Bali, Sumatra, Java and Thailand, as well as in the desert of Arizona. Years later, she developed an important relationship with the Mediterranean island of Sardinia: attuning to the force of the sea, the rocky landscape and rich pastoral culture steeped in ancient legends, many of which are set in caves inhabited by magical presences.[10] She returned from these places full of impressions, bringing back not only objects, but also memories destined to emerge in the totemic appearance of many of her works. This is also evident in the evocative names of works from the *War Games* series: *Anasta* (pp.168–9), *Baz, Kos, Kuka, Runa, Ukon* and *Zyk*. Likewise, Grotowski focused on the theme of rituals, including some still alive in various areas of Poland, and in Haiti, India, various African countries, and Mexico. For instance, in his *Theatre of Sources*, the actor searches for contact with the absolute, appeals to the power and vigour of the originary cultures. Here, too, the natural environment – very often the forest – is the scene of the action.[11] Thus, both artist and director were driven not only by the Polish political situation but also by the changing cultural climate that was prompting European artists to come to terms with the non-Western world beyond their immediate European sphere of reference.

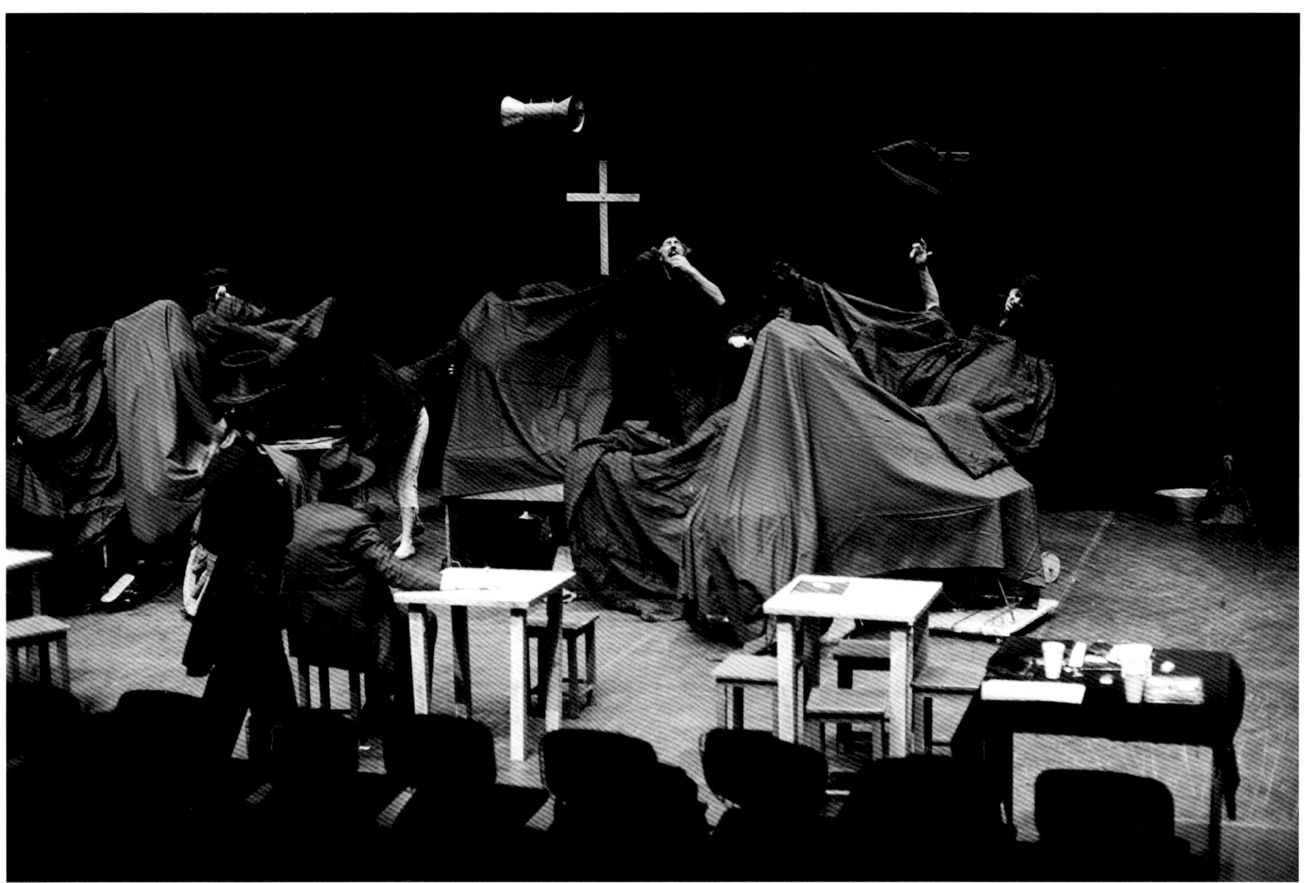

Above: *Assemblage for the End of the Twentieth Century*, photo of sequence in *I Shall Never Return* 1988, directed by Tadeusz Kantor.

Abakanowicz's affinity with forms of expression developed far away in time and space is also revealed in her interest in the Butoh dance of Tatsumi Hijikata (1928–86), which was carried on after his death by his wife and collaborator Akiko Motofuji (1928–2003). Born after the devastation of the atomic bomb, this avant-garde dance form incorporates echoes of the darkest, most ghostly Japan that, in the face of the erasure of life, expresses an intense, dramatic physical reaction. Characterised by stillness, economy and extreme tension – by a rigour that is already on its own, critical and resistant – Butoh combines spirituality and expressive impact based on muscle memory and spasmodic concentration. It asserts the need to begin anew through the body, honouring and employing its energetic properties akin to ascetic or shamanic development. Abakanowicz grasped the force of protest of this dance, conscious of the bombing of Warsaw just one year before the nuclear tragedy of Hiroshima and Nagasaki. In response, with Motofuji, she created a Butoh dance score that was performed in 1995 in Tokyo, Hiroshima and Warsaw. In this piece, nude, faceless bodies moved slowly, expressing a sculptural character reminiscent of *Backs* or *Garments* and perhaps even – with the cramped bodies – the *Embryology* nuclei. Once again, the theme of strenuous, visceral resistance to devastation intertwines with a performative component and an interest in an animistic-magical perception of nature: 'For many years while leaving my studio at night, closing the door, I had the impression that now, left alone my stiff standing sculptures will start to behave in their own way. Liberated from the pressure of my imagination they will begin to move, to walk, to dance, to dress into heads to adapt faces. With time I created real dances.'[12]

While the concept and expression of 'poverty' in Polish theatre is rooted in the country's history, in the contemporary art world *povera* is identified as an Italian visual art thanks to the adoption of Grotowski's term by the art theorist and critic Germano Celant. In 1967, Celant used arte povera to identify an emerging group of artists from Turin and Rome who, in 1959–60, were responding to the postwar climate and reconnecting to nature.[13] They remained known thusly even as their careers matured and varied from each other. Cultural exchange between Poland and Italy is evident as early as 1968 when Polish theatre directors were assiduous presences in Italy with performances, workshops and lectures. In this period, the country was a reference point for international artistic research and a destination for theatre companies from all over the world. Kantor's Cricot 2 was a fairly regular guest of cultural events and institutional theatres in various Italian cities. Grotowski's *Laboratory Theatre* visited the centres associated with what Eugenio

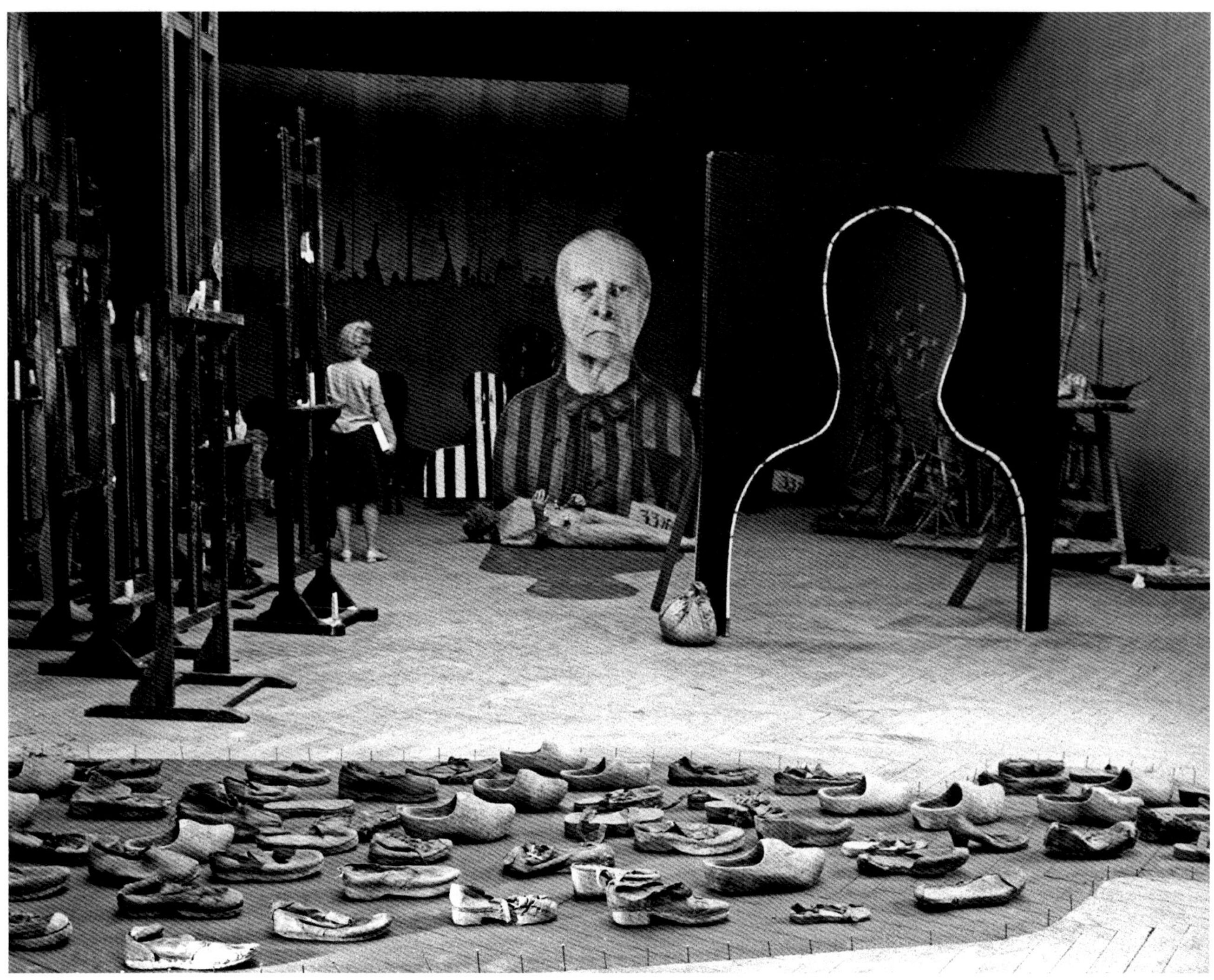

Above: A woman observing *Reminiscences*, directed by Józef Szajna, at the 35th Venice Biennale, 1970.

Barba would call the 'Third Theatre'. According to Barba, this term signified the area where different modes of dramatic expression that live in the fringe meet and intertwine as a breathing social fabric.

Yet in Italy, arte povera came into being in an atmosphere radically different from that of postwar Poland.[14] During this period, Italy was governed by the Christian Democrats installed under the aegis of the Marshall Plan[15] through which the United States exerted a decisive political, technological and cultural influence over Italy. Throughout the 1950s and 1960s, Italy grew quickly yet disjointedly, triggering protest movements punctuated by the uprising of 1968. This explosion of social and political dissent resulted in strikes on the part of workers, students, intellectuals and artists. Theatrical and artistic expressions during this time directly critiqued the institutional system, conventional codes of behaviour, the invasion of technology, and the pervasive influence of the market's commodification of Italian culture. The term '*povero*' offered an alternative: the pursuit of the essential, primary energies and meanings; a return to the centrality of human beings and authenticity of feeling and perception; and a focus on a physical, sensorial, unmediated relationship with phenomena and materials.

For Abakanowicz the use of 'poor' materials was a way to respond to the imposition of administered thoughts. Her powerful objects draw their force from a direct connection with the magic and the energies of the earth. Like Abakanowicz, the Polish theatre directors experimented with non-traditional processes and contexts and made use of basic materials, investigating their structure, deeper energies and connections. For them, too, this was an attempt to break free of a politically questionable present and to develop new modes of action from cultural and artistic conventions they considered restrictive and isolating.

While they revealed profoundly different sensibilities, the importance of the concept of poverty was shared by Poland and Italy: they sought a vitalistic dimension connected with the exploration of the art-life relationship and the role of the artist in an industrialised society. Italian arte povera critiqued the current social conventions of a world increasingly seduced by consumption. Meanwhile the Polish art scene had to come to terms with a traumatic, unresolved individual and national experience: a context that frustrated and depleted the individual towards demanding a critical, impersonal acceptance. Thus, dialogue with memory, reality, the forms of the human body, and subjective experience run throughout the political theatre of Grotowski; the sense of transcendence of Kantor moves 'between the dustbin and eternity';[16] and the excruciating chaos of uprooting and suffering are in motion in Szajna's installations.

Though sharing in this same atmosphere, impulses and histories, Abakanowicz stubbornly asserted her independence and the singular character of her work. She concentrated on systematic everyday labour based on an incessant dialogue with herself, her own personal mythologies and history. Yet she was of her time, as art cannot help but express itself in relation to the cultural climate and vicissitudes of its time. An unmistakable expression of awareness, in this sense, is her reaction to a query posed by the American critic Michael Brenson about the relation of her works and Pompeii: 'I think that it is important to inform people that I was fully aware of all Western trends like Minimalism and Conceptualism. It was my conscious choice not to follow these trends which were in contradiction with my philosophy.' And then:

> *As regards the influence of the 'ashes of Pompeii'. My country is covered with mass graves. Still new graves are discovered and opened, filled with stiff bodies of thousands of murdered soldiers or civilians dressed in colourless clothing or rags. These discoveries are shown in television news. I have been in Prague in 1968 when the Soviet Army entered to crush the liberation movement. Trying to escape back to my country, I spent the whole day at the railway station. Everywhere the floor and platforms were covered with sleeping Russian soldiers in their uniforms made out of linen. These breathing linen bundles left on me an unforgettable impression. Only a person completely ignorant about the experience of Eastern Europe and the country of Auschwitz could suppose that I have to look for inspiration in Pompeii ashes.*[17]

Indeed it was the sum of such experiences, of existential fears and a shared sense of loss from which Polish avant-garde theatre emerged. Meanwhile poor materials in Italian art of the postwar period was a means to rebuild from roots in the past and the eternal in nature. This, too, was the world from which Abakanowicz arose. While this experience made for powerful art and performances, this crude reality was hard to fully feel for those outside as Abakanowicz observed:

> *Here, art never became merchandise ...*
> *The war was long ago, but images of it are our companions every day when we watch the news on TV. Dull-brained we watch, drinking tea, some people killing other people in the East or West, terrorists lynching the innocent, or whole settlements of quiet people killed with poison gas. Anyway, news of this kind evokes emotions and is viewed in different ways in my country and yours.*
>
> *Art tells about reality because it springs from the reality from which it develops. Mine could never be born in America, just as Warhol could never create his vision of the world in Poland. Our mentalities are shaped differently. We have different passions perceived differently, and we exclaim different things.*[18]

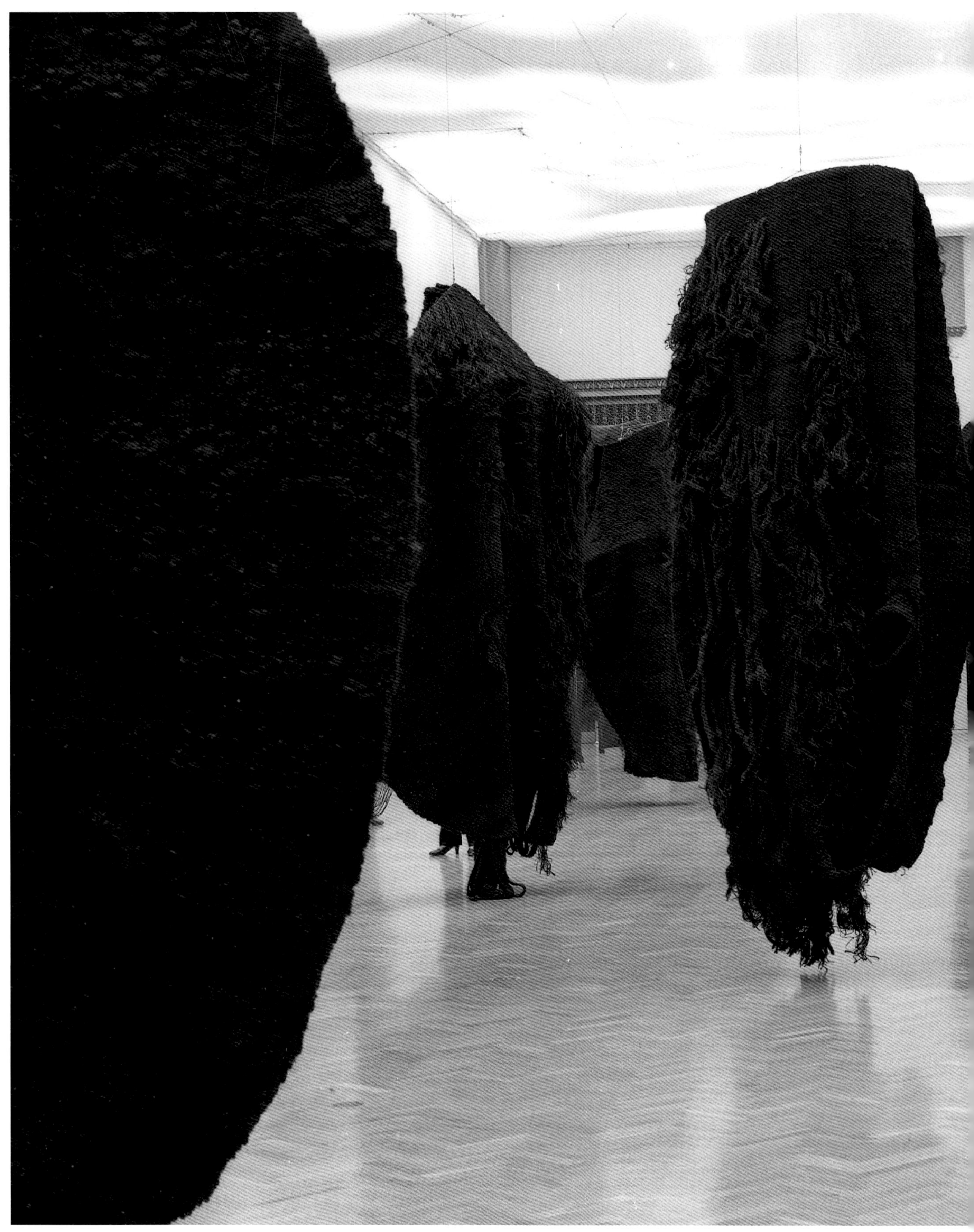

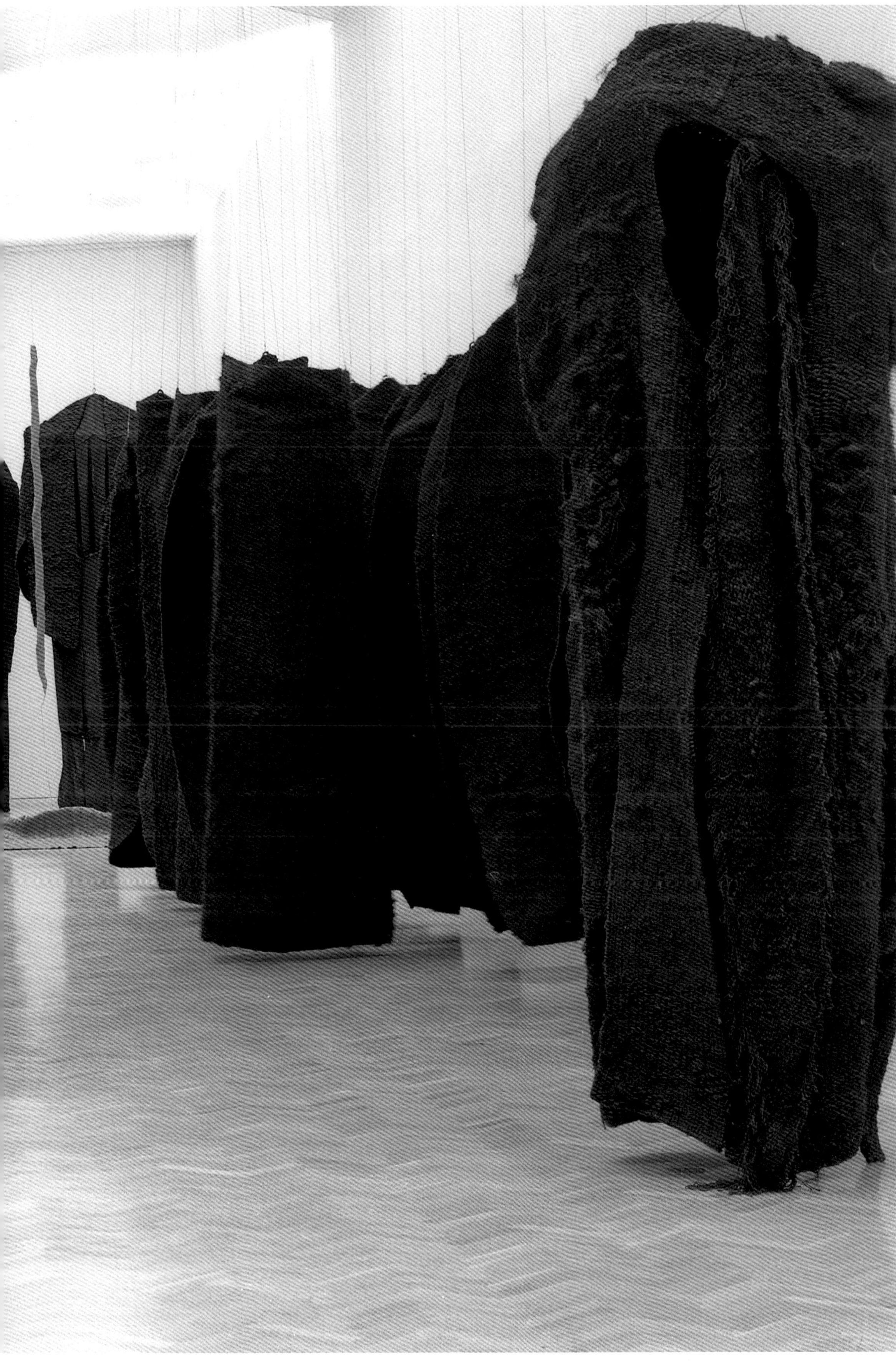

From left to right: *Abakan Winged* 1967, *Black Garment* 1968, *Great Black Abakan* 1967–8, *Abakan Round* 1967–8, *Black Garment Rounded* 1973, *Abakan Orange* 1971, *Black Garment with Sack* 1971, *Black Forms* 1970–8 and *Abakan Open* 1967–8. Installation view, Museum of Contemporary Art Chicago exhibition at the Chicago Cultural Center, 1982.

Abakan étroit **1967–8**
Sisal and wool
320 × 100 × 100

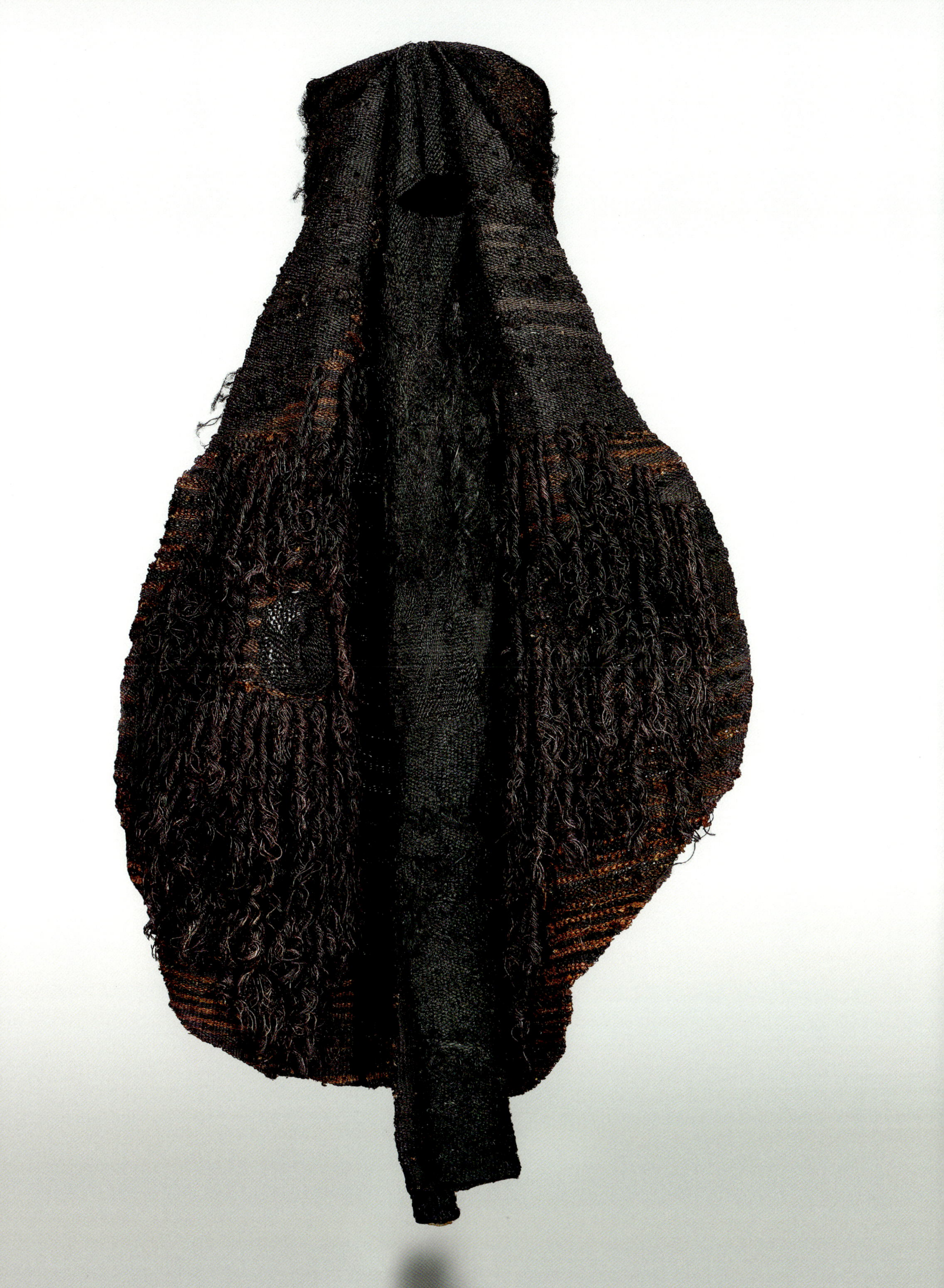

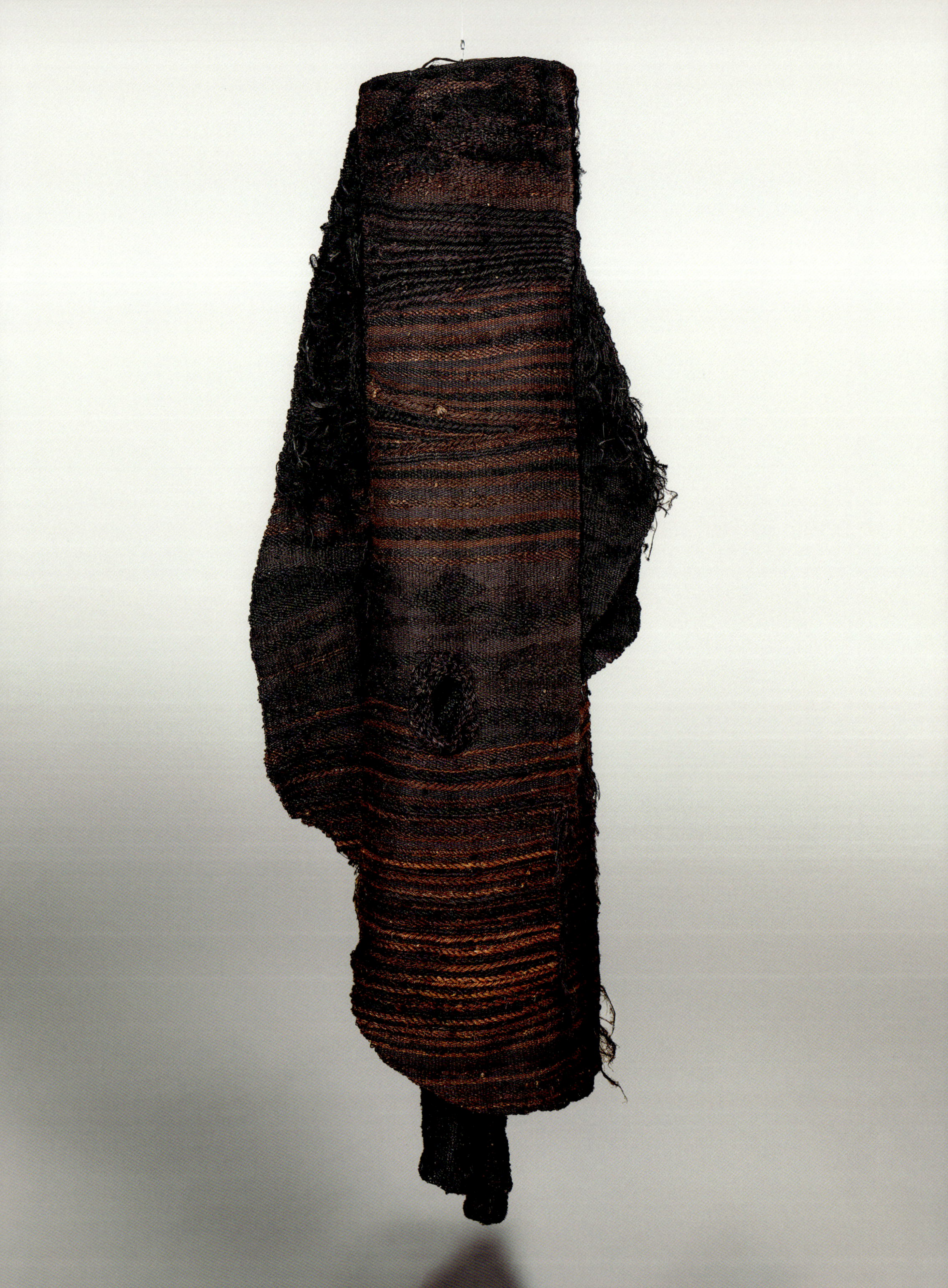

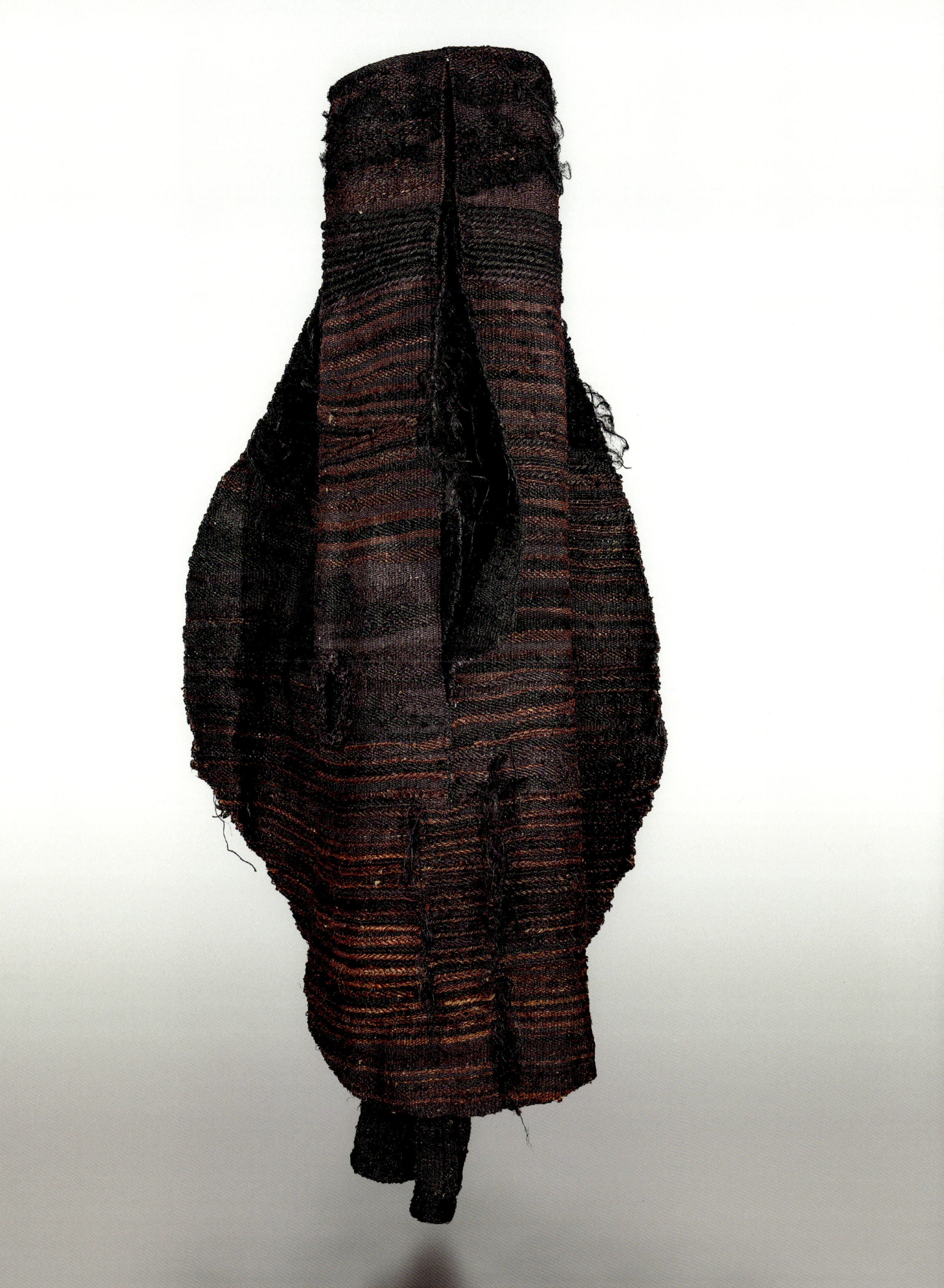

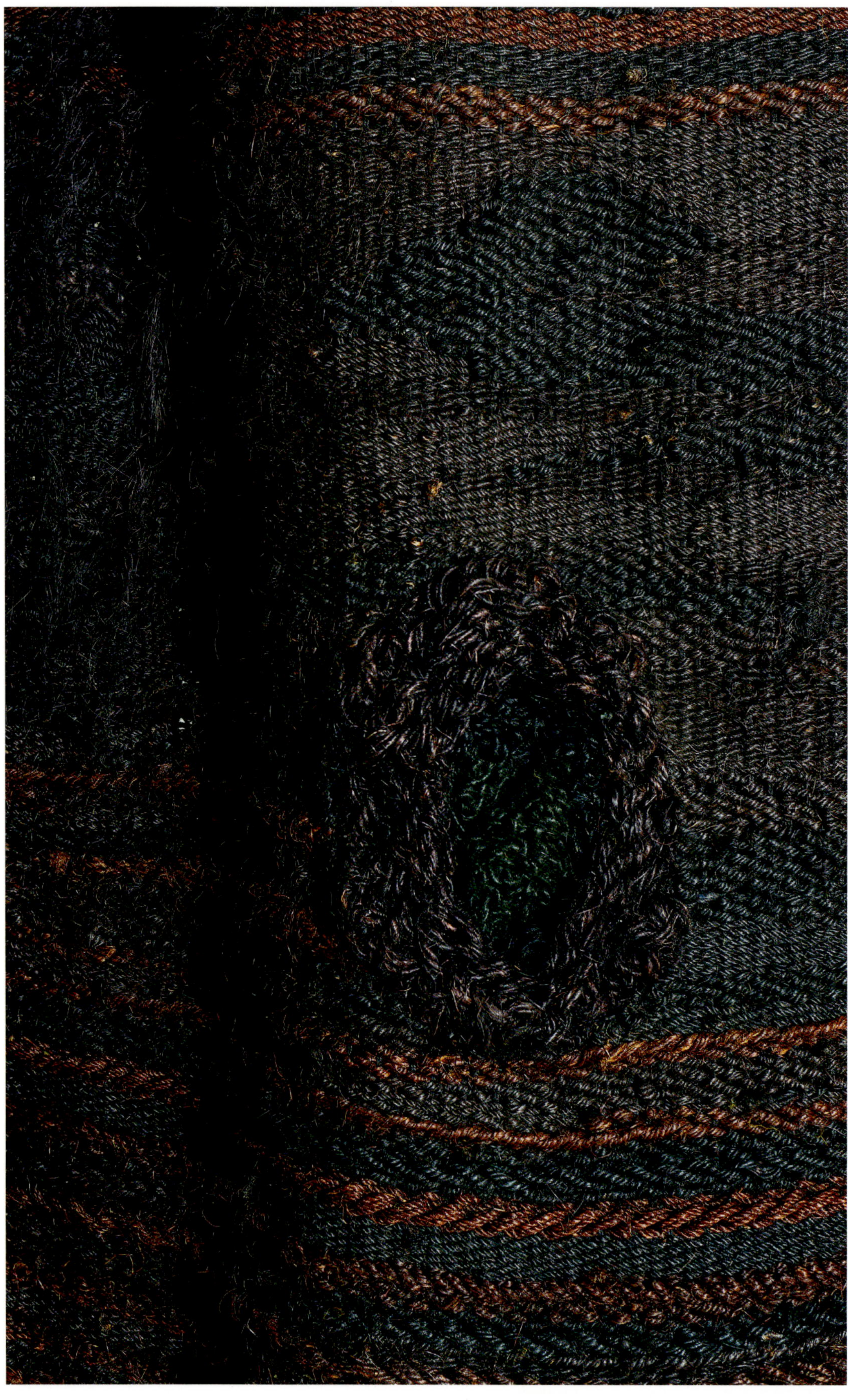

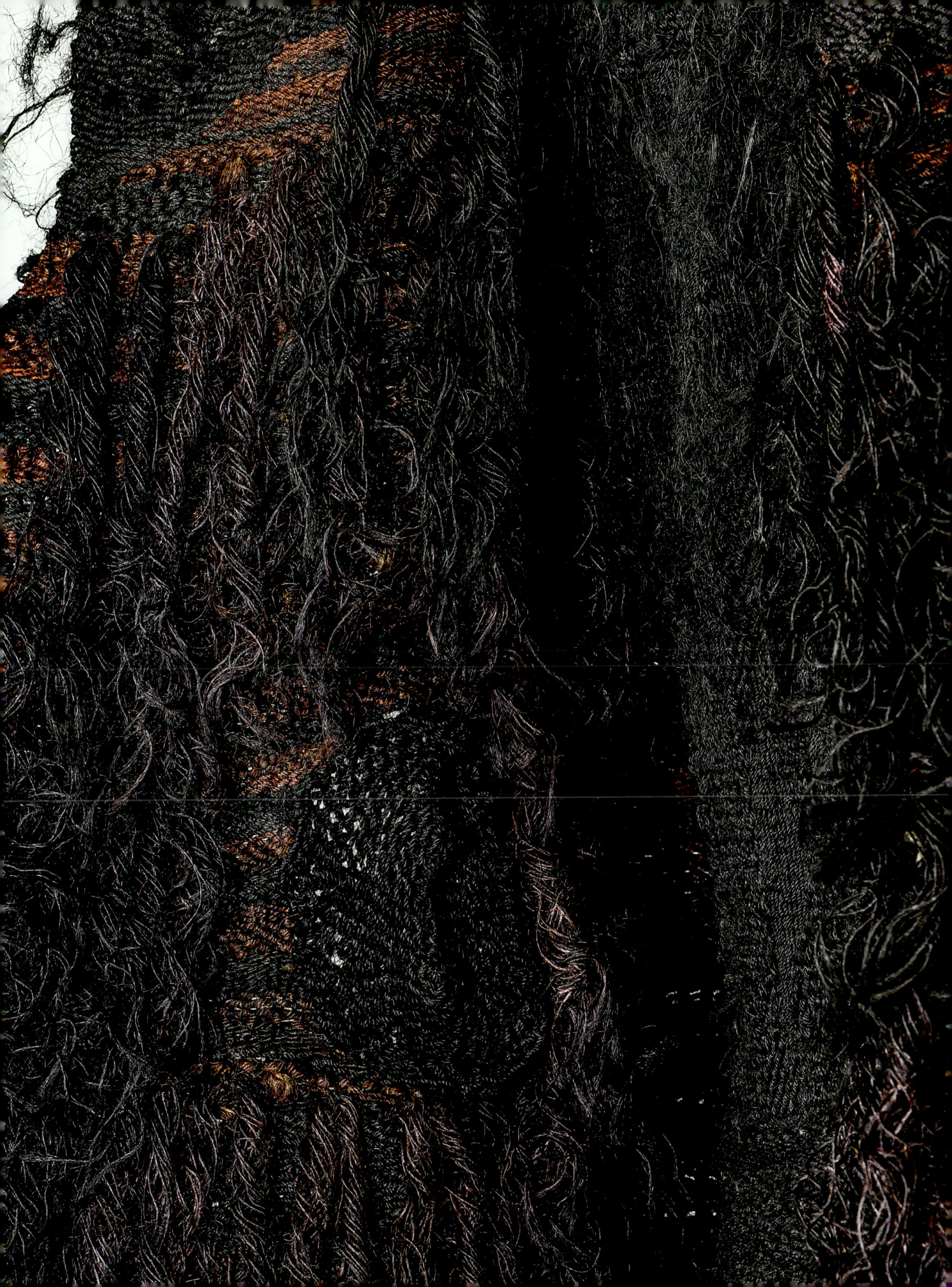

Abakan Round **1967–8**
Sisal
340 × 150 × 100

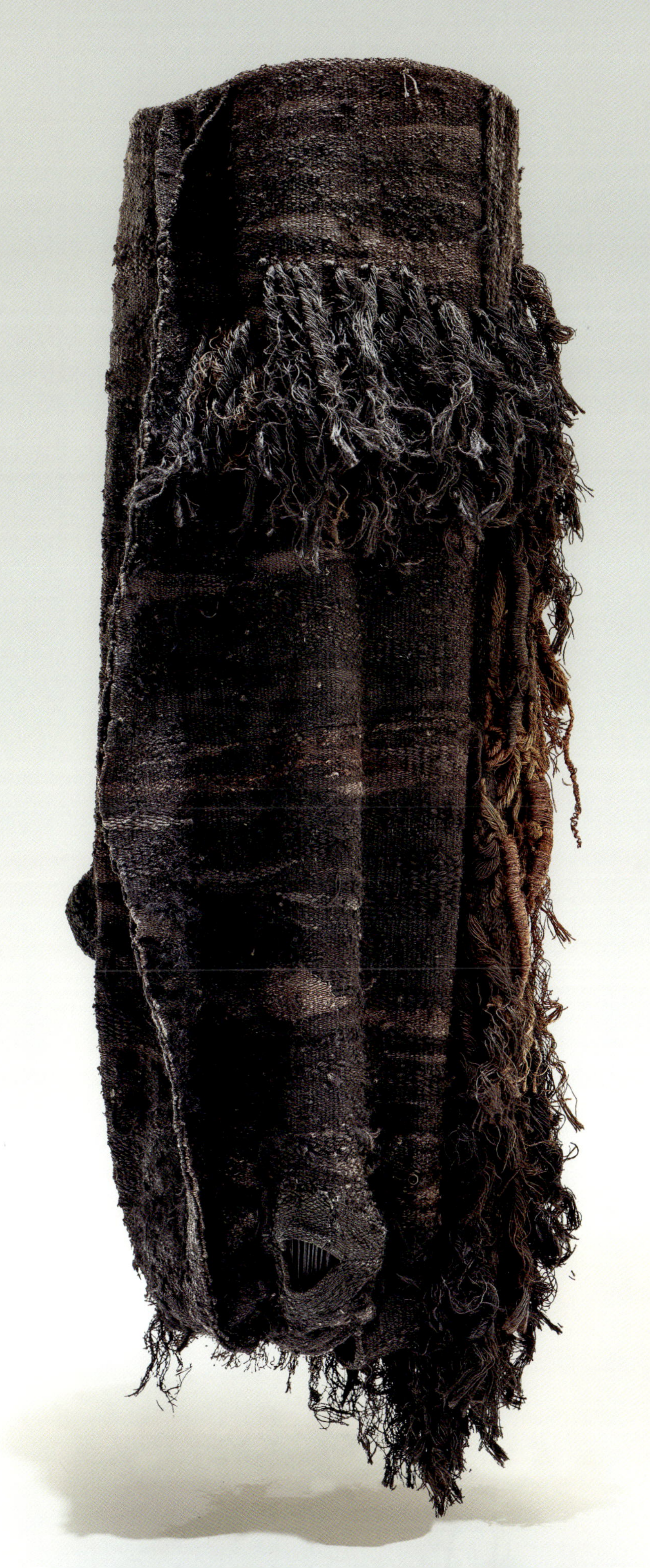

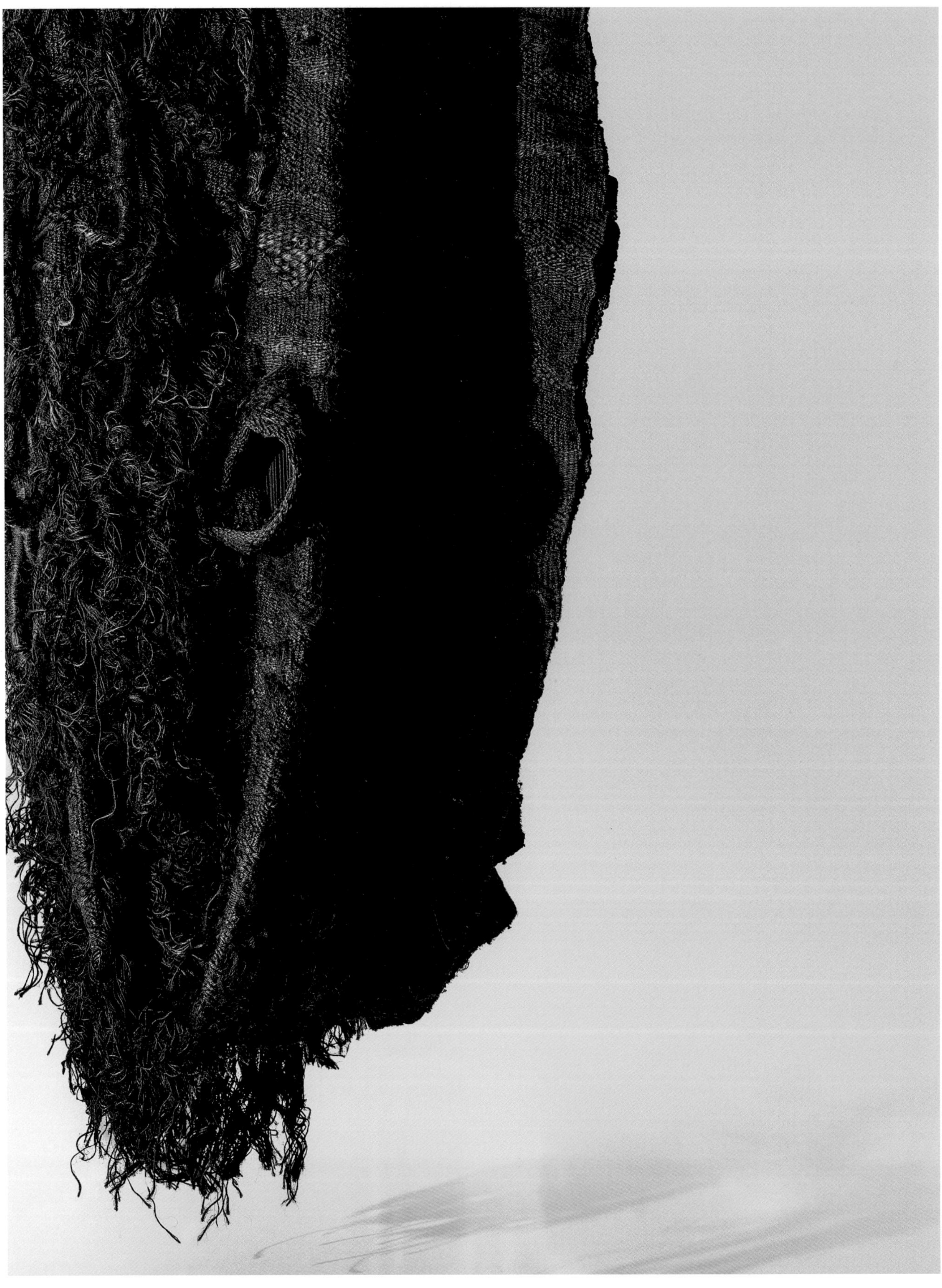

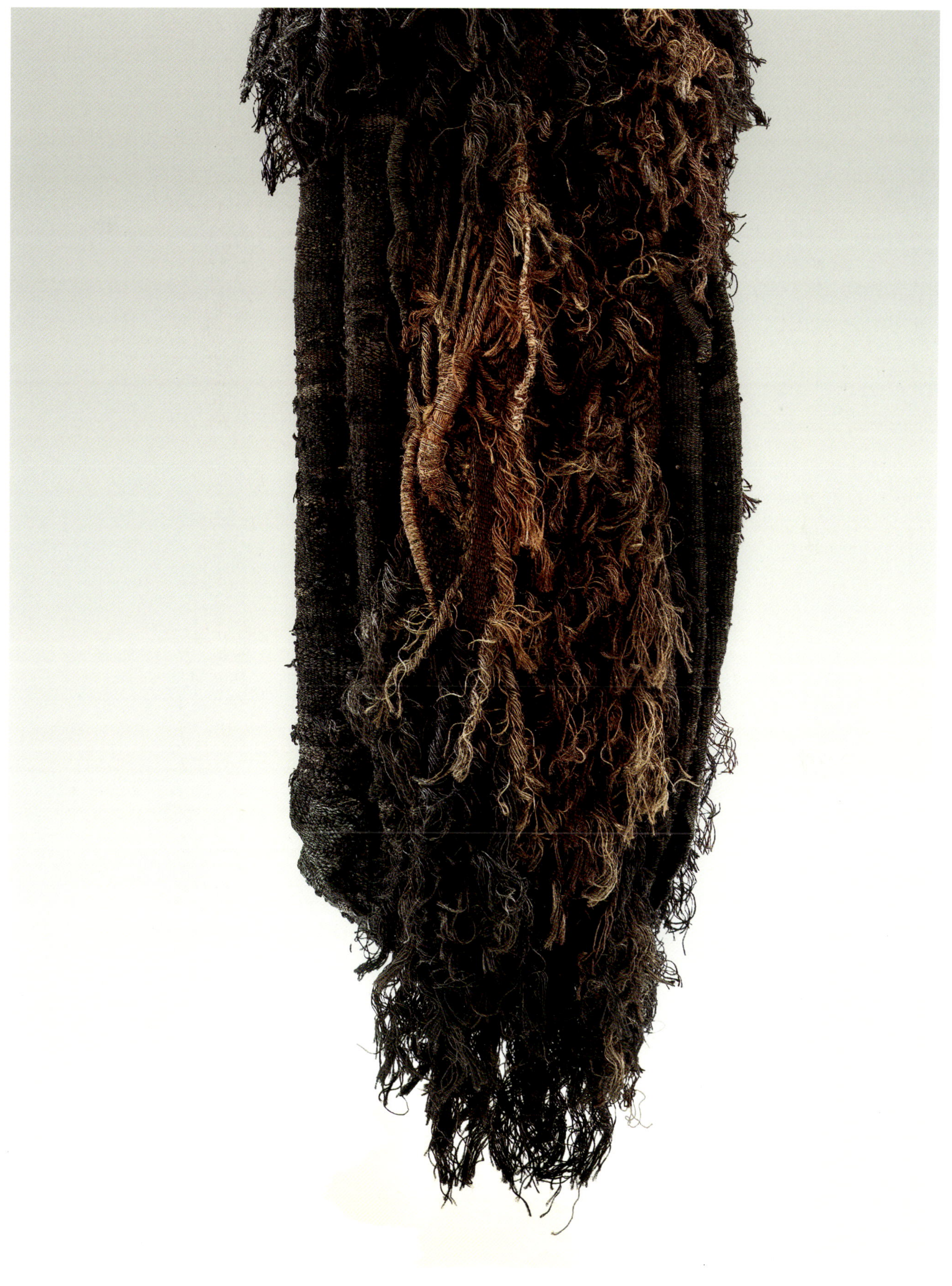

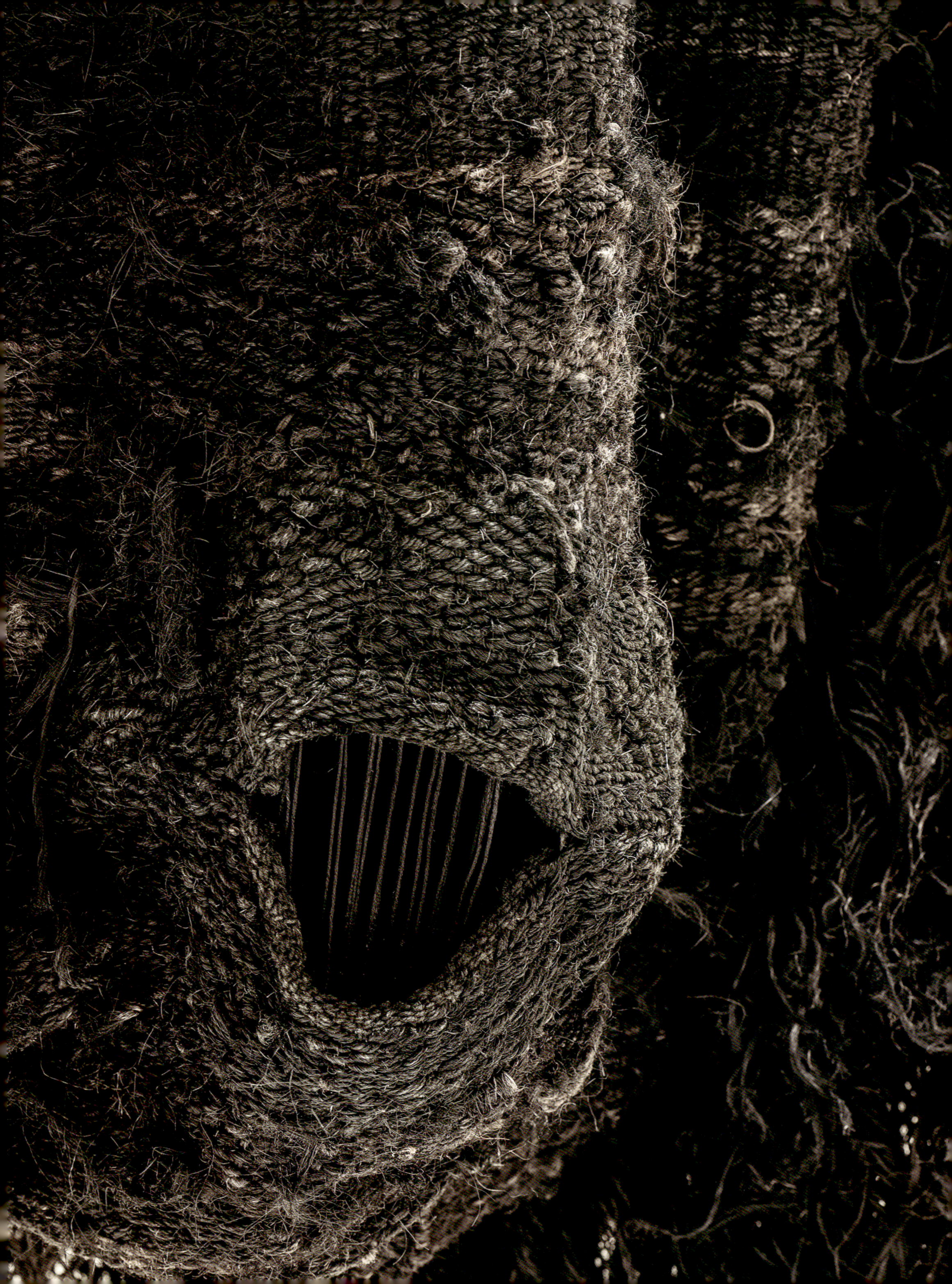

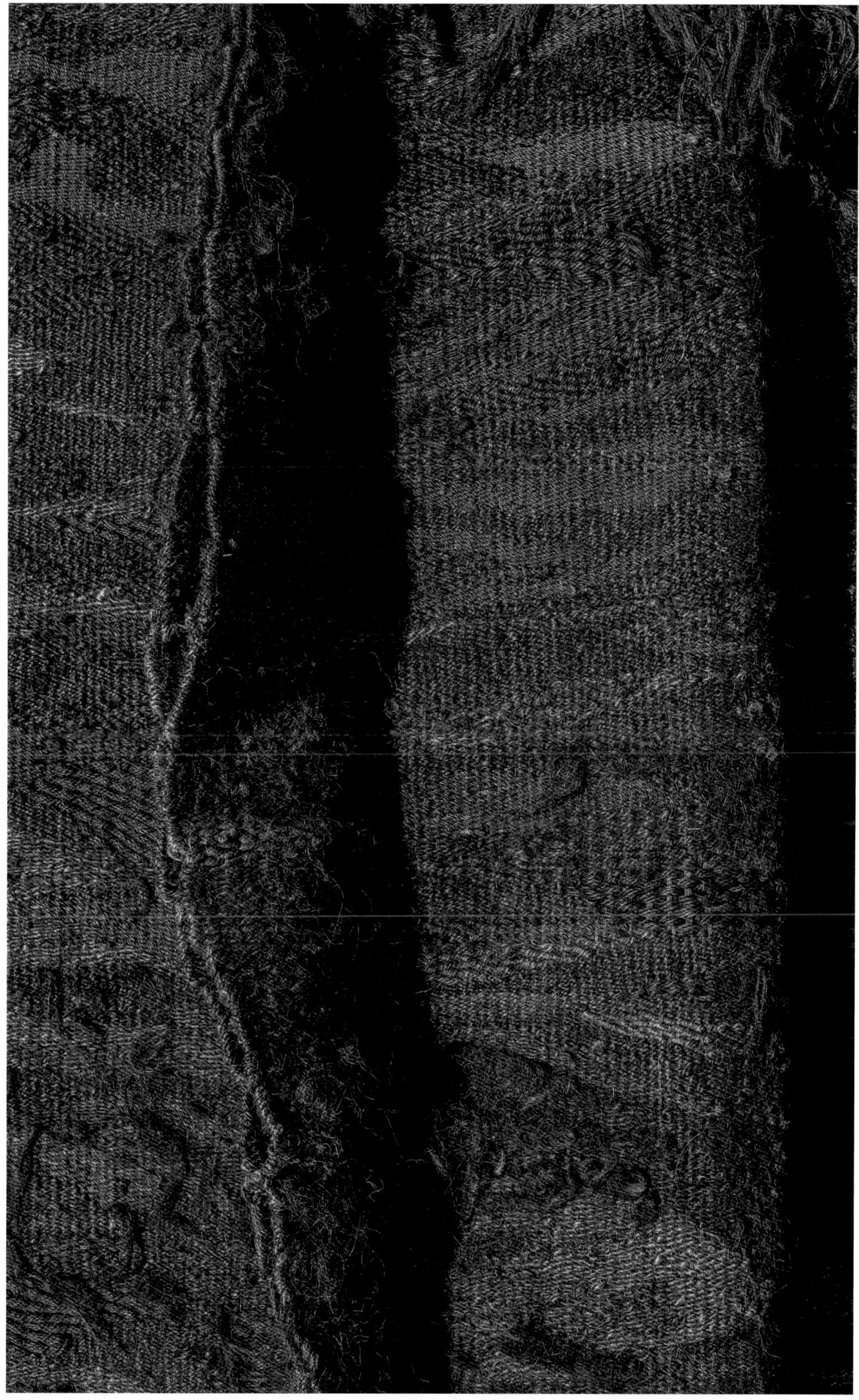

Abakan Open **1967–8**
Sisal
330 × 150 × 100

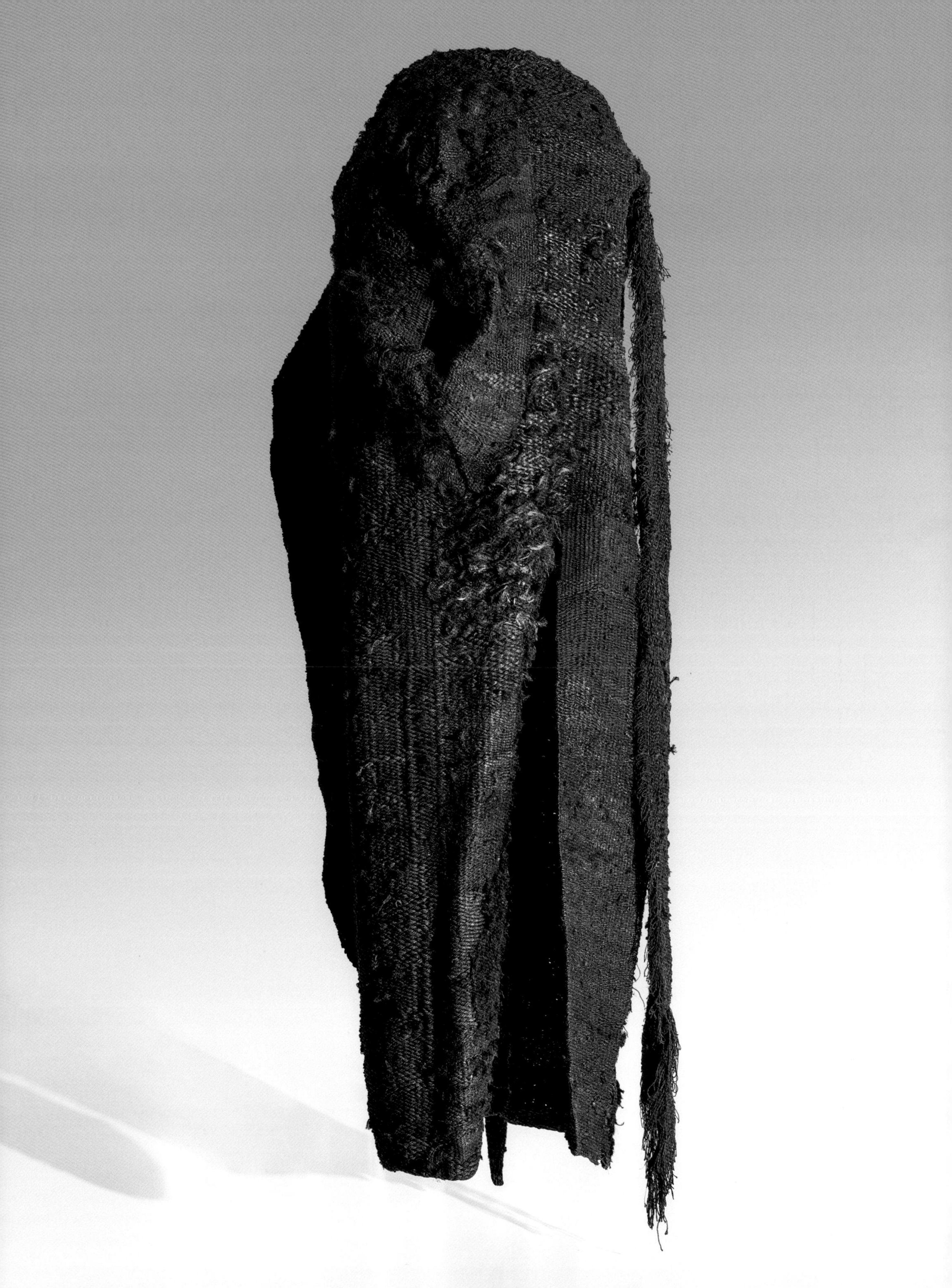

Abakan Festival **1971**
Sisal
370 × 100 × 100

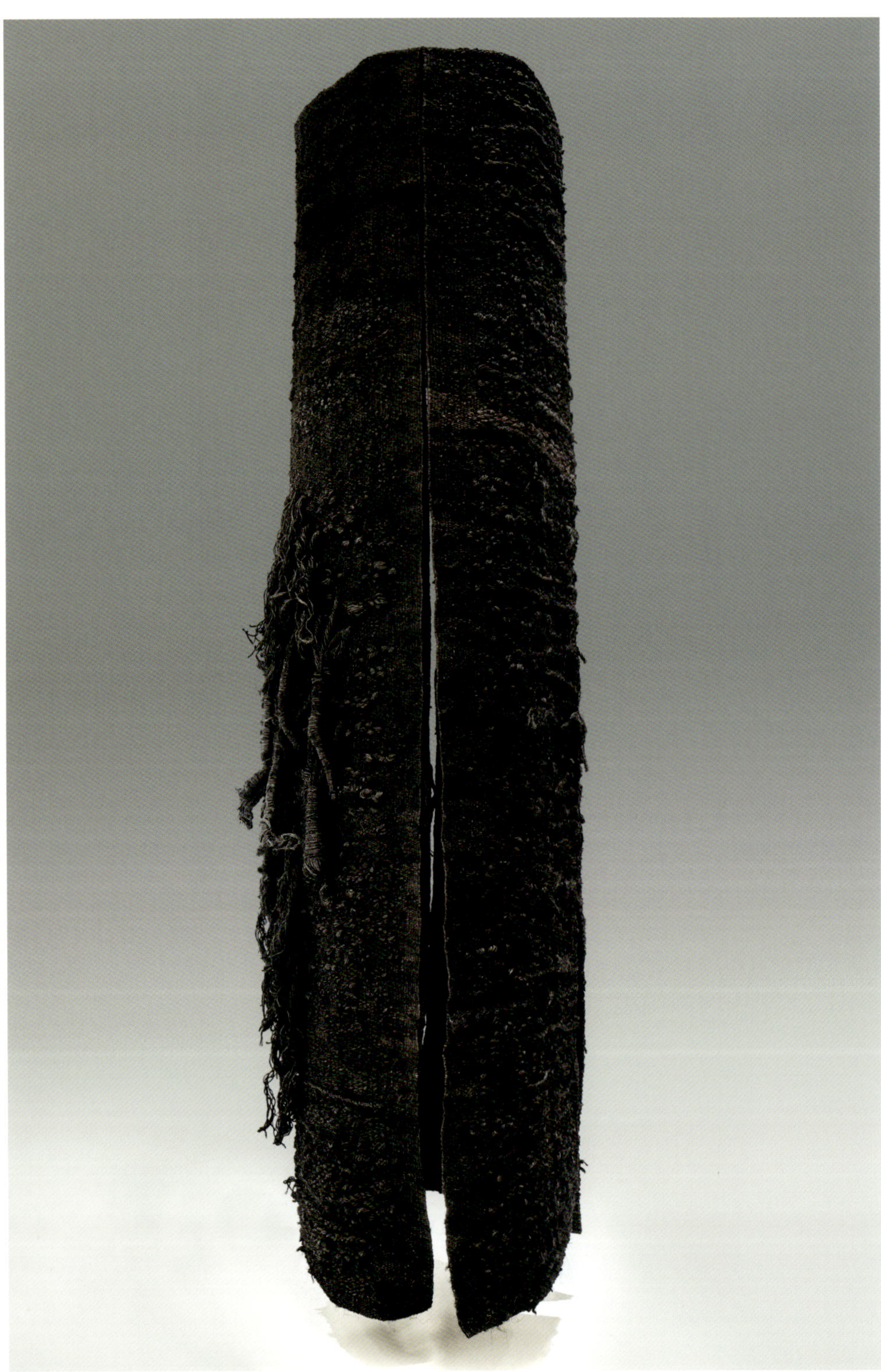

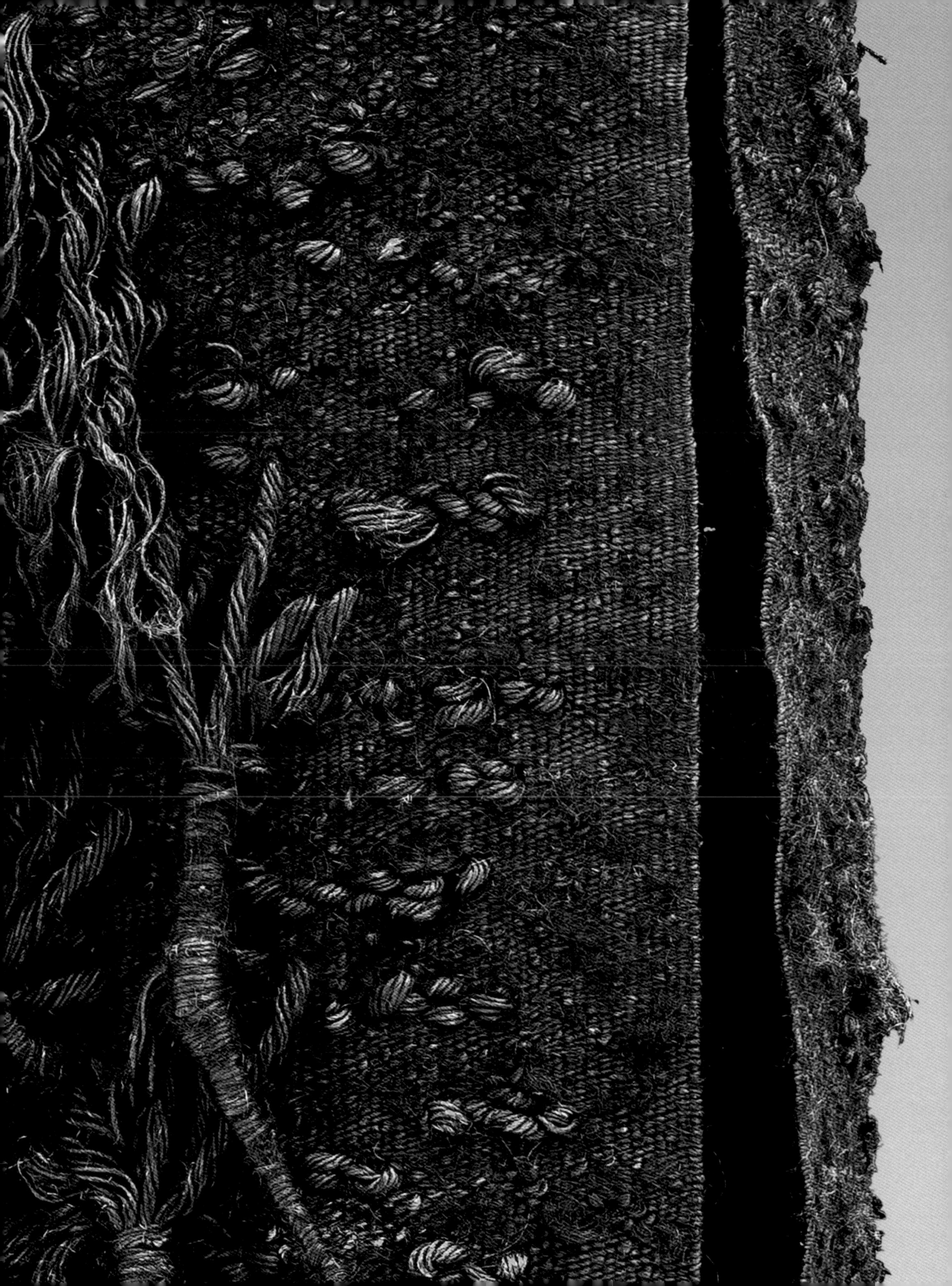

***Brown Coat* 1968**
Sisal
300 × 180 × 60

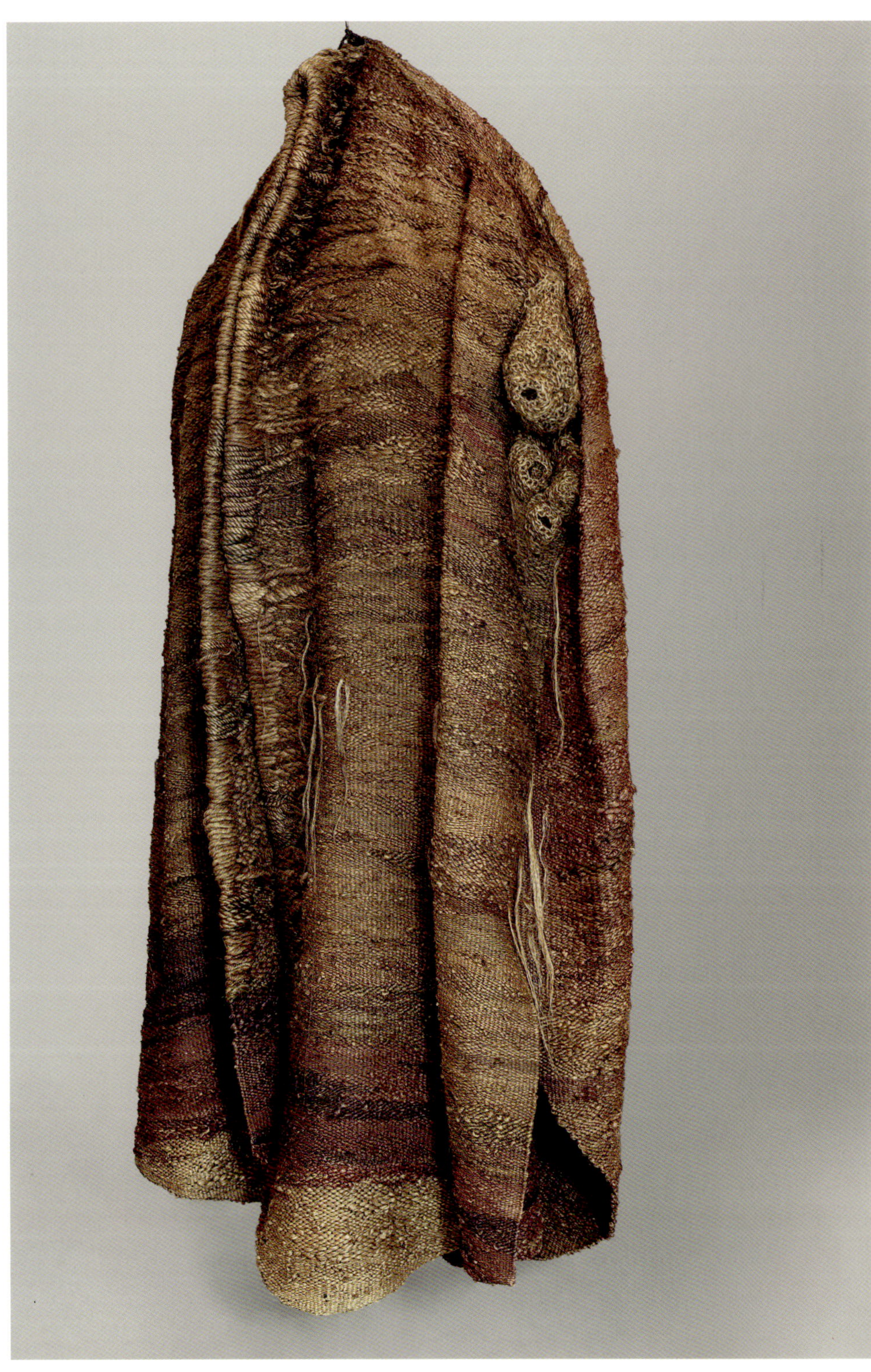

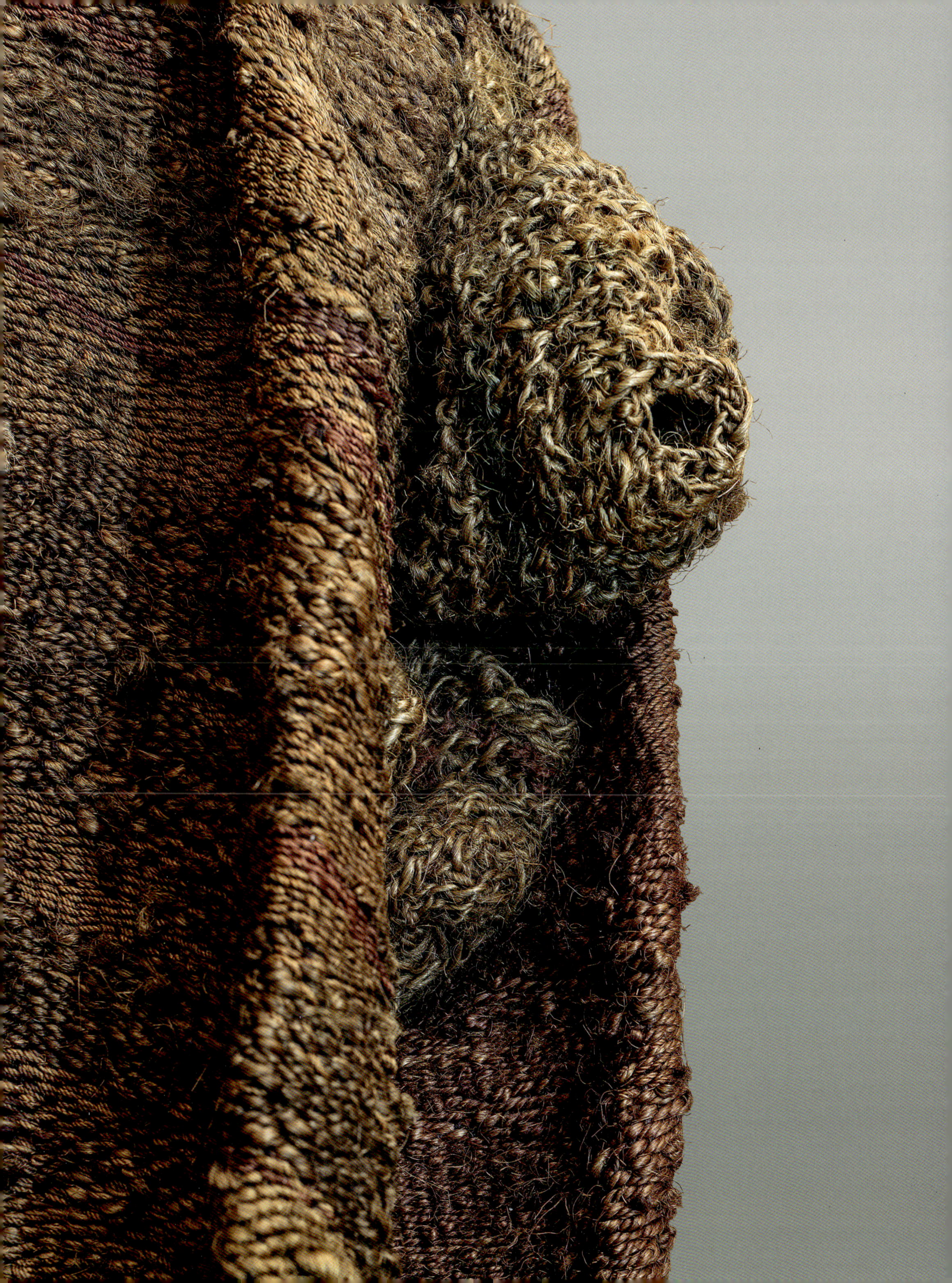

Black Garment **1968**
Sisal
350 × 250 × 250

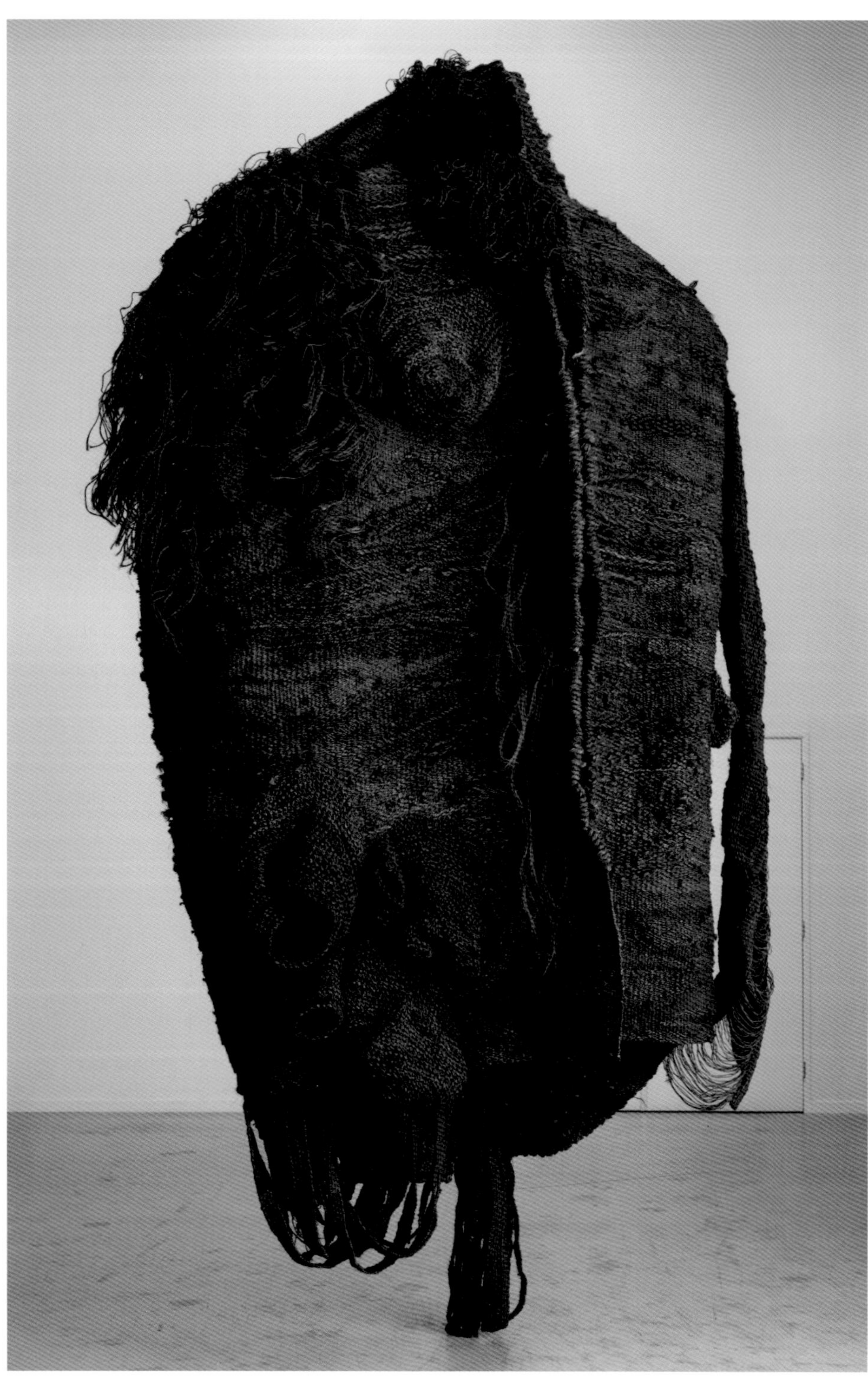

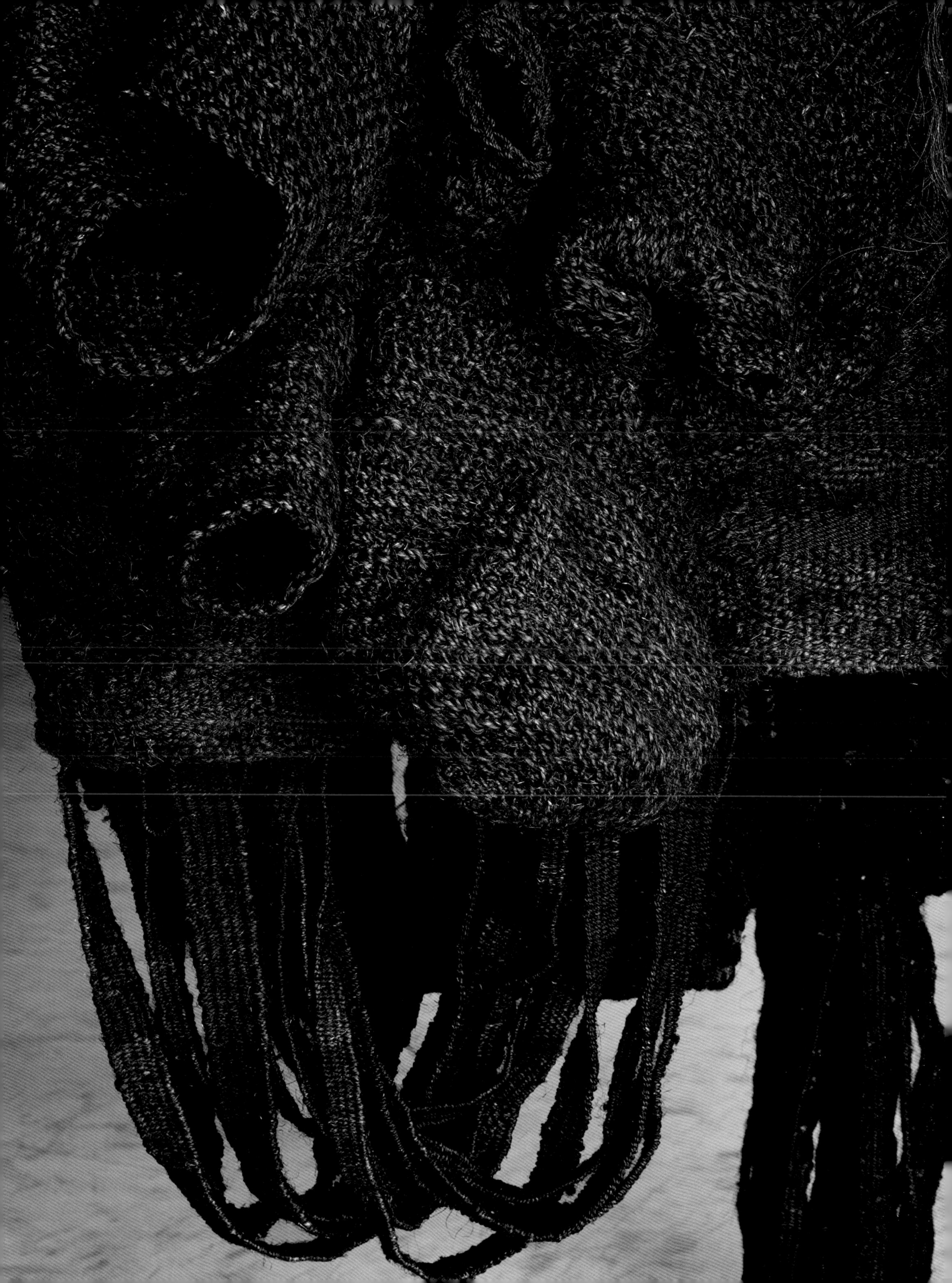

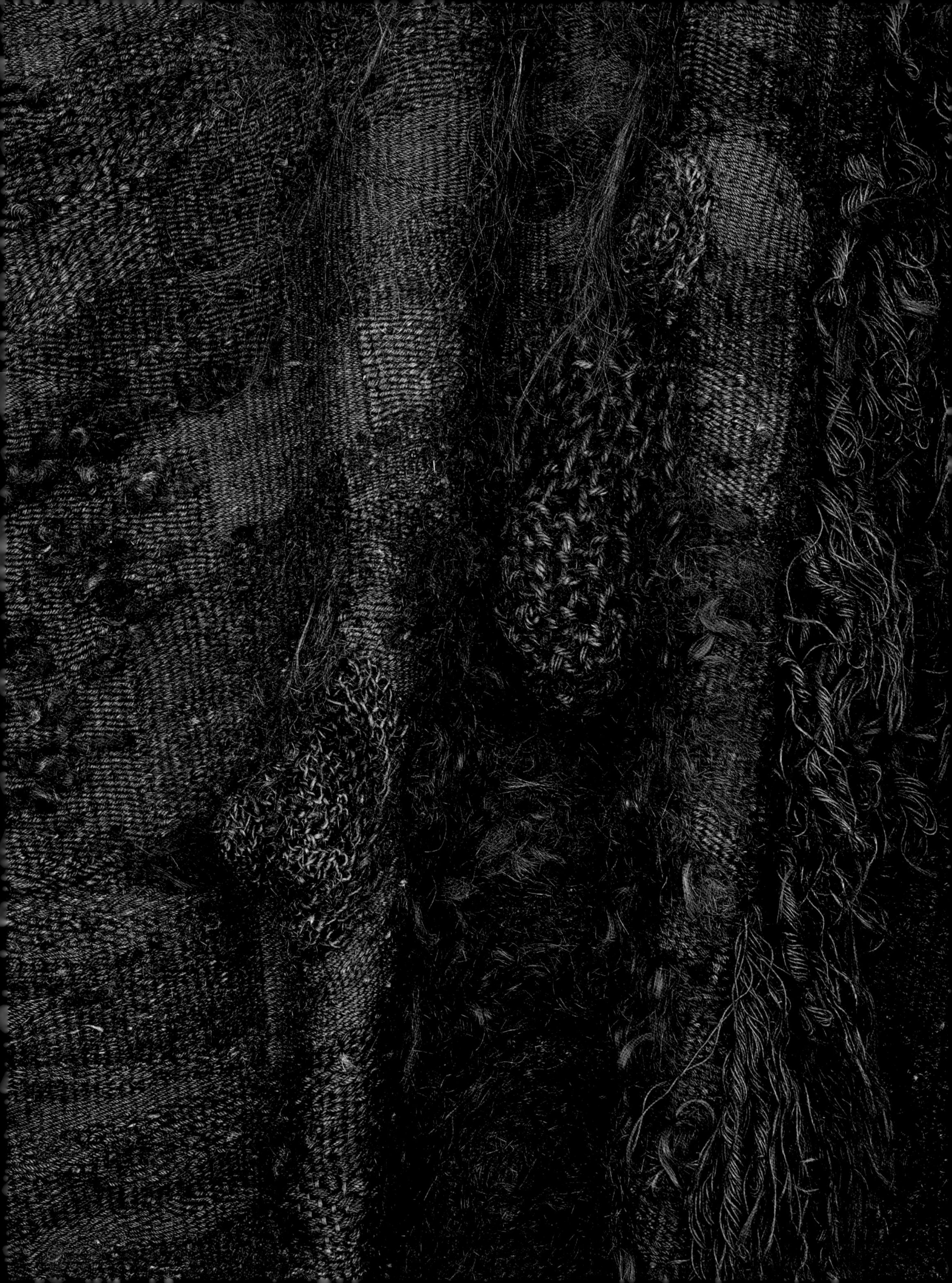

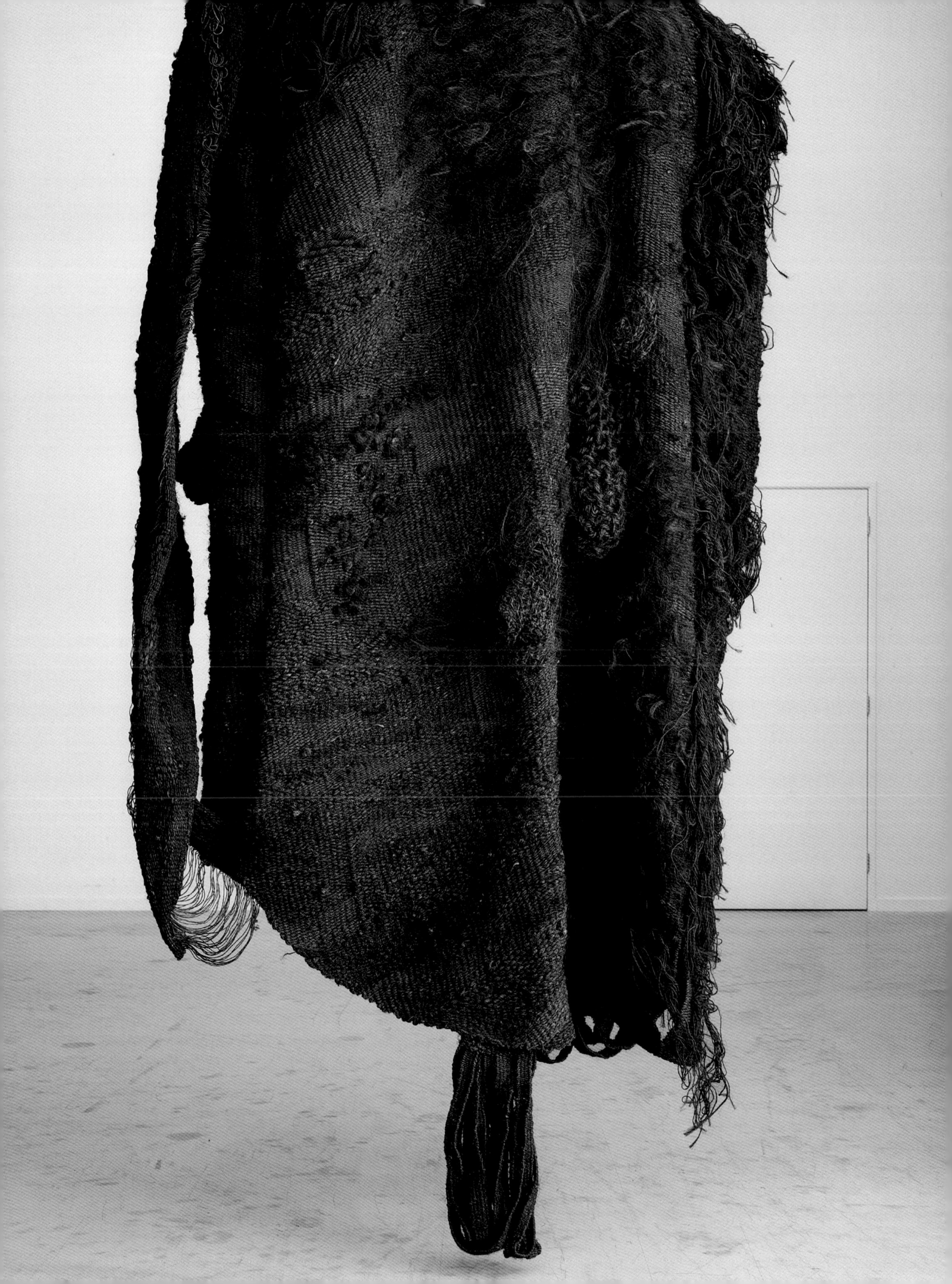

***Abakan – Situation Variable II* 1971**
Sisal and rope
400 × 250 × 100

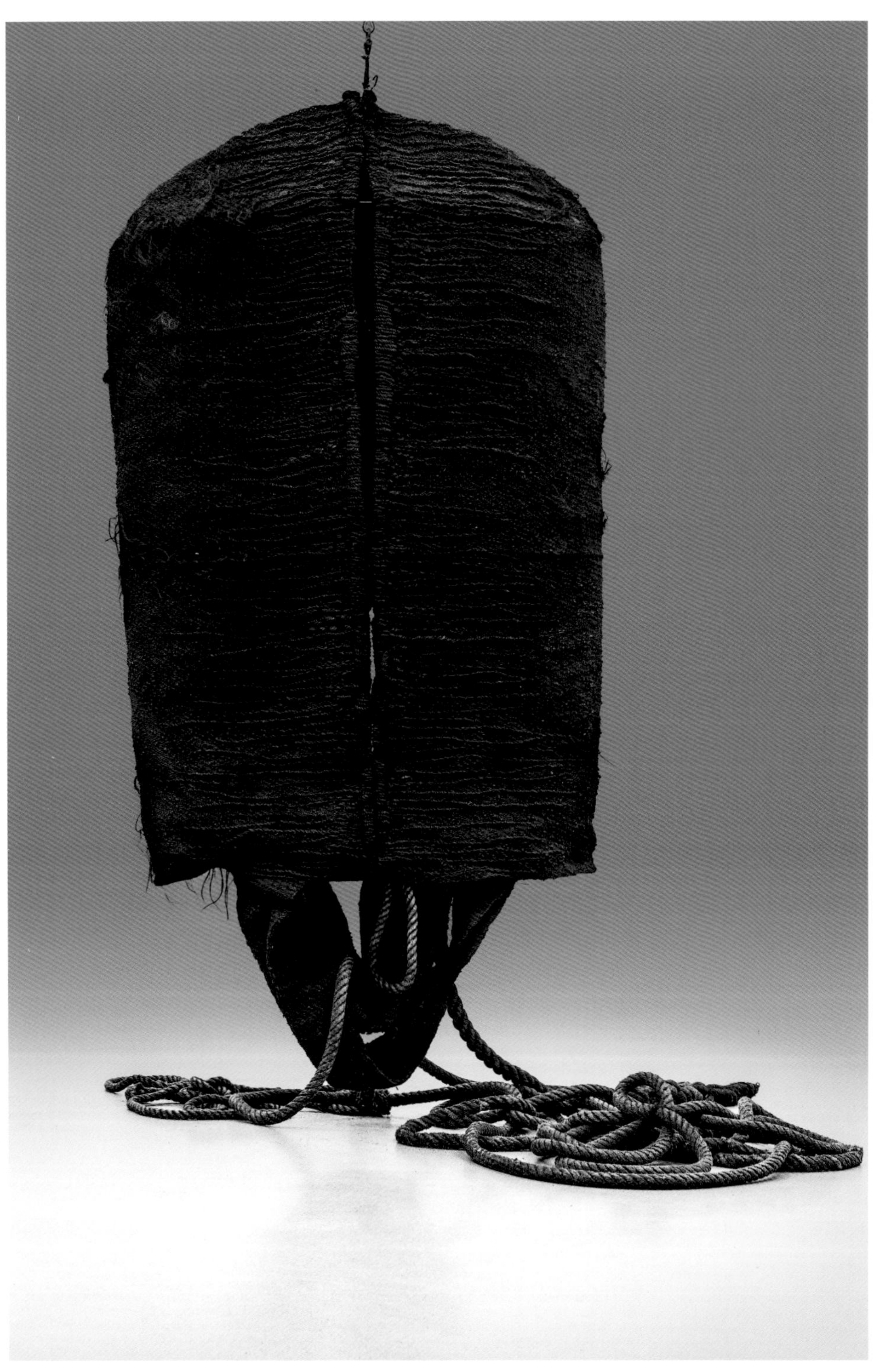

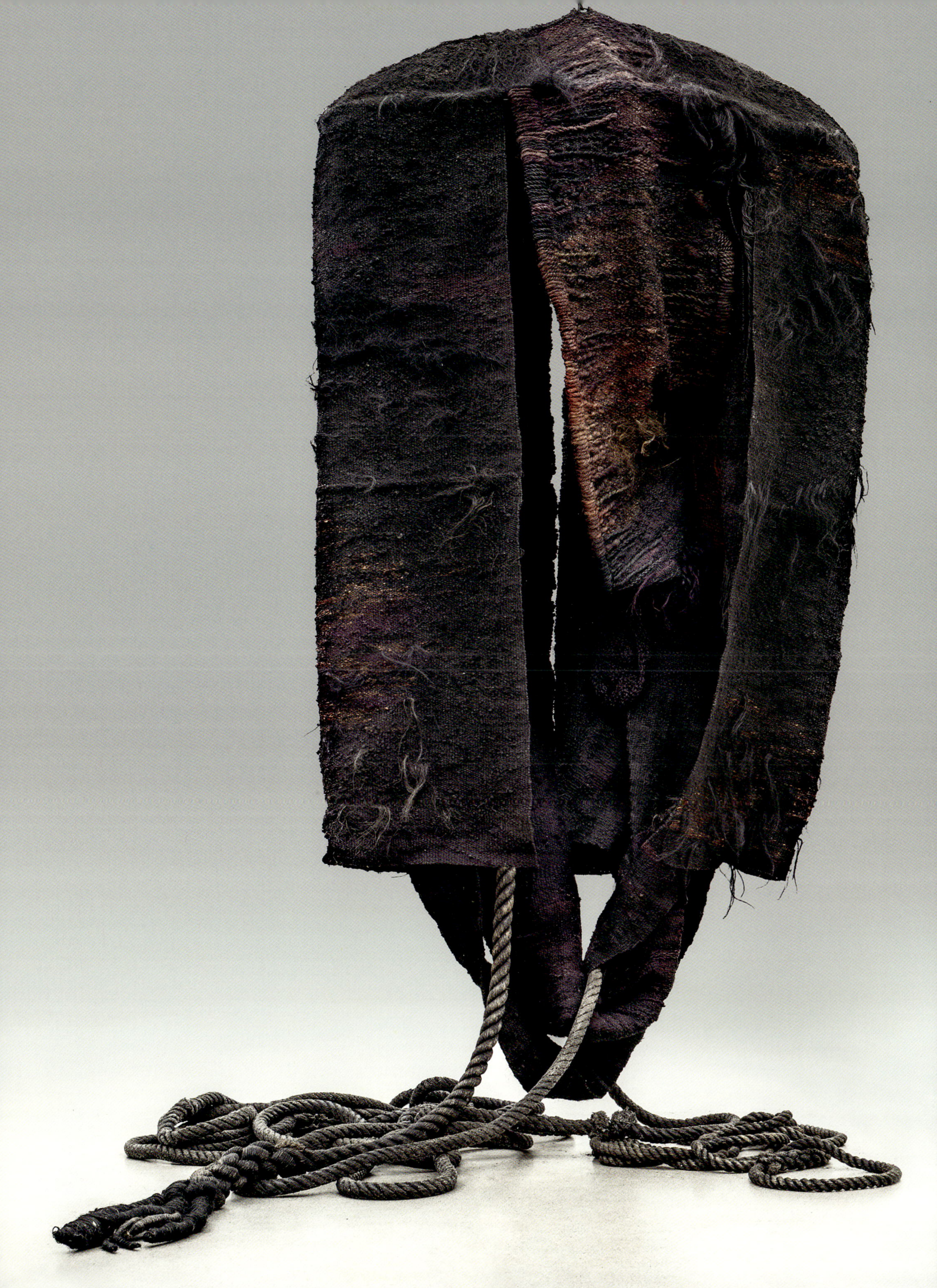

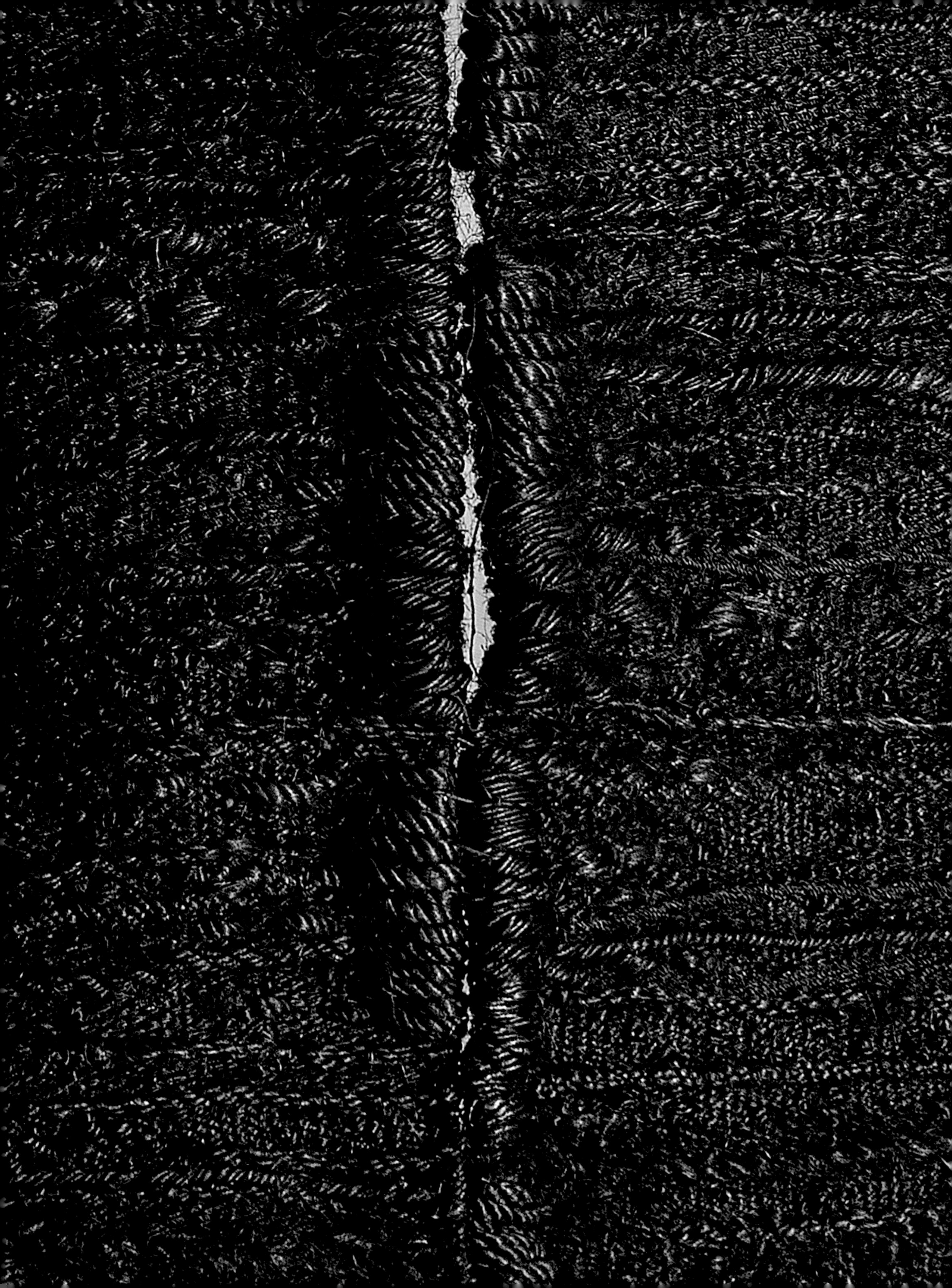

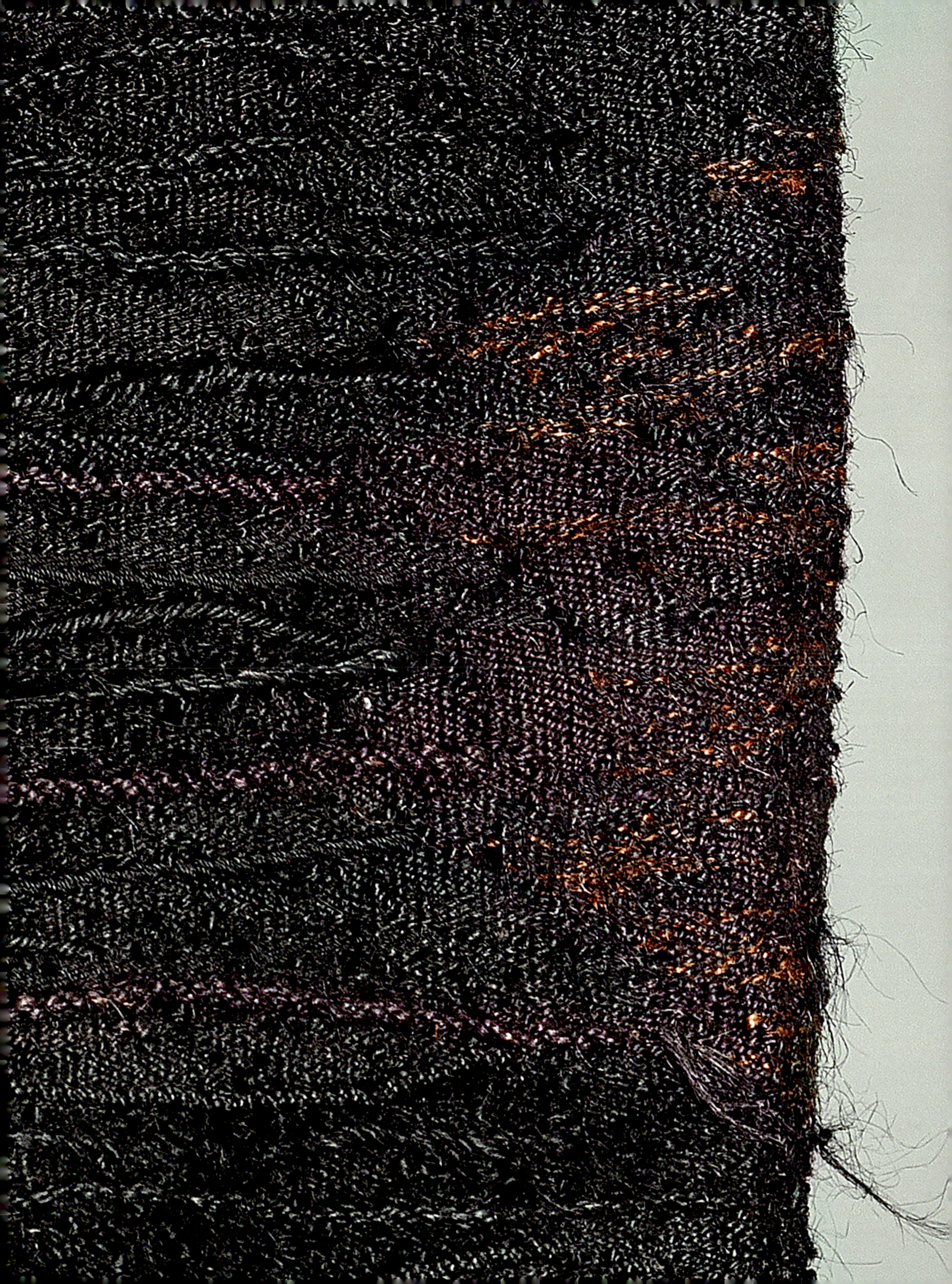

Black Garment VI **1976**
Sisal
330 × 220 × 100

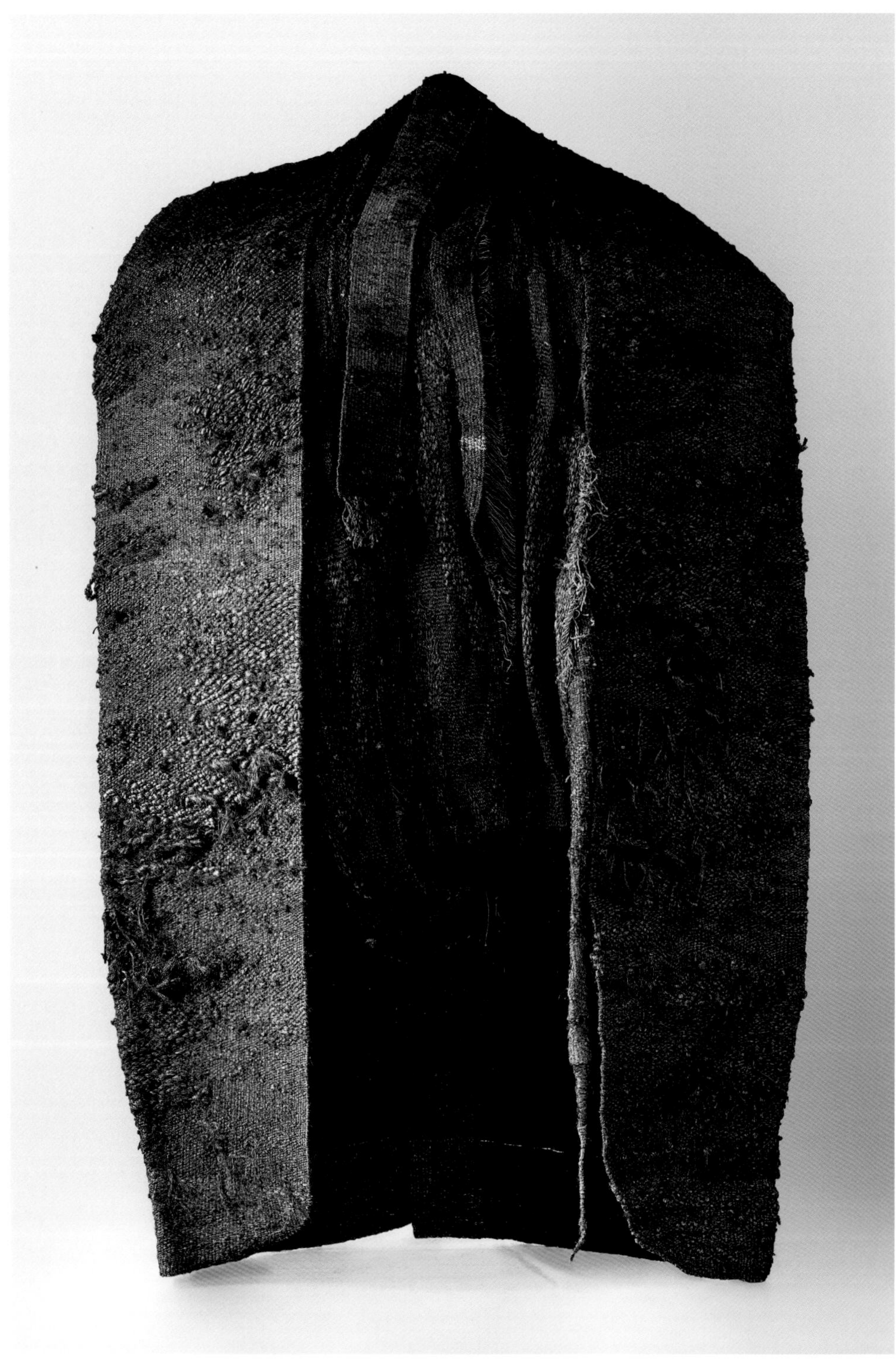

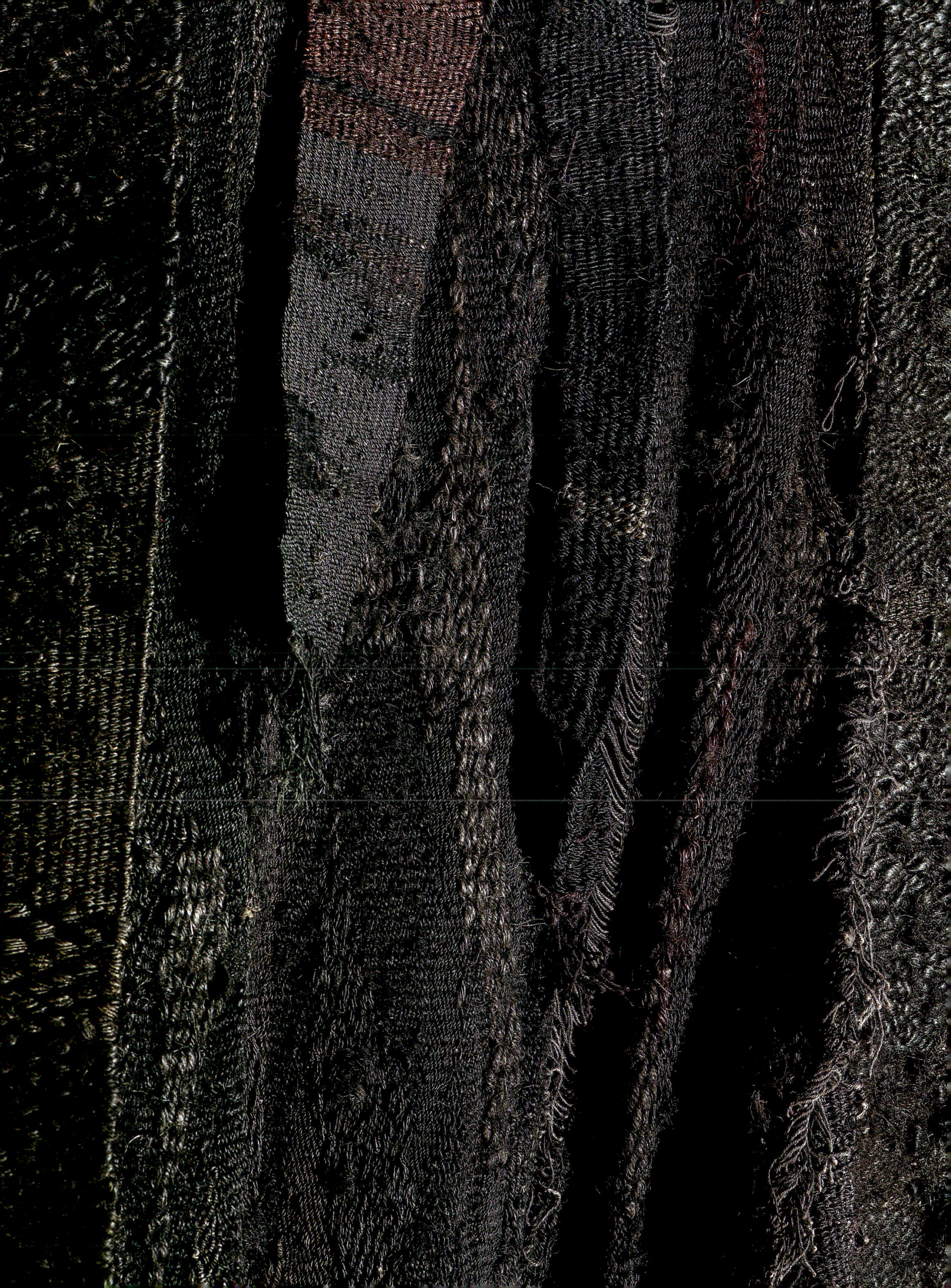

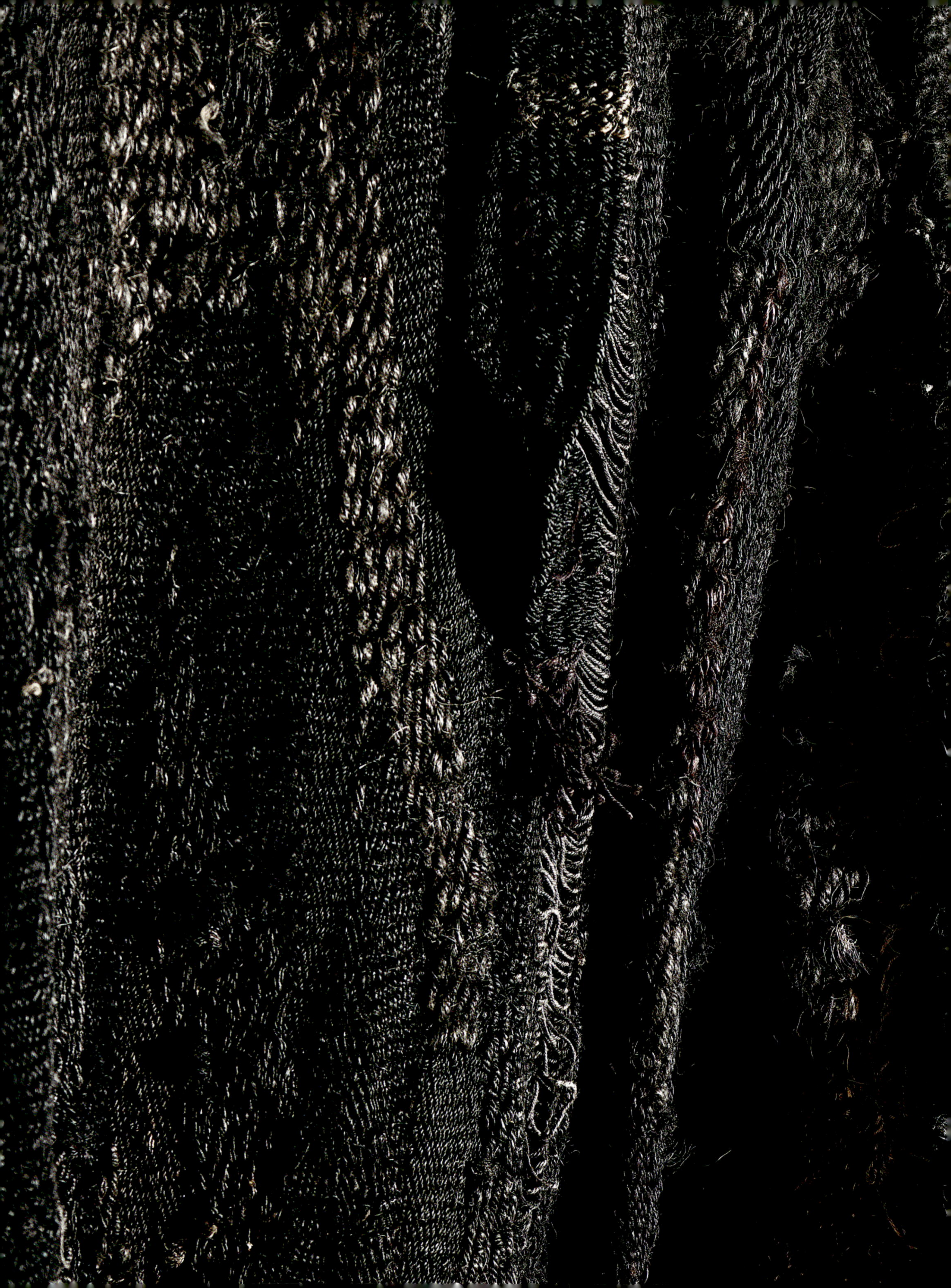

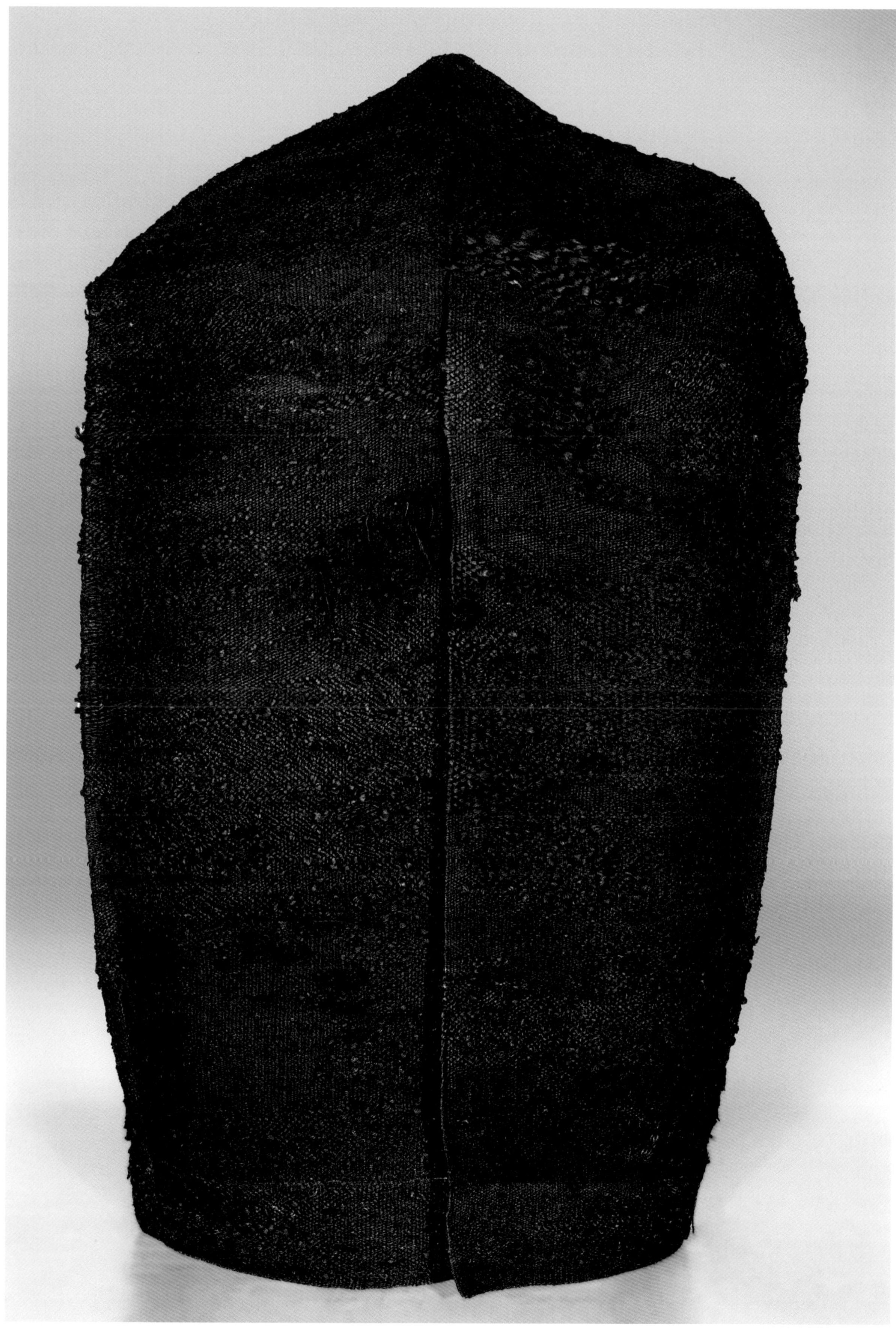

***Abakan Brown* 1969**
Sisal
300 × 300 × 150

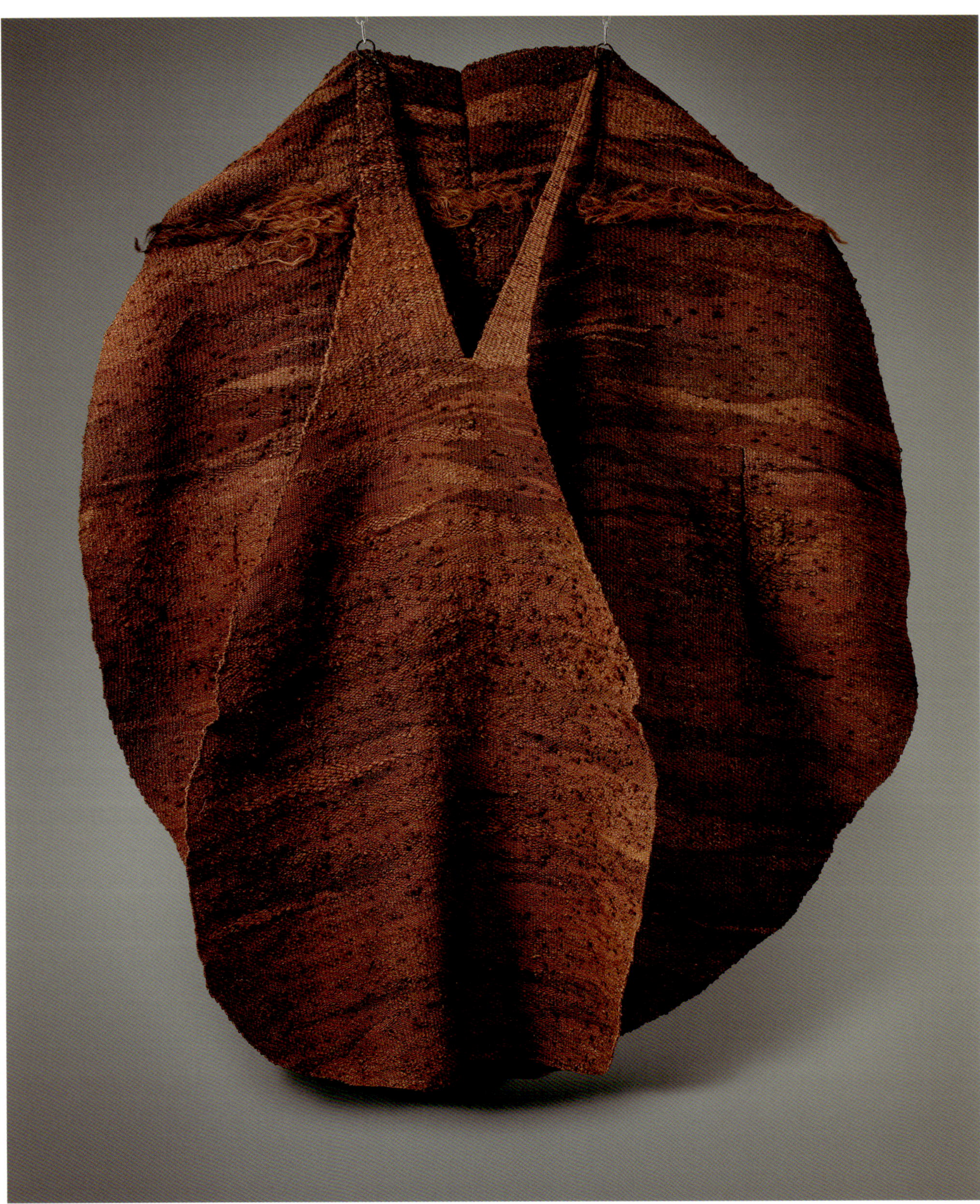

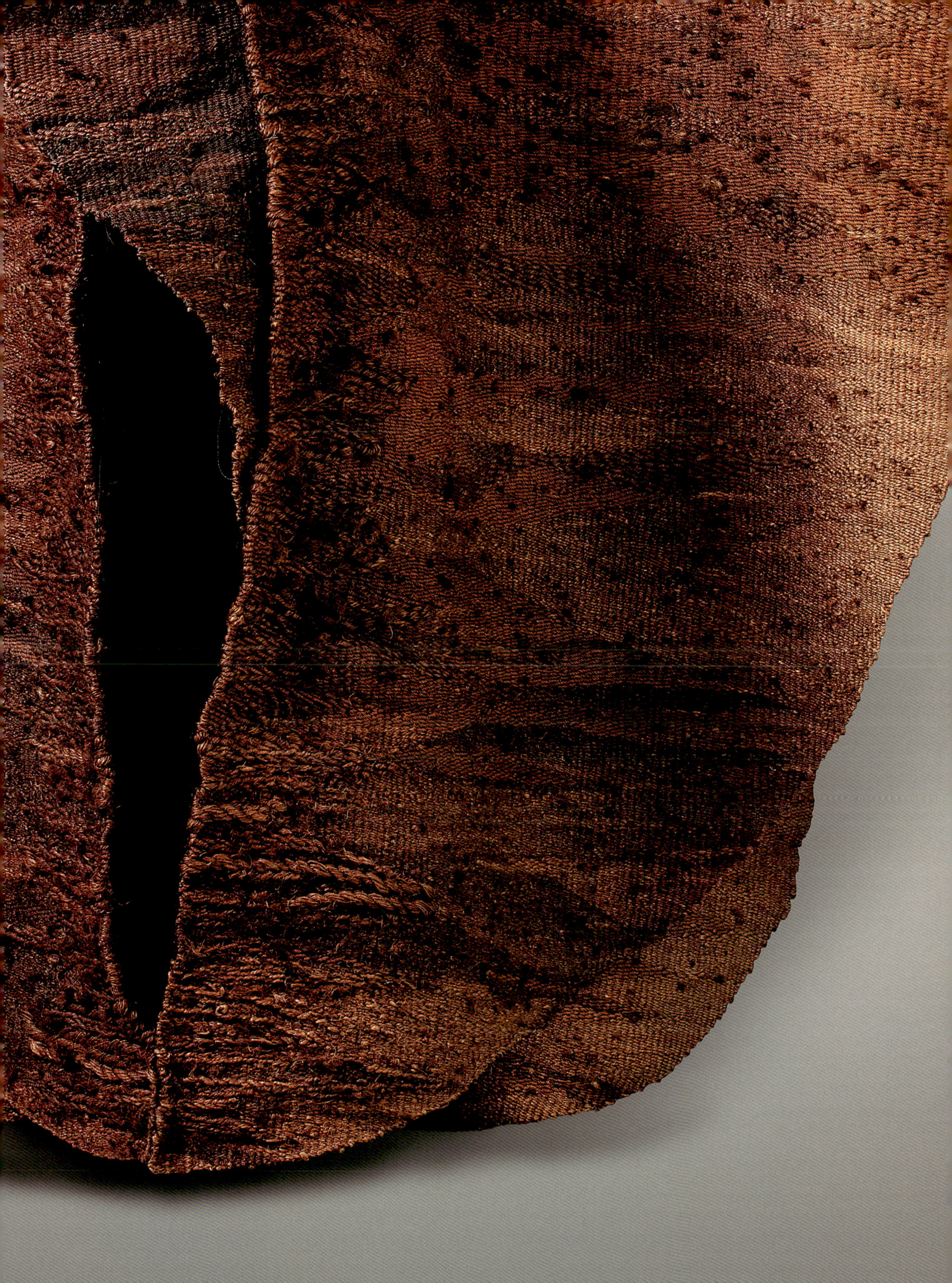

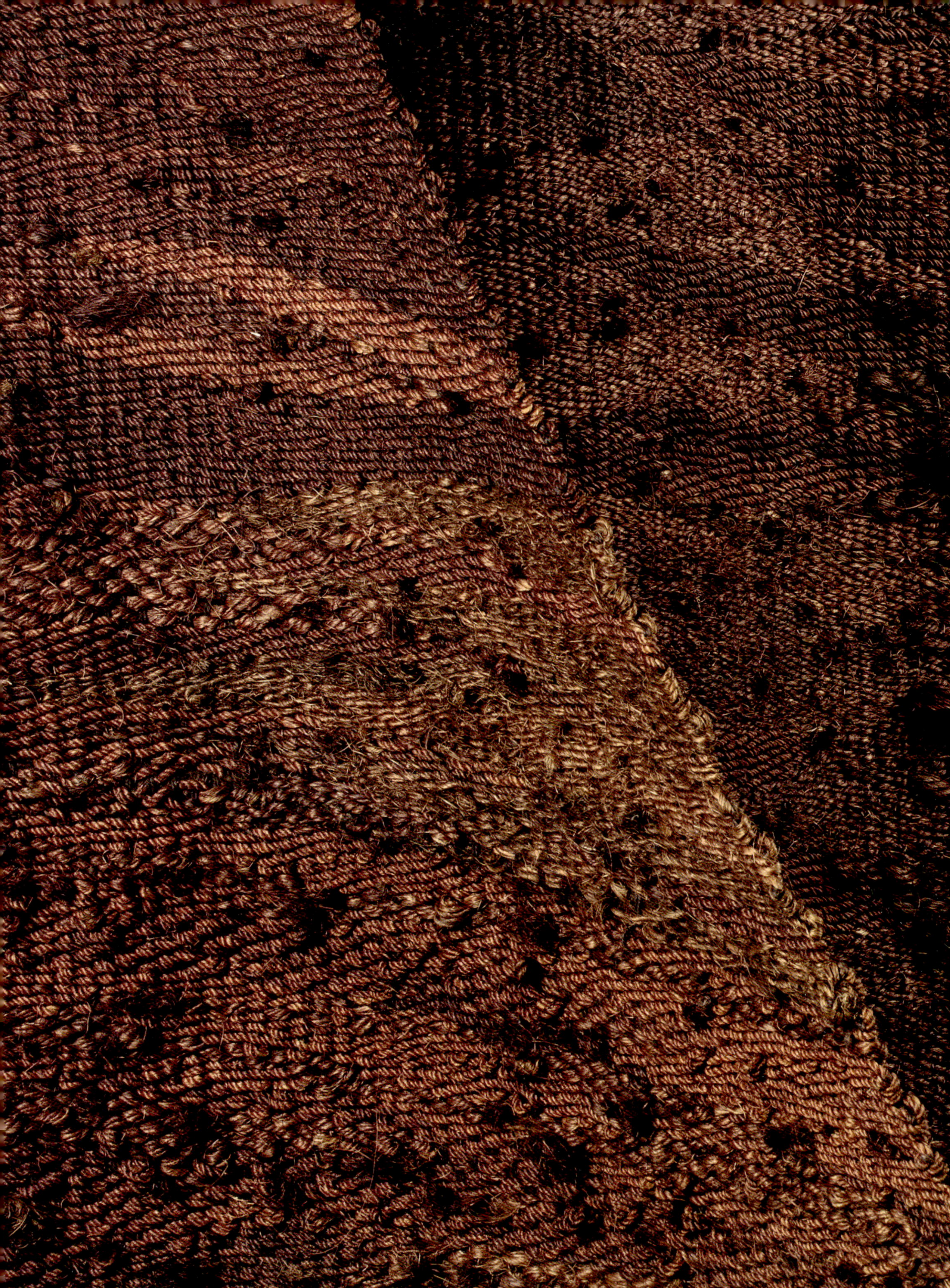

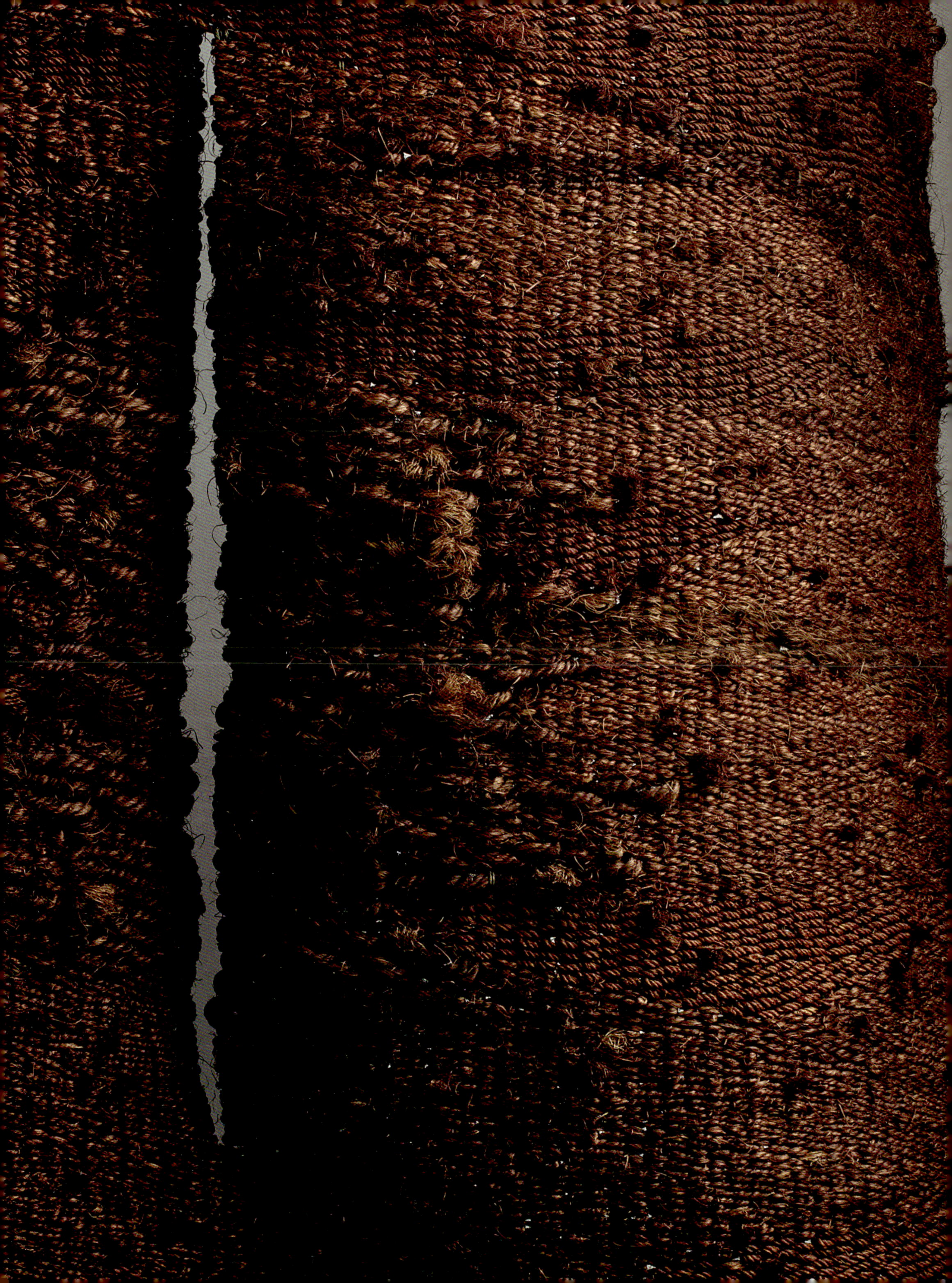

***Abakan Brown IV* 1969–84**
Sisal
290 × 300 × 30

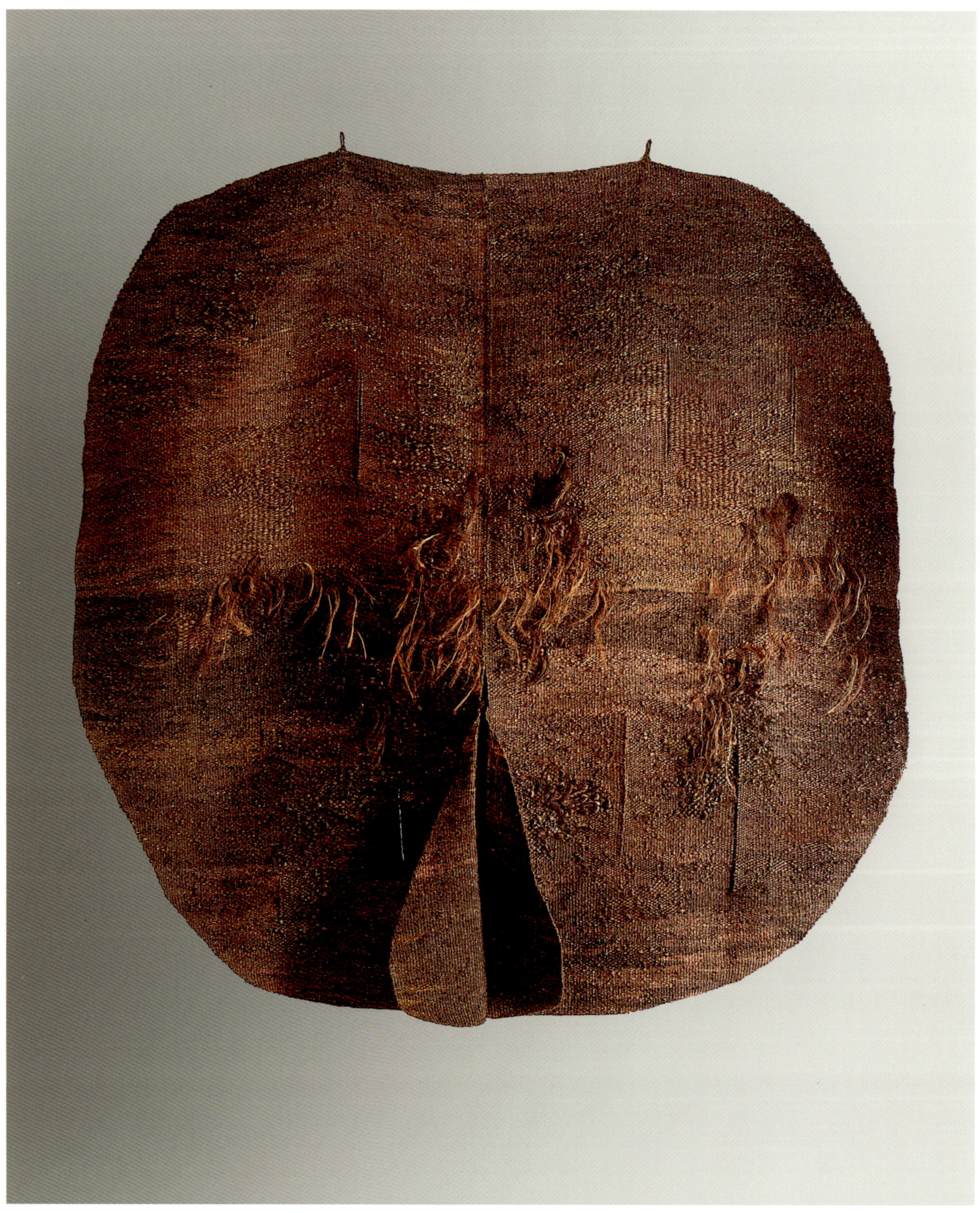

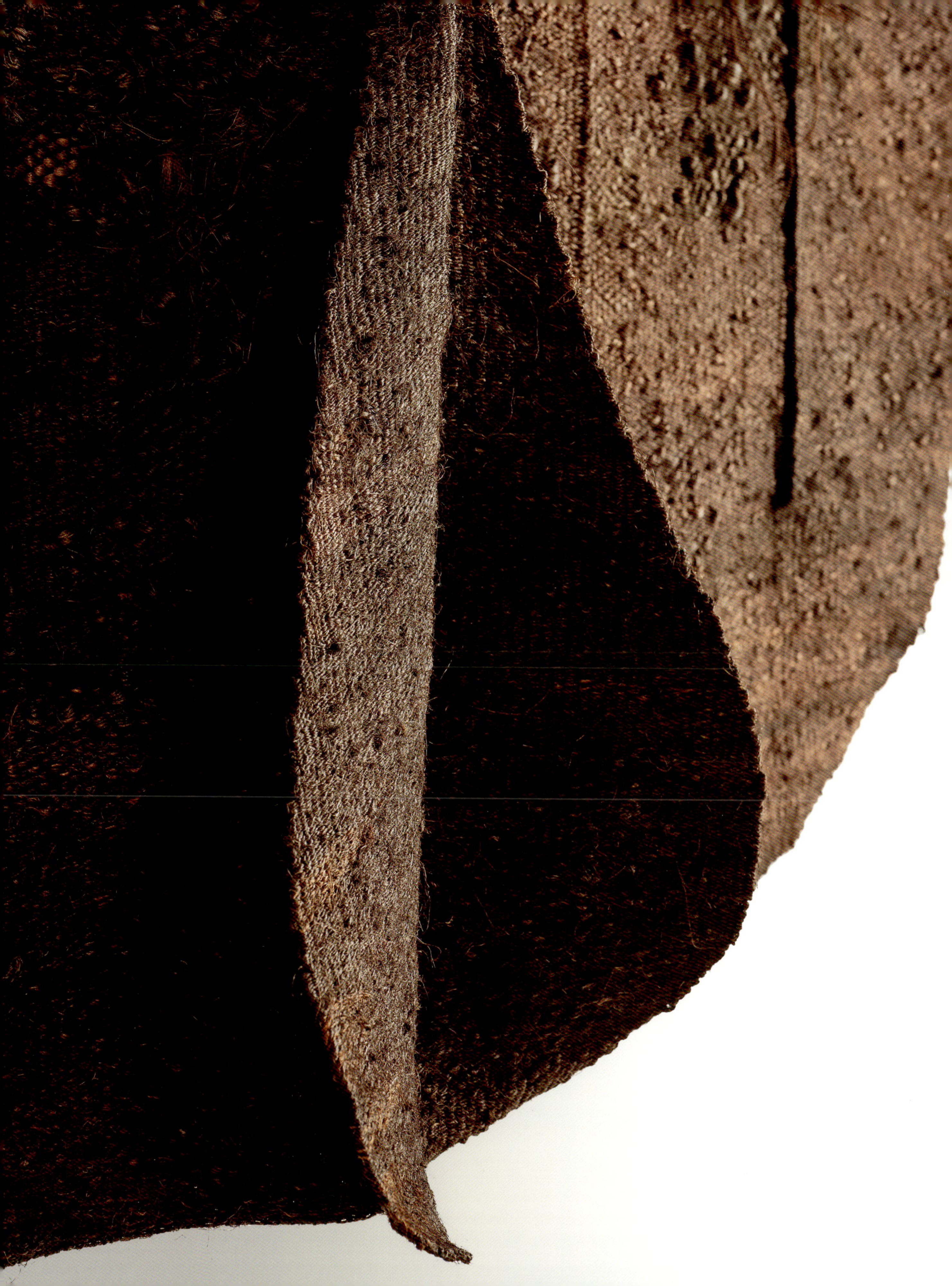

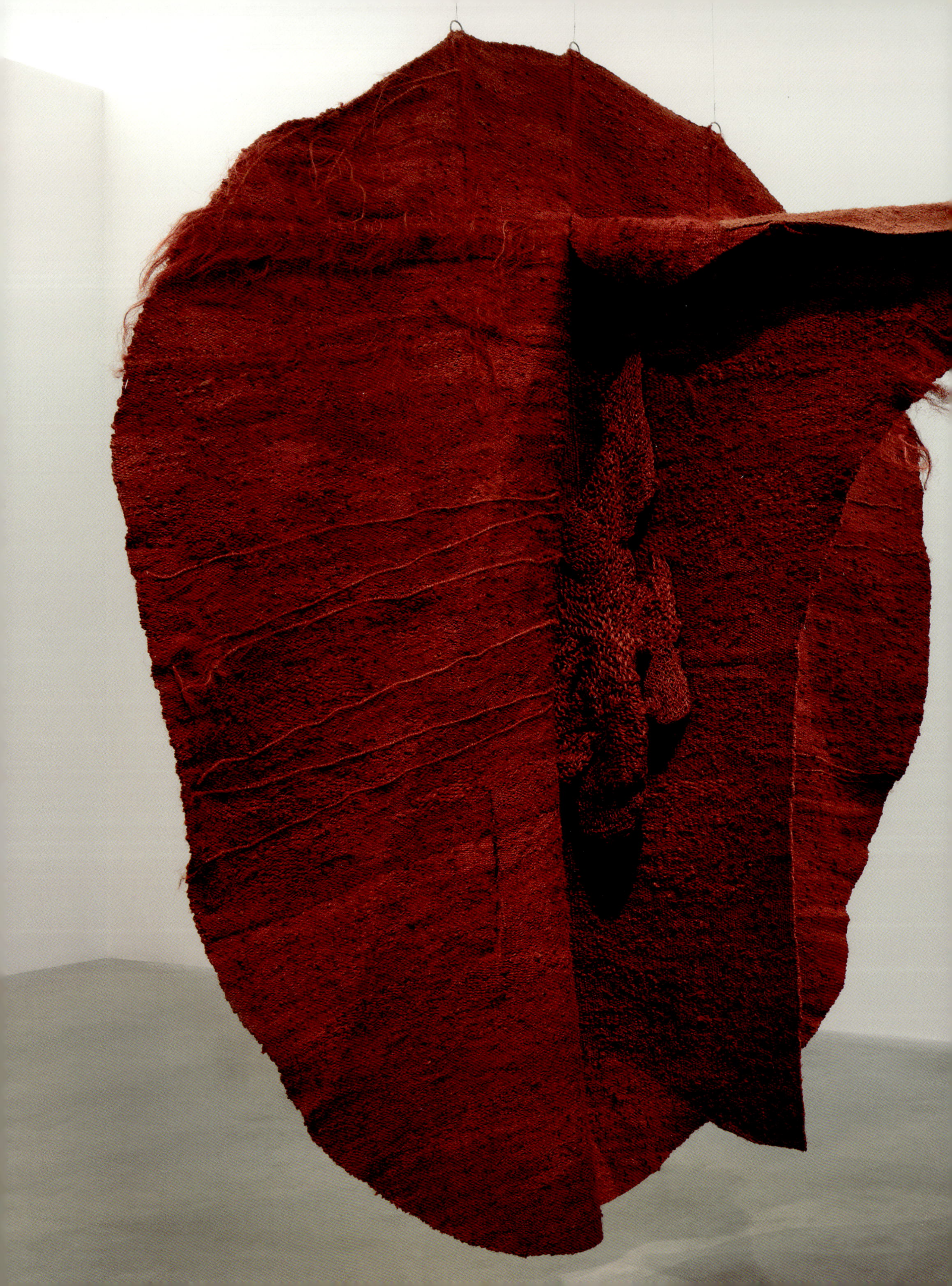

Abakan Red **1969**
Sisal
405 × 382 × 400

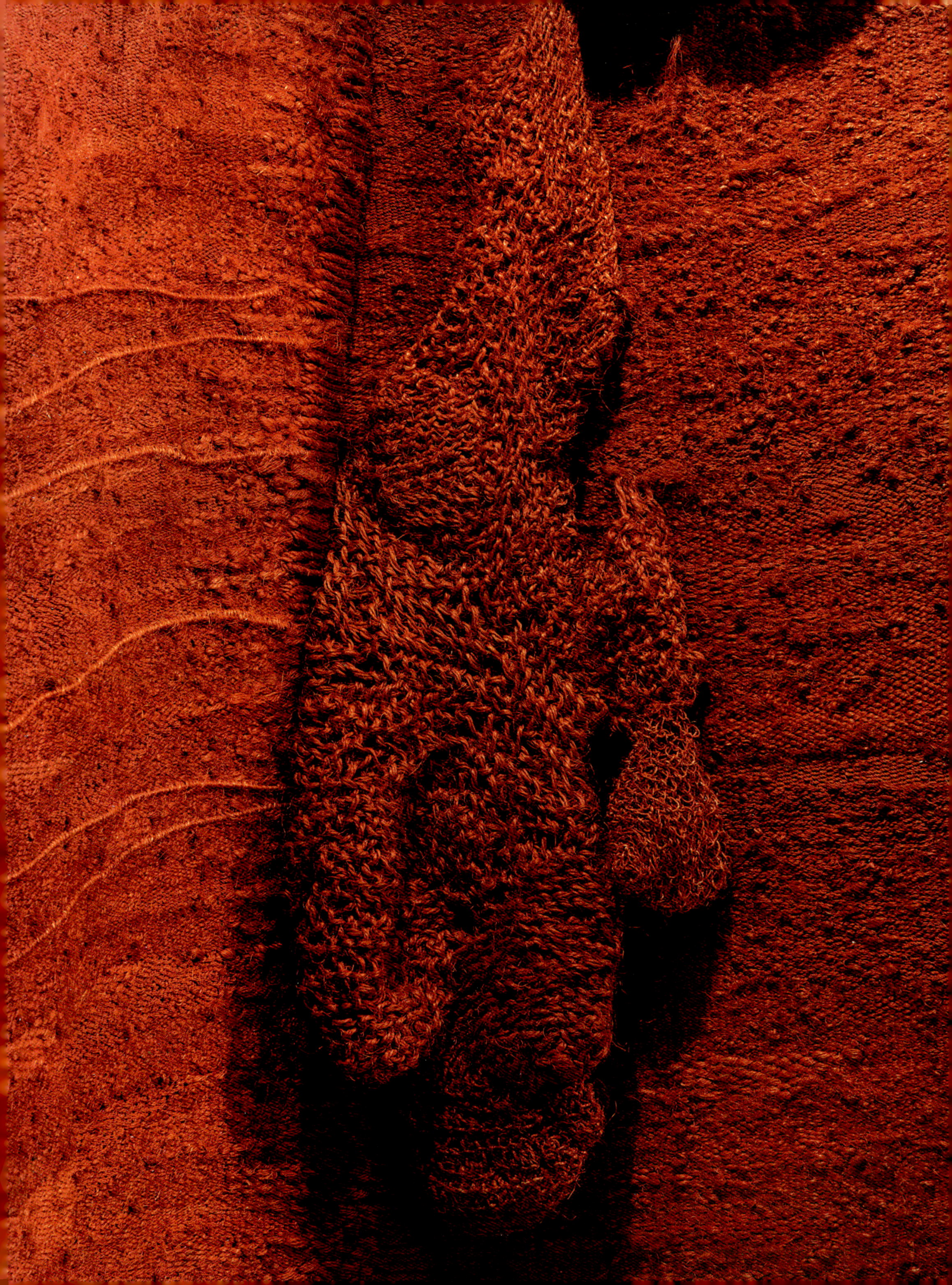

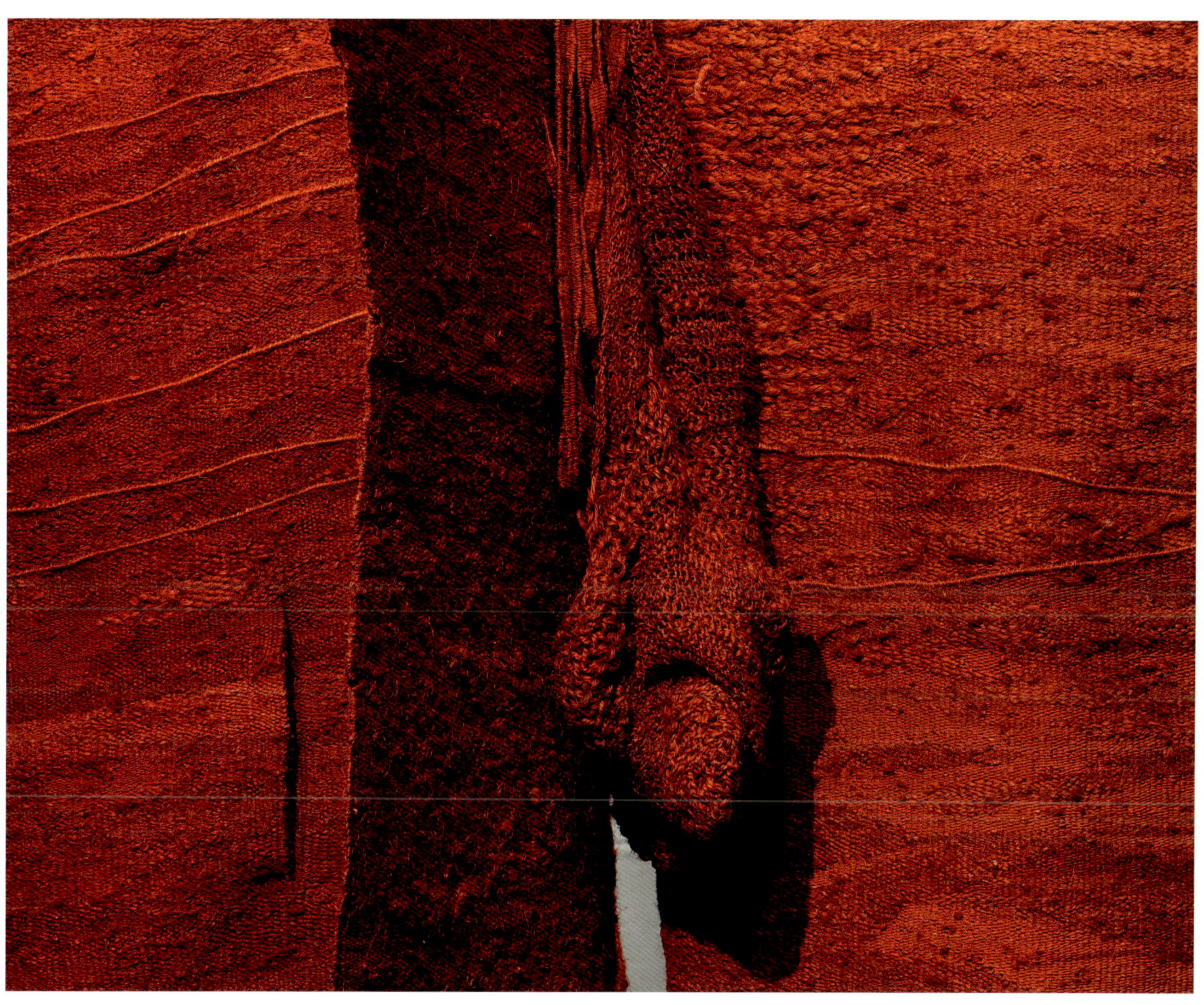

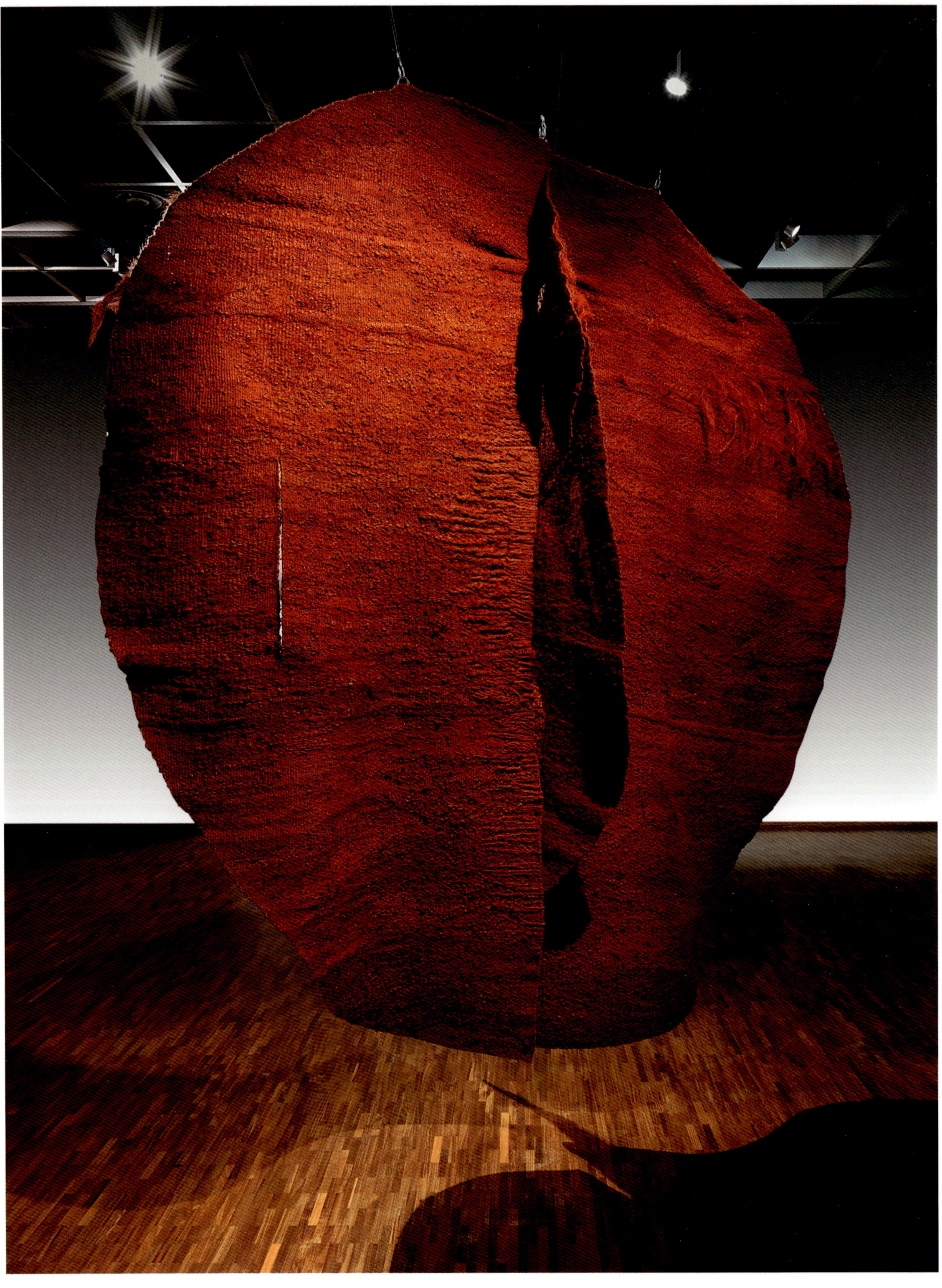

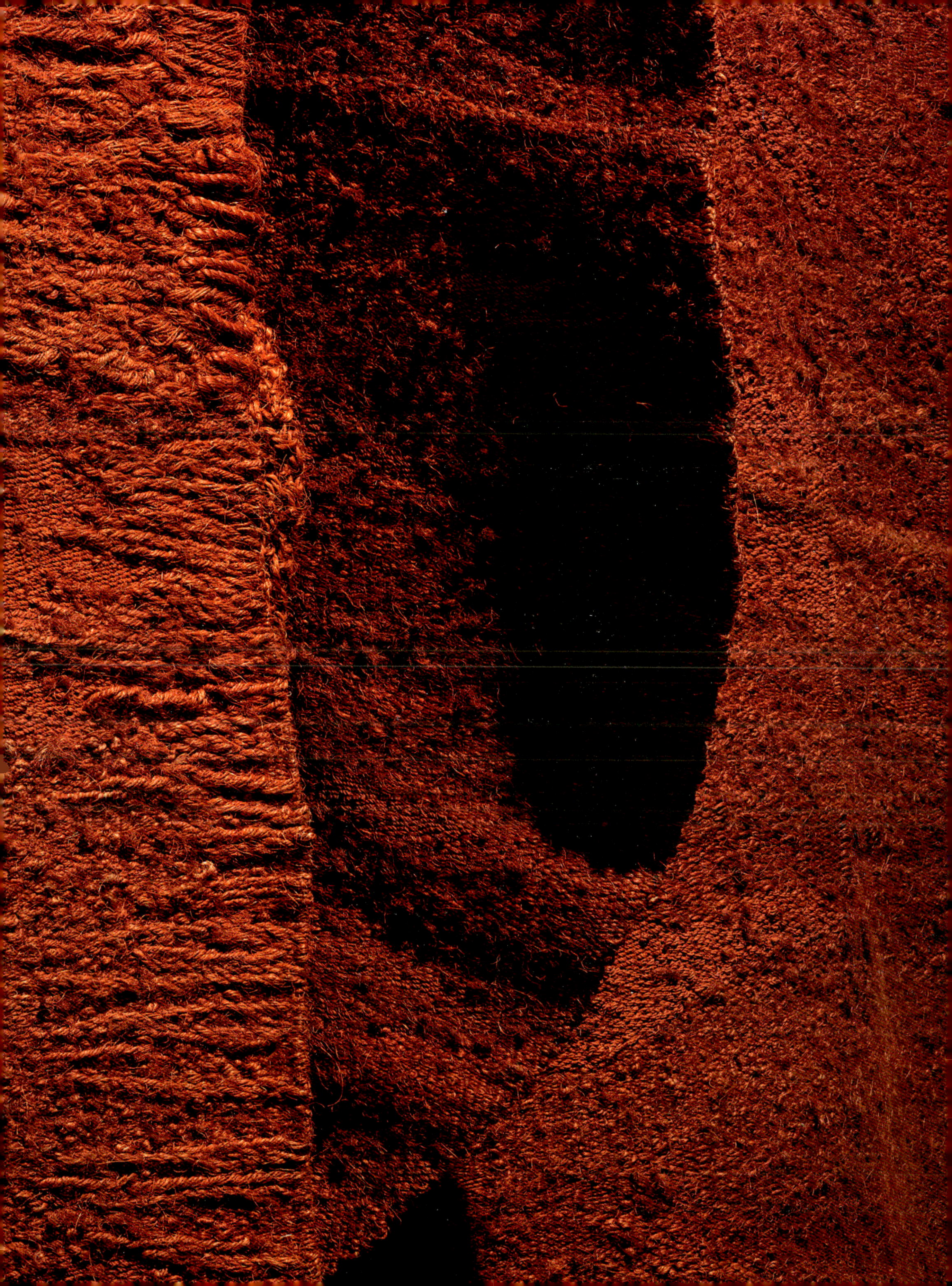

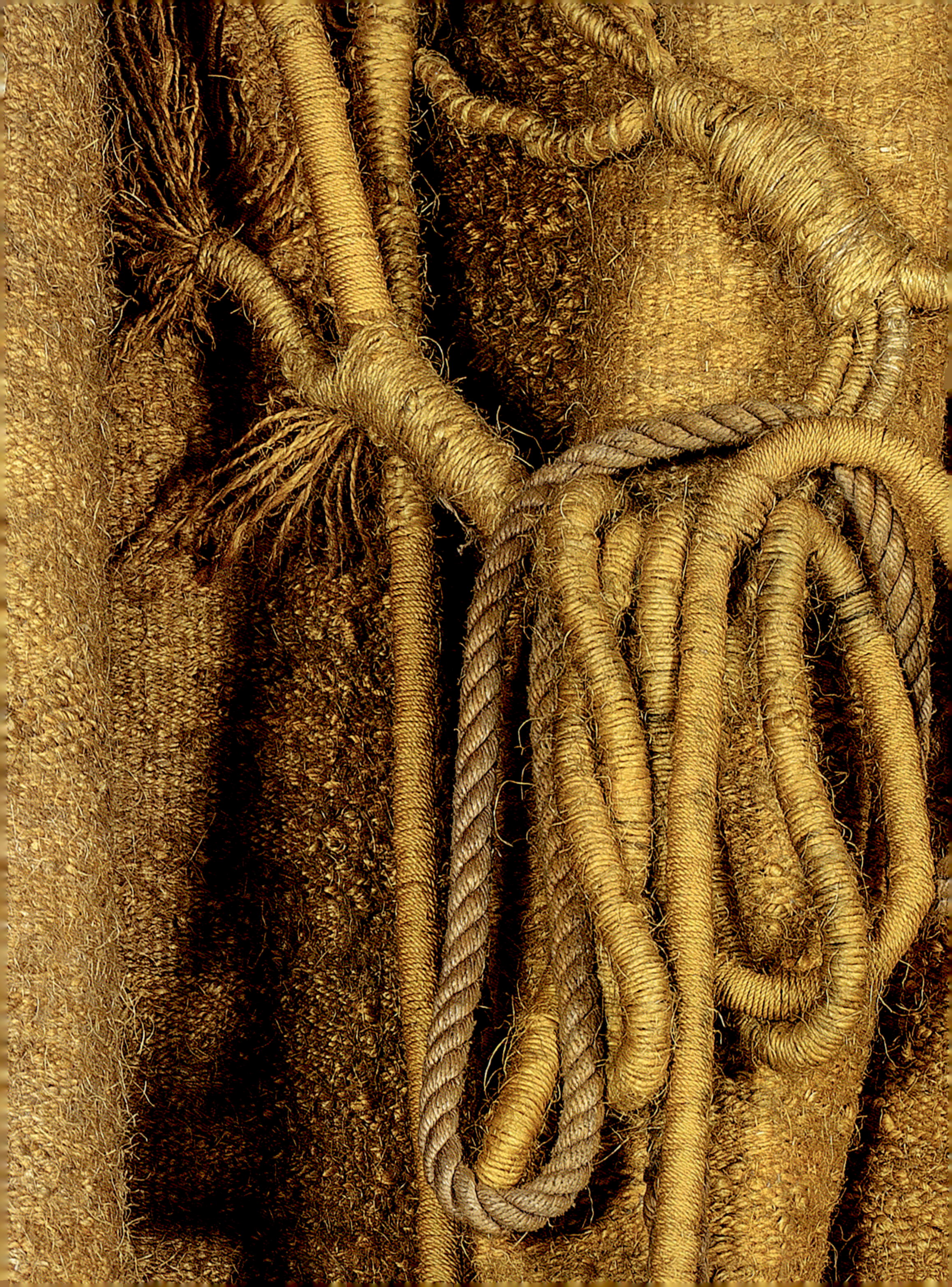

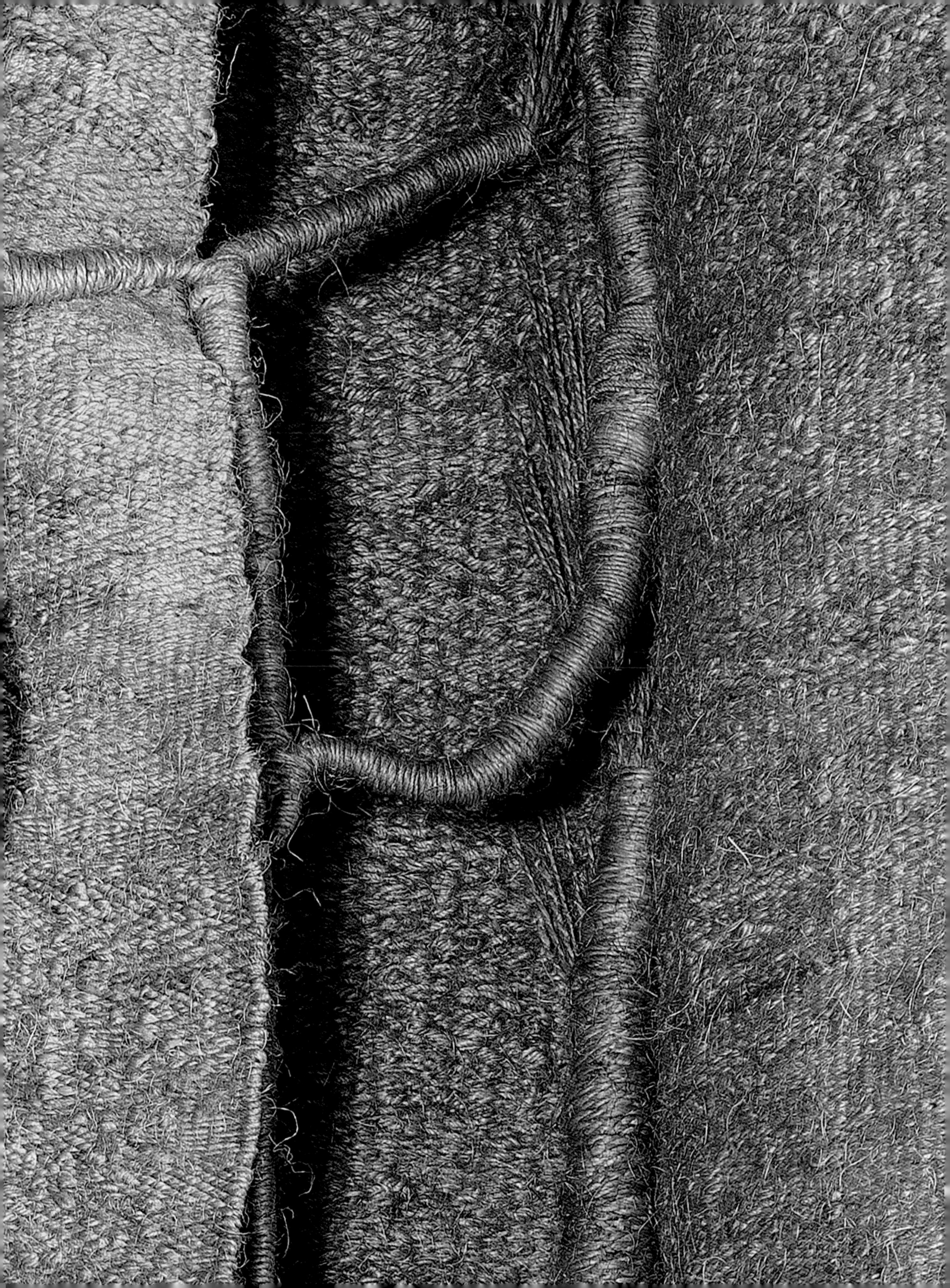

***Abakan Yellow* 1970**
Sisal and rope
380 × 380 × 70

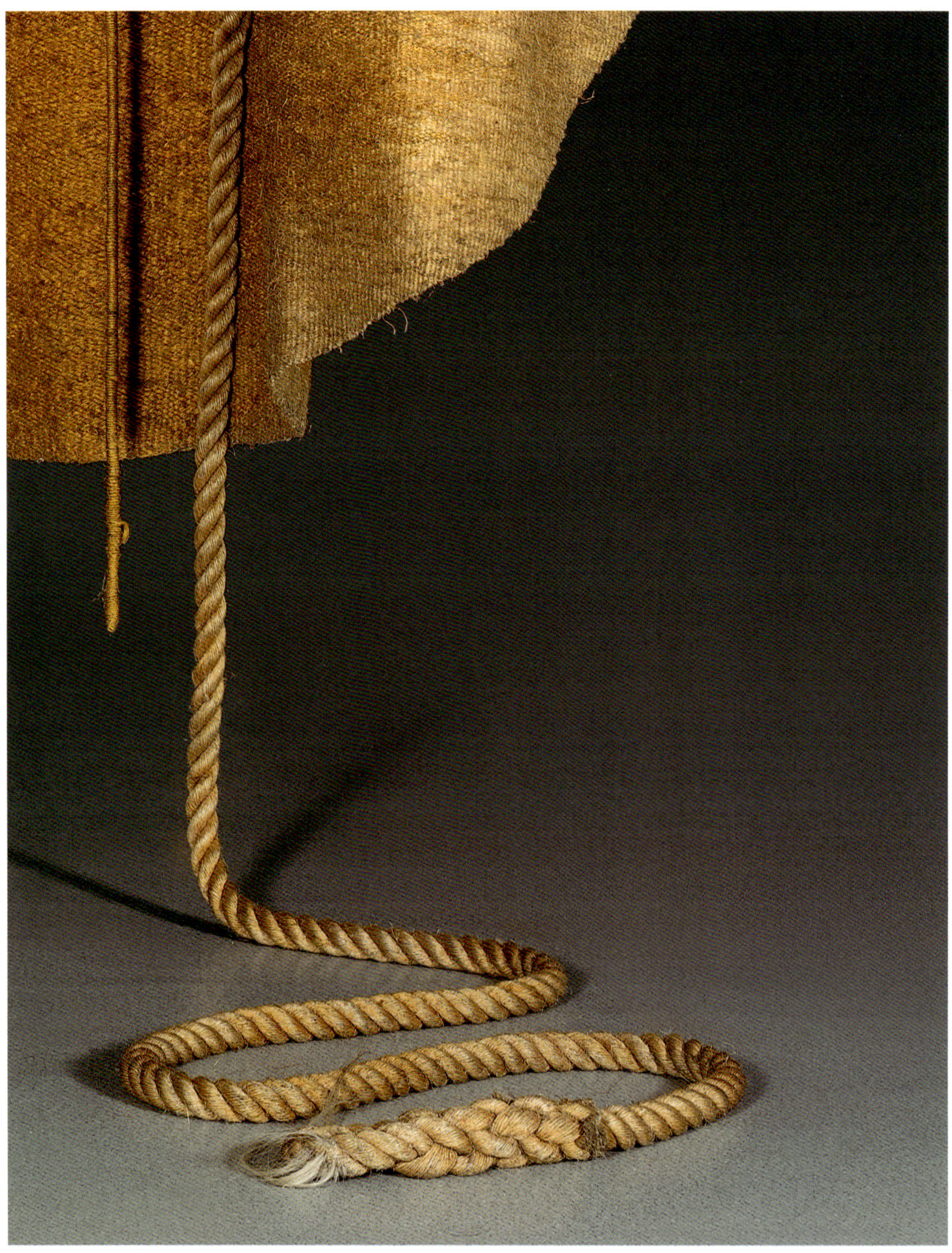

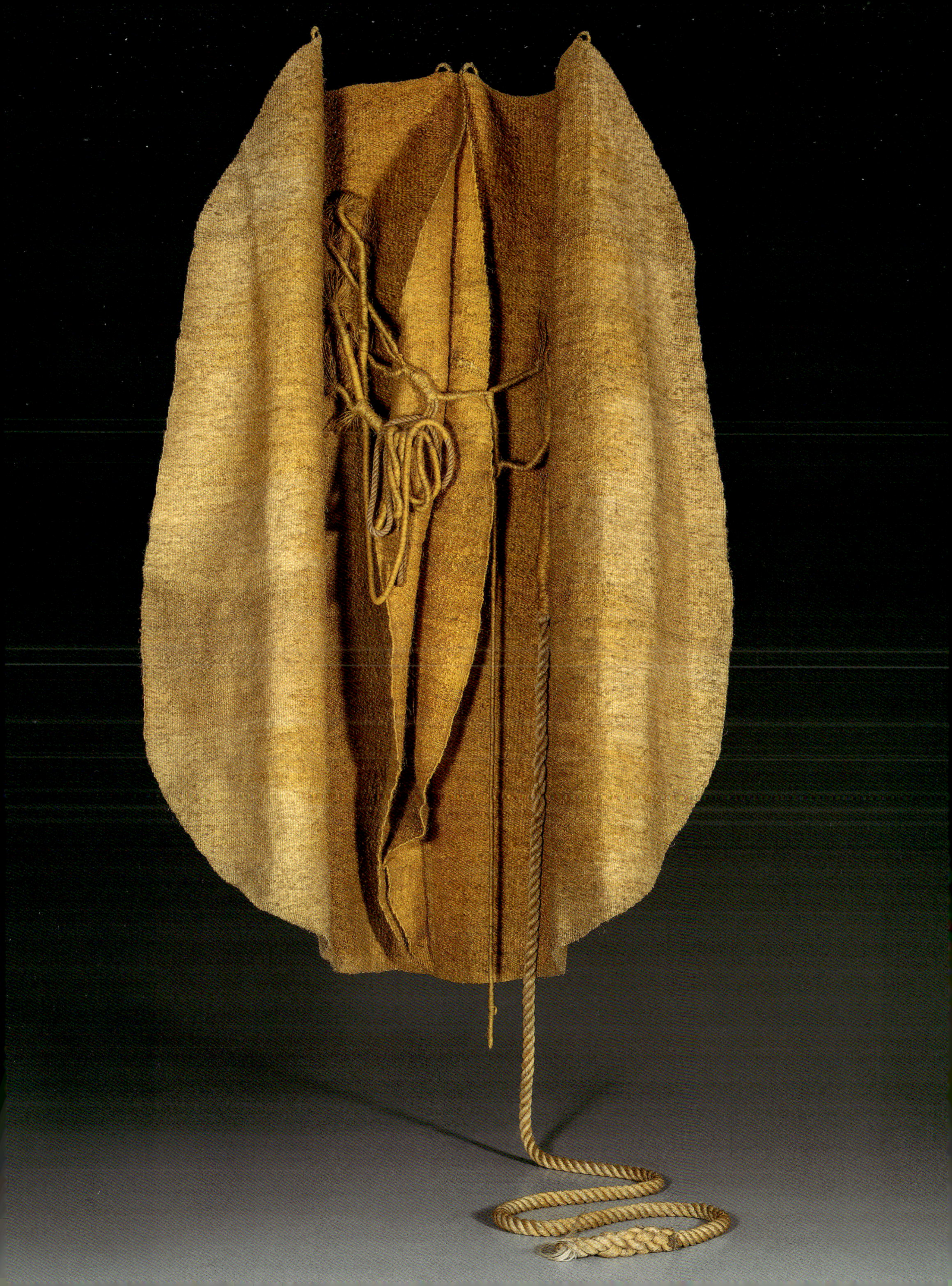

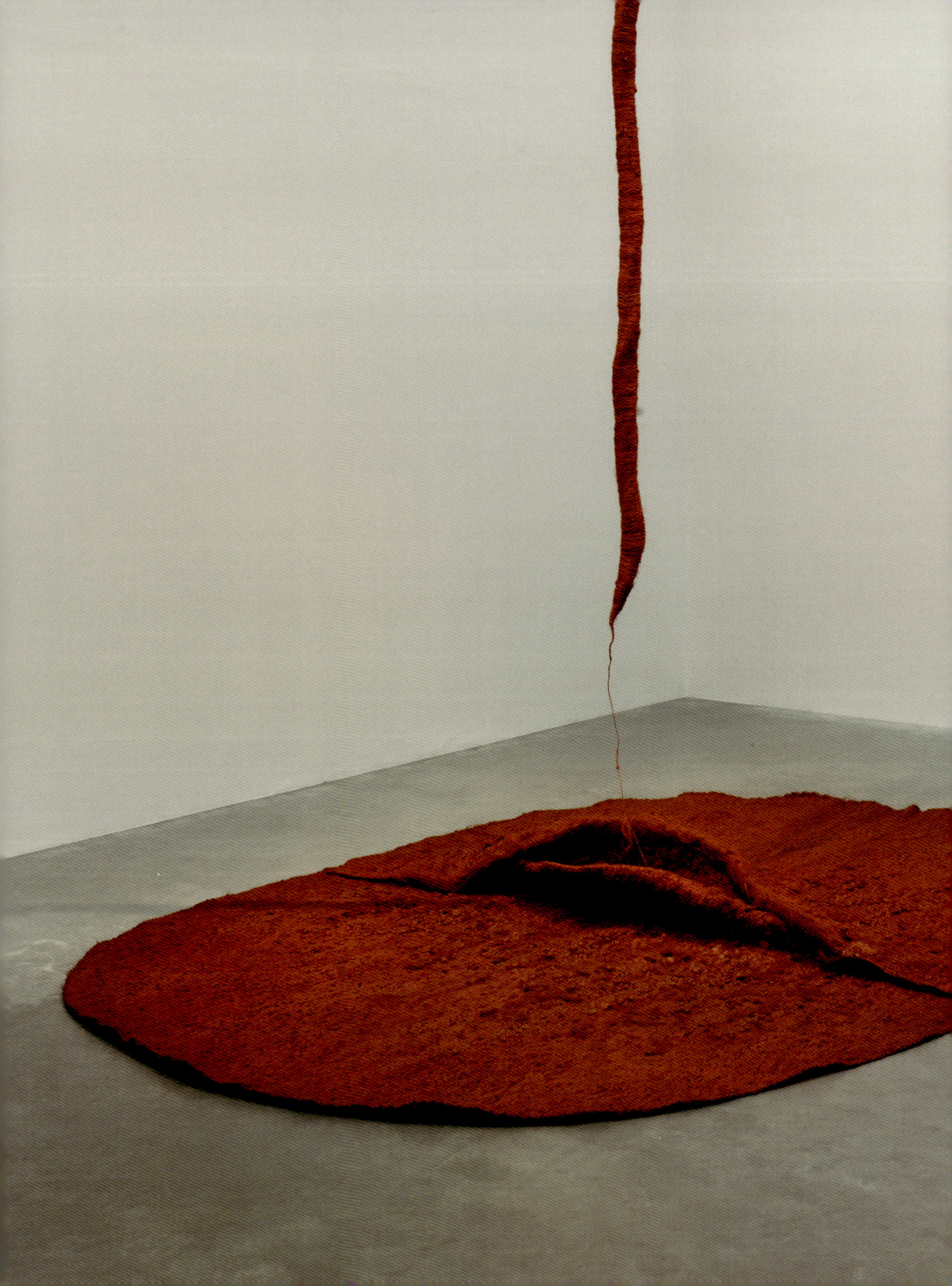

Abakan Orange **1971**
Sisal
401 × 290 × 370

Abakan January–February
1972
Sisal
330 × 325 × 55

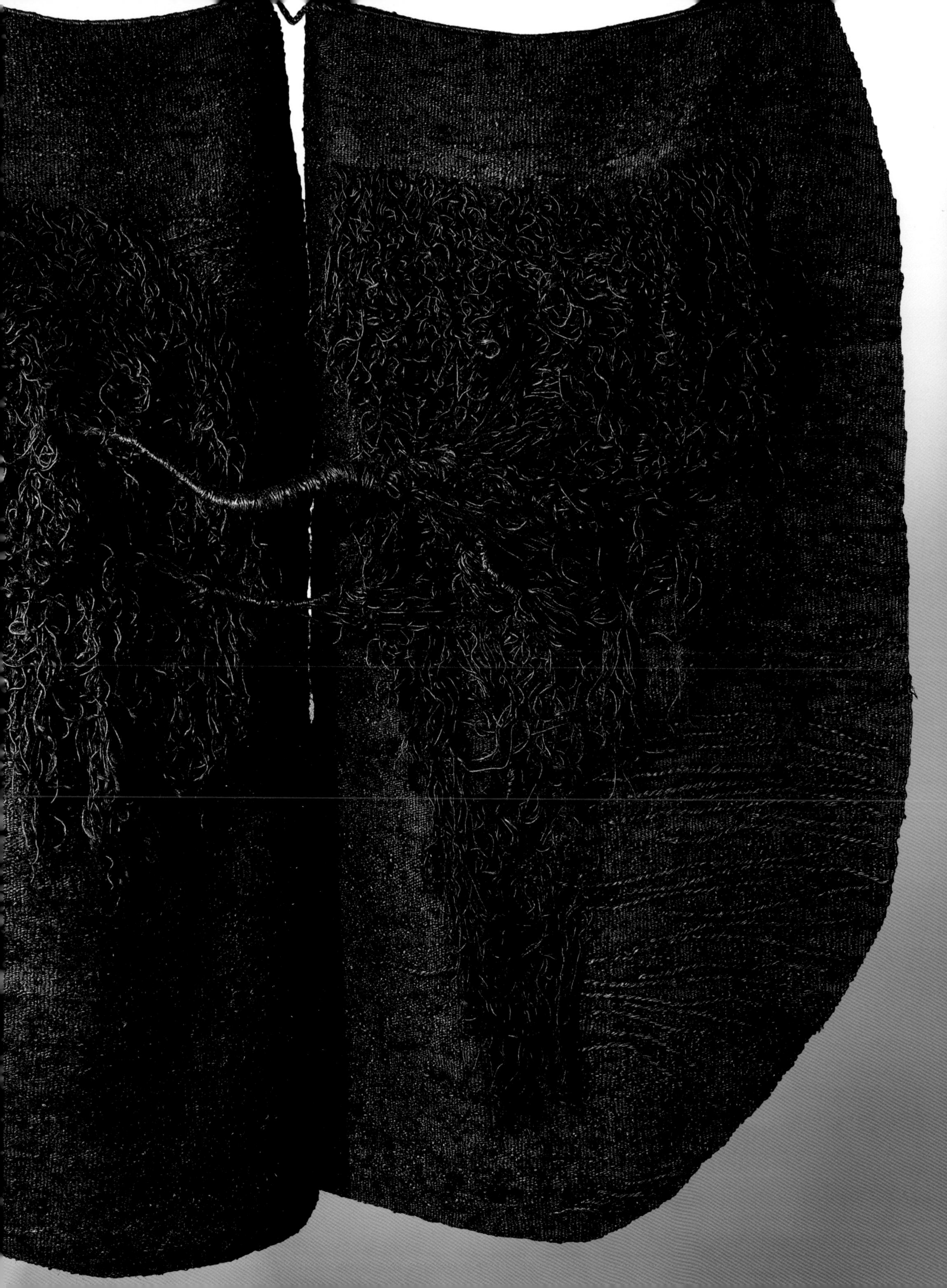

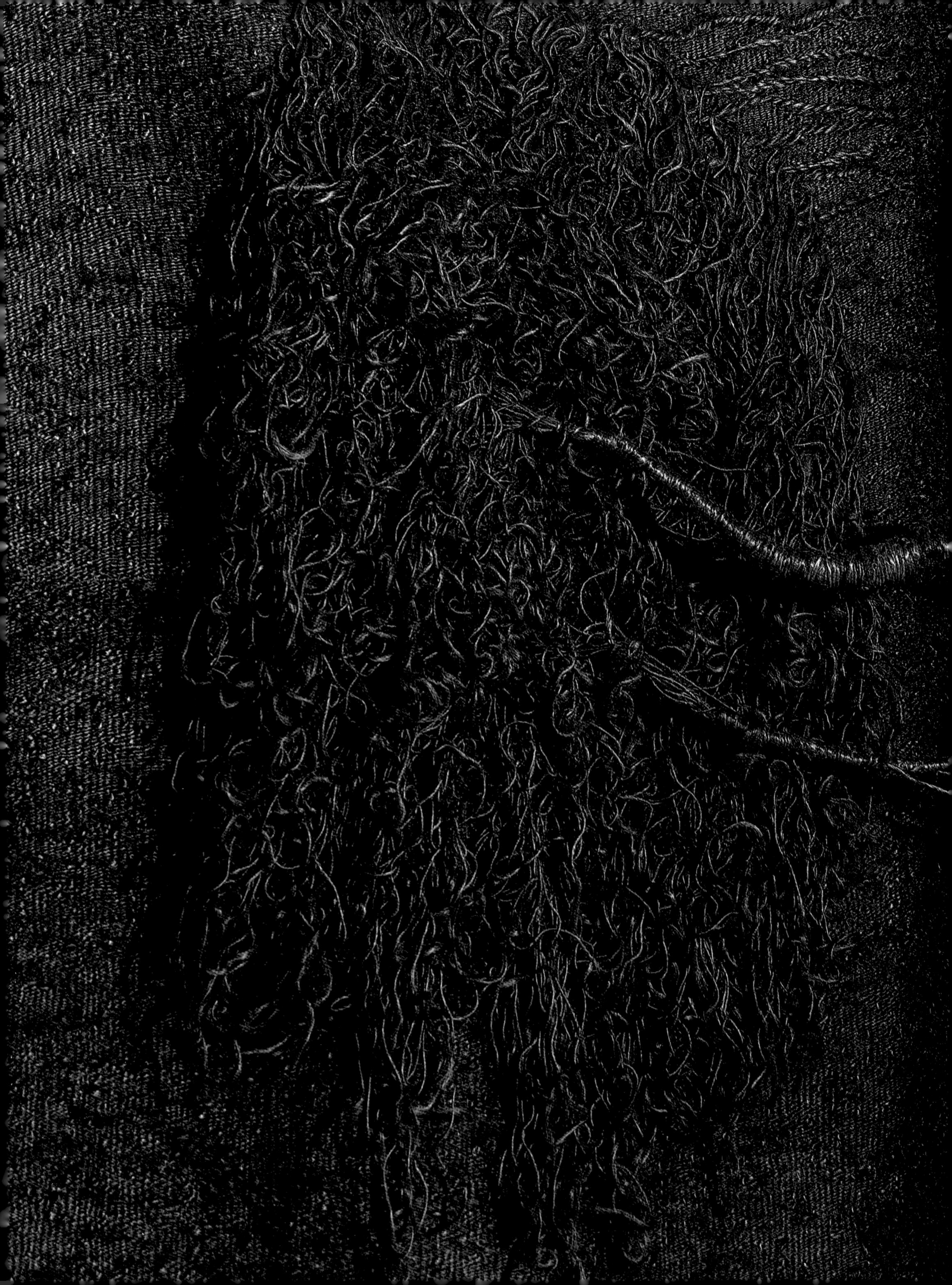

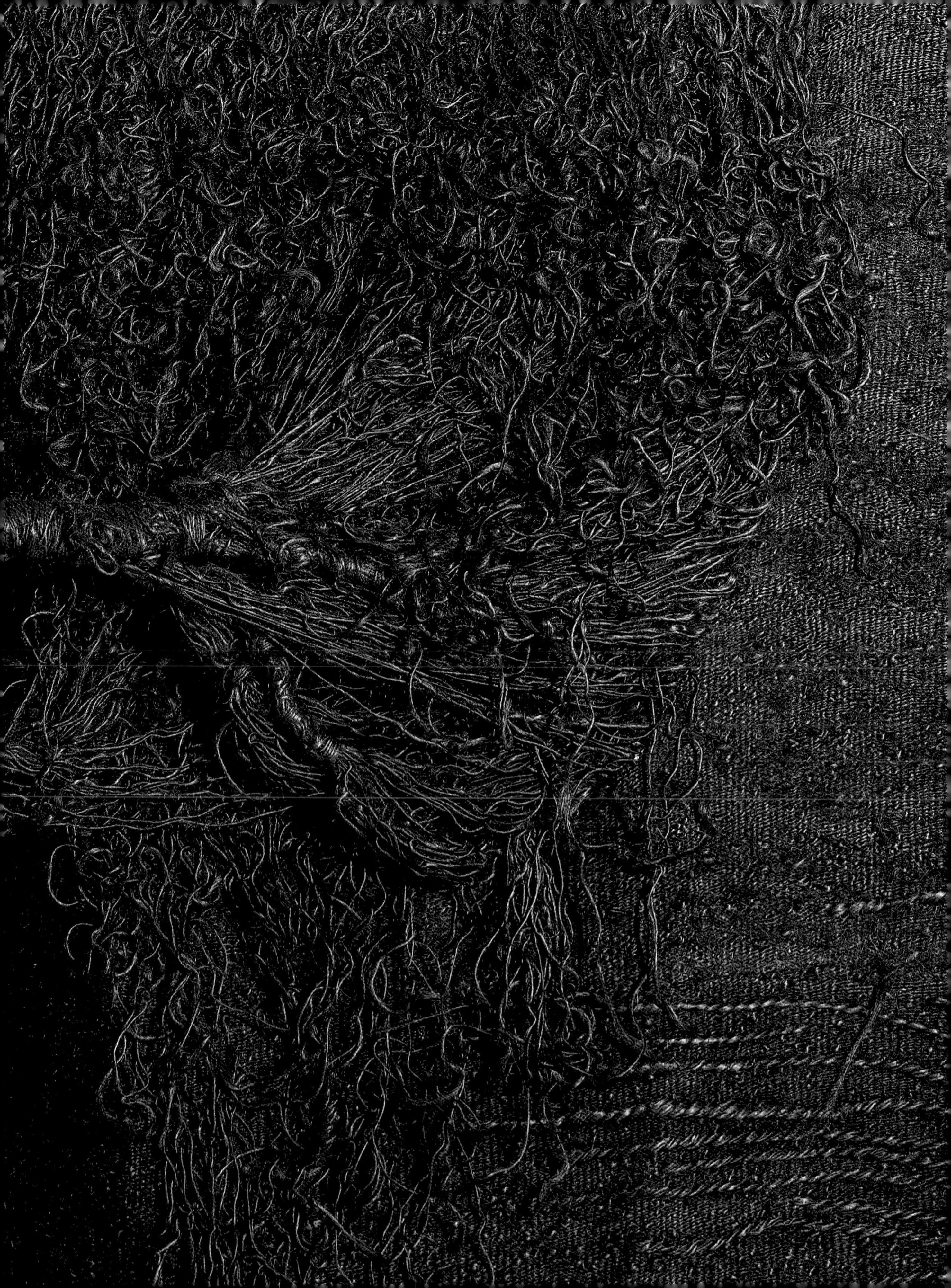

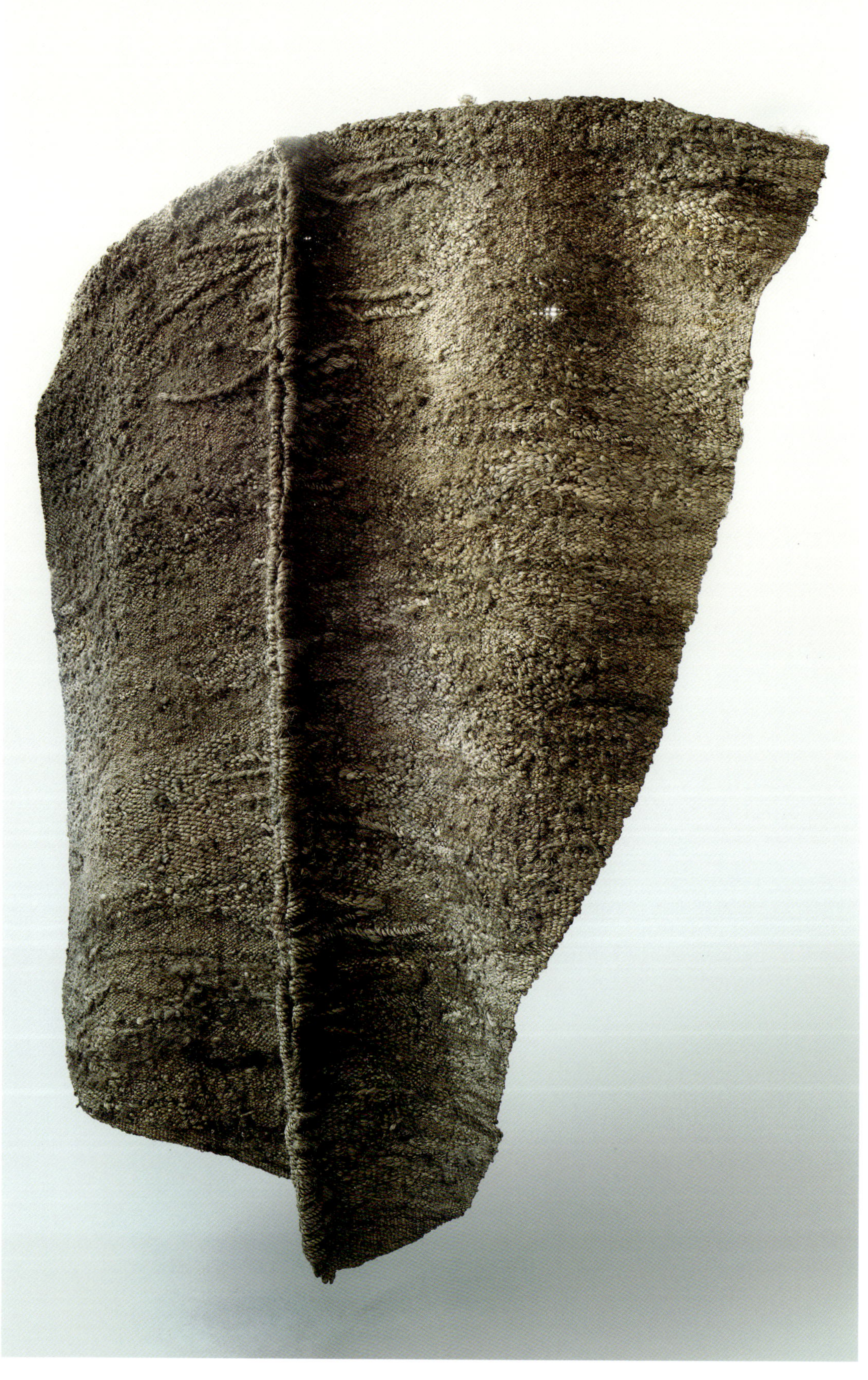

***Winter* 1975–80**
Sisal
320 × 360

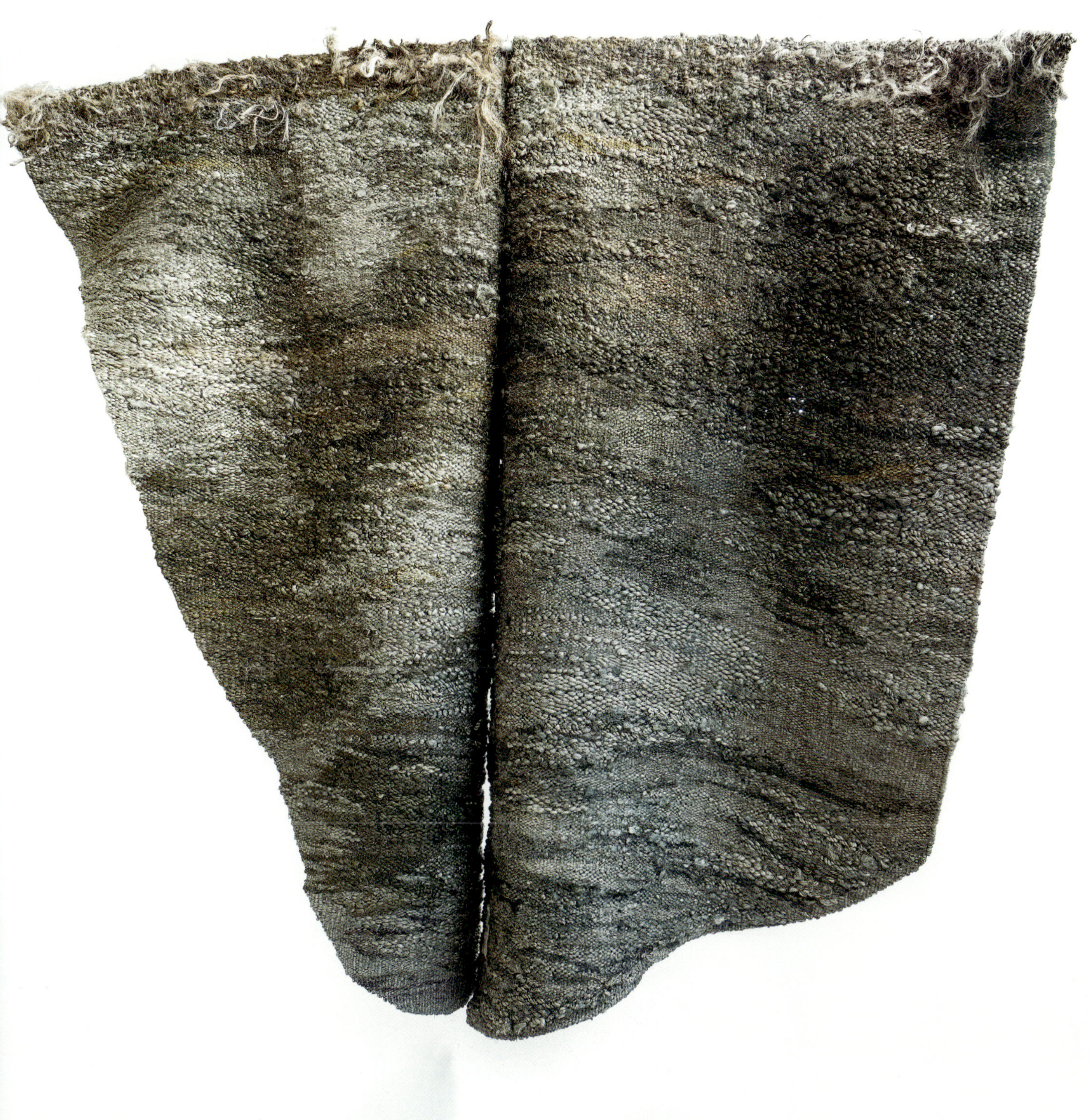

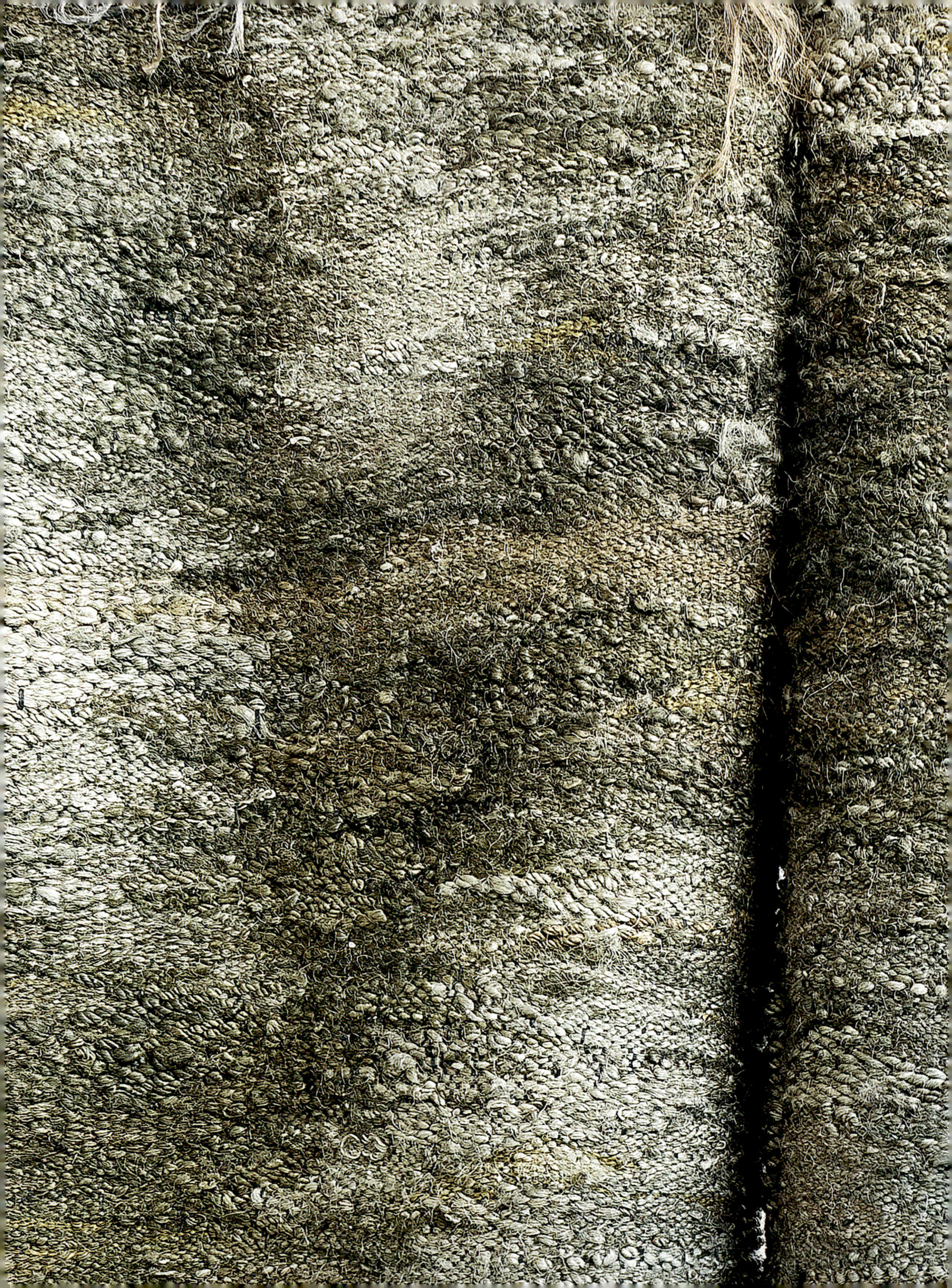

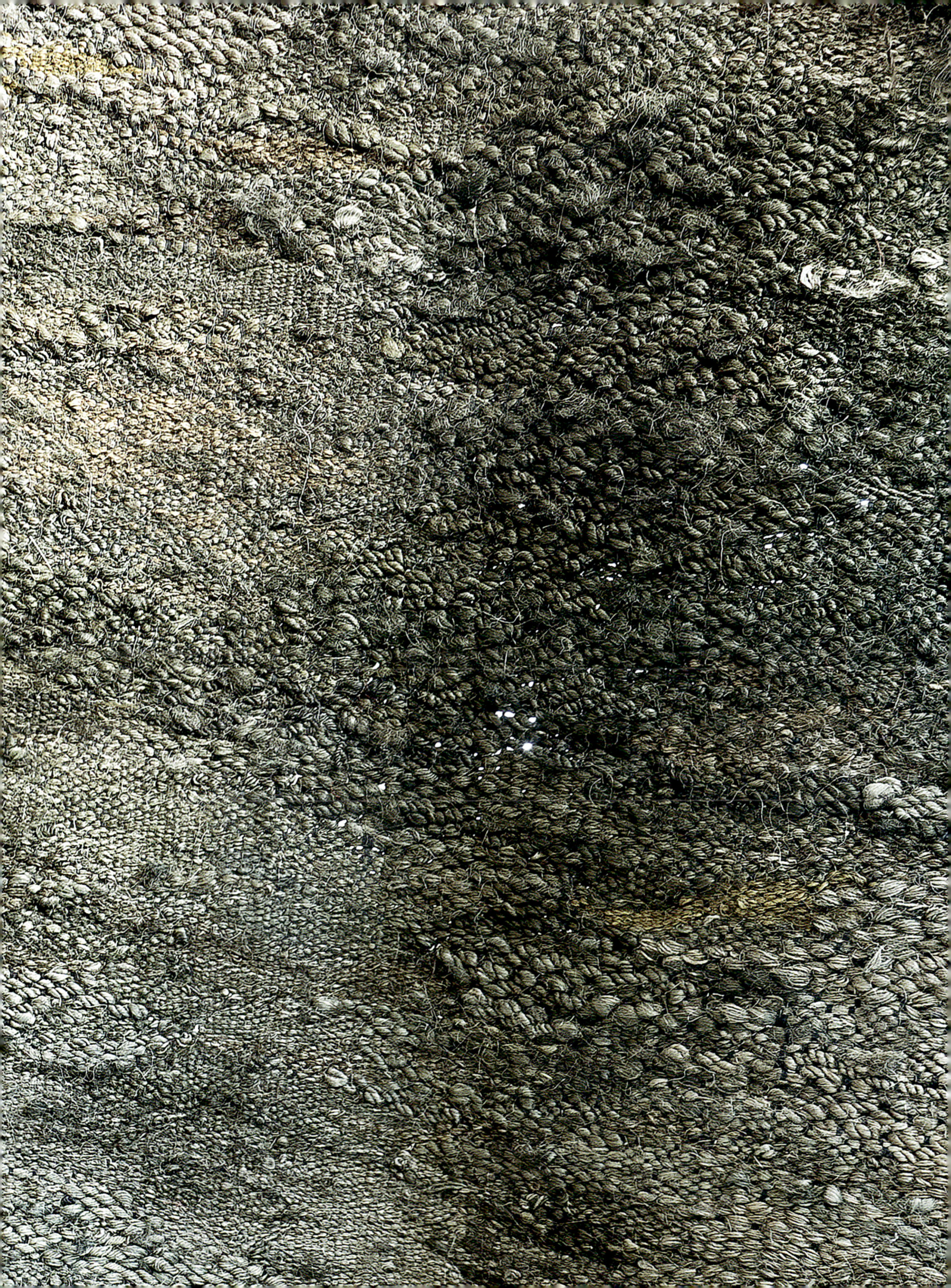

Pregnant **1970–80**
Sisal and horsehair
135.9 × 106.7

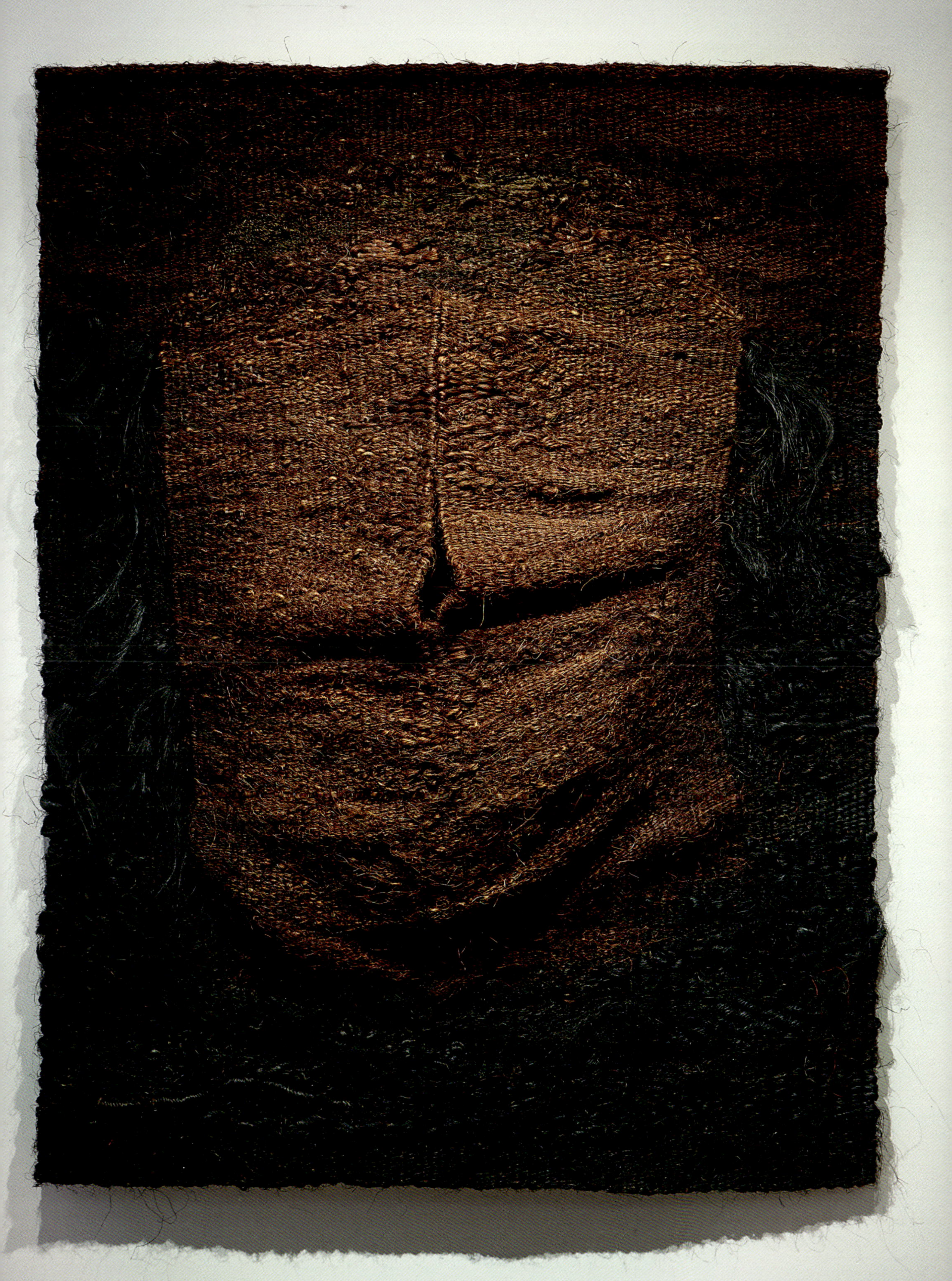

Black Ball **1975**
Sisal
140 × 110 × 100

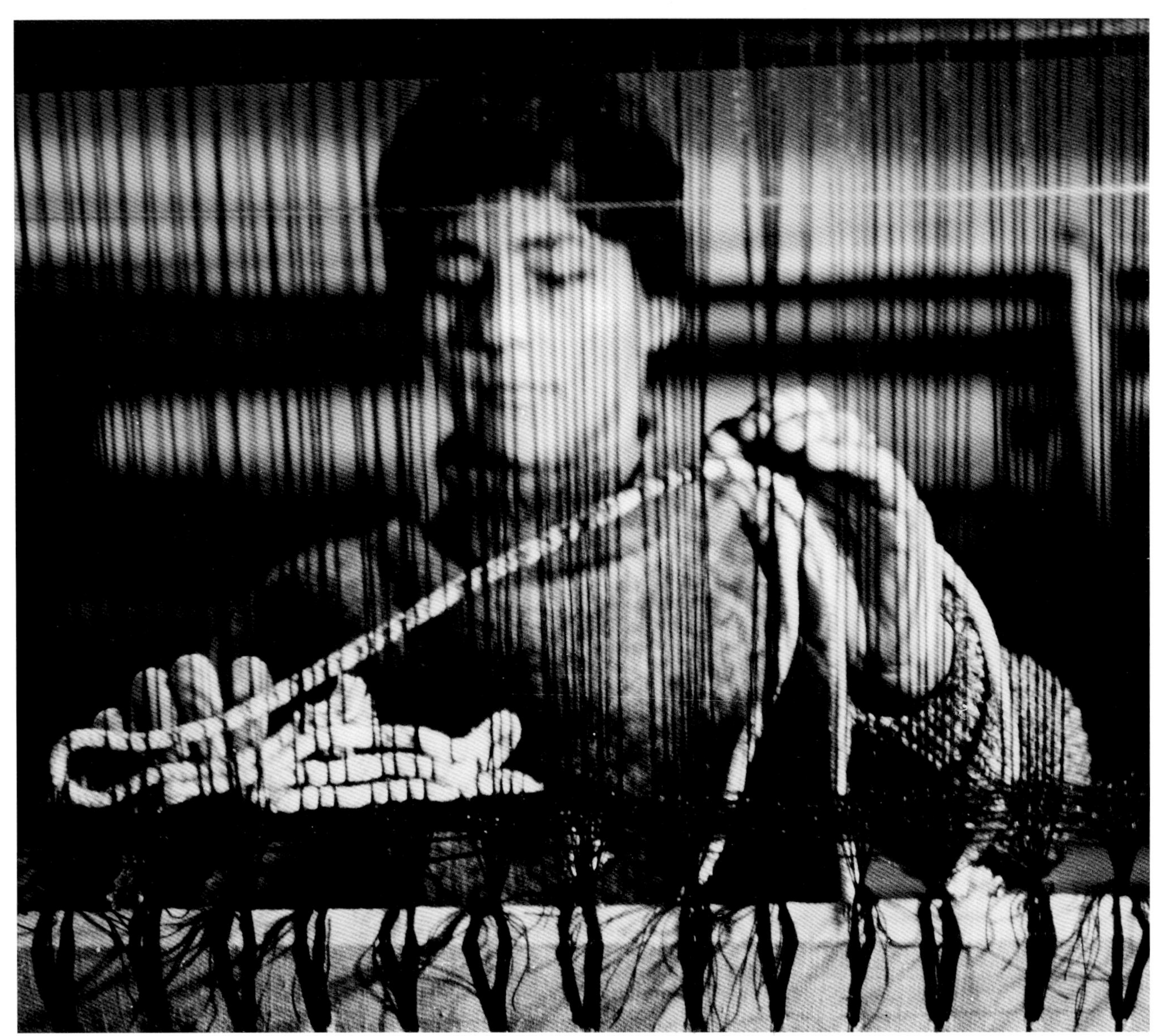

CRAFTING AN ART PRACTICE
THE POSTWAR POLISH ART SCENE

MICHAŁ JACHUŁA

Opposite: The artist at her loom, 1966.

Emerging from the struggles of the Second World War, Magdalena Abakanowicz embarked on the studies she needed to become an artist in Poland. Upon graduating from the Secondary School of Plastic Arts in Gdynia[1] in May 1949, where she obtained her high school diploma, she enrolled at the State Higher School of Fine Arts in Sopot on 20 September 1949. When the textile department was eliminated at the school – textiles was the very discipline in which she intended to specialise – Abakanowicz transferred to the Academy of Plastic Arts in Warsaw.[2] In addition to being one of the few schools in the country that recognised textiles as a form of art and area of study, being a student at the Academy placed Abakanowicz in the centre of cultural change.

In Warsaw, her studies focused on textile-related subjects, such as weaving theory and design, the history of textiles and fabric, as well as manual weaving. Other classes included painting, drawing and art history, but also a state-sanctioned indoctrination class called 'The Issues of Marxism and Leninism', mandatory at all Polish universities at the time. In 1954, Abakanowicz received a diploma in weaving from the department of painting at the academy. Though she took courses with several painting professors, importantly, she also studied with Eleanora Plutyńska (1886–1969), whose weaving studio was a specialisation within the department. Additionally, she was also influenced by the jacquard studio led by Anna Śledziewska (1900–79), with whom she had initially started her studies.[3] In addition to Plutyńska and Śledziewska, Mieczysław Szymański (1903–90) also played a key role in educating the first generation of textile artists in Poland following the war: Jolanta Owidzka (1927–2020), Wojciech Sadley (b.1932), Barbara Falkowska (b.1931) and Krystyna Wojtyna-Drouet (b.1926), among others.

Although Plutyńska, Śledziewska and Szymański had different teaching methods, they all stressed respect for the use of traditional weaving techniques in the creation of contemporary experimental works, and their influence is visible in Abakanowicz's work. Plutyńska emphasised spontaneous methods of creation, drawing from the power of imagination, and through the understanding of properties inherent in the material. Preparatory stages of weaving, including dyeing and the use of organic materials, were also explored. Plutyńska's method was influenced by the time she spent with folk weavers from the Eastern territories of Poland, and from 1934 onwards she played a pivotal role in the revival of Polish folk weaving. Specialising in jacquard technique, Śledziewska demonstrated to her students the subtle difference in designing repetitive patterns through her masterful approach to composition and selection of chromatic scales. Szymański's practice, on the other hand, focused on tapestry and carpentry. A demanding professor in terms of technical precision, he is generally acknowledged as the first and most important figure when it came to encouraging students to experiment with their weaving materials. Under his tutelage, students began to incorporate in their projects materials such as paper, rope and metal wire, as well as naturalelements such as straw.

In order to understand artistic life in the People's Republic of Poland, it is crucial to consider the role of the most important visual artists' organisation – the state-run Association of Polish Artists and Designers, known in Polish simply as ZPAP. Often called an artists' union, the organisation was established in 1945, although its roots go back to 1911 with the establishment of other artist organisations in Kraków, Lviv and Warsaw.[4] All-encompassing, ZPAP was 'a complex bureaucratic structure, supporting ministerial control of artistic life'.[5] Members of the union practised fine and applied art: painting, sculpture, graphics, interior and set design, as well as conservation.[6] ZPAP enabled artists to obtain the raw materials needed to create artwork, which at the time required official documents from the state[7], and it also handled the assignment of studio spaces, and social and health insurance. In addition, ZPAP provided guidance in copyright law in conjunction with the Polish Society of Authors and Composers.[8]

Crucially ZPAP membership entitled artists to pursue their learned profession and take up paid employment in places managed by the state.[9] Being a member of ZPAP also allowed artists to receive major commissions from the state as well as participate in state-run competitions, which essentially guaranteed work for artists. Furthermore, it needs to be noted that the free art market in the People's Republic of Poland was practically non-existent. The main patron, commissioner and client of art was the state, which operated through the Ministry of Art and Culture, as well as its owned enterprise, Desa State Enterprise for Artworks and Antiques. Known simply as Desa, the enterprise mainly made purchases for the country's museums and art institutions.[10] Its organisational structure also included the Desa Foreign Trade Office, which was officially in charge of mediating the sale of artworks aboard. The possibility of selling one's work in Poland and internationally was limited to those who held membership with ZPAP, or persons who had obtained a permit from the Ministry of Art and Culture, allowing them to practise art professionally.[11] Most importantly, ZPAP offered artists the opportunity to exhibit their work in state galleries. In addition to organising open-air artistic events and workshops, the organisation arranged financial support for Polish artists to travel. In fact, some of Abakanowicz's most important exhibitions, spanning over fifteen years of her career (1960–75), were organised in cooperation with ZPAP, alongside Zachęta Centralne Biuro Wystaw Artystycznych (Zachęta CBWA) in Warsaw.[12]

Below: *Jacquard project for* Polish Textiles *book cover* 1952
Graphite on graph paper 14.5 × 16

Opposite: *Untitled* c.1958. Screenprint and paint on cotton 136 × 78

Abakanowicz applied for admission to ZPAP in 1955, and was entered as a candidate for the interior design and decorative arts section: ZPAP categorised each member according to their education, achievements and interests. She became a full member in 1957. In the documents submitted to ZPAP, her difficult housing conditions were noted – a room of eight-and-a-half square metres – and her referenced speciality, fabric, placed her within the area of applied arts. Under the heading 'future artistic intentions', she wrote: 'designing and manufacturing textiles [that are] decorative, painted, printed and woven'.[13] As a source of income, she cited her work at Central Natural Silk Plant 'Milanówek', Warsaw, where she was employed from 1 August 1954 on a part-time basis as an artistic manager of the weaving mill; her tasks included designing ties. Abakanowicz was also briefly associated with ŁAD, the Artists Cooperative of Plastic Arts,[14] as well as the Cooperative-State Central Agency for Folk and Art Industry, known as Cepelia,[15] which effectively carried on the ŁAD tradition of working with fabric designers, who were to find employment primarily in industry.

Abakanowicz's early modernist works, such as *Iris* 1955 and *Butterfly* 1957, were painted on fabric. The expressiveness of these works pushed the boundaries to verge on abstraction. Applied arts, including decorative textiles, were not bound by the dogmatic aesthetic doctrines of the Polish state at the time. Such works enjoyed even greater freedom than paintings on canvas. Shown at exhibitions of interior design, they were received in the context of 'innocent' decorative art.[16] Abakanowicz even won, among other awards, a distinction in the competition for decorative painted fabric organised by ŁAD in 1954, in addition to first prize of the Institute of Industrial Design and for the ŁAD 30th anniversary exhibition, both in 1956. These successes were, in part, enabled by the artist's membership with ZPAP.

Such national exhibitions of interior design and decorative art were an attempt to show artistic achievements, as they related to architecture, craftsmanship and industrial design, as well as stage design. These exhibitions sought to raise material culture to the high status of art. Yet they were also propagandistic and political in character, referring to the formation of a new lifestyle in the People's Republic of Poland. However, in 1960, when Abakanowicz presented a group of such works – fabric designs using oil paint or gouache – at the Kordegarda Galeria Narodowego Centrum Kultury, in the building of the Ministry of Art and Culture in Warsaw, the authorities closed the exhibition before it had a chance to open to the public.

By 1961, the nature of Abakanowicz's work shifted to weaving, and by the following year, she found an artistic home in the Atelier Expérimental de l'Union

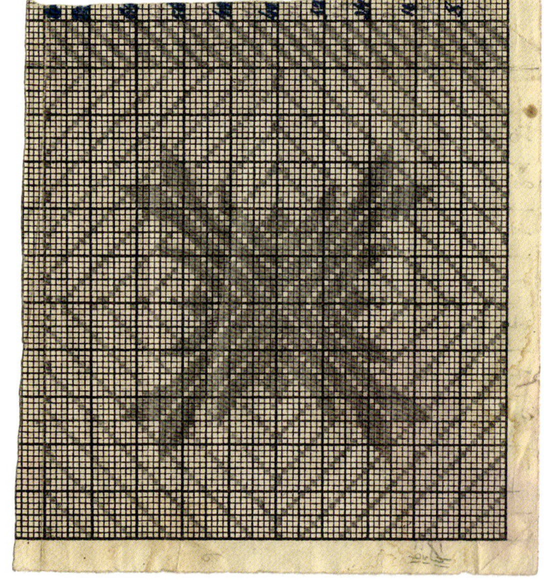

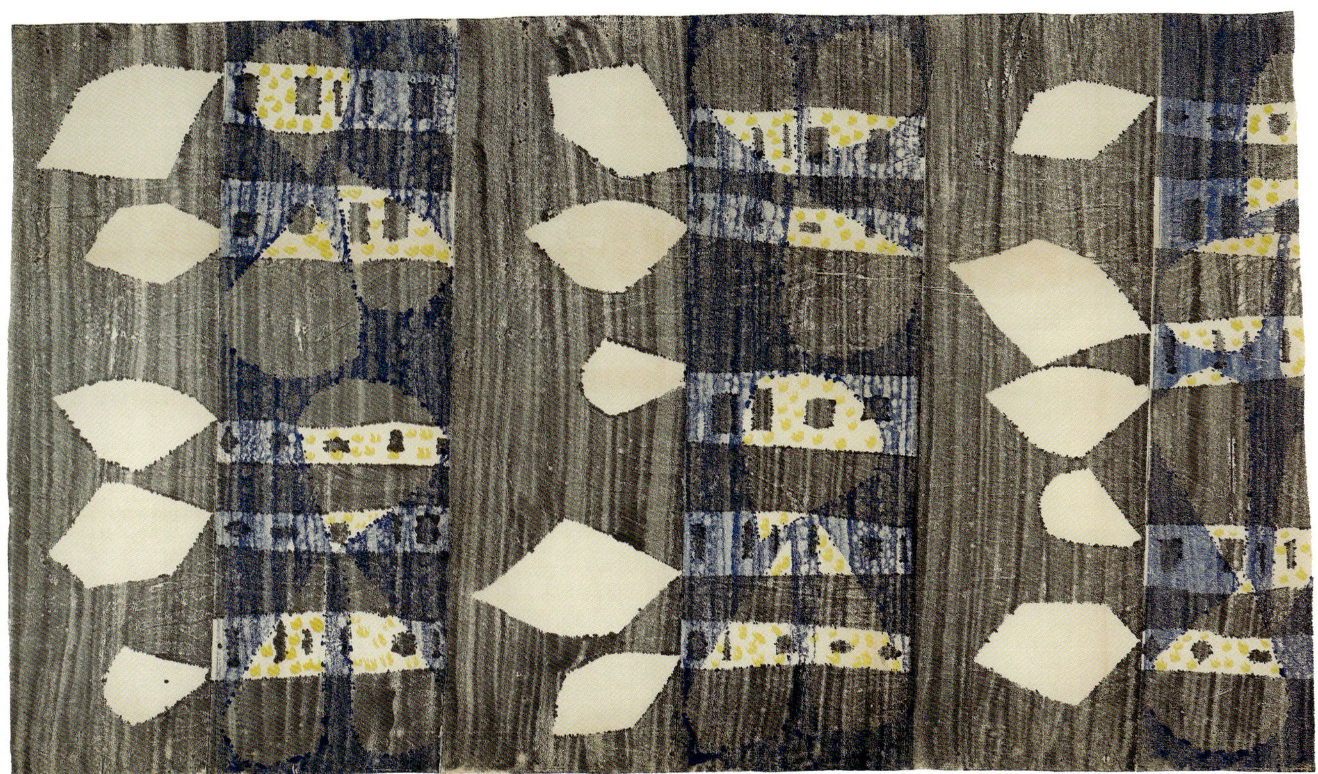

des Artistes de Polonais, an independent operation initiated by weaver Maria Łaszkiewicz (1891–1981), whose name was registered in French. Łaszkiewicz's modest studio, located originally in the basement of her house, offered a haven for artists, including those from the first generation of postwar academy graduates who did not have their own weaving workshops or studios. Although Łaszkiewicz was not a formal teacher, she was very influential for a number of textile artists, because of her sculptural approach to woven matter. Considered to be a pioneer of incorporating three-dimensional sculptural objects into woven textiles, Łaszkiewicz's practice was undoubtedly a significant influence on the development of Abakanowicz's own.

In the 1960s and 1970s press articles about Abakanowicz buzzed with confusion as to how to name her art and creative method, with labels including 'painting-like textiles' (*Zwierciadło*, 22 December 1963); 'painter at the looms' (*Express Wieczorny*, 9 March 1965); 'sculptor in fabric' (*Zielony Sztandar*, 27 August 1972); 'carpet-creatures' (*Gazeta Krakowska*, 9 April 1971); and 'sculpting with textile' (*Fakty 79*, 17 July 1979). In a biographical dictionary published by the ZPAP Warsaw District in 1972, Abakanowicz was strictly classified as an artist associated with textiles.[17] The text mentioned Abakanowicz's numerous awards, including state-awarded ones which, after the publication of the dictionary, increased in number.[18] It was not until 14 March 1979 that the Board of ZPAP, Warsaw released information about the change of Abakanowicz's affiliation, moving her from the interior design section to the sculpture section.[19]

It was in the mid 1960s that her work gained the name of *Abakans*. This neologism, derived from her name, is still a rather capacious term, and one that is understood and used in different ways. One of the first testimonies to the appearance of the name *Abakan* was the 1964 article in *Zwierciadło* magazine, in which it was used in reference to all her work.[20] Its broad meaning encompassed the medium, technique and Abakanowicz's authorship. It should be noted that *Abakan* was initially used in regard to her woven works that were hung on the wall. With the emergence of Abakanowicz's three-dimensional work in the mid 1960s, *Abakan* came to describe objects that were soft and sculptural in form, finally becoming part of the works' titles. So exceptional was this moniker in understanding the artist's work, that some continue to use it today to describe all her woven work, while others have continued to call Abakanowicz a fibre artist in spite of the varied materials she has employed over the decades. While Abakanowicz's name remains bound to the medium of fibre, her later works reveal broader sculptural ambitions, reflecting the diverse influences of her educational and personal origins.

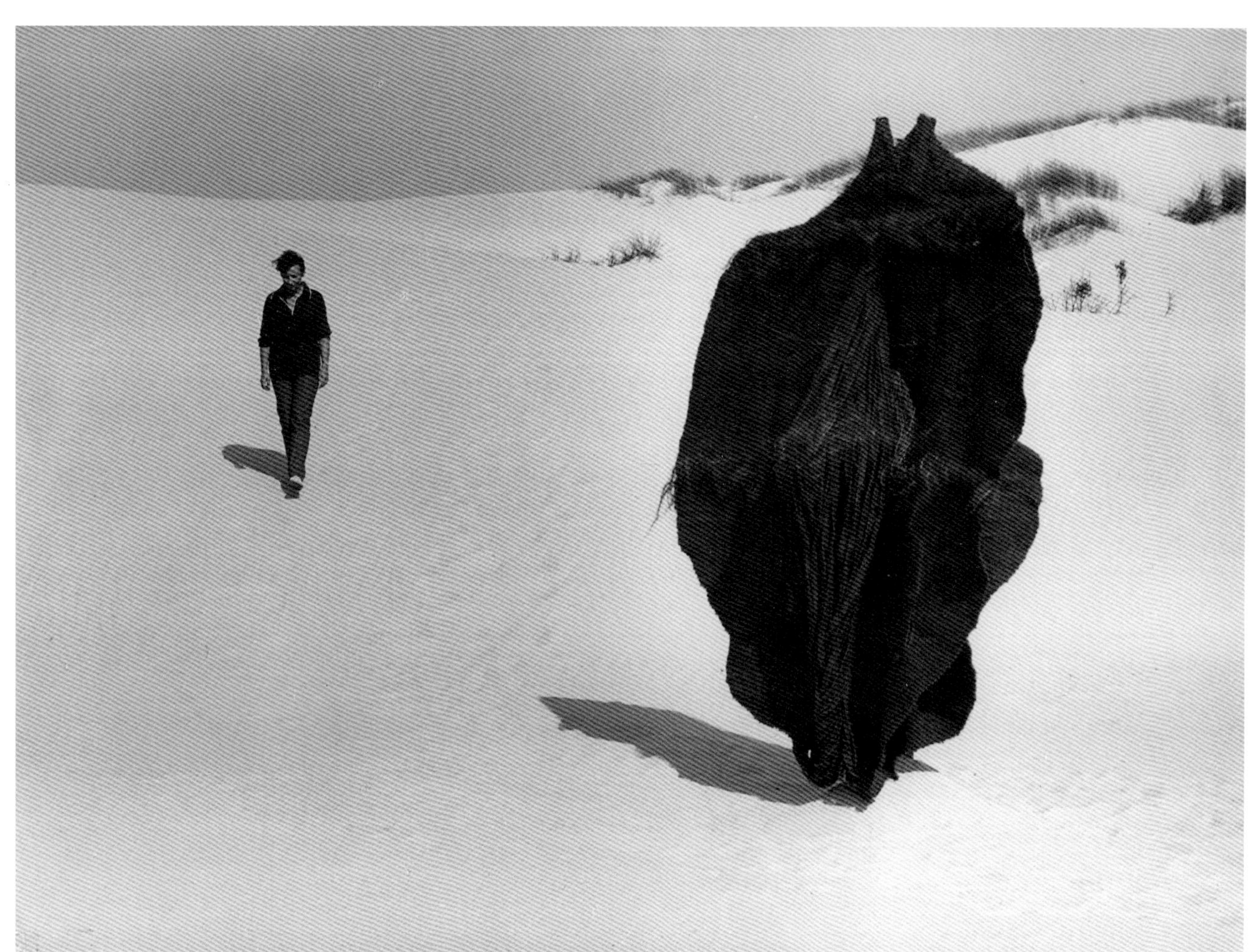

ABAKANY
THE ESSENCE OF TIME AND SPACE

MARTA KOWALEWSKA

A solitary figure traversing barren, gently sloping dunes. It is a mesmerising landscape, difficult to locate in time and space, and one that appears to be lunar. It is all the more hypnotic because it fills up with organic forms that defy all definition. At first glance, these open-air scenes from the 1970 film *Abakany* may appear loosely conceived. In fact, they carry a powerful truth about the work of Magdalena Abakanowicz.

Abakanowicz's works are the protagonists of this thirteen-minute film, shot partly by filmmaker Jarosław Brzozowski (1911–69). Twenty years her elder, he had lived through turbulent times, experiencing the Second World War in his own way as the artist had in hers. They shared the need to make a new world almost *ex nihilo*, out of shattered fragments. They had to find an entirely new language to describe the harsh reality that surrounded them.

Brzozowski produced films of unusual emotional intensity that entered the canon of Polish cinematography as outstanding examples of documentary study. Focusing on themes such as wartime reality, social issues, and the harshness of the Siberian landscape, his films were concerned with the pursuit of truth. He understood art, just as Abakanowicz spoke of it, as a manifestation of the internal need to create, as rendering the work 'in the medium closest to the truth'.[1] He sought a deep understanding of the way in which creative energy takes concrete shape. He wanted to access the 'primary source of each work of art: that unknown plasma from which new worlds and new material qualities are formed and which possess special capacities to evoke and engage feelings and imagination'.[2] And for him, the only way to comprehend the genesis of art is through its creators.

Given the distinctiveness and ambiguity of both the artist herself and her work, Abakanowicz made for a perfect subject, but one that also presented a challenge. As Brzozowski's assistant, Barbara Stopczyk, recalls, the idea for *Abakany* took shape as a result of many hours of discussion between the director and the artist, and was the product of the ideas of two powerful personalities, two artistic visions. As Brzozowski explained to Abakanowicz, 'I do not want any generalisations. Generalisations are only made when we search our memories for things that are resolved ... What I am interested in is a description of a problem that seeks resolution now.'[3]

At the time the film was begun, in 1969, Abakanowicz declared that the prevailing view stating that her primary interest lay in the texture of a work was wrong, since she had already turned her attention to the exploration of three-dimensional space. The first *Abakans* had only begun to populate exhibition spaces in 1967, barely a year before the filming of *Abakany*. She had freed her woven forms not only from practical functions, but also from the wall or base.

Sharing her desire to liberate the *Abakans* from restrictions, Brzozowski proposed that these works be shown outdoors – within the natural environment. He found a suitable setting in the Słowiński National Park, home to Europe's largest tract of shifting sand dunes, and occupying approximately 500 hectares on a narrow, desert-like spit of land between the Baltic Sea and Lake Łebsko. Untamed nature can exert a powerful attraction on the unbridled artistic soul. At the beginning of the twentieth century, when part of Germany, the area became a favourite haunt of German bohemians. Since being assigned to Poland after the Second World War, it witnessed the rapid growth of the town of Łeba, which became a popular holiday destination for Poles during the 'little stabilisation' of 1956–68, and remains so today.[4] In nearby Ustka, the Association of Polish Artists and Designers had a studio and workshop, which was frequently visited by artists in the 1960s.

The region has a unique terrain where the human struggle with the elements takes on a special significance. The eroded vegetation was destroyed by a man-made fire in the first half of the sixteenth century. The sands, then subjected to unceasing blasts of wind, shift constantly creating dunes that reach heights of several dozen metres. Over time they have assimilated forests, bogs and even residential areas. In this wild landscape nature has fought for its autonomy and won. The uncanny calmness, the mood of contemplation and the beauty of nature make it seem as if this place exists outside of time and space. And it is the very place where the *Abakans* gained a new dimension by drawing an almost mystical breath of vital force into their immense bodies.

Eschewing the documentary approach by which he had made his mark, in *Abakany* Brzozowski used allegory and lyrical suggestiveness to interpret Abakanowicz's work. These scenes make up its most original sequence and are the last that Brzozowski committed to film before his death. It is not only the Saharan-like setting that surprises in the film *Abakany*, but also its cinematographic vision. The fable opens with shots of the artist striding alone in the boundless expanse of the dunes' gentle curves. Then in the final, closing sequence a group of men walking in pairs enter this landscape of dunes carrying the bodies of the *Abakans*. At first this association evokes *Faraon* (Pharaoh), a classic 1965 film set in ancient Egypt, directed by Jerzy Kawalerowicz (1922–2007), with its grand *mise en scène*, its cast of thousands and its exotic landscapes, that succeeded in arousing the imagination of the Polish public. Cast slipshod onto long, wooden poles that they support on their bare shoulders, these woven forms are denied monumentality and grandeur, as if lifeless.

Opening page and right: Stills from Jarosław Brzozowski and Kazimierz Mucha's film *Abakany* 1970
35 mm film transferred to digital, colour, sound, 13 min 5 sec

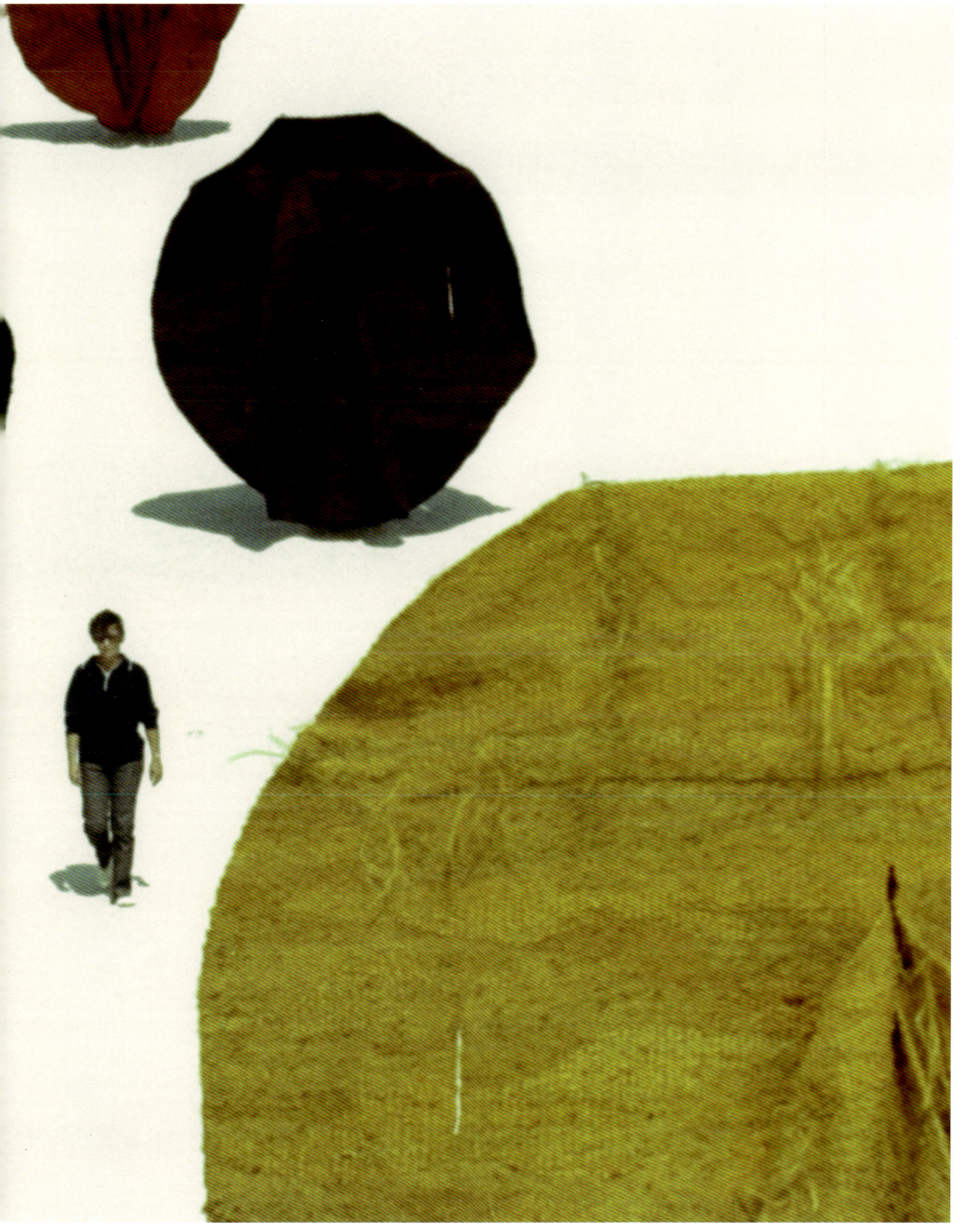

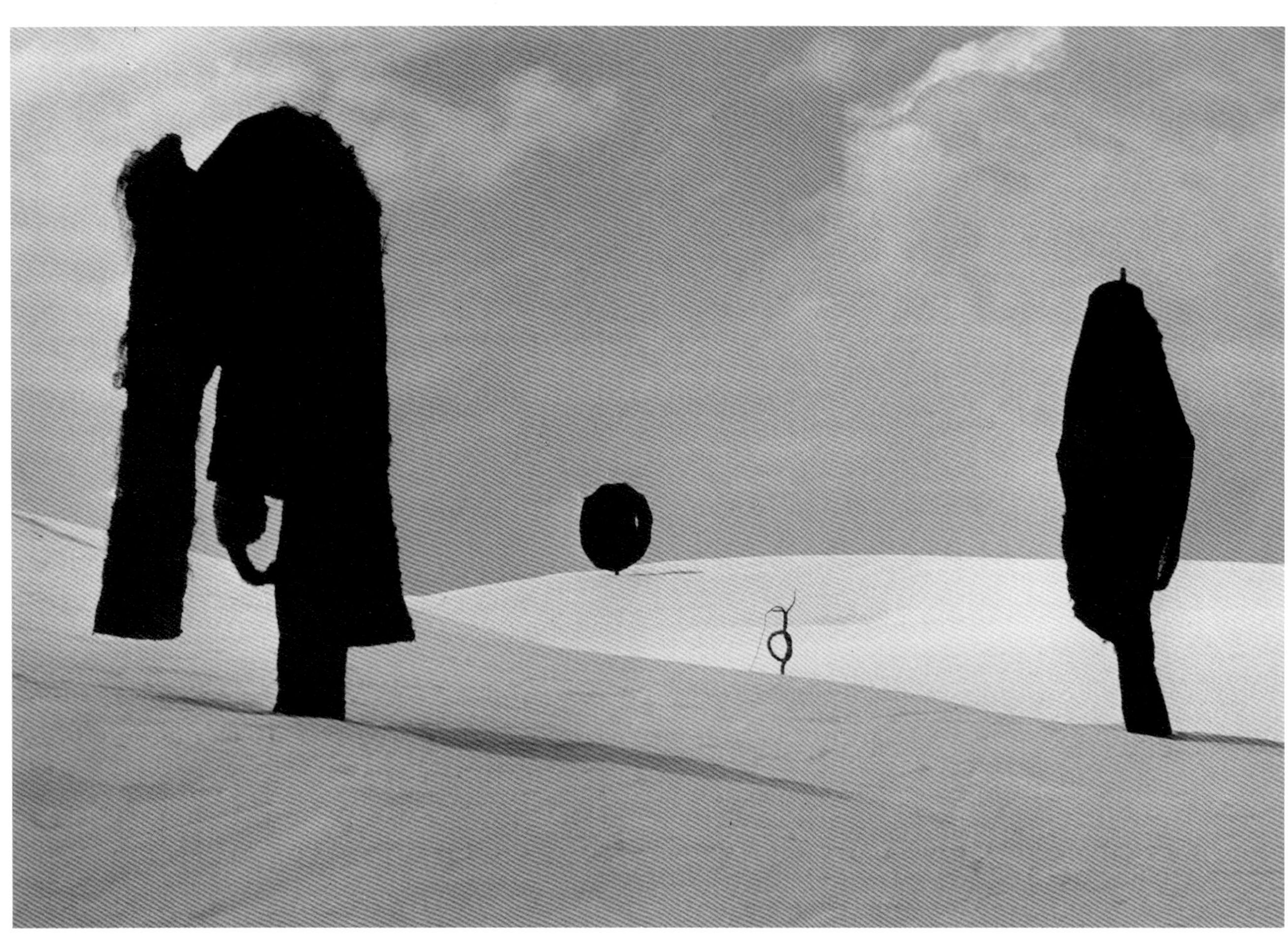

Above, opposite and overleaf: Stills from *Abakany* 1970

Yet once upright in the limitless sandy landscape, the sea breeze fills their bodies with breath. Liberated from restrictive gallery spaces, and now among the slopes stretching away in gentle arcs, they begin to pulse with an inner energy.

Unfortunately, soon after shooting at Łeba, Brzozowski died, and the Polish director Kazimierz Mucha (1923–2006) took up the task of completing the film at the request of the Educational Film Centre in Łódź, which produced the film. Mucha complemented Brzozowski's captivating open-air scenes with a sequence of shots of the artist at work. It is evident that conveying the movement and tactile nature of the monumental sisal compositions was very important to him too. In these sequences Abakanowicz touches, presses, examines, shapes the sisal surfaces and also goes inside them. This is a different type of poetry. Mucha's approach is to experience that which exists, penetrate the structure of the material, and explain the genesis and meaning of the work to viewers so that they can undergo the 'secondary' (as he called it) experience of engaging with art.[5] Mucha, who had made many films about art and poetry, always remaining faithful to the personality of the artist, sought to capture the vibrating energy between the creator and the work, and between the work and the audience.

In this cosmically inflected context, the music of avant-garde composer Bogusław Schäffer (1929–2019) resounds powerfully. Only one year older than Abakanowicz, he belonged to the same generation of artists who, having survived the war, were searching for a new formal language, one that would best reflect the complexity of the world and the burden of their experiences. What captivated him was the essence of sound: drawing nearer to its beginning. He achieved an enormous change in the texture and structure of sound itself by cutting apart and collaging together magnetic tapes he had recorded, as well as introducing new contexts and creating new forms. He was always near the centre of avant-garde artistic movements and events. It was no accident, then, that the 'father of new music in Poland' was invited by Brzozowski to work on a film connected with the progressive art of Abakanowicz.

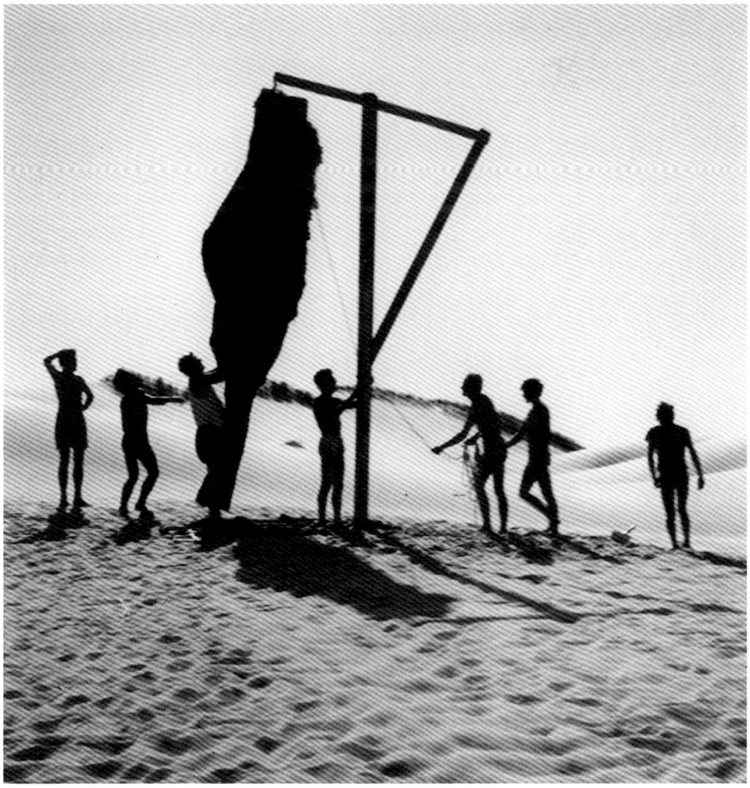

The score for the film – an original sound collage reminiscent of the traces of radio waves set off by the Big Bang – is captivating in itself as it interprets the images. It was recorded in the Polish National Radio Experimental Sound Workshop, founded in 1957. An exciting and innovative place, it was (after Milan, Paris and Cologne) the fourth centre devoted to electronic music in Europe. Here Schäffer could concentrate exclusively on experimentation.

Still, the film's protagonists are the eponymous *Abakans*. Irena Huml, Poland's foremost authority on textile and fibre art who had witnessed many groundbreaking events on the postwar art scene, described them as 'an allegory for depicting our dread of the unknown and inescapable'.[6] She saw them as a representation of the state of mind of the postwar generation. She wrote:

> *These striking objects, which were first made in cycles and then included in systems of similar but varied forms, were designed to reflect states of high tension, changeable moods and the adversities of fate, that is, the complex internal world of contemporary human beings. On the one hand they emanated brutality, and on the other the pursuit of even momentary contemplation. They expressed the painful dilemmas and the multitude of possibilities that usually exceed ordinary human needs.*[7]

Rather than originating in inspiration drawn from the forces of nature alone, the *Abakans*, which were exceptionally biological and full of pulsating, inner energy, were the product of a desire to confront those forces. 'I do not go to the lakes or to the forests for inspiration,' said Abakanowicz, 'I go there to relax in that eternal logic, in something everlasting, in something that, above all, is immutable in the face of the changeability that we are constantly subjected to. It is wonderful ... To look upon living things and to consider what I am attempting to add to that which exists: really it's confrontation rather than inspiration.'[8] Thus, the grand forms of the *Abakans*, seem apart from nature, as *Abakany* reveals: they are the product of the imagination and hands of the artist who breathed life-giving energy into them.[9]

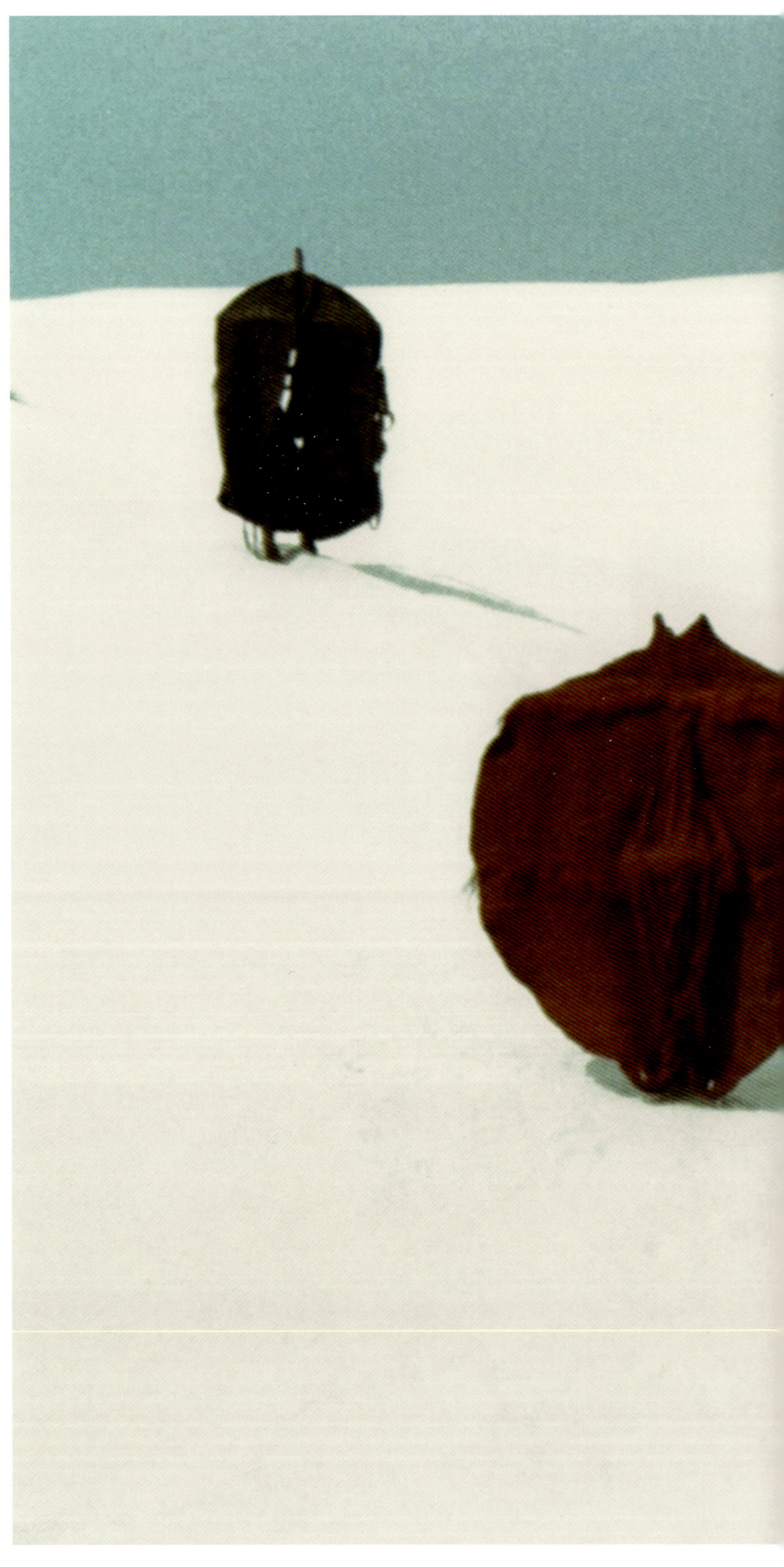

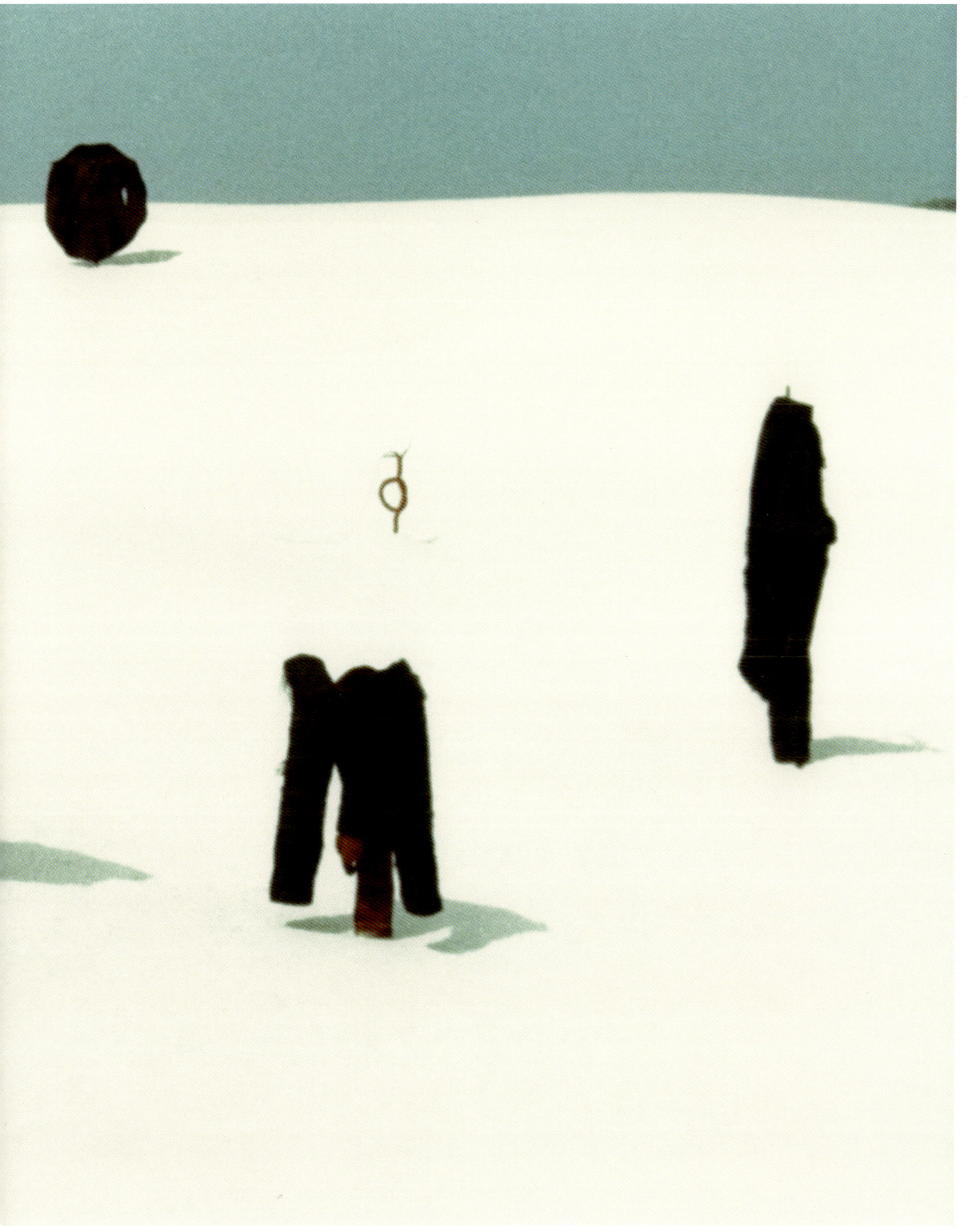

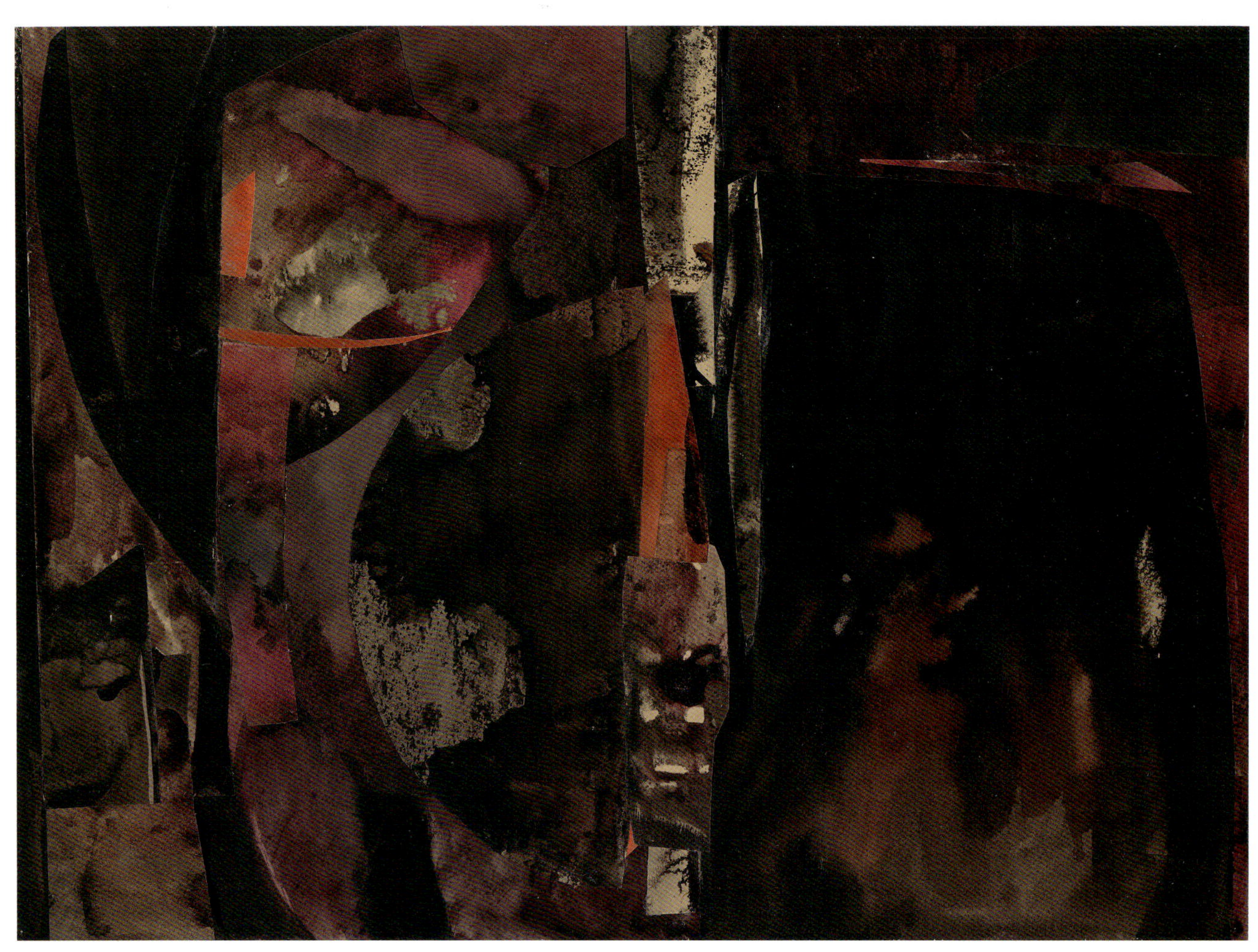

SPACES UNGUARDED
ABAKANOWICZ'S DRAWINGS

MAGALI JUNET

Opposite: *Untitled* 1965
Ink and gouache on papers on paper
50 × 69.5

Below left:
Embryology 1981
Ink on paper
63 × 49

Below right:
Embryology 1981
Ink and charcoal on paper
63.5 × 49

Although less often displayed and critiqued than her woven works and sculptures, Magdalena Abakanowicz's drawings, which included gouache, ink, collage and charcoal, fulfilled the same imperative need to express a state of transition and becoming. Together with her more renowned mediums of expression, drawing featured in the artist's practice for almost sixty years, bearing witness to her ongoing research in the visual arts and illustrating her reflections on the natural world and its metamorphoses.

At the beginning of the 1960s, Abakanowicz adopted weaving as her principal artistic language, a discipline that, unlike painting, allowed her to explore materiality and texture. Characterised by abstract compositions in a style that was more lyrical than geometric, her first weavings distinctly shared common aesthetic qualities with her painted works.

In the years 1962–5, Abakanowicz sketched small models that she used as a guide for making large-format tapestries. She also created collages of cut-out pieces of paper, painted beforehand in a rich range of shades, translated into weaves using different types and thicknesses of wool as well as less common materials such as flax, cotton and rope, and later sisal and horsehair. These collages were an integral part of the design process, with each piece providing an essential shape, tone or rhythm for structuring the composition on paper before commencing work in thread. In this respect, Abakanowicz seemed to attach as much importance to the various conceptual stages of her work as to its final aesthetic form.

But these complex collages, composed of dozens of pieces of paper, can hardly be perceived only as preparatory precursors to her woven, sculptural works. The artist had always recognised the value of collage and drawing for their own sake,[1] further demonstrated when, in 1965, at Zachęta Centralne Biuro Wystaw Artystycznych (Zachęta CBWA), in Warsaw, some of her graphic and fibre works might have been displayed side by side – at a time when preparatory processes were not considered worth exhibiting.[2] Among the fifty works by Abakanowicz preserved by the Fondation Toms Pauli, there are three collages created in 1965 which are close in spirit to her textural composition, *Desdemona* (pp.52–3). Untitled but signed and dated on the back, these collages in deep and dense colours, covering the entire surface of the paper, are important works in their own right. (One of these is illustrated on page 160).

Between 1969 and 1971, Abakanowicz produced a series of expressive, almost hastily outlined, black drawings in gouache and ink. These abstract images resemble cosmogonic visions, as for example, one in which the ovoid forms divided into two hemispheres is reminiscent of the first maps of the world, or the spherical surfaces in a depth of black that suggests eternity (pp.164–5). The artist had already explored rounded shapes and contours in her *Abakans*, which had the effect of bringing life to the weavings. But these drawings vibrate with an inner energy which comes from rapid, extended brushstrokes that overlap and intertwine. The seemingly spontaneous combination of strokes and their watery forms create an illusion of three-dimensionality, just as the white spaces of the paper give an impression of depth and volume.

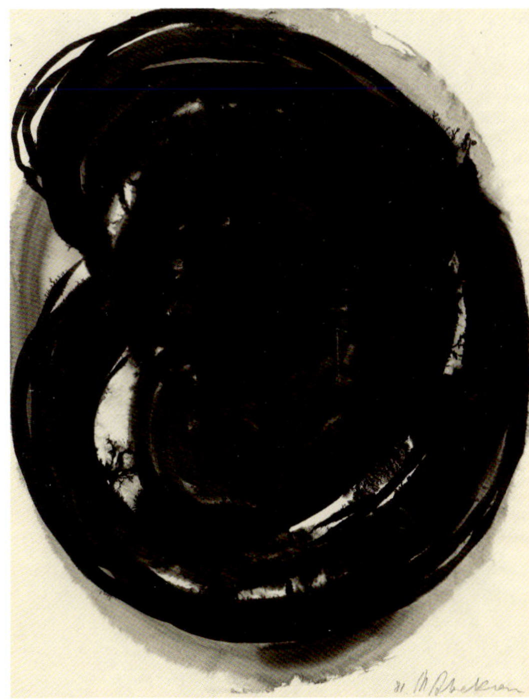

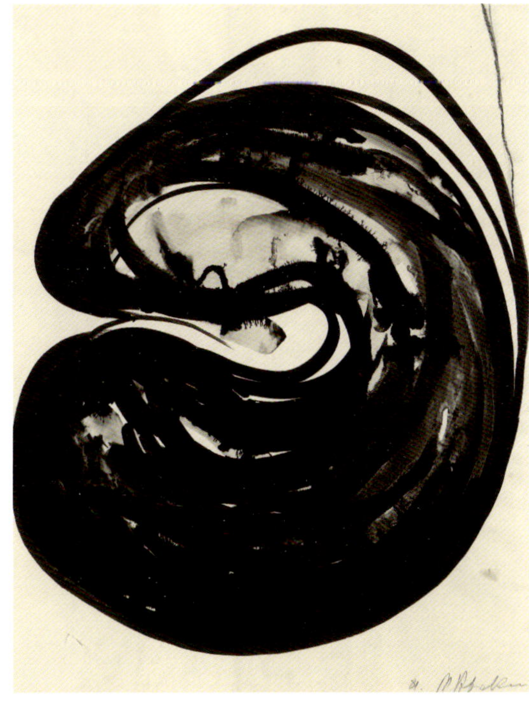

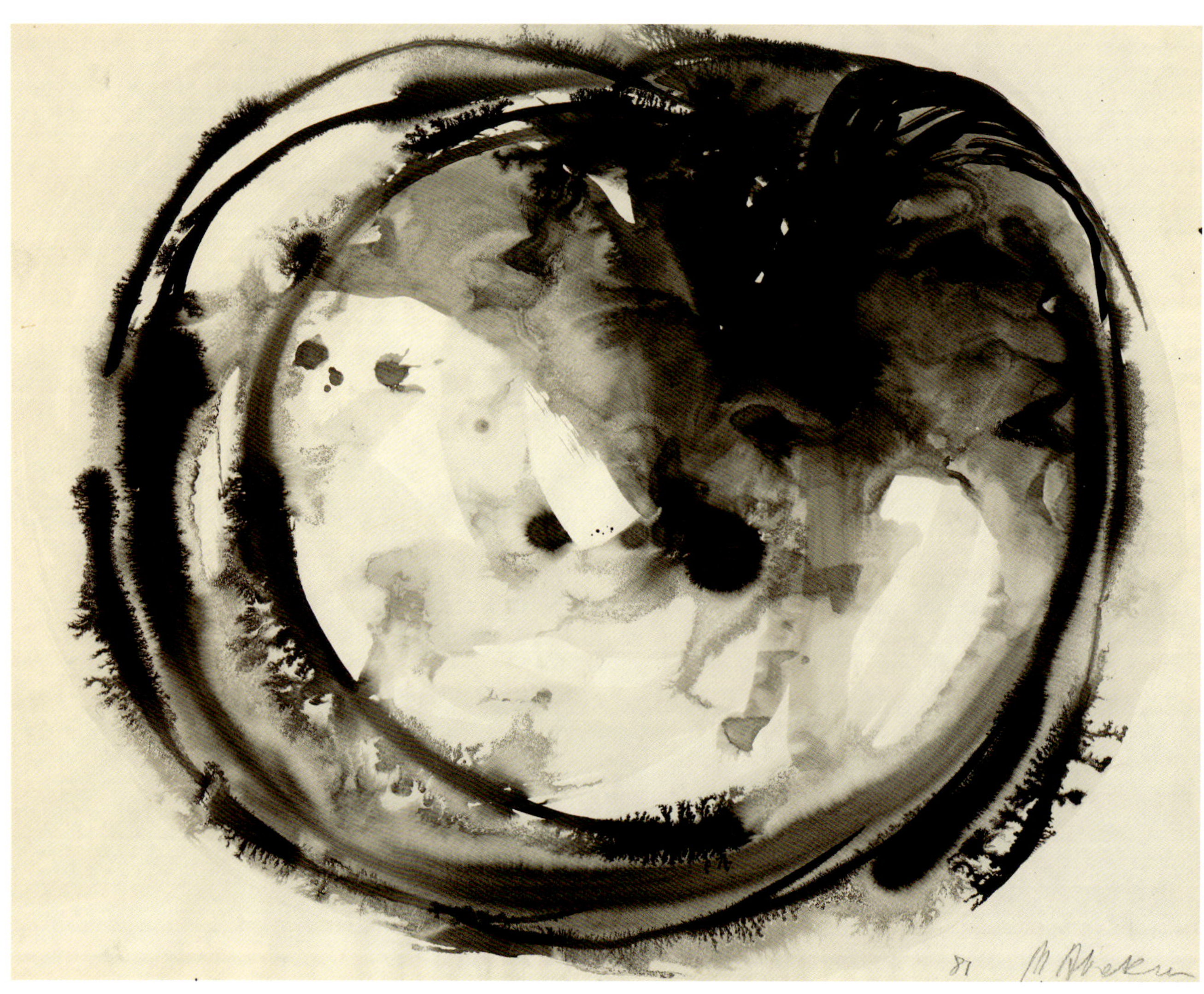

Above: *Embryology* 1981
Ink on paper
49 × 63

Below: The artist in her studio, 1981.

In 1973, through a cycle of work known as *Alterations*, Abakanowicz began exploring the human figure. She produced moulds of hollow and fragmented bodies, often grouped together in gripping scenes, laying bare the structure of the human species. By extension she also dealt with the biological world, as embodied in the *Embryology* series in 1978 (pp.174 and 176–7). The cocoon-like elements in cloth, stuffed with all manner of materials, were then captured in 1981 in black-ink drawings featuring spots, ink washes and blotches, and occasionally filled in with charcoal or graphite (pp.161–2 and 165). While relatively unknown compared to some of her other works on paper, such as *Bodies* and *Faces* created the same year, the *Embryology* series is nonetheless undeniably relevant and pregnant with symbolic power. Between figurative and abstract art, Abakanowicz sketched biomorphic images that resemble specimens that have been magnified under a microscope. The expressive gesture of these images suggests a notion of growth, inherent in nature and significant in her work.

Rather like snapshots, these paper versions of *Embryology* illustrate the development of biological forms (plant, animal and human), while the drawing technique contributes to the alchemy of the composition. On a partially damp sheet, the line drawn in ink dilates and prolongs the impulse given by the artist. The drawing thus takes on the surface aspect of cellular tissue; in relief, the blistered paper resembles living skin. Her drawings capture an astonishing vitality even though, most certainly due to the use of dark shades, her abstractions exude a sense of ominous threat, even death. However, in Abakanowicz's work black represented light and not darkness. In addition to the metaphor of an organic world that grows and changes, the circular repetition of brushstrokes seen in some of her drawings in the *Embryology* series is reminiscent of wound yarn out of which a textile object emerges, as in the work *Hand* 1975, also part of the *Alterations* cycle.

From the early 1980s, Abakanowicz's drawings began to enjoy a new status and were presented at several exhibitions.[3] In the 1990s and 2000s, alongside her increasingly monumental sculptures and environments, Abakanowicz's drawings maintained their relative importance: gouaches applied with a brush or fingers; webs of vivid and multidirectional lines in charcoal; and subtle ink and gouache washes. Some of her later drawings, which include the *Flies* and *Flowers* cycles, foreshadow her large-scale sculptures and installations in stainless steel. The *Flies*, *Embryology* and *Birds* ensembles bring to mind the insects, animals and flowers that characterised her early gouaches on linen executed in plain, bright colours in the second half of the 1950s.

In retrospect, the mental and physical link between Abakanowicz's drawings and the other mediums she used seems obvious. There was no border between them. Whichever discipline she employed, it enriched the others with its concept, execution and its respiration. It was one and the same driving force that ran through them all: the power of metamorphosis – that of the natural world from which the artist drew her inspiration, and that of an artistic practice forever developing and reinventing itself.

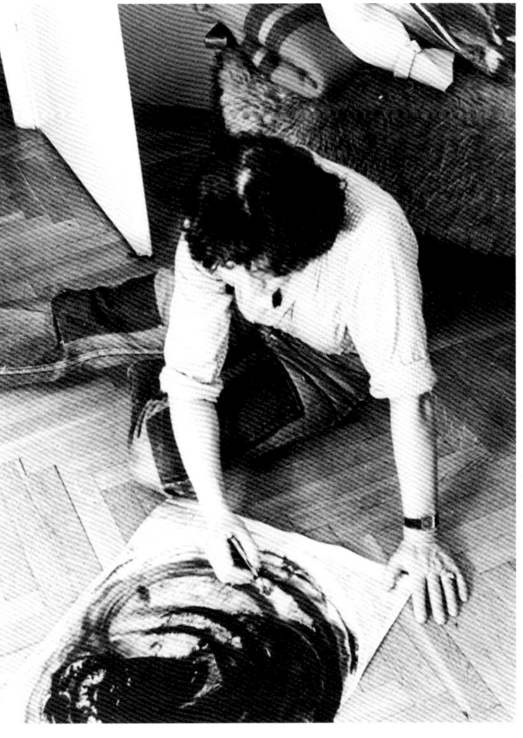

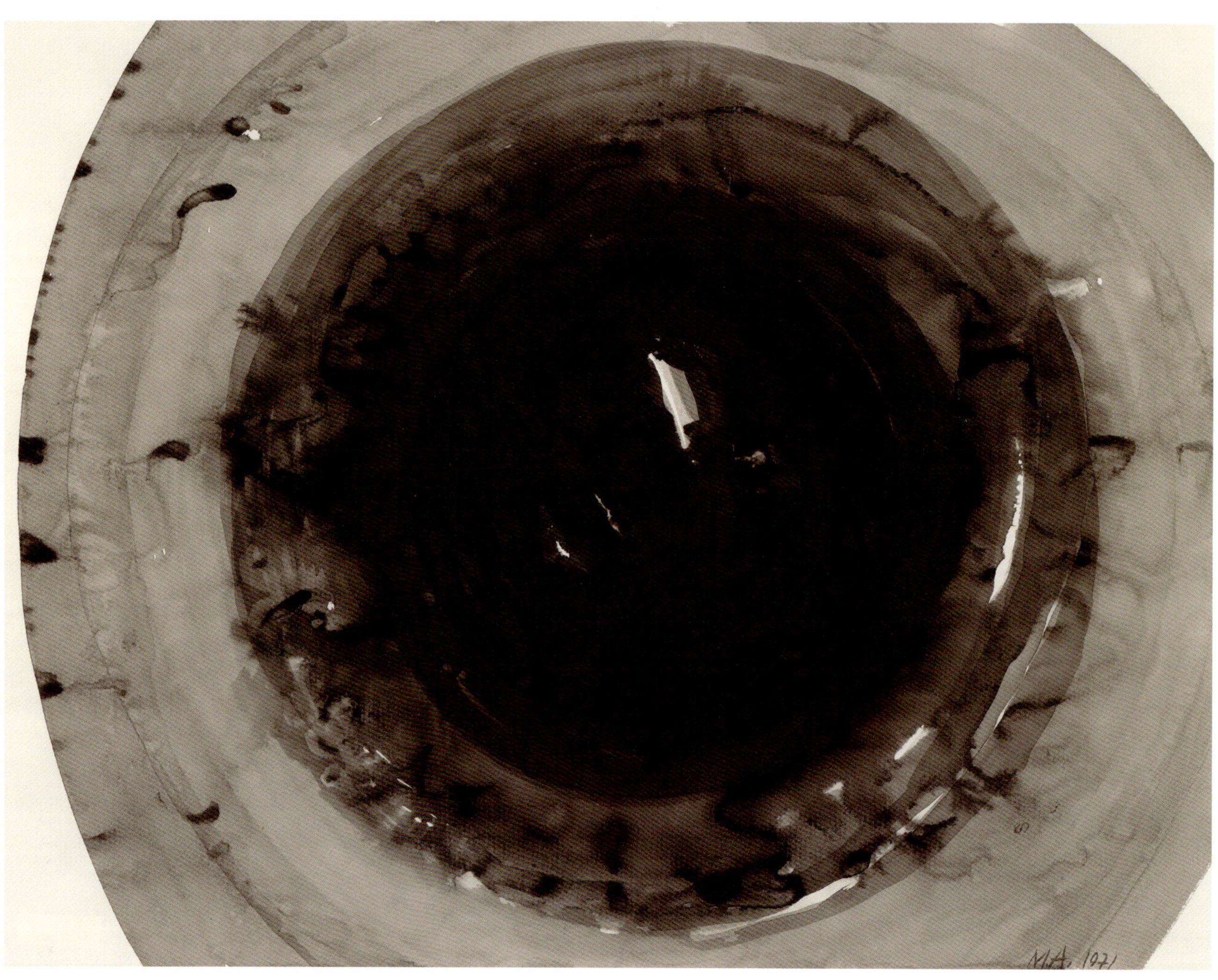

Above: *Untitled* 1971
Ink on paper
53 × 70

Right: *Untitled* 1971
Ink on paper
50.5 × 73

Below: *Embryology* 1981
Ink, charcoal and graphite
on paper
48.5 × 63

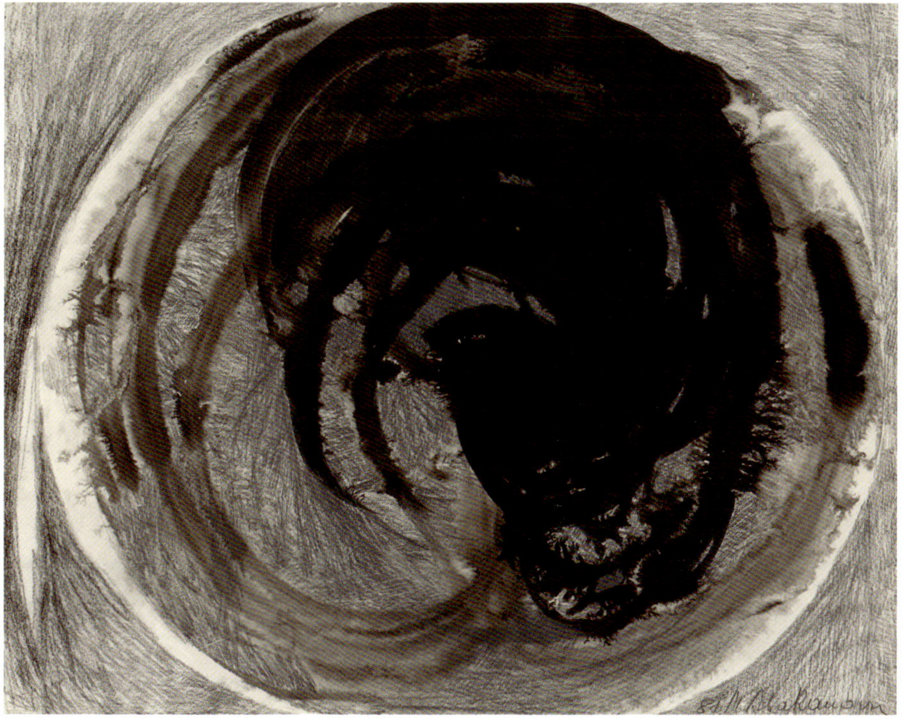

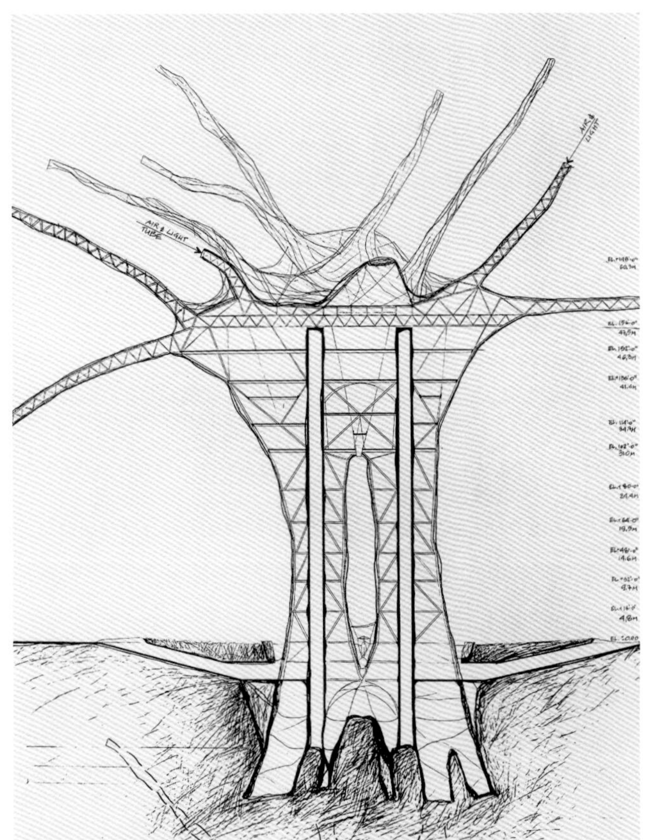
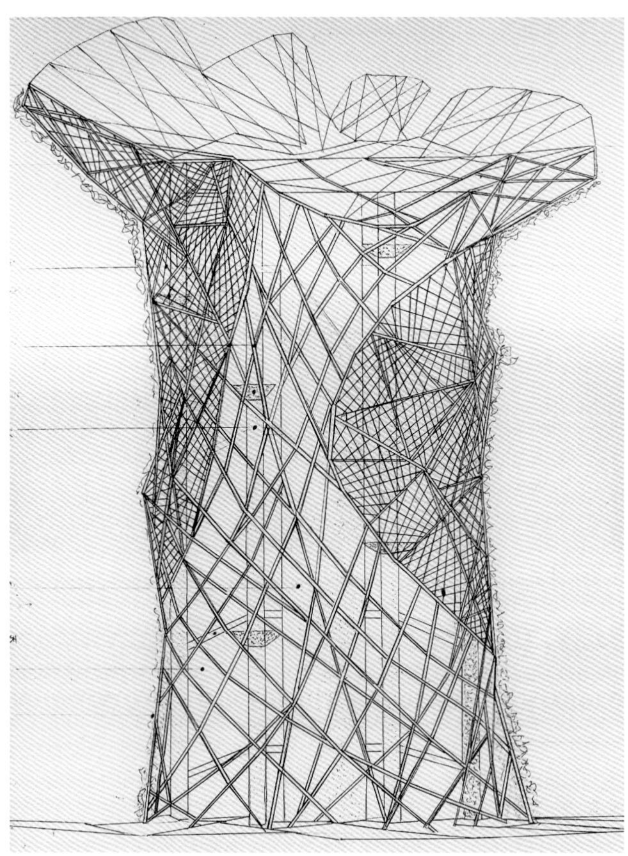

RETURN TO PARADISE
CONCERNING ARBOREAL ARCHITECTURE

CLARE LILLEY

Opposite: *Arboreal Architecture* 1991. Vertical sections of a 25-storey building showing the system for planting and irrigation.

Below right: *Inside Dwelling Trunk I* 1992 Charcoal and gouache on paper 100 × 75

Overleaf: *Anasta* 1989 from the series *War Games* Wood and steel 159 × 600 × 210

Throughout her life, Magdalena Abakanowicz emphasised the imperative that the natural world played in all facets of her being and work. She spent her childhood on her family's countryside estates outside Warsaw where her observation of biological cycles and an acute sense of animistic energies were activated. There she experienced companionship, apprehension and succour: 'Strange powers dwelled in the woods and lakes that belonged to my parents. Apparitions and inexplicable forces had their laws and their spaces.'[1]

The extreme trauma of Abakanowicz's childhood played out in the raw, uncompromising vision of her art, which unrelentingly explores man's inhumanity to man, animal and earth, yet speaks of the profound potential of mankind's other more beneficent nature. The Nazi invasion of Poland in 1939 wrenched Abakanowicz not only from her childhood but also from the peace of her marshlands and woods: 'Among the plants and the animals, everything was good. Man, I was unable to fathom.'[2] The parallel Abakanowicz drew between the good in human nature and nature itself – and similarly the harm inflicted – was established early in her life and expressed in a 1994 text, 'Banished from Paradise': 'Perhaps at that time in Paradise while eating the forbidden apple they lost the balance proper to nature – as one loses the sense of smell or eyesight. And perhaps at the same moment they acquired the instinct of destruction of the surrounding world and of themselves.'[3]

The solemn belief in the life-affirming essence of the natural world was quickly established as a constant in Abakanowicz's work and remained at the core of her practice; conflating machine, mankind, nature and the animal world, while highlighting man's misalliance with the earth, drawing on the sanctuary and innate truths that nature promises. Her early monumental paintings, such as *Butterfly* 1957, are immersive interpretations of creation and by the late 1960s the textile *Abakans* were objects of an immense scale and rich animalistic sensuality. Of these, perhaps none more so than the enormous sisal and wool *Bois le Duc* 1970–1: measuring over seven metres high and twenty-two metres long, it is a veritable forest (pp.75–7) as its name implies. Crucial to an understanding of Abakanowicz's identity, and indeed to the psyche of many Polish people, is the fact that more than a third of Poland is forested, with the UNESCO protected Białowieża Forest the last remaining primeval forest in lowland Europe. Playing a powerful role in the country's history, mythology and everyday life, the actuality and mystique of Poland's forests is deeply ingrained.

The monumental scale of *War Games* also owe their origin to the forest. These dark, menacing, sensual sculptures, which Abakanowicz created between 1987 and 1995, are made of felled trees that had been discarded by woodsmen in Poland's Masurian Lake district, a region that in adult life she loved deeply and to which she repeatedly returned, staying in the house of her dear friend, Artur Starewicz. The *War Games* works came directly from the rejected forest trees that lay close to the road: 'I looked at these huge bodies, muscular, wounded, but full of strength and personality: trunks with amputated limbs, in gestures of pain or protest or helplessness.'[4]

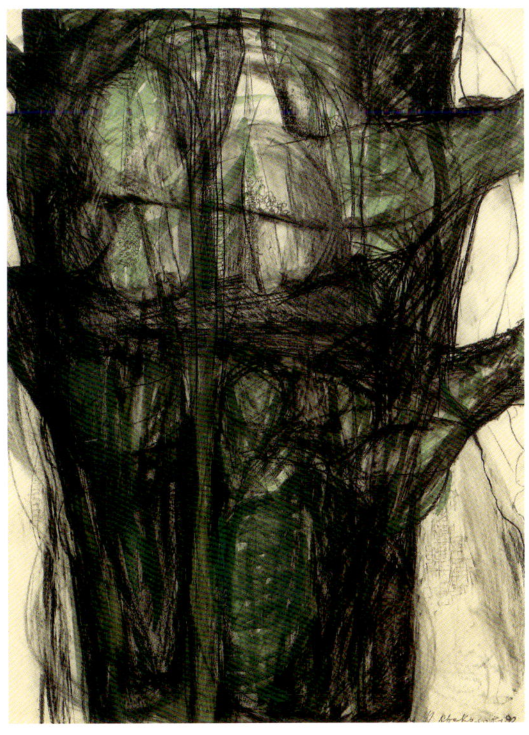

These she shackled, collared, extended, bound and stunted with weighty steel so that they allude variously to abattoir carcasses, medieval torture weapons, missiles or fighter planes. The decision to work with noble timber was not taken lightly; 'For a long time I couldn't use wood. I saw it as an entity finished in itself. Some years ago, suddenly I discovered the inside of an old tree trunk with its core like a spine entwined by channels of juices and nerves. I discovered the carnality of another trunk with its limbs cut off, as if amputated.'[5]

This series of seemingly inimical sculptures came in the wake of two years of martial law in Poland, at the start of which, on 13 December 1981, Abakanowicz re-experienced the terror of tanks rolling through the streets of Warsaw. The decade ended with Poland's first democratic elections since 1946, but also the appalling recognition of the devastation wrought by decades of acid rain, for many of Poland's once pristine forests are within the coal-fired industrial 'black triangle' of Dresden, Wrocław and Prague, and thus are particularly degraded. *War Games*, together with such series as *Coexistence* and *Mutants*, express Abakanowicz's understanding about the incompatibility between living beings and their environment. Meanwhile her *Space of Unknown Growth* 1998 (pp.170–1), firmly plants a group of twenty-two monstrous lumps of concrete sculpture into the Europos Parkas in Vilnius, Lithuania – brooding, malformed sentinels of the forest.

In 1990 Abakanowicz was selected by the Etablissement public pour l'aménagement de la région de la Défense to develop a public project for the Parisian axis that runs from the west of the Grande Arche to La Défense. Her ensuing conception, resulting from many years of enquiry into architectural forms and sustainability, was not a sculpture alone but a vast, living ecological architecture, which she named *Arboreal Architecture*. As early as 1968 Abakanowicz had travelled in the US, where she was captivated by the form and scale of canyons, deserts and skyscrapers alike. In the early 1970s she visited the radical eco-architect, Paolo Soleri (1919–2013) at Arcosanti, his experimental micro-city near Scottsdale in Arizona, after which they continued a correspondence and friendship. Still in development, for fifty years the feasibility of creating densely populated, low-impact built environments had been explored at Arcosanti. In 1980 Abakanowicz noted, 'I went to the desert of Arizona to talk to Paolo Soleri about the future of society',[6] indicating the depth and scope of her thinking. However, she rejected his theories related to social interaction in the city: 'Being raised in socialism, I knew the difference between theory and life. In the 1950s, we had in Warsaw a research center about housing development based on philosophy too close to that of Soleri. The practical results were negative.'[7] Naming the concept of the Paris project, *Bois de*

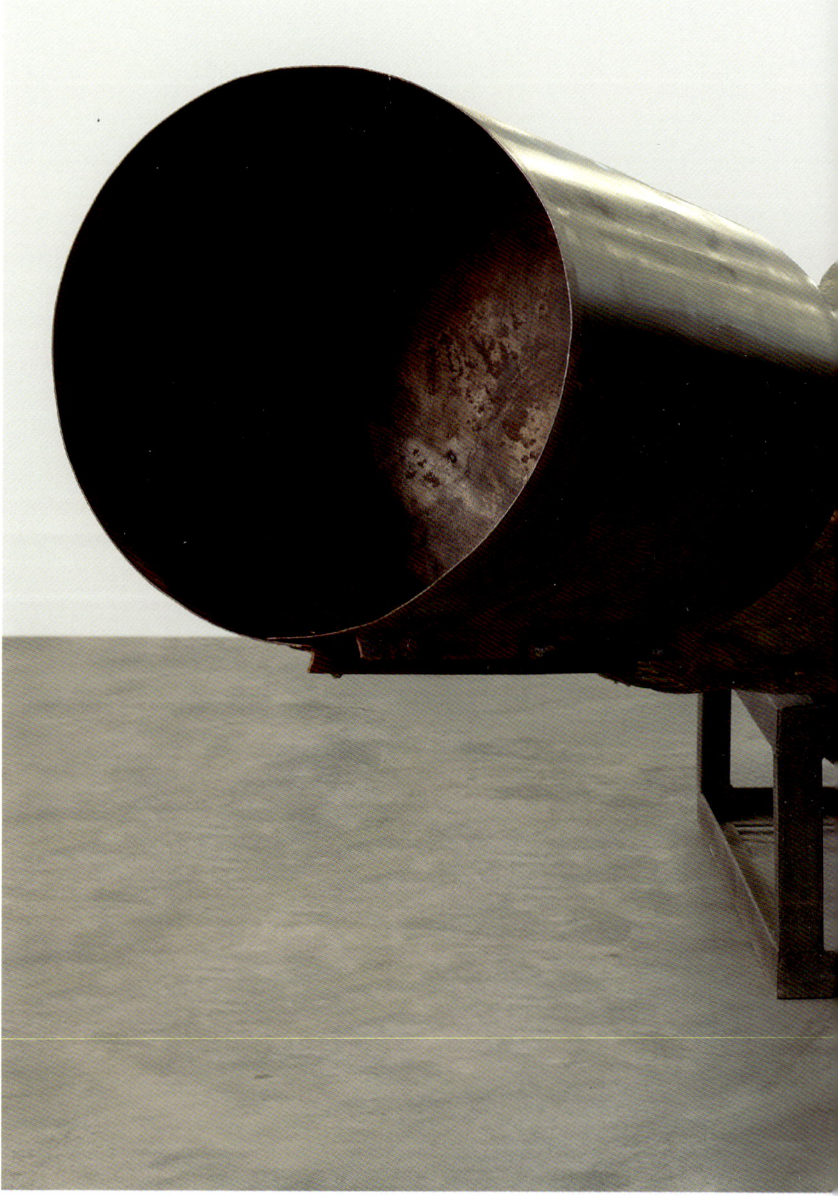

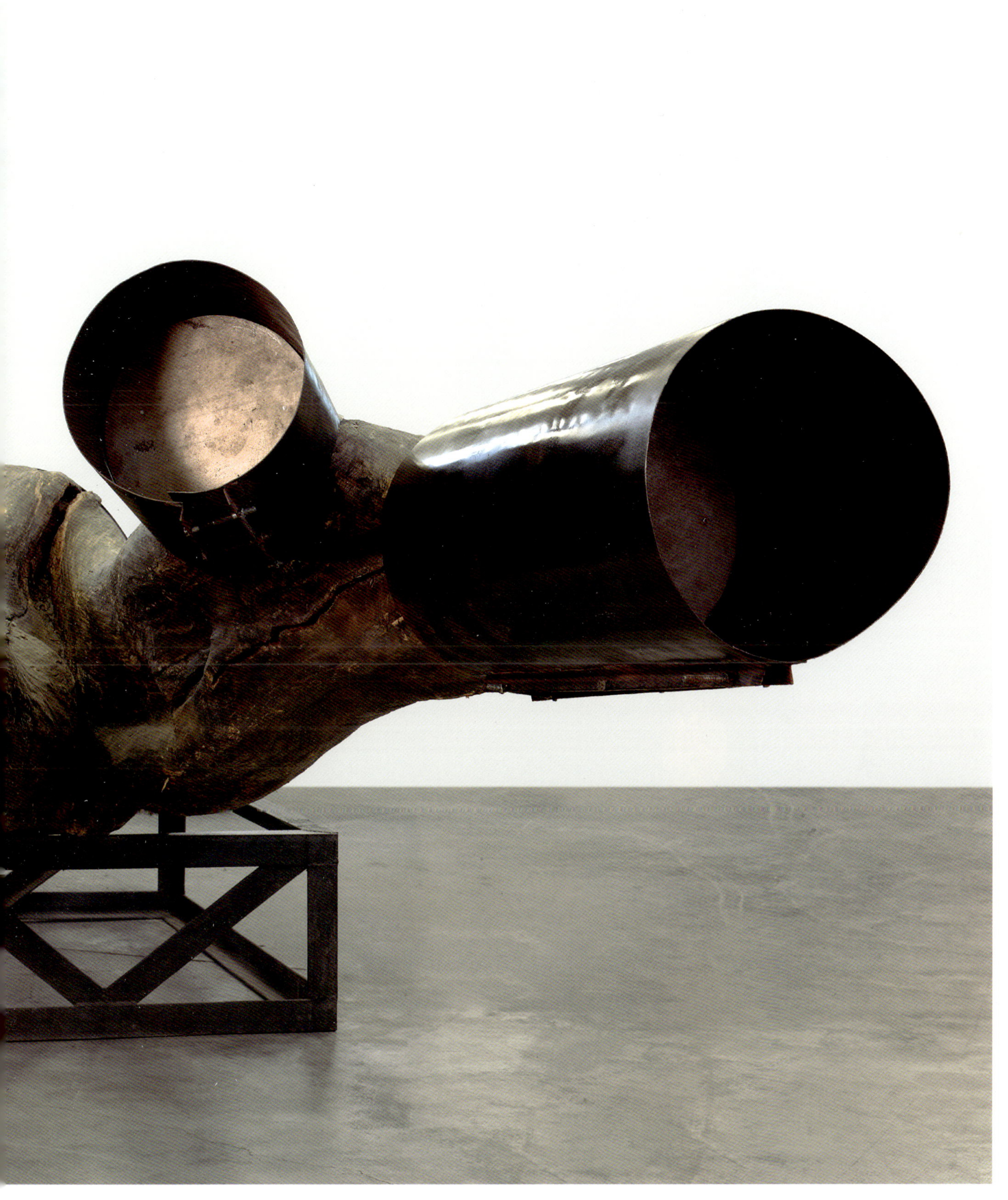

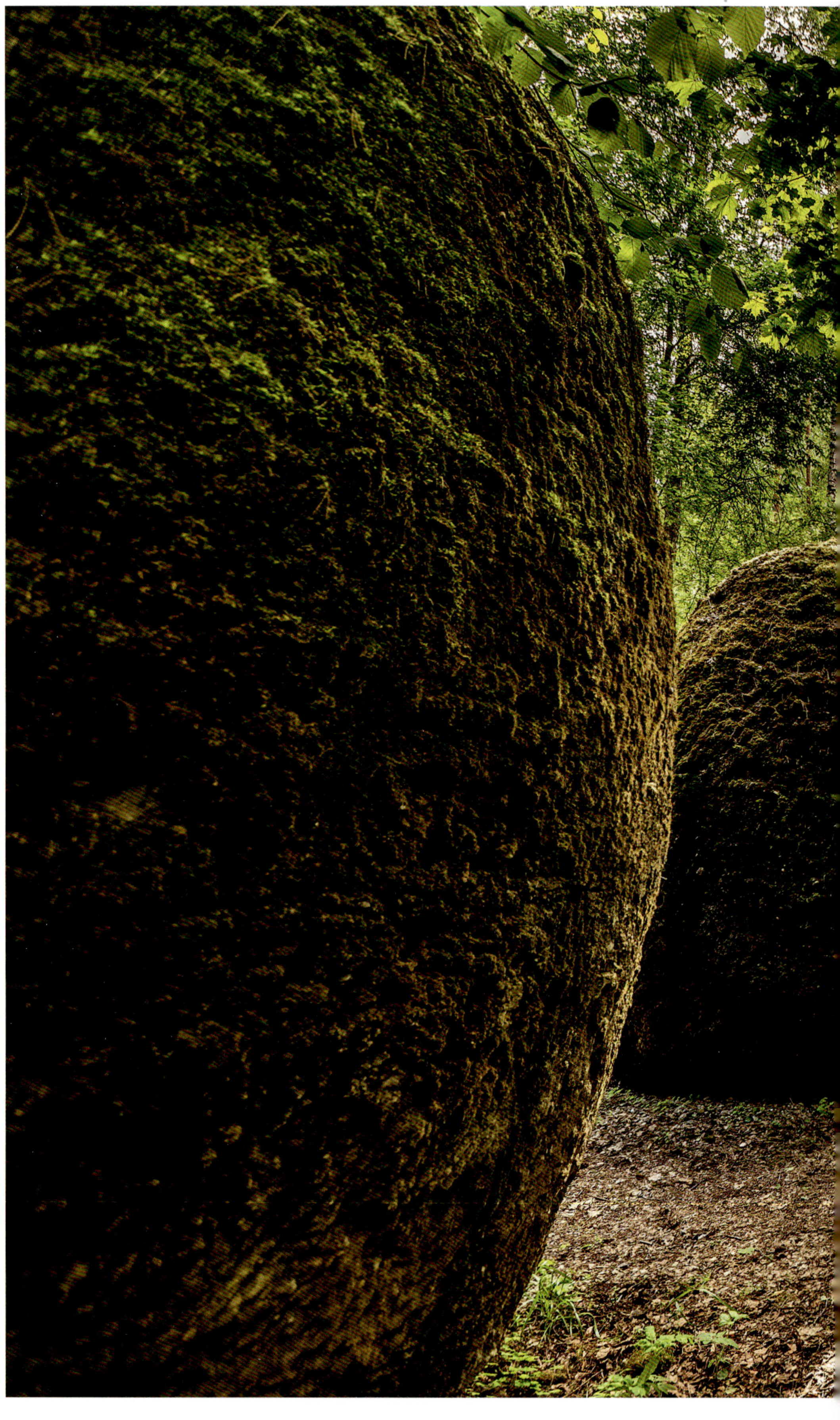

Space of Unknown Growth 1998
22 concrete elements in Europos Parkas, Vilnius, Lithuania.

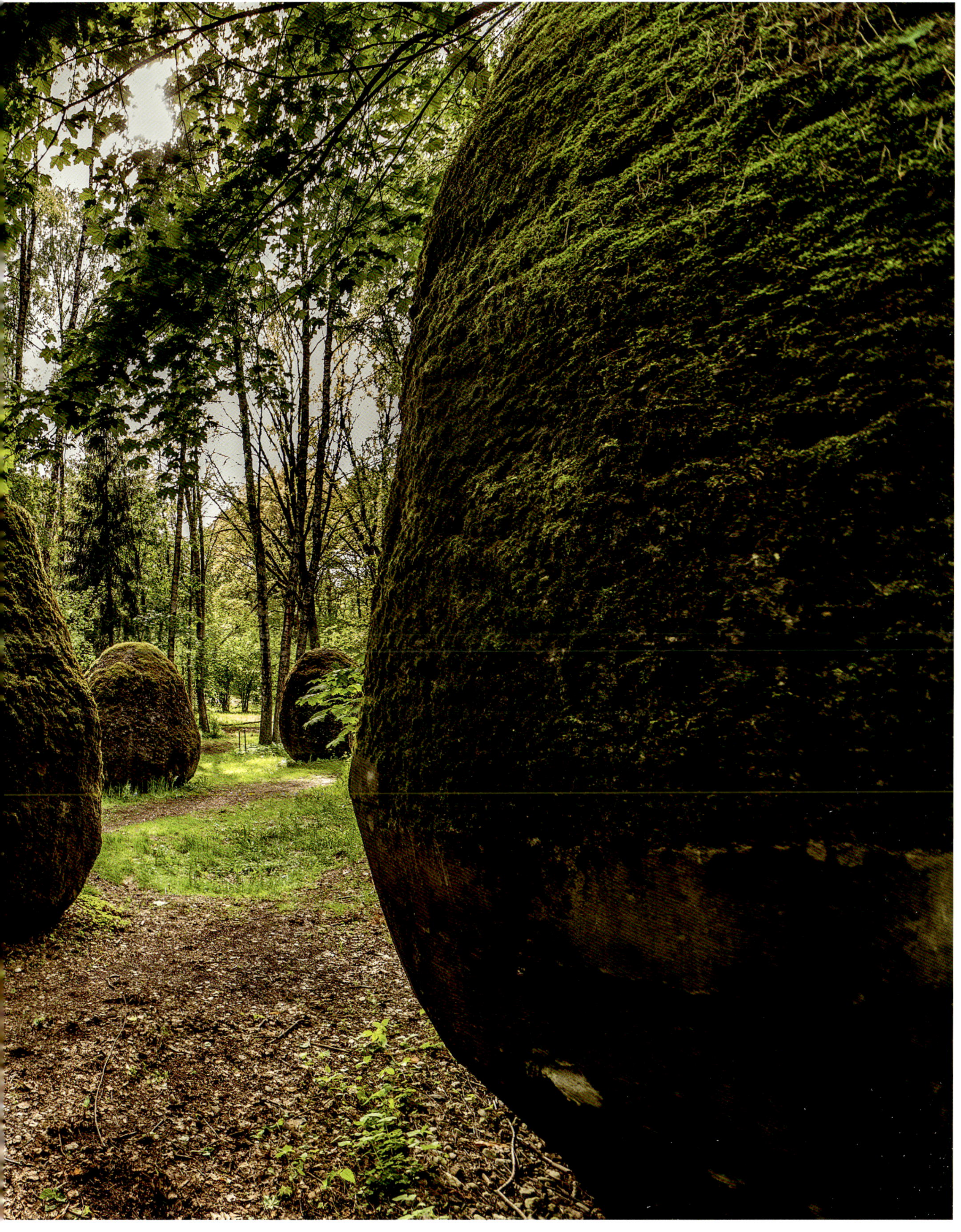

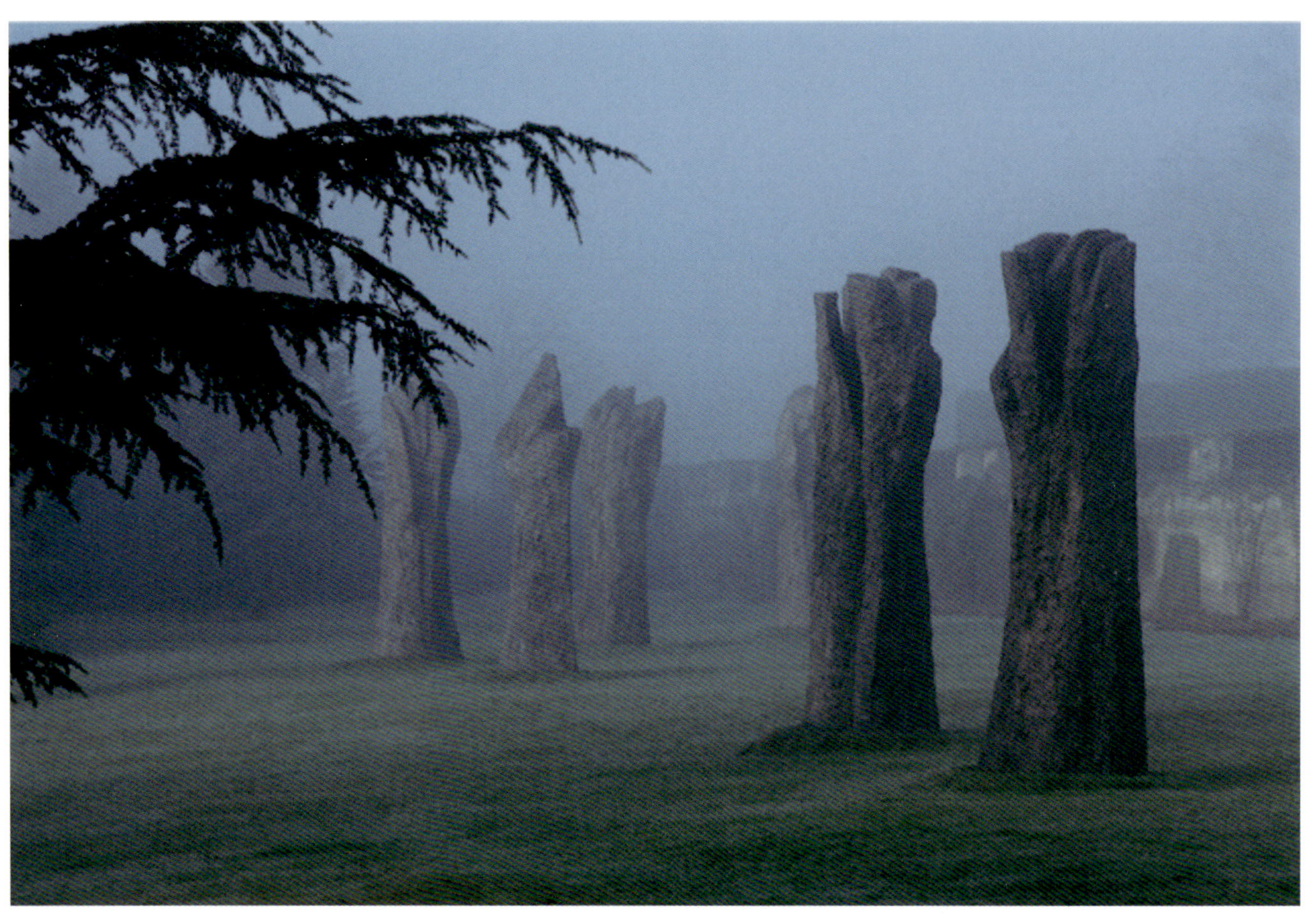

Hand-like Trees 1992–3
Bronze; each c.4 metres in height.
Installation view, *Magdalena Abakanowicz: Bronze Sculpture*, Yorkshire Sculpture Park, Wakefield, England, 1995.

Nanterre, she described it thus: 'I knew the shape must be organic, vertical, huge, 100 metres tall, a tree-like-building. And it must be followed by other tree-like-buildings. Many of them. An area of organic shapes. This should be the new western entrance to Paris: *Arboreal Architecture*!'[8]

> *Each of the arboreal buildings is a vertical garden. The façade is enveloped by trellises that support vegetation and are its irrigation system. Creepers and other plants would grow, beginning at the bottom and then at different levels of the façade ... The greenery produces oxygen. There are recreation areas with swimming pools on the top of each building, as well as wind turbines and solar energy collectors. In the underground, in the 'roots' are garages, commercial spaces, subway stations.*[9]

The scheme demonstrates the artist's understanding of environmental change and its causes – she refers specifically to the devastation of the rainforest – as well as experiments in sustainable architecture:

> *For the* Arboreals *I don't create any theory. Life shows what everybody needs and I try to answer to that. I also have the experience of the results of atomic disease: many people and animals suffered in my country after the Tscharnobyl [Chernobyl] accident. That's why I cover all branches of* Arboreals *with solar batteries. We also think about use of wind energy collectors placed on top of the building among branches. In this way each building could have its own source of energy.*[10]

But the artist also added: 'The *Abakans* and *Arboreals* have a similar richness in shape and surface, like a living organism. In the *Abakans* I am responsible for it. In the *Arboreals* I ask nature to do it following my design with full liberty'.[11]

Intensive research into the practicability of creating *Arboreal Architecture*, as well as growth platforms, irrigation, photovoltaic cells and other technologies, lasted for six years. Abakanowicz engaged with and was supported by many collaborators, including her cousin Andrzej Pinno (1927–2006), a philosopher and architect from the University of Texas at Arlington, and Boston-based architect Halina Starewicz who worked for the firm Gruzen Samton Steinglass in New York, and was the daughter-in-law of Artur Starewicz. Ultimately, the exceptionally forward-thinking scheme was not adopted and, following the death of President François Mitterrand (in 1996), neither was any other on such a scale in Paris. Enormously ambitious in concept, there is no doubt that *Arboreal Architecture* was ahead of its time, informed by technical research, an acute appreciation of form, scale and space, and imbued with understanding of the human condition. In a 1994 text, the art historian Michael Brenson wrote:

> *If the project looks ahead to what the planet may need to survive and if it demands the most advanced technology, it also acknowledges the world of ritual, magic, cruelty and wonder that Abakanowicz believes human beings must face and understand in order to have a better chance of leaving the destructiveness of our world behind. It looks far ahead and way back in time. It is a city, a forest, a body, a prayer.*[12]

In 1995 when the artist and I worked together at Yorkshire Sculpture Park, Abakanowicz spoke ardently about her *Arboreals*, describing them as green buildings able to nurture a mass of plants and trees and to be the lungs of a city. In my ignorance, I supposed she dreamed of a distant utopian future but in 2014, two towers (one of twenty-six floors, the other eighteen), conceived by Stefano Boeri Architetti (b.1956), opened near Milan. They are home to more than 20,000 trees and plants which are intended to convert carbon dioxide to oxygen while protecting the interior from noise and dust pollution and massively expanding the biodiversity of the locale. While there is some scepticism on the actual ecological effects of this project, it does bring to fruition something of Abakanowicz's vision from two decades previously.

While Abakanowicz's *Arboreal Architecture* was not realised, she developed in parallel the *Hand-like Trees*, a group of sculptures of around four metres in height, some with more branch-forms than others and most referencing the seemingly cruel labour of pollarding or the savagery of amputation (p.172). The severed form is one to which Abakanowicz repeatedly turned and its brutal metaphoric meaning is clear, particularly from an artist whose first-hand experience of war and totalitarianism was so barbaric: the coupling of such forms seems indissoluble with the artist's childhood memory of witnessing her mother's arm shot off entirely and the dismembered hand on the ground.

Abakanowicz's approach to Yorkshire Sculpture Park's eighteenth-century designed landscape and centuries-old trees was both informed and fine-tuned. Of the ninety-two sculptures installed there, including *Puellae*, *Standing Figures* and *Backs*, the six *Hand-like Trees* were the first to be sited. Comprising massive bronze trunks riven by gashes and cavities, these sculptures stood in stark contrast to the cultivated mature specimens of cedar of Lebanon, sequoia, beech, oak and more, yet they quickly asserted themselves in the garden and anchored the entire exhibition. Their truncated hand/arms – stumps or clenched fists – thrust into the sky in a powerful series of gestures, both vulnerable and defiant, were in tune with Abakanowicz's compulsion to make 'sites of spiritual shelter, of meditation, responding to the very old needs of the human existence'.[13] The work with Abakanowicz was intense but the exhibition reflected her consummate skill in handling sculpture and her adroit understanding of space and place. My first time in the installation entirely alone was early on a foggy October morning in 1995; jutting out of the earth and lit by a hazy autumn sunrise of pink and gold, these sculptures – poised, subtle, indefatigable – summoned the viewer to join their maker in her forbearance to endure, witness and prevail.

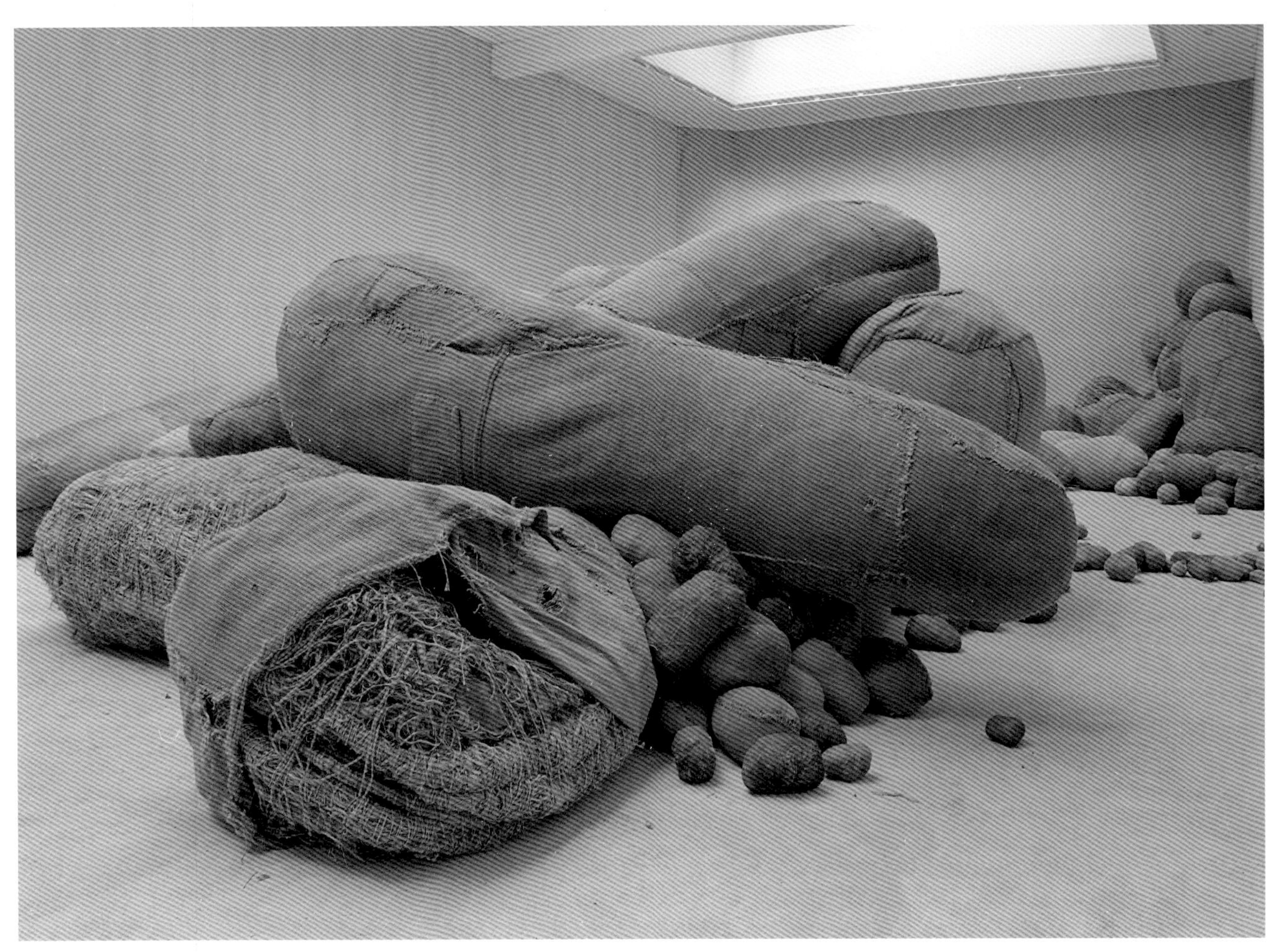

CELEBRATING AN ARTIST
ABAKANOWICZ IN WROCŁAW

IWONA DOROTA BIGOS

Left and overleaf: *Embryology* 1978–81 Burlap, cotton gauze, hemp rope, nylon, and sisal. Dimensions variable. Opposite: Installation view, Venice Biennale, 1980.

In the Four Domes Pavilion, the contemporary art branch of the Muzeum Narodowe in Wrocław, Poland, one can see some of the best examples of Magdalena Abakanowicz's work. This modernist building was designed by the German architect Hans Poelzig (1869–1936) for the exhibition to celebrate the centenary of the Prussian victory over Napoleon.[1] Since 2016, it has housed part of the museum's collection of modern and contemporary Polish art, including the world's largest number of works by Abakanowicz. The collection, which has extraordinary scope and coherence, came to the museum due to the enduring professional relationship between the artist and the museum's former director Mariusz Hermansdorfer.[2] It was he who, very early on, recognised the universal and timeless significance of Abakanowicz's work and what it communicates about the human condition.

Hermansdorfer first met Abakanowicz in the late 1970s,[3] but it was not until the 1990s, when they worked closely together to organise a series of exhibitions across Japan and Europe (primarily in Wrocław),[4] that mutual trust was truly established. He had been pursuing a determined policy of acquiring the work of outstanding Polish artists of the second half of the twentieth century and beginning of the twenty-first. By 1986 he had already bought two very important works by Abakanowicz: *Embryology* 1978–81 (opposite and overleaf) made up of more than 200 of the elements first shown in 1980 in the Polish Pavilion at the Venice Biennale (opposite), and twenty-six figures from the poignant series *Backs* 1976. Both these formally very different works still surprise with their deep message and testify to the artist's insight into both nature and human nature. The egg-like forms of *Embryology* belie the artist's lifelong interest in that shared among living things and with this work she explores the edges between gestation and decay using guaze and stockings, as well as coarse sacking, to give a view of an interior world of indefinite origin. By contrast, the *Backs* are recognisable not only by their human form but also expression. Likened to meditation, prayer, obedience or despair, they remain nonetheless enigmatic. The range of their significance and interpretation possibilities is profoundly demonstrated by the creation of forty bronze elements titled *Space of Becalmed Beings* 1993, created as a memorial for the Hiroshima City Museum of Contemporary Art, in Japan.

From the beginning, Hermansdorfer sensed the strength and timelessness of Abakanowicz's works and watched her career with interest.[5] Over the years, their dialogue led to the expansion of the collection, enriched through both acquisitions and gifts from the artist to include the notorious *Abakans*. In the 1960s, *Abakans* were revolutionary, their three-dimensionality and complex forms were difficult to categorise and shook the world of Fiber Art. They emanated with magical strength and allowed the artist to break artificially imposed boundaries between art from within and outside the Iron Curtain. The *Abakans* were not only a breakthrough in thinking about art, but also in Abakanowicz's career, enabling her to appear on the world art scene. The ambiguity of her works, their dimension and their timelessness made her one of the most interesting artists of the 1970s. To a large extent, this enabled her to create other, very experimental and, at that time, unpopular sculptural forms, using man, his entanglements and tragedies as the starting point.

The museum's collection encompasses twenty-eight *Abakans* including *Abakan Open* 1967–8 (p.101), *Abakan Round* 1967–8 (pp.95–9), *Abakan Festival* 1971 (pp.102–3) and *Black Forms* 1970–8 (later called *Black Environment*), consisting of fifteen parts. Yet exceptional among these is *Abakan January–February* 1972 (pp.136–9) for its unique form, its richness of colour, and its commanding presence.[6] A bifurcated work, these two mirror images seem at once tenuously connected and determinedly strong. Like the bicameral heart, its focalpoint is the sinuous threads that pulsate with life, keeping beings alive.[7] As the artist wrote in 1978: 'Our heart is surrounded by the coronary plexus, the plexus of most vital threads. Handling fiber we handle mystery ... The threads I weave make up homogeneous fabric, the expression of which depends on the tension or the relaxation of my nerves. On the inner circulation of the juices under my skin.'[8]

The museum continues to build upon the great foresight and exceptionally diligent work of its former director. His intention and dedication were evident in these words with which he bade farewell to the artist at the Powązkowski Cemetery in Warsaw on 27 April 2017:

> *No Polish artist, and very few others, have equalled her achievements. Thanks to her, Polish art asserted its presence in various countries on every continent, in renowned museums and art galleries, in private collections, and in public spaces.*
>
> *Thanks to her, there was a revolution in artistic weaving, which for centuries had been decorative, flat and designed to embellish walls and floors. Instead Abakanowicz positioned her woven works in space – strong, biological, soft sculptures that are symbols of life.*
>
> *Thanks to her, there arose a terrible vision of societies subordinated to totalising systems and crowds of brainless, headless and hollowed-out figures arranged in prison gangs and queues.*[9]

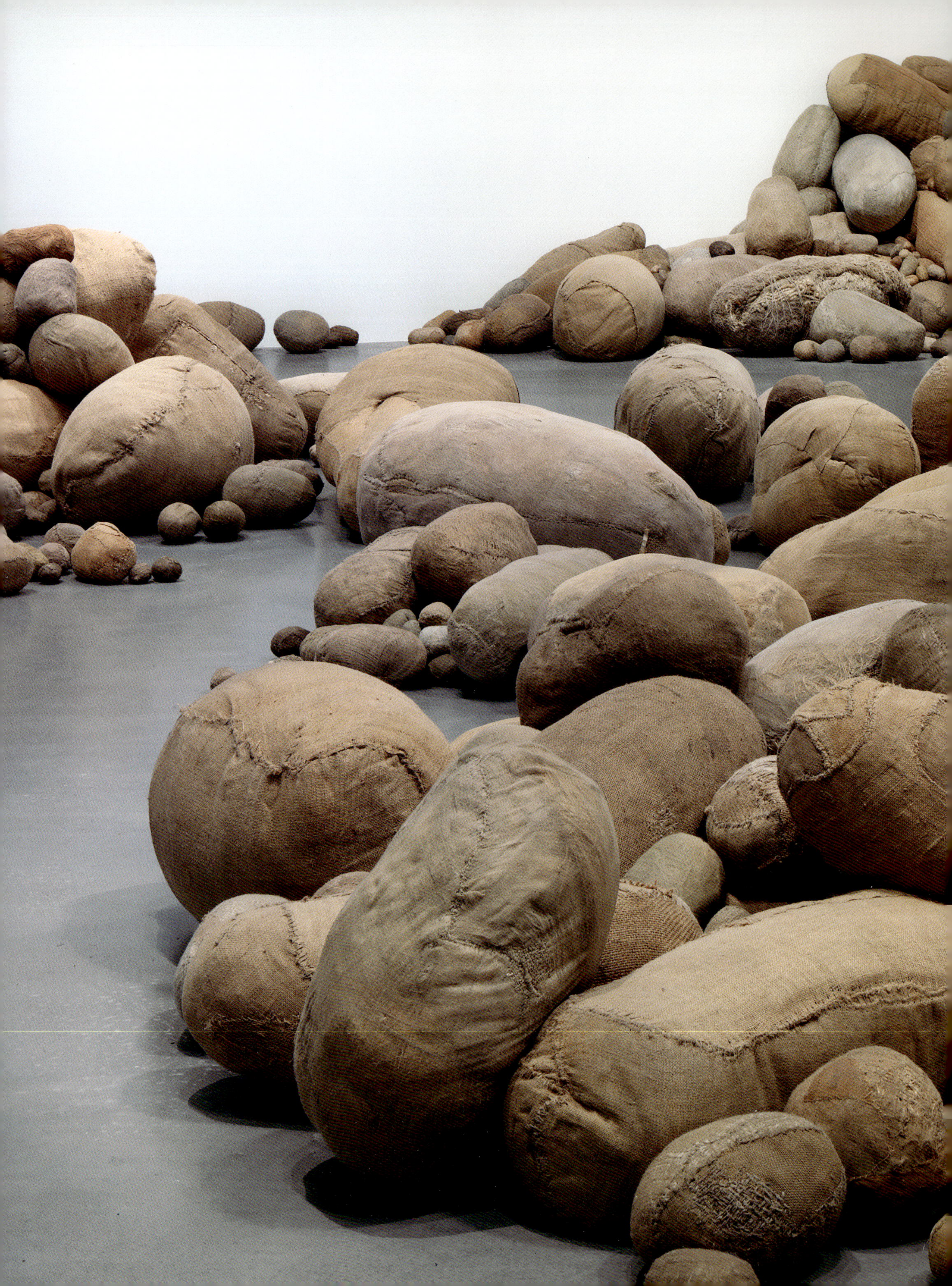

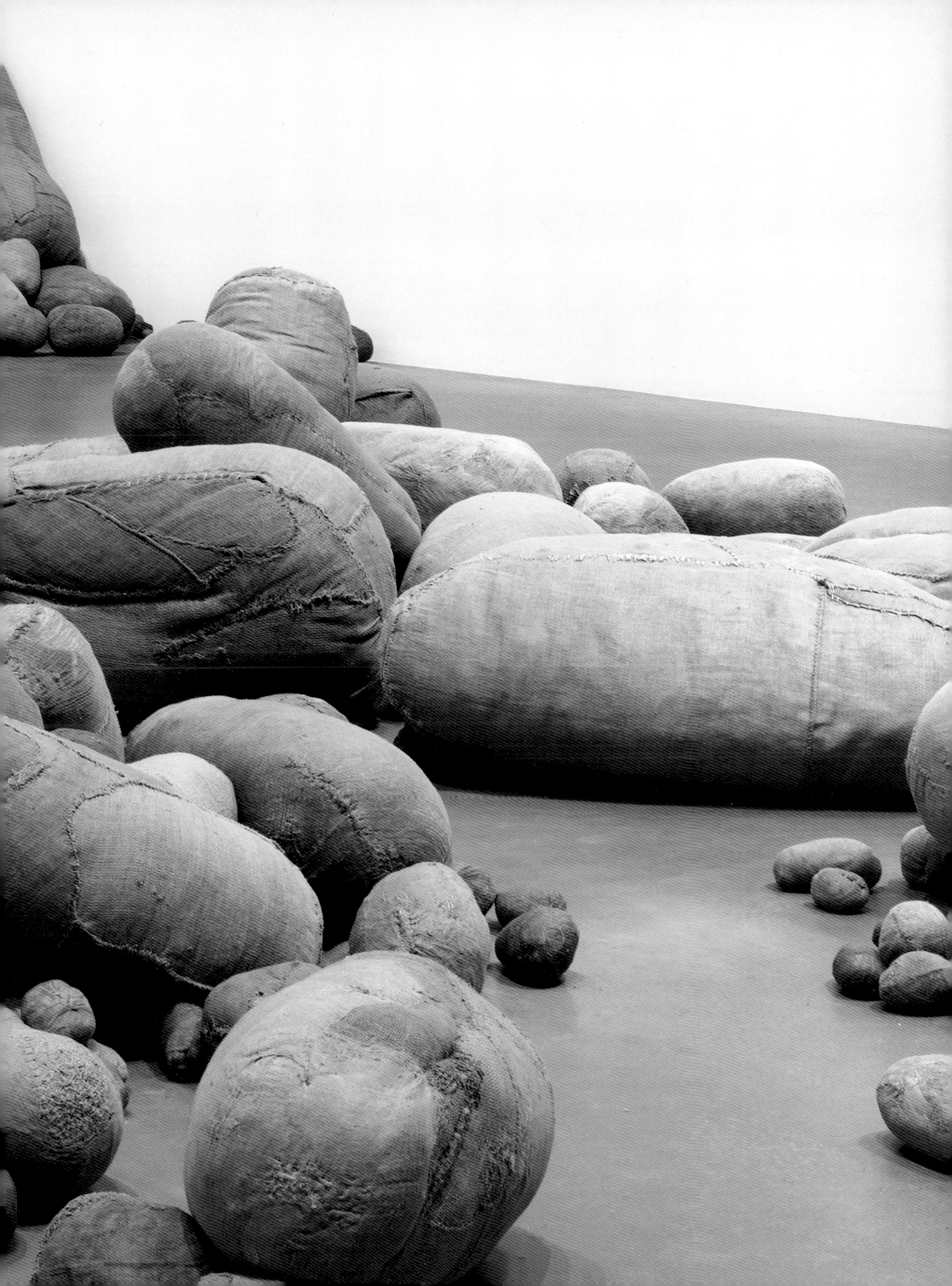

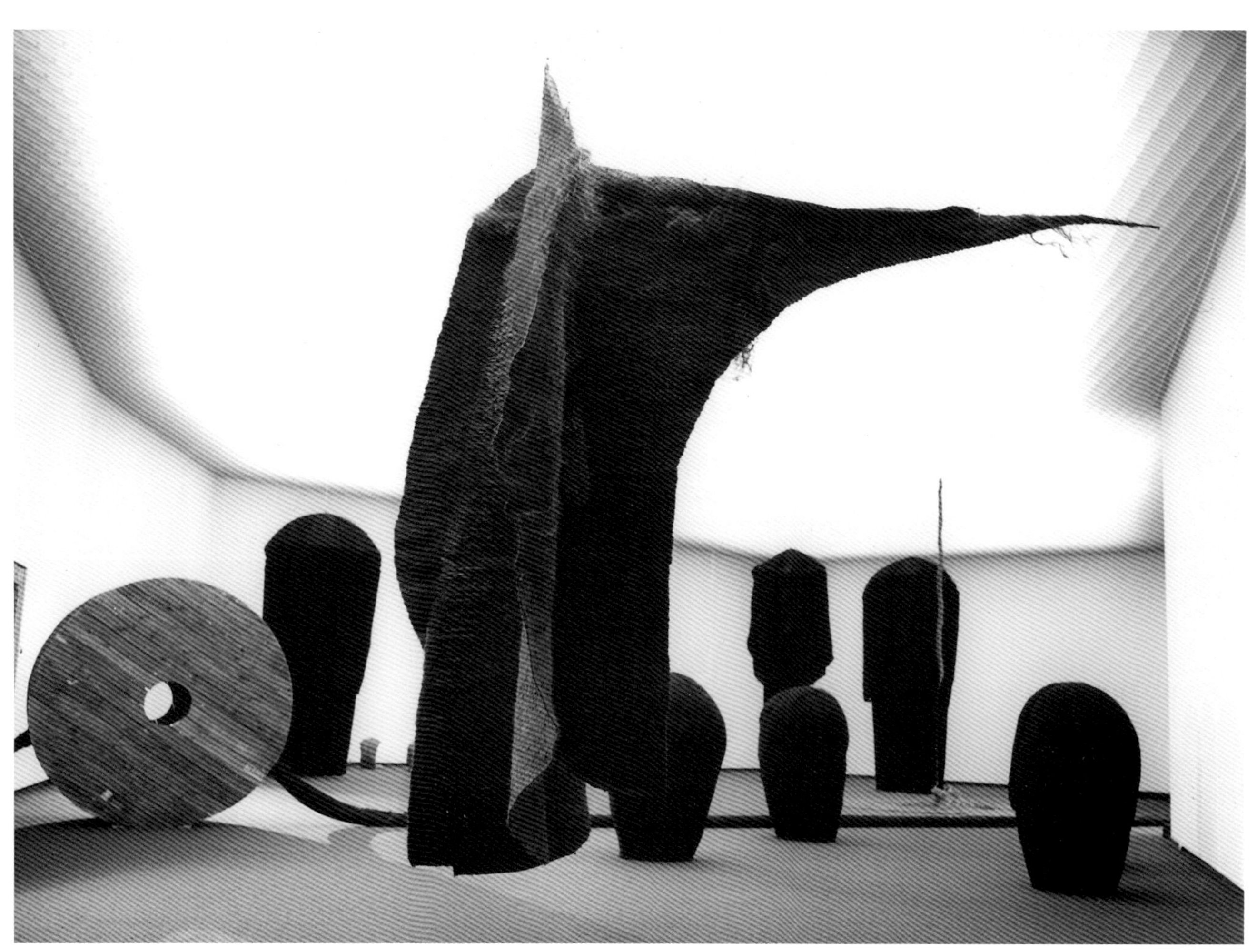

ORGANIC STRUCTURES
ABAKANOWICZ IN NORWAY

CAROLINE UGELSTAD

Opposite: *Abakan Red* 1969. Installation view, *Magdalena Abakanowicz: Organic Structures*, Henie Onstad Kunstsenter, Høvikodden, Norway, 1977.

Two of Magdalena Abakanowicz's first solo shows took place in Norway, in 1967 and 1977. The exhibitions of this pioneering artist presented something entirely new for Norwegian artists and audiences and incited strong reactions. Within ten years, one could witness the surprising and powerful development of Abakanowicz's work,[1] and why it had such a remarkable impact on the fields of sculpture and Fiber Art.

The art of weaving was not, by any means, unknown in Norway. In the years around 1900, a tapestry renaissance occurred, spearheaded by Gerhard Munthe (1849–1929) and Frida Hansen (1855–1931). Munthe made templates for tapestry, drawing inspiration from Norwegian folk tales, Norse history and mythology, art nouveau and the English arts and crafts movement. Hansen was interested in rediscovering and preserving Norwegian tapestry traditions. Hansen, and later, Hannah Ryggen (1894–1970) were the first women in Norway to be recognised as both artists and craftswomen working with weaving. Hansen is considered the first practitioner of modern Norwegian fibre art, while Ryggen's efforts in changing the perception of weaving into an expressive visual art, which could comment on world events, were no less pioneering. Together with Ryggen, Synnøve Anker Aurdal (1908–2000) also contributed to a new era for Norwegian fibre art in the early 1960s.

In 1962, Abakanowicz had her international breakthrough at the 1st International Tapestry Biennial in Lausanne, Switzerland. The Norwegian art historian, Alf Bøe, at this time chief curator at Kunstindustrimuseet in Oslo, and later director of the Munchmuseet, in the same city, was among those she impressed. Abakanowicz's large work, *Composition of White Forms* 1962, which received immediate attention at the biennial, had, according to Bøe, an unusually rich texture. He remarked upon the spontaneous expression that Abakanowicz had achieved by weaving without using a cartoon (traditionally, weavers used the cartoon as a guide to weave the coloured threads on the loom, replicating the chosen pattern), and he noted the absence of the smooth surface in the artist's work: 'The technique is rough, and the carpets are far from flawless – the surfaces bulge, and the weave is uneven. Yet, the composition and colour of these tapestries work together with an expression that is embedded in the texture of the material itself, so that we are, to some extent, facing compositions in material.' According to Bøe, these were lush works with great uniqueness. 'They mean something new in the great European tapestry tradition and have given artists from other weaving countries something to think about'.[2]

Woven Works

Abakanowicz's approach to fibre would become an important source of inspiration to Norwegian artists, just as it was for the international development of fibre art throughout the 1960s and the 1970s.[3] At this time, Norwegian artists were particularly aware of Polish fibre art, which was exhibited in Norway as part of Poland's propaganda for Polish art and culture abroad,[4] with some artists choosing to leave Norway to continue their studies in Poland. These were pivotal years during the struggle to transform the understanding and categorisation of woven objects as mere craft rather than fine art. A new radical feminism and a time of political change helped pave the way.[5]

Upon an invitation from Alf Bøe, Abakanowicz held her first solo exhibition in Oslo. *Woven Works* was presented at the Kunstindustrimuseet, travelling thereafter across the country to Bergen, Stavanger and Trondheim. The exhibition's twenty-six works, primarily made between 1966 and 1967, were mounted on the wall like large paintings. Among the works on display were the abstract compositions *Dorota* 1965 and *Desdemona* 1965 (pp.52–3), works that were rich in colour, in earthy tones, light beige, reddish-brown and black. Yet, there were also white colour variations, such as in *White* 1966: interspersed with an open, vertical slit, this was an example of how Abakanowicz began to sculpt her works in relief. One work, *Column* 1967, 380-cm high and shaped like a cylinder, was mounted from the ceiling as a free-hanging sculpture. This marked the start of Abakanowicz's three-dimensional works called *Abakans*, which she presented in Oslo ten years later at Henie Onstad, to critical acclaim.[6] The exhibition would prove significant in the ongoing struggle to recognise textile art as fine art. Indeed, many reviewers believed that Abakanowicz's work had abolished the distinction between the two.

Organic Structures

The 1977 Henie Onstad exhibition *Organic Structures* included fifty-eight works from the last decade, and two of the most notable groups of works in Abakanowicz's oeuvre: the large, three-dimensional woven objects known as the *Abakans*, which were hung from the ceiling, and defined as textile sculptures, and the *Alterations* – human forms, torsos, heads and hands woven or sewn in sisal and sackcloth and placed on the floor (opposite and overleaf). One of the most significant works on display was *Abakan Red* 1969 (opposite and pp.124–9), which at a monumental size of four by four metres, must have looked imposing. Another key work was *Black Forms* 1970–8 (later called *Black Environment*), which consists of fifteen high-rise cylindrical objects resembling trees and hung from a wire-shaped structure. Also featured was *Black Garment with Sack* 1971, a five-metre-high sculpture, suggestive of a human monster, judge or god, a giant without a head – a ritual figure perhaps, or a totem, extended from floor to ceiling (p.180).[7]

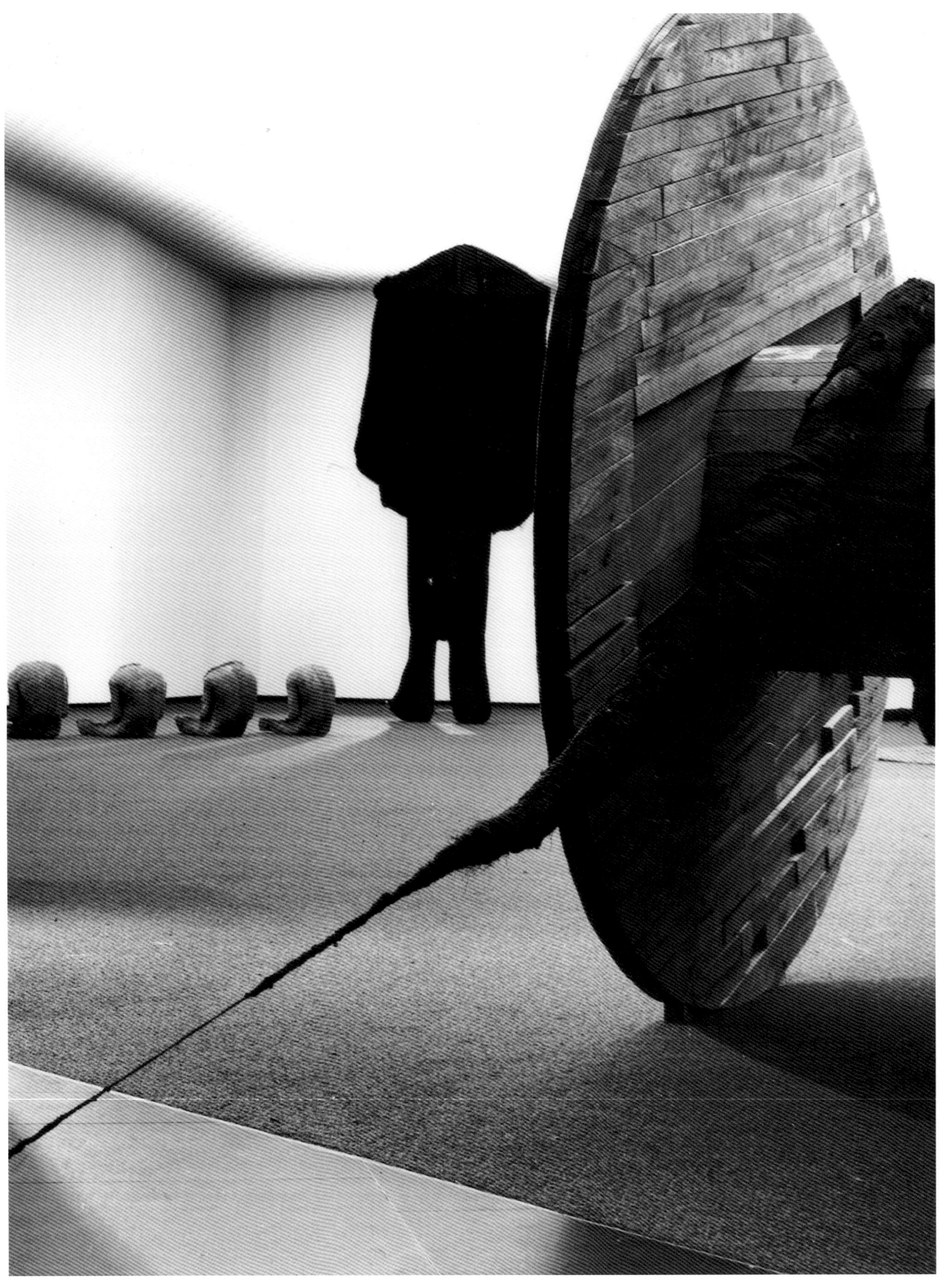

Opposite: *Wheel and Rope* 1973, with *Black Garment with Sack* 1971 and *Backs* 1976–7. Installation view, *Magdalena Abakanowicz: Organic Structures*, Henie Onstad Kunstsenter, Høvikodden, Norway, 1977.

Right: *Heads* 1973–5 and *Seated Figures* 1974–5, from the series *Alterations*, in the same exhibition.

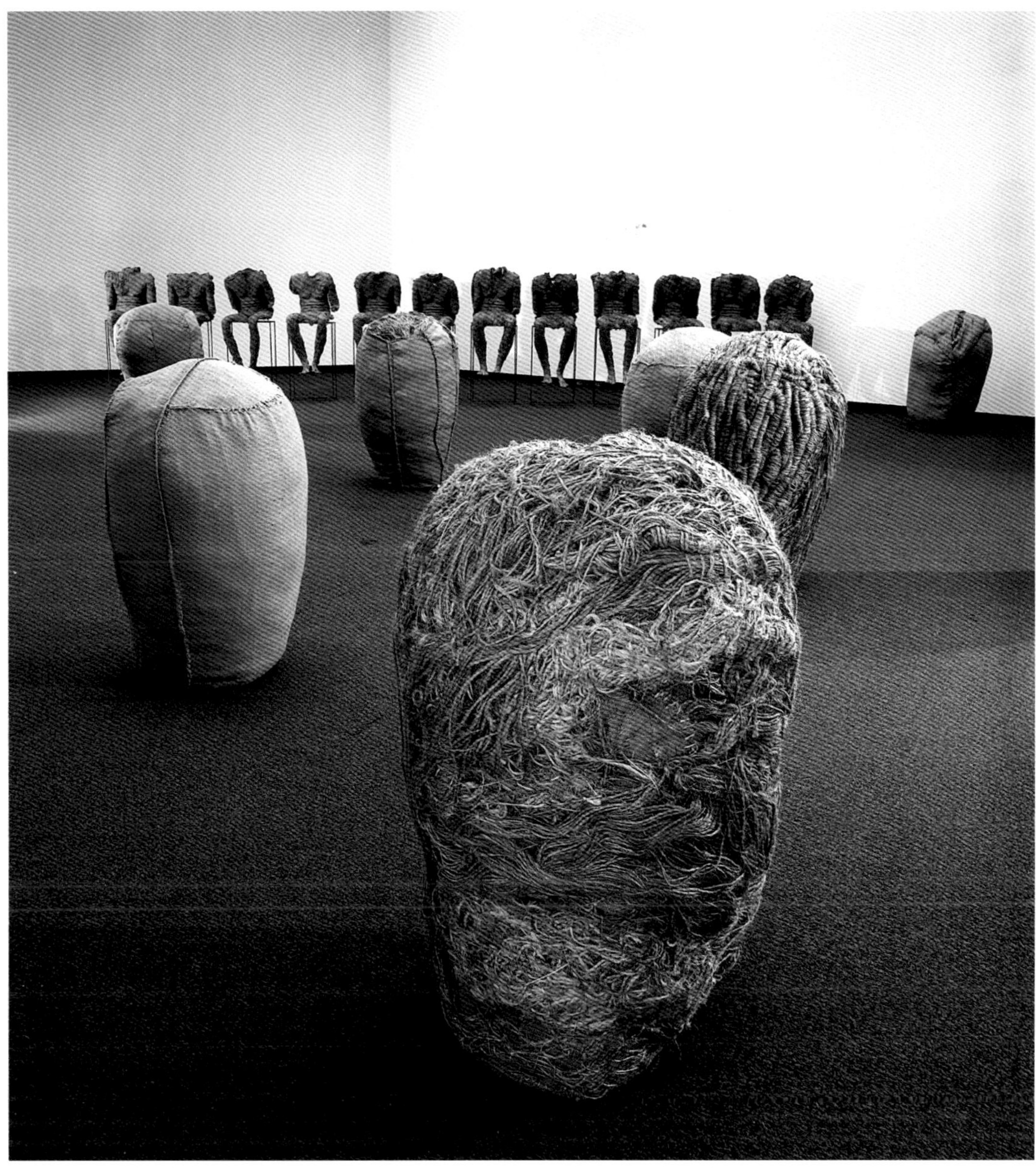

The *Organic Structures* exhibition is said to be one of the first examples of installation art in Norway, where the space, work and environment merged.[8] This interplay between the artworks and the architecture was deemed particularly successful. Some critics called the artistic quality and the innovation of the works into question.[9] Others declared Abakanowicz's work an 'earthquake in the visual arts', which had created a set of unforeseen and new dimensions.[10]

Monumental Terms

Abakanowicz was one of the first women artists to gain international recognition. In Norway, her exhibitions contributed to an increased interest in fibre art and helped to establish it as an independent artistic medium. Her use of materials, such as sisal, ropes, wool and horsehair to build monumental three-dimensional sculptural works, brought something new. As an exhibition, *Organic Structures* was particularly groundbreaking in the way it built up a scenic space for the artist's own works. It demonstrated a self-confidence that stood out among the practice of her contemporaries.

In the 1980s, a new generation of fibre artists emerged in Norway, who experimented with new materials and made three-dimensional works for display in the exhibition space and not necessarily on the walls.[11] If these artists were not directly inspired by Abakanowicz, her legacy is indirectly present precisely in the fact that fibre art continues to be a medium of increasing importance in Norway, which has gradually also become a part of the art institution's collections and programming.

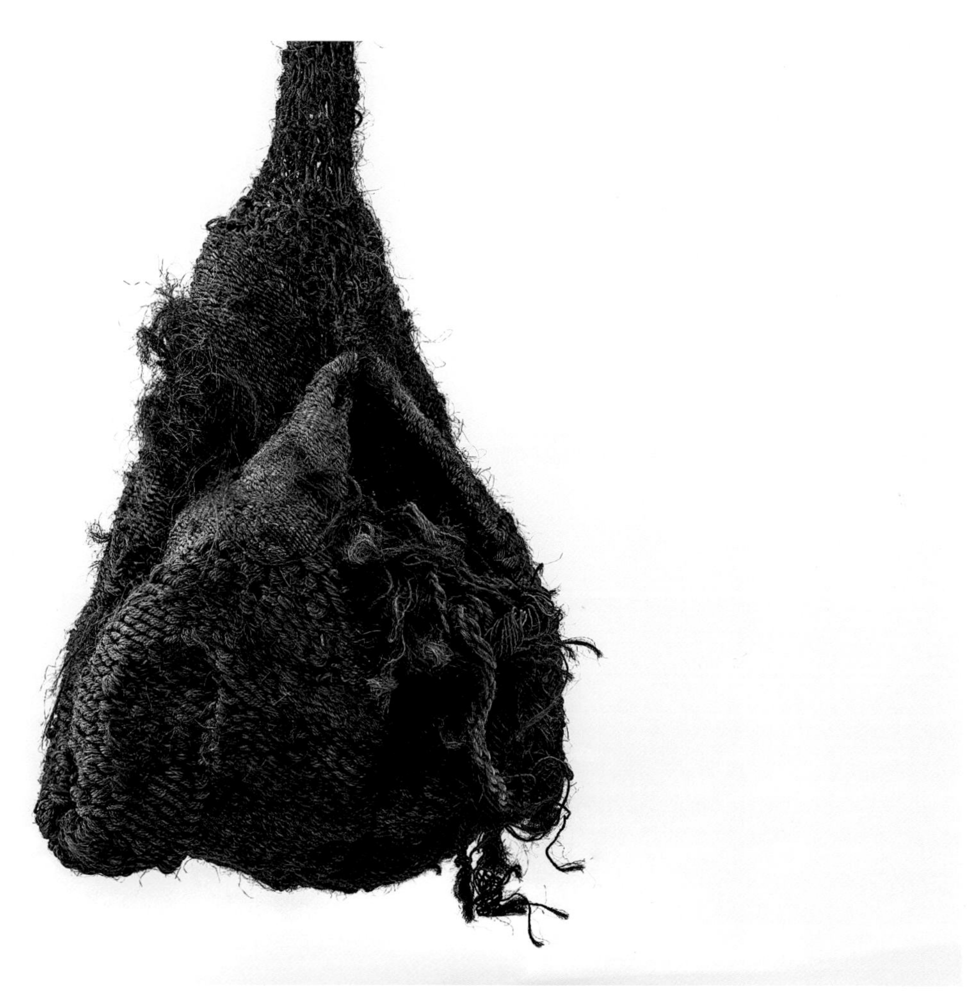

THE LIVELINESS OF MATTER
CONTEMPORARY DIALOGUES

DINA AKHMADEEVA

Opposite: *Abakan vert* (detail) 1967–8 Sisal 260 × 60 × 30

Below: Vivian Suter *Above the crater Stephano* 2016 Pigment and oil paint on canvas, volcanics, earth 200 × 352. Documenta 14 Athens project, Nisyros, Greece,

Magdalena Abakanowicz's universe is one distinctly filled with the creaturely bodies of the *Abakans*. Their roots and tentacle-like protuberances reach out towards the viewer. Others open up their orifices within layers of 'skin' to reveal the complex interior of ligaments, knots, holes and folds. Others, still, seem to ooze the contents of their form onto the floor. Folding in on themselves, cocoon-like, or stretching out their rippled, puckered surfaces that suggest a fleshy malleability surrounding a more rigid skeleton, they offer glimpses of features, limbs and organs belonging to amorphous living beings.

They are borne of a mentality that perceived an interconnectedness between the human body and the living earth, seeing energy, life and vitalism in matter. For Abakanowicz, the connection between the human body and the living earth was visible in a shared physical structure, as she stated: 'the fibre, which I use in my work, derives from plants and is similar to that from which we ourselves are composed,'[1] and that 'it is from fibre that all living organisms are built, the tissue of plants, leaves and ourselves'.[2] This connection was likewise a boundless continuity and synergy between her own body and the bodies of the *Abakans*. 'My forms are like successive layers of skin ... Each time they belong to me so much, and I belong to them, that we cannot exist apart.'[3] In these layers, Abakanowicz recognised the *Abakans*' liveliness and responsiveness to the environment, explaining, 'Woven material can move. It can react to people and they react, when they touch it. It can move too in the wind when I put it outside. It has a life which no other material has.'[4] This capacity of the *Abakans* is at its most vivid in the film *Abakany*, where the slow pans of the camera capture with great care how each *Abakan* ripples as it stands in the wind of the Baltic coast (see pp.152–9). The vitalism with which the *Abakans* vibrate within Abakanowicz's cosmology is one that also imbues a world larger and more ancient. Her imaginary is filled with the presence of 'inexplicable forces', informed by folk beliefs about the Polish landscape glimmering with rye hags and noon witches belonging to fields, bodies of water and forests.[5] This cultural imaginary gives rise to a world in which forces beyond full knowledge and control refuse the human mastery over nature and matter acts back.

With ecological and political stakes growing ever more acute in the twenty-first century, it is this necessary reconfiguration of the relationship between humanity and the world around it, materialised through the *Abakans*, that reverberates with renewed relevance in our contemporary world. Through the liveliness of matter, a set of transgenerational connections emerge organically between the *Abakans* and contemporary artistic practices. This kinship is neither linear nor genealogical; rather, a larger web or constellation of artistic practices coalesces around a shared engagement with materialist thinking. Within it, the works of Vivian Suter (b.1949), Tamara Henderson (b.1982), Daiga Grantiņa (b.1985) and Nairy Baghramian (b.1971) point to the multiple lives that matter has come to live within a contemporary context.[6] In parallel, the

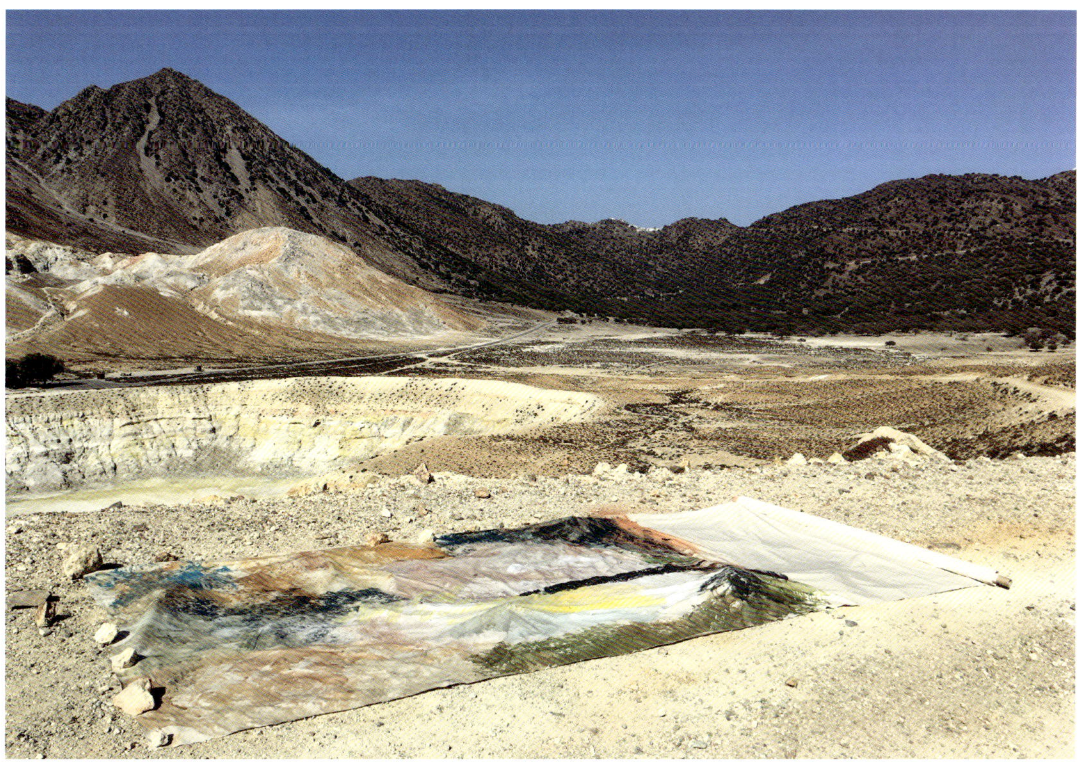

Below: Tamara Henderson *Garden Photographer Scarecrow (dehydrated)* 2016 Brass, plaster, Spandex, canvas, paint, photo reflectors, wood (skeleton), sand, glue, plastic, 35mm film, seashells, weights, lace, rope, ribbon, feathers. Dimensions variable Installation view, REDCAT, Los Angeles, 2016.

Opposite top: Daiga Grantiņa *Buff in Bloom, Glow and Thumos* 2016 Elastane fabric, resin, wire mesh, nylon, aluminium, plastic, acrylic sheet and other materials. Dimensions variable. Installation view, *Adhesive Products*, Bergen Kunsthall, Norway, 2016.

Opposite bottom: Nairy Baghramian *Scruff of the Neck (LL 23/24b & LR 26/27/28)* 2016 Aluminium, plaster, beeswax and rubber 213.5 × 225 × 110 and 200 × 255 × 127. Installation view, Tate Modern, 2019.

Abakans are a pertinent reminder of a geographically dispersed set of worldviews and practices in which materialist thinking is deep-rooted.[7]

The agential force of the environment is evidently present in the work of Vivian Suter, whose distinctively colouristic canvases emerge through the confluence of her own hand and the intervention of nature when the works are 'given over' to the landscape on Lake Atitlán, near Panajachel, Guatemala, where Suter has lived since 1982 (p.183). When the unstretched canvases are left outdoors, volcanic ash, wind, dirt, plant matter, rain and animal life find their way onto them, leaving their prints and traces, and becoming comingled with Suter's paints. Prompted by a landslide that engulfed her canvases in rubble and mud as a consequence of Hurricane Stan in 2005, Suter's method shifted with the realisation that she 'had to start working with nature and not against it'.[8] Giving her works over to the environment is as much an acknowledgement of humanity's need for submission to nature, as it is to co-exist with it in planetary terms.

The spiritedness of matter, meanwhile, underpins the practice of the Canadian-born artist Tamara Henderson. Her own cosmology, which includes explorations into the transmigration of the soul (the movement of the soul from one body to another), has birthed a cast of characters in the part-installation, part-film, part-performance *Seasons End* 2016–18 (below).[9] 'Scarecrow' was a four-metre high creature of upholstery, foliage and keepsakes within the project's centre which charted a cycle of life, sickness, death and reincarnation as the work moved between exhibition locations. In a state of decay and cared for by the figure of 'The Doc' having reached Los Angeles, Scarecrow was cremated on a beach by the artist and lived on as ashes in the belly of a newly formed figure in Dublin, where it was transformed into ceramic glaze for future works. Henderson honoured systems of belief that simultaneously require being acknowledged in order to show her work, speaking to a shifting landscape within art historical and curatorial discourse and pointing to wider recognition of beliefs, ritual and spirituality.[10]

Recalling a set of amorphously fleshy, bodily forms in flux, Daiga Grantiņa's ongoing series of works *Buffs* emerge in an uncertain primordial or futuristic temporality, invoking forms of life prior to or beyond the human species. Through these voluptuous abstracted forms of plastic and taut Lycra suspended from the ceiling, resting on the floor or emerging from the wall, Grantiņa has blurred the boundaries between the industrially and technologically made on the one hand, and the corporeal on the other. Her *Buff in Bloom, Glow and Thumos* 2016 (opposite) borrows the Ancient Greek term *thumos* –'spiritedness', 'soul', 'life' and 'breath' – evoking the presence of the animate within the synthetic substances of these hanging forms. It is part of Grantiņa's larger artistic universe of sculpture and installation that has engaged with vitality in an expanded way: through the growth and decomposition of organic substances such as lichen, or through light as an agential, life-giving substance.

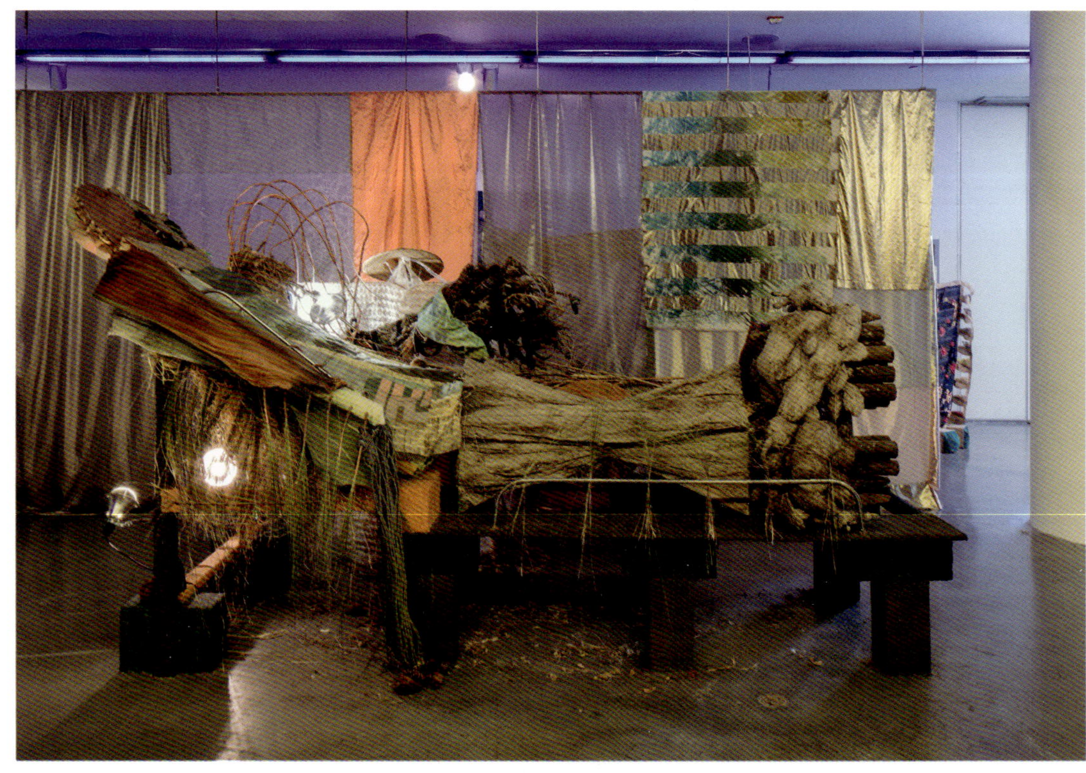

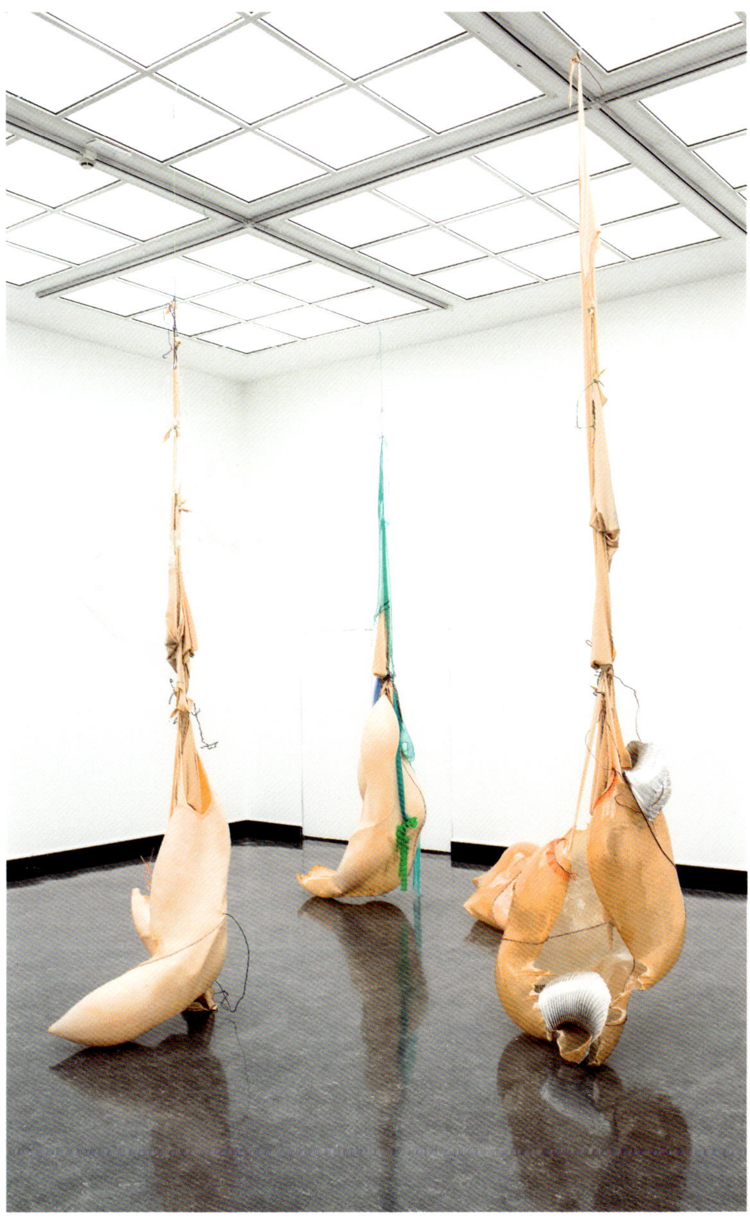

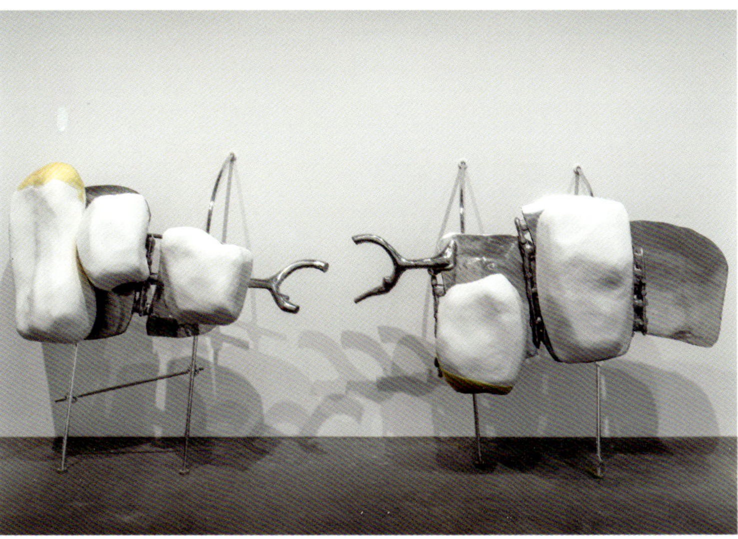

The sculptural practice of Nairy Baghramian taps into explorations of the non-human body to engage in a playful form of institutional critique, imagining the space of the exhibition as a parallel bodily form. Objects that abstractly, or more explicitly, recall prostheses, braces and supporting structures for the human body, appear on an enlarged scale resting on, or propping up architecture. A particular strand of Baghramian's sculptures continues her interest in prostheses used for medical purposes, and specifically orthodontic dentistry equipment and procedures made to alter the body. *Scruff of the Neck (LL 23/24b & LR 26/27/28)* 2016 (below) and *Scruff of the Neck (UL9/10, E)* 2016 form a pair of objects made of matte white plaster, beeswax and polished aluminium. With one work resting on the floor and the other hung just below the ceiling, Baghramian has turned the exhibition spaces where they have been shown into an oral cavity, with the presence of orthodontic treatment acting as a reminder of the ongoing institution-wide remedial work required.

As points in a larger constellation, each of these artists' practices sets in motion a new direction in materialist thinking. Whether honing in on ecological catastrophe, or on the cosmological reconsideration of inhabiting or co-habiting, or on the agential and animate potential of the synthetic or human-made as well as the natural, each suggests a dislodging of the human from the centre of the world. Bringing these practices into an associative conversation holds up a mirror to Abakanowicz's practice. Baghramian's holistic conception of her works in space speaks to Abakanowicz's idea of the rope as a muscle,[11] as a way to connect spaces and act as a guiding 'thread' through what became her expanded practice of installation. Henderson meanwhile prompts further consideration of the 'inexplicable forces' within Abakanowicz's universe in relation to indigeneity, including her invocation of a Tatar heritage. Grantiņa's nuanced theorisations of the creaturely, synthetic body prompt a conjectural consideration of the kind of life form contained within the *Abakans*; Suter's position on nature as agential creator in a planetary context also speaks to the expanded body of Abakanowicz's work in the environmental realm. This is evident in her public commissions symbiotic with nature, especially the ambitious *Arboreal Architecture* proposal as an architectural living organism (p.166). This shared commitment to thinking about matter as animate, and about things as vital players in the world alongside and in dialogue with their human counterparts, animates the *Abakans* with a renewed vital energy in a contemporary context that, in turn, reminds us of the multiple long lives the liveliness of matter has had.

A LIFETIME OF EXPERIENCES: A NARRATIVE CHRONOLOGY

JENNY DALLY

The emergence of an object is accompanied by a lifetime of experiences, by an imaginary world, by many questions one asks, while looking for answers.

—Magdalena Abakanowicz[1]

1930-9

Born Marta Magdalena Abakanowicz on 20 June 1930 in Falenty, a small village eleven kilometres southwest of Warsaw, Poland. Her father, Konstanty (late nineteenth century–1972), is a landowner of Russian and Tartar heritage, well respected by the residents bordering his estate. Her mother, Helena Domaszowska (1901–90), is descended from Polish nobility, and described by the artist as elegant yet intimidating. The artist's sister Teresa ('Terenia') (1929–2010) was born one year earlier. To this noble family hoping for a boy, Abakanowicz later wrote:

My birth was a terrible disappointment.[2]

In 1932, she moves to the family's seventeenth-century manor, set deep in the forest, near the village of Krępa, around 140 kilometres southeast of Warsaw. There the family hunt and have a logging operation on the grounds. Abakanowicz recalls trophy heads and hides with fangs and hooves inside. They live between there and the Falenty house until the outbreak of the Second World War when they settle in the forest house exclusively. Abakanowicz is tutored at home.

I had no companions of my own age. I had to fill the enormously long and empty days alone, minutely exploring everything in the environment. Learning about all that was alive – watching, touching, and discovering – was accomplished in solitude.[3]

1939-44

Nazis invade Poland on 1 September 1939, and Soviet troops follow on 17 September. These invasions mark the beginning of the Second World War.

I was nine. It was autumn. German tanks were coming. We stood on the terrace, taken by surprise, watching. They were looking at us, standing as if on parade. I saw them for the first time, faces, uniforms. I did not know how to hate. I did not believe it. I could not understand why they should hate the four of us on the terrace. They fired, aiming, probably on purpose, at a wall. I stood fearless, suddenly humiliated by their violence, helpless in the face of injustice and the impotence of my parents ... The house exposed us, it ceased to be a shelter. The forest also became alien. I no longer went there to talk to it as before.[4]

We all had a childhood broken by the war. We had to take responsibilities which are not for children. We had to act not like children, we had to get the knowledge [of] of what life is and how to defend it, ours and the lives of other people. We learned what country means, what liberty means, what pressure means, what prison means and all this when we were nine or ten years old.[5]

In 1943, German soldiers wound Abakanowicz's mother in the family home. The family flees to Warsaw in 1944.

As our home and the countryside receded, I felt increasingly hollow. As if my insides had been removed and the exterior, unsupported by anything, shrank, losing its form.[6]

On 1 August 1944 (after the Germans had occupied Warsaw for nearly five years), the Warsaw Uprising begins, led by the Polish resistance. Planned to be supported by the Red Army, instead Soviet troops stay outside the city. After sixty-three days of conflict, Germany razes Warsaw.

I do not remember the beginning, the firing from all sides, mother and the two of us lying in the street. Later everyone was running, we too. Suddenly, I was alone in a crowd of people ... Afterwards, we were with father in Milanówek, and mother was cut off from us somewhere in Warsaw. The city was closed ... I dreamt about [mother]. Not maimed. I willed her to have hands again. So that what had happened would be undone ... Two months later, she arrived. Embracing her, thin and shrunken, I could feel her infirmity very precisely. An empty sleeve.[7]

For a period during 1944–5, Abakanowicz works in a makeshift hospital.

1945-54

At the demand of the Soviet Union, the second German Instrument of Surrender is signed in Berlin on 8–9 May 1945, marking the end of the Second World War in Eastern Europe.

The family remains in the Warsaw area and Abakanowicz attends the gymnasium nearby in Milanówek, then relocates to Tczew, near Gdańsk, and she transfers to the gymnasium there.

In 1948, she enrolls in the Secondary School of Plastic Arts in Gdynia. Then she enters the State Higher School of Fine Arts in Gdańsk, based in Sopot, in 1949. When in 1950 the textile department is eliminated in Sopot, Abakanowicz transfers to the Academy of Plastic Arts in Warsaw and graduates in 1954, defending her diploma in Faculty of Painting, in the field of textile under the supervision of Anna Śledziewska, and presenting both paintings and jacquard fabrics and designs.[8]

During the early 1950s, Abakanowicz meets Jan Kosmowski (1930–2018), a student of engineering at Warsaw University of Technology. They go on ski outings in the Tatra Mountains and camping trips. She also visits the Masurian Lake District for the first time, which becomes an inspirational landscape.

On 5 March 1953, Stalin dies. The Khrushchev Thaw begins, relaxing repression and censorship in the Soviet Union and in Soviet Bloc countries until the early 1960s; this included opening up opportunities in the fields of education and culture.

In Warsaw, in 1954, takes up residence in an attic room of a three-storey, partially destroyed house on the east side of the Vistula River. She takes a job at Central Natural Silk Plant 'Milanówek', Warsaw, where she paints organic designs on cloth for production.

1955-9

Develops a close friendship with avant-garde painter Henryk Stażewski (1894–1988).

I was brought up by a Polish Constructivist who was the friend of Mondrian, and who worked in the Cercle et Carré in Paris and so on. His name is Henryk Stażewski. I was very close to him and his group of intellectuals in Poland for many years and this influenced me. But you can't see any Constructivism in my work.[9] *He was my dear friend. In his one-room flat on the twelfth floor of an apartment building the intellectual Warsaw used to come together and talk: poets, musicians, theatre people, historians, visual artists, also writers and politicians. Everything was questioned, and the search for new reality, for answers to existential problems touched all areas of human thoughts and intellect. This was my school.*[10] *It was really a fantastic group for many years and they accepted me, and I had this marvelous feeling that because they criticised me they were interested in my work.*[11]

In 1955, Jerzy Sołtan (1913–2005), a professor at the Academy of Plastic Arts, Warsaw, suggests she enter a competition for furniture and fabric designs at the Cooperative-State Central Agency for Folk and Art Industry, known as Cepelia. This show in 1956 – *30th Anniversary of the Artist Cooperative of Plastic Arts 'ŁAD'* held at Zachęta Centralne Biuro Wystaw Artystycznych (Zachęta CBWA) – is her first group exhibition. Sołtan is among the judges. She is awarded a prize for *Iris* 1955, a large, brightly coloured image of a centrally placed, explosive flower. The condition of winning is that the work would be executed as a tapestry in the ŁAD workshops.

I was glad to have the prize, but I could already see a basic misunderstanding. The Cepelia competition was for fabric design, but these plants painted on paper had nothing to do with the designs for tapestry. They simply were. They were not at all intended to be repeats or for decoration. Because they found their way to Cepelia, suddenly they became something that should be practical and utilitarian. If it had been a painting competition – what would have happened then?[12]

In the mid to late 1950s continues to pursue designs for industrial production, an activity begun during her student years. Still, discontented with her work at the silk factory, she leaves that job in 1956. In autumn of the same year, she marries Jan, now a civil engineer, and they live together in the attic room. It was so small, the couple took turns working on large paintings and construction drawings.

When I am married, mother told me: '... but I don't think you should have children.' She could not imagine a child being raised in a one-room apartment with both parents in the same room. No nanny to help, none of the basic comforts. She suffered because of our living conditions and was afraid that we would turn our life into a torture. She also felt that I, as a determined artist, would never be happy giving up my passion for any reason.[13]

From 1956–89, participates in more than fifty solo shows and well over 100 group shows internationally; a dozen solo shows and more than fifty group shows took place in Poland. This was indicative of the vigour of the Polish art system and the extent of international cooperation during the communist period. A further testament to Abakanowicz's artistic curiosity and tenacity, she also has twenty-seven solo shows in Europe which travel to forty venues during this time.

Travels outside Poland for the first time in 1957, for a two-week trip to Italy organised by the Association of Polish Artists and Designers (abbreviated to ZPAP in Polish) of which she became a member that year.

What unbelievable excitement on the bus, what joy and what a shock crossing the border with Austria and Italy: unknown, colorful, quiet, clean, and abundant life. For us every day began with comments by our art historians about what we would see and experience in each town. Art and architecture, political, social, and religious events that took place during European history and shaped the culture. I repeated to myself, 'I must see all I can, I will never have the possibility to come back here.' We managed to travel all the way down to Rome, through Perugia, Pisa, Siena, Pistoia, Florence. [14]

In 1958, Abakanowicz and her husband move into a one-room apartment, number 36, at al. Waszyngtona 30, its limit of eighteen square metres dictated under socialist rules (each person was allocated nine square metres). They live there for seven years.

1960-5

In 1960, her first solo exhibition, *Exhibition of Artworks by Magdalena Abakanowicz-Kosmowska* is organised for the Kordegarda Galeria Narodowego Centrum Kultury in Warsaw. It includes gouache paintings on unstretched cloth and oil paintings and gouaches on canvas and fibreboard.

The first show – what an excitement. I came one hour before the opening to check all the details. I could not enter; the door was locked ... The next day we learned that the authorities found the show to be 'formalistic,' that means not engaged with building socialism, thus a tendency disapproved in art. The show was closed before it ever opened. We realized that the 'thaw' that had come after Stalin's death was over. The old rules returned. [15]

Based on this showing, Maria Łaszkiewicz (1891–1981), a professional weaver, puts forward Abakanowicz to represent Poland in the 1st International Tapestry Biennial in Lausanne, Switzerland. She is accepted. In order to provide access to a loom, Łaszkiewicz invites the artist to her Atelier Expérimental de l'Union des Artistes Polonais, a nod to her formal training in France as officially registered with ZPAP, a workshop which she operated in the basement of her home at ul. Cegłowska 62 in the Bielany district of Warsaw. Here Abakanowicz makes her first weavings and continues working there for the next four years until she is able to purchase a home and studio of her own in 1965.

I did not know much about weaving – and that allowed me to invent my own technique. And Maria Łaszkiewicz was an extraordinary friend – thoughtful, helpful ... She knew life; she was tough and strong-minded. [16]

I made a decision to intertwine everything with everything else in my own way, with a tense anger, until I acquired the logic of this entanglement ... There were many of us working there. One had to wait for his or her turn to use the loom. Fighting against difficulties and struggling to survive stimulated us. It was becoming clear to me that I could build a three-dimensional reality: soft, full of secrets, protecting me, being a shield to me, and at the same time being my own creation, an integral part of myself. [17]

Shows for the first time internationally in 1962 when she exhibits *Composition of White Forms* 1962 at the 1st International Tapestry Biennial and travels to the opening at the Musée cantonal des Beaux-Arts in Lausanne. She meets Pierre Pauli (1916–70) and artist Jean Lurçat (1892–1966), co-founders of the biennial. (She shows in subsequent editions of this biennial in 1965, 1967, 1969, 1971, 1973, 1975, 1977, 1979 and 1985.)

Receives a grant in 1962 from the French Ministry of Culture to travel to France, during which time she has her first solo show outside of Poland, *Magdalena Abakanowicz: Tapestries*, at Galerie Dautzenberg, Paris, and spends four months visiting tapestry centres.

I was invited to lectures by Jean Lurçat, the man behind the revival of French tapestry ... That is when I realised that our textile art came into being quite independently, and its development has been singular, original, and rooted in different traditions ... Technically speaking, [Polish designers] explore texture, an approach that is completely unknown in France. I have also noticed with some inexplicable joy and pride that we, the Poles, are starting to be seen as a problem that arose in the wake of the Lausanne Biennial. Here is a serious rival that has unexpectedly surpassed them when it comes to innovativeness. [18]

In March 1963, Pierre Pauli, with art critic André Kuenzi (1916–2005), travels to Poland for the first time and visits Abakanowicz in Łaszkiewicz's atelier. Pauli returns that year to prepare group shows of Polish weaving in Germany, Norway, and the Netherlands (1964–5), always including Abakanowicz.

Her first one-person show of weavings in Poland, *Magdalena Abakanowicz: Gobelin* (Tapestry) (1963), opens at the Centrum Sztuki Współczesnej Zamek Ujazdowski in Warsaw.

In 1964, Abakanowicz is invited to exhibit in the 8th São Paulo Biennial, Brazil (along with artist-weavers Jolanta Owidzka [1927–2020] and Wojciech Sadley [b.1932]). In preparation, Abakanowicz builds a special loom with Łaszkiewicz and hires Stefania Zgudka, a sixteen-year-old graduate of the Vocational School of Arts and Crafts in Zakopane; she becomes her lifelong assistant and dear friend. Abakanowicz creates five large-scale wall weavings, some named after great women in history: *Andromeda* 1964, *Ana II* 1965, *Dorota II* 1965, *Cleopatra* 1964 and *Helena* 1964–5 (pp.50–1). She is awarded the Gold Medal in Applied Arts at the biennial. Unable to attend because of travel restrictions, this recognition would nonetheless have a major effect on her career.

The name *Abakans* is invented. It appears publicly for the first time in 1964 in a caption for an article by art critic and theatre historian Elżbieta Żmudzka. [19] While initially ascribed to wall-hung, rectangular works, the artist states: *I began to use the name 'Abakans' after a year or so for the three-dimensional woven works.* [20]

In 1965, Abakanowicz and her husband move to one of three cooperative housing blocks along al. Stanów Zjednoczonych. The building has studios for artists on the top floor, with big windows facing the north. They live there until 1989.

Jan and I received the necessary permissions to buy a space, that consisted of three very small rooms and a larger one, with a ceiling about four-metres high. This would be my studio. All on the tenth and top floor of an apartment building. It was a kind of recognition for my achievements. I paid for it with the prize money I had received from the São Paulo Biennale. The balcony ran the length of the whole apartment with a view of the Vistula River and the western part of the city. The sunsets were an endless spectacle, no building in front of us. We were ecstatic at our luck. [21]

Shows *Desdemona* 1965 (pp.52–3) in the 2nd International Tapestry Biennial in Lausanne (1965).

Participates in the *1st Biennial of Spatial Forms* (1965), in Elbląg, Poland, for which she creates *Untitled* 1965 (p.39), her first permanent public outdoor work and first in metal.

In 1965 she is also awarded the annual Minister of Culture's Award – First Degree. Other Polish government awards follow from 1966–98.

Appointed a professor at the State Higher School of Plastic Arts in Poznań in 1965.[22] At first declining, she came to understand that teaching art was an honourable profession in Poland, one imbued with the responsibility of passing on history, culture and tradition, especially important after years of foreign occupation. Under Abakanowicz, the Weaving Studio (in the Department of Sculpture and Graphics) becomes a place for innovation, attracting aspiring artists from around the world. She continues to travel monthly to the Poznań school until her retirement in 1990, in the early years often with colleague Stanisław Zamecznik (1909–71), an artist and stage designer. They talk about space, the relation between objects and the radiance between various matters:

The idea of 'spaces to experience' which I created later in many countries was born on the train to Poznań.[23]

1966-9

Her first group exhibition in the US, *Contemporary European Tapestries: The Collection of Mr. and Mrs. J. L. Hurschler*, opens in 1966 at the Santa Barbara Museum of Art, California, and travels to at least seven venues across the country.

Executes her first fully three-dimensional woven forms in 1967.

The fabric I made was stiff, its surface grew into reliefs similar to tree bark or animal fur. I liked the fact that I was creating an object from its very beginning, from the outer shell to the total shape. I sewed several surfaces together to form a huge three-dimensional object. I could not see it in its entirety. I could only control it with my imagination and then examine it suspended in an exhibition room. Monumental, strong, soft, and erotic, these objects were once again my reality, a protest against the established definitions of sculpture.[24]

In 1967, Alice Pauli offers Abakanowicz the first of many fourteen solo and group exhibitions at her gallery in Lausanne.

The same year her first touring solo show, *Magdalena Abakanowicz: Working in Textiles*, goes to four venues in Norway.

In 1968, *Abakanowicz: A Polish Textile Artist* is staged at Helmhaus, Zürcher Kunstgesellschaft, Zürich, while from 1968–9 *Magdalena Abakanowicz: 2- and 3-Dimensional Fabrics* tours six cities in the Netherlands; the term *Abakan* appears in an exhibition catalogue for the first time for this exhibition.

In 1968, Abakanowicz and her husband take their first trip to the US, travelling across the country by car for one month with her sister Terenia and her husband, both who at that time worked in the foreign trade division of the Polish Embassy in Washington and could arrange the necessary invitations which, to the artist, was 'an incredible miracle'. She was:

stunned by the fact that this one country spans the whole continent. And this whole continent uses one language, although people of various nationalities have gathered there. That this diversity of cultures was transformed into one. That the dynamics of competition and social responsibility created a society of great determination and imagination, in which every day you take an exam in your values against others.[25]

Two major museum group exhibitions introduce the US and Western Europe, respectively, to the emerging textile art movement. Beginning in March 1968, the Museum of Modern Art (MoMA), New York, circulated *Wall Hangings* (1968–9), curated by Jack Lenor Larsen (1927–2020) and Mildred Constantine (1913–2008). Including artists from eight countries, the press release cited developments in weaving over the past ten years that 'caused us to revise our concepts of this craft and view the work within the context of twentieth-century art'. It was showed at MoMA in February 1969. There its presentation broke institutional barriers and later confounded departmental identities when *Yellow Abakan* 1967–8 (p.68) was proposed for purchase. Yet, in keeping with the show's title, this work, was placed in a niche.[26]

I felt deeply depressed. The whole three-dimensionality of my work, its movement in space, was lost; its female character of a dress with a vagina, its many meanings, had disappeared.[27]

Meanwhile, in January 1969, *Perspectives in Textile* opened at the Stedelijk Museum, Amsterdam. Abakanowicz is one of only two artists to be given her own room. She shows three works: *Black Garment* 1968 (pp.106–9), which later enters that museum's collection; *Abakan Orange* 1968 (also known as *Baroque Dress*, p.69), acquired by the Nationalmuseum in Stockholm, where she also has a solo show the following year; and *Abakan Round* 1967–8 that later enters the collection of the Muzeum Narodowe in Wrocław, Poland (pp.95–9).

Magdalena Abakanowicz: Tapestries and Spatial Textures opens in 1969 at the Kunsthalle Mannheim, Germany.

She shows *Abakan Red* 1969, now in the collection of Tate, at the 4th International Tapestry Biennial, Lausanne (1969) (pp.124–9).

In the same year, with film director Jarosław Brzozowski (1911–69) and experimental composer Bogusław Schäffer (1929–2019), she creates *Abakany* 1970 on the sand dunes of Słowiński National Park in Łeba along the Baltic coast of Poland. The next year, following the death of Brzozowski the film is completed by Kazimierz Mucha (1923–2006) with indoor sequences of the artist working.

1970-3

During the 1970s Abakanowicz travels frequently, making exhibitions onsite as installations.

With my exhibitions around the world, I wanted to make people aware that my captivated [captive] country still has a high level of old culture contributing to the world heritage, and at the same time is able to speak about the recent reality with the very personal strong voice of modern art ... I travelled probably more than any other artist. So important was the dialogue with the whole world.[28]

Creates her first installation work in 1970 at the Södertälje Konsthall, Sweden, naming the exhibition *Textile Sculpture, Textile Environment*. She explores for the first time rope as a medium, joining it with her *Abakans* to produce a single, all-encompassing temporary work. A version is next undertaken at the Nationalmuseum in Stockholm.

In 1970, receives her first major public commission for the theatre at the Provinciehuis van Noord-Brabant in 's- Hertogenbosch, in the Netherlands. Measuring 7.2 metres high by 22 metres long by two metres deep, and suspended from the ceiling, *Bois le Duc* (pp.75–7) is an extraordinary undertaking. Completed in 1971, this dense and mysterious environment is a tribute, as the title suggests, to the origins of this place, while also suggesting Polish forests of the artist's youth.

In February 1971, she creates a highly improvisational temporary environment of *Abakans*, hanging them from scaffolding and employing rope, stuffed linen elements, and a chair at Galeria Współczesna KMPiK 'Ruch' in Warsaw.

In November, travels to California to undertake her first solo show in the US, *The Fabric Forms of Magdalena Abakanowicz* (1971) at the Pasadena Art Museum. The show affords her the opportunity for greater experimentation with space and found objects.

I wanted to make something in this space. I was always putting a knife into this established thing of weaving. So, I borrowed an old, king-size immense iron bed. I went to the harbor and got an incredible, enormous rope. I put part of the rope on this bed in the main space of the museum and it looked like an open belly. One rope just cut the space, went through the roof and came down as one thread only. [29]

With her inclusion that year in *Dimension of Fiber* (1971), an exhibition at the California College of Arts and Crafts, Oakland, California and a lecture for the symposium 'Fiber as Medium', Abakanowicz's status within the international Fiber Art movement is cemented for a new American audience.

By 1973, the first anthologies detailing the rise of the Fiber Art movement are published, each with extensive chapters on Abakanowicz and her *Abakans*: André Kuenzi, *La Nouvelle Tapisserie*, Geneva 1973 and Constantine and Larsen, *Beyond Craft: The Art Fabric*, New York 1973.

Abakanowicz further explores rope as a material in the 5th International Tapestry Biennial (1971) with *Abakan – Situation Variable II* 1971 (pp.110–13). The rope from her Pasadena show is featured the next year in solo shows at the Kunstverein für die Rheinlande und Westfalen, Düsseldorf (1972) and Aberdeen Art Gallery (1972), but undoubtedly most impressive as its use at city-scale when invited by Richard Demarco to Atelier '72: Edinburgh International Festival (1972; p.72).

The gallery space wasn't large enough to show all the works I'd brought over. So, sitting there and thinking, suddenly I saw Edinburgh as a monumental city. I looked at the façade of the Demarco Gallery and I thought I would bring the rope through it into the gallery and out again of the window where my exhibition was. It disappeared on the top of the building. Then it reappeared on Edinburgh Cathedral, which you could see from the exhibition room. From the top of the Cathedral it went to the Chapter House, and from the Chapter House it went in a straight line to the garden and then disappeared ... My work is always connected with thread and sewing. And this was sort of sewing through a building, through one building and then through another. [30]

On this occasion she collaborates again with Schäffer, composer for *Abakany*, who presents five concerts in her installation at Richard Demarco Gallery.

She continues to create temporary environmental installation projects with rope in 1973: *Rope Structures* at the Arnolfini Gallery in Bristol, England; *Rope: Penetrations, Location in Space* at the Lausanne Biennial in which rope extends from the *Wheel and Rope* inside the gallery, out of a window, to the grounds of the building; and a project for *October in Bordeaux: 8 Artists in the City*, Bordeaux, France. In 1976 she uses the rope again in Sydney and Melbourne. It threads through the Polish Pavilion at Venice in 1980.

In a series of exhibitions I had in the last four years, I used the woven material just like fabric. I also used a run of rope which for me has been one of the most meaningful and flexible materials. With the woven material and the rope, I create different shows in different places depending on the space. I use the gallery space and also the landscape ... every situation inspires me as a result of working in that situation ... I wanted to establish a definite link with the outside by means of this run of rope. [31]

1974-6

Begins several series based on the human form which she calls *Alterations*: *Heads* 1973–5 (her first objects to stand and not hang in space) and *Seated Figures* 1974–9 (her first figures from reclaimed materials and resin), giving like forms their own individuality.

My constant dream about large scale was suddenly embodied in a landscape consisting of shell-like human shapes, negatives of the bulk ... I observed the body liberated from the face, free to demonstrate, to express things not seen before ... Sleepless nights of uncertainty – I would get up, look at, pace around this untamed stranger, this intruder. But I wanted him. I had to arrive with him at an agreement without which we would have remained strangers to each other. I finally came to understand that he did not want to become a starlet, that in a series of figures he would become the span of a bridge, that his fate was to be a member of a crowd as I was. [32]

Receives an honorary doctorate in 1974 from the Royal College of Art, London. [33] There meets Artur Starewicz (1917–2014), Poland's ambassador to Great Britain from 1971–8. A chemist by training, Starewicz worked in the Polish political system after serving in the Second World War, ultimately rising to the post of Secretary of the Central Committee. He becomes a lifelong friend of the artist and her husband and, upon his retirement in 1978, becomes her photographer.

Begins to show *Abakans* with *Alterations*, first in her second one-person show in Warsaw at Zachęta CBWA (1975), having had a previous solo show ten years earlier.

Stages *Organic Structures and Human Forms* (1975) at Whitechapel Art Gallery,

London, curated by Polish-born director Jasia Reichardt (b.1933), who remains a friend and in 1982 writes one of the first comprehensive texts on the artist's career (*Abakanowicz*, Chicago and New York 1982).[34]

In 1976, creates the environmental exhibitions *Organic Structures and Soft Forms* at the Art Gallery of New South Wales, Sydney, which travels to the National Gallery of Victoria, Melbourne. Two films are also produced by Film Australia for the Crafts Council of Australia: *Abakanowicz in Australia* (on her Sydney exhibition) and *Divisions of Space* (based on a student workshop in Sydney).

Staying in Australia for the two months between showings, she undertakes a profoundly inspirational visit in the rainforest in Papua New Guinea with German-born Australian artist Jutta Feddersen (1931–2022), travelling in a twelve-metre canoe just wide enough across for each person and handled by two local men. She desires to go to the seat of 'nature's magic power' and is struck by Sepik art as 'an expression of man's interaction with his physical and supernatural environment'.[35]

With support from the Asia Council, she also travels with her husband to several islands in Indonesia (Sulawesi, Bali, Sumatra, Java) and Thailand.

In 1976, gives a lecture at the National Museum of Modern Art in Kyoto on the occasion of *Fiber Works Europe and Japan* (1976–7), which travelled to the National Museum of Modern Art, Tokyo.

1977-9

In 1977, creates variant installations of *Organic Structures* shown at Malmö Konsthall, Sweden; and returns to Norway to install a version of the show at the Henie Onstad Kunstsenter, Høvikodden.

In 1977, Pontus Hultén (1924–2006) invites Fluxus artist Daniel Spoerri (b.1930) to create a special project for the inauguration of the Musée national d'art moderne, Centre Georges Pompidou, Paris, where he is director. In turn, Spoerri invites Abakanowicz to *La Boutique aberrante du Musée Sentimental* (1977) an exhibition of works displayed and multiples for sale. Abakanowicz contributes four unique works, the cycle she calls *Decisions*, providing the accompanying explanation:

I sweep my studio from time to time. What I put on my shovel constitutes a document of decisions taken and a psychic state. The objects, that is, sets of objects sealed in jars. Attention! Do not open! The things are eliminated because:
No. 1 a distaste for a long, spiral shape
No. 2 a repugnance for fibers, the same of which we are made
No. 3 a spontaneous anger at the newspaper and all sorts of entanglements
No. 4 a joy born at the sight of empty space after removing a half-started work[36]

Additionally she includes *Everyday Music*, a cassette tape to be duplicated and sold as a multiple:

A magnetic tape, ten-minutes, recorded in the spring of 1975 at the window of my studio, of peripheral voices. Everyday Music *is a considerable stimulant of my artmaking. I hope to place it within the reach of others.*

P.S. The magnetic tape can be copied fifty times and numbered in the tapes from 1 to 50.[37]

Begins writing an autobiographical prose poem in 1978 entitled 'Portrait x 20', which is first published in 1982 in the book accompanying the touring retrospective mounted by the Museum of Contemporary Art Chicago (*Abakanowicz*, Chicago 1982).

In November 1978, she is included in a group show, along with Louise Nevelson (1899–1998) and Maria Helena Vieira da Silva (1908–92), at Galerie Jeanne Bucher in Paris. Hultén acquires for the museum *Great Black Abakan* 1967–8, one of two *Abakans* shown.

Participates in *Fiberworks: Symposium on Contemporary Textile Art* (1978), Oakland, presenting one of her most powerful lectures (see excerpt p.15).

Furthers her study of the forms and meanings of the term 'soft' in 1978, while she begins her series *Embryology* 1978–81 (pp.174, 176–7).

The contents, the inside, the interior of soft matter fascinated me. I suspected I could find there the explanation for the character and nature of the soft object. By 'soft,' I meant organic, alive. What is organic? What makes it alive? In which region of throbbing begins the individuality of matter, its independent existence? ... meanings and associations centered on the body, any kind of body, and belly, any kind of belly, and life which seems to need soft, organic matter to exist. I carried these thoughts and the need to visualize them.[38]

In 1979, *Soft and Plastic: Soft Art* opens at Kunsthaus Zurich, an exhibition about the meaning of soft materials and human creativity. Organised by director Erika Billeter (1927–2011) who was inspired by a conversation with Abakanowicz, works of influential modern artists are shown along with ethnographic objects. The artist contributes a poem '"Weich= Leben" (Soft = Life)' to the catalogue (see pp.22–3) and starts to use the term 'soft art' to describe her work.

During these years, Abakanowicz develops a close personal relationship with Paris-based critic Pierre Restany (1930–2003), known in part for coining the term nouveau réalisme, and Geneva-based art historian and author Jean-Luc Daval (b.1937). Curator Mary Jane Jacob makes her first visit to the artist's studio in February 1979 and offers the artist a major retrospective in the US.

Receives in 1979 the Herder Prize, Germany and Austria, awarded annually to scholars and artists from Central and Southeast Europe who have contributed to the cultural understanding of European countries and peaceful interrelations.

1980-2

In June 1980, represents Poland at the Venice Biennale.

To the last moment we did not know whether we would be able to exhibit in our pavilion – the Polish curator for the Biennale [Aleksander Wojciechowski (1922–2006)] and I, the exhibiting artist. The political tension between the Soviet Union and Poland could be felt in the air. Our participation at the Venice Biennale could be forbidden at the last moment. The Polish curator was very nervous, not knowing what to expect. The Solidarity [Solidarność] movement, standing in opposition to the Communist regime, had gone underground ... Jan could not come as he was involved in the Solidarity movement. Artur was with me.
This was the first time he helped me with an installation.[39]

She announces her work with *Trzepaki* 1980 in the garden flanking the entrance of the Polish Pavilion, then creates an itinerary inside starting at the door with the *Hand* 1975 on a pedestal at the foot of which begins the rope leading the visitor as it threads to the left at the imposing *Wheel and Rope* 1973 (p.180), then continuing into the voluminous *Embryology* 1978–81 (pp.174, 176–7), consisting of 800 objects and shown for the first time here, finally ending with the solemn rows of 40 *Backs* 1976–80.

Also shows 40 *Backs* in *ROSC '80: The Poetry of Vision* (1980) at the National Gallery of Ireland and School of Architecture, University College, Dublin. This work becomes the most iconic of her *Alterations* series.

When I investigate humans, I investigate myself. When I yield to my curiosity, I do not expect rational explanations. I have not really disturbed the original image I carry within myself. The man I deal with in my work is man in general. At the Venice Biennale, at ROSC in Dublin, in Paris and elsewhere, people who saw the Backs would ask me: Is it Auschwitz? Is it a religious rite in Peru? Is it a dance from Ramayana? The answer to these questions is affirmative, because it speaks about the human condition in general. [40]

Begins to make large-scale drawings, a medium that she employed, on a smaller scale, in its own right several times earlier in her career but which now took on greater significance.

I got these sheets of paper and I put one on the floor and asked Jan to lie down on it. I drew along his body. This was such a regular sheet of paper, one meter by seventy [centimetres]. I drew along his body and then he stood up and I filled the contour. This was the first drawing, then I began to make my own vision out of it. [41]

By 31 August 1980, Solidarity, the first independent trade union in a Soviet Bloc country, led by Lech Wałęsa, is officially formed in opposition to the government.

The situation in Poland is very dangerous – like never before. And every day can be the last day of our liberty. In this situation we decided with Alice Pauli to organize the transport of my works to Switzerland. This is the only possibility to make sure that the exhibitions you are planning can happen without unexpected difficulties ... There are real problems in my country, but I think I will be always free to go away and work with exhibitions – but to get the works out can become an enormous problem or just impossible and we must send everything as quickly as possible. [42]

Martial law is declared in Poland on 13 December. It would not be lifted until 1983.

Jan and I ... looked out our window. We were completely terrified. They were coming right along the highway next to our house. We did not know if this was the Polish or Russian army; if it is the Russian, then we were finished. We counted twenty-five tanks and then we knew they were Polish because if they were Russian there would have been hundreds. So, this was only to block the town and to impose the martial law. In a country where law does not exist, anything can happen, and we had martial law and the tanks came into Warsaw. War games came every day because here they were fighting with the Russian monuments and they were killing and putting people into prison, and this and that, and it was happening all the time, everyday. [43]

Because he was an active member of the Solidarity movement, Jan loses his position as a general director of industrial development where he supervised the construction of ports, steel mills, water reservoirs, dams and power plants. He begins to travel with the artist and assist with the technical planning of her exhibitions and public art projects.

Creates her last rope installation in 1981 for *Malmoe*, Malmö Konsthall, Sweden, in which artists were to react to the context of the southern Swedish industrial port city. Presented at the Malmö Konsthall, Sweden, she brought old tarpaulins from Poland and gathered six-metre-long poles from the docks to create a massive installation.

In January 1982, she and Jan, along with Artur Starewicz, are among the first cultural travellers to be granted permission under martial law to travel out of Poland to install the exhibition *Abakanowicz: Alterations* at ARC, Musée d'Art Moderne de la Ville de Paris.

In May, she is the only woman included in the thirty-artist show *Art Becomes Material* (1982) at the Nationalgalerie, then West Berlin, showing *Seated Figures* 1974–6; 206 objects from the cycle *Embryology* 1978–80, 30 *Backs* 1978–80, *Trunks* 1981, *Pregnant* 1981–2 and *Monads* 1982.

In October 1982, returns to Japan to lecture at the Abakano-Kai Foundation that had been formed after her 1976 trip and was spearheaded by Kuniko Lucy Kato, an art historian who had served as the artist's interpreter. Abakanowicz and Kato enjoy a close, ongoing relationship.

In November 1982, her first major retrospective opens in Chicago, staged in two venues to accommodate the great scale: *Abakans* at the Chicago Cultural Center; and *Alterations* and new works at the Museum of Contemporary Art. The show travels to eight locations in North America.

1983-9

Begins to undertake major public projects.

The outdoor works began in the most difficult period of the martial law in the 1980s. I got commissions after my success at the 1980 Venice Biennale. At that time, it was extremely difficult to get the passport and visas. This fight, this desperate struggle against these restrictions has finally created such a stimulus to the work, whether it was Italy or Jerusalem. Every moment was unusually precious. [44]

Invited by French cultural authorities, in 1983 visits Schneider-Creusot company, that was disposing of nineteenth- and early twentieth-century casting models, and offered them to artists to transform. Abakanowicz chooses giant wooden forms used for casting big engines.

I discovered this engine was made on the principles of the human body. You have a belly that covers everything moving inside, all the energy moves inside.

She encases them in glass structures:

in which things are growing, greenhouses. They stand in the middle of nature, and it is there you feel the sunshine on the object – and if the object doesn't grow, it's very mysterious. This is a situation not of death, but of expecting life. [45]

In 1983, while in Massachusetts installing her Chicago retrospective at the deCordova Sculpture Park and Museum, she has her first experience casting metal with the sculptor George Greenamyer (b.1939), a professor at the Massachusetts College of Art. In autumn of 1984, Abakanowicz is a Visiting Professor at University of California Los Angeles, and an artist-in-residence at California State University, Fullerton, where she further develops skills in casting metal, both bronze and aluminium, with Jim Jenkins. A film is made by the school about her time at Fullerton.

Included in the inaugural show at the expanded MoMA, *An International Survey of Recent Painting and Sculpture* (1984), organised by Kynaston McShine (1938–2018), where she shows *Monads* 1982. Later *Pregnant* 1981–2 is acquired by the museum and the artist installs it in the galleries in 1986.

MoMA curator Ann Temkin commented: 'One has to remember how rare it was at that moment for the visiting artist to be a woman, and for that woman to be a person of such strength and conviction as Abakanowicz. One must remember the context within which she worked.'[46]

In 1985, begins to show at the gallery of Xavier Fourcade (1926–87) and works with him for two years until his death.

At the invitation of collector Giuliano Gori, who first saw her work in 1980 in Venice, she undertakes her first major permanent outdoor installation, *Katarsis* 1985, for the sculpture park, Spazi d'Arte, at Fattoria di Celle, Santomato di Pistoia, Italy, employing bronze for the first time, which she is introduced to at the Venturi Arte Foundry in Bologna.

Begins the series *Crowds*, initially in burlap, later in various metals (1985–2008). She remained resolute that each figure was unique, the product of her own hand.

It happened to me to live in times during which the population of the planet increased three times, during which millions were killed in wars, nations were and are manipulated by leaders. Crowds behave like a brainless organism and act like a brainless organism. I suspect that under the human skull, instincts and emotions overpower the intellect without us being aware of it. I wanted to confront man with himself, with his solitude in multitude. I visualize my fears in the metaphoric language of my art. I am building the fence of my immobile crowds between my reality and the existing one. I bewitch the phenomenon of crowd. I change it into the bridge between human and nature.[47]

Creates *Incarnations* 1986–2008, in bronze based on her face, and *Anonymous Portraits* 1985–2008, in cotton and linen.

Begins the series *War Games* 1987–95. Coming upon trees in the Masurian Lake District, she creates a total of twenty-one huge forms from discarded tree limbs that are alternatively weapons and bodies, some of which the artist described as:

Erotic, with large spread legs, nearly naturalistic, nearly too female – like shameless effrontery. I walked among trunks, moved by this dramatic scene. I touched them to feel their temperature and smoothness, excited as if touching real bodies. An anatomy as real as my own. How to give them another existence? As if obsessed, I returned and returned to this place.[48]

Creates *Negev* at the Billy Rose Art Garden, Israel Museum, Jerusalem, in 1987. Impressed by the aliveness of the local limestone, filled with fossils, a record of time, she proposes a group of seven 12-tonne wheels. Each is to be more than 2.7 metres in diameter and installed on the very edge of the Hill of Tranquility. The most abstract work since the *Abakans*, it draws from the spirituality of the barren desert, the silence of its rocks, and the prehistoric shores of the Mediterranean while its round form evokes humankind's basic tool or millstones for olive crushing. Its number is symbolic of the seven days of Creation, seven ancient gates of Jerusalem and more.

In 1988, a major survey of her work is staged at Műcsarnok, Budapest.

For the 1988 Olympic Games, she is commissioned to make a work for Olympic Park in Seoul, South Korea. In an area surrounded by hills she makes *Space of the Dragon*, ten enormous, prehistoric-like bronze skulls.

Sagacious Heads 1989 continue the form of the skull, finding homes in 1992 at both the Walker Art Center's Minneapolis Sculpture Garden and Nagoya City Art Museum, Japan.

Like pieces of rock, like big stones, like organisms that do not exist ... The head is the place where we have our brain. The head is first to see, to react, to inform the whole body. But these heads also have this quality of growing out of the earth. I think they are rather mysterious because you don't see the whole, you see only a part of them.[49]

After more than fifteen years of bureaucratic negotiations, in 1989 the artist and her husband move into a new home and studio in an area south of Warsaw's city centre, where they live out the rest of their lives. This was a moment of tremendous change, punctuated by the fall of communism that began peacefully in Poland on 4 June 1989 when Solidarity was victorious in a partially free election. By November of the following year its leader, Wałęsa, became the first President of Poland elected by a popular vote.

Meets Pierre Levai, President of Marlborough Gallery, and has her first New York show there in 1989, and one at Marlborough London the following year, beginning active decades of representation with over twenty solo exhibitions.

1990-9

Under François Mitterrand (1916–96), a programme is launched in 1990 to redesign La Défense, a business district in Paris that forms the westernmost stretch of the Axe historique. Établissement public pour l'aménagement de la région de la Défense invites proposals from twenty-two international artists; four finalists are chosen: Abakanowicz, Piotr Kowalski (1927–2004), Jean-Pierre Raynaud (b.1939) and Alan Sonfist (b.1946). Abakanowicz proposes *Bois de Nanterre*, her vision of a vertical garden/housing and commercial tower, which would become a series she calls *Arboreal Architecture* (see pp.166–73). Abakanowicz's drawings and maquettes for the project were later shown at Marlborough Gallery in New York in 1992 and in Warsaw and Łódź in 1994, each accompanied by a publication.

My Abakans, *magic totemic forms, similar to tree trunks and animal bristle. They and* Bois de Nanterre *are, in fact, the result of the same fascination by organic corporeality; the same necessity to touch the mystery of nature by intermediary of something similar, created by me. In my old statement about* Abakans *I said: I want people to enter my forms, to penetrate into them. I wanted to share the mysteries of shapes and of the matter. Now I think about the longings of humans living in cities ... I imagine so well the landscape of huge vertical shapes as powerful as in the rainforest.*[50]

In 1991, a major solo show takes place at the Muzeum Narodowe in Wrocław. Her growing friendship and respect for the director Mariusz Hermansdorfer (1940–2018) leads to the museum acquiring the largest collection of the artist's work and ultimately a catalogue raisonné.

That same year, a solo show tours four museums in Japan including the Hiroshima City Museum of Contemporary Art. There she is struck by the memory of the Second World War, reflecting on her own experience of war in Poland.

I was fifteen when the atom bomb hit the town. In my dreams I visualised what happened there, I heard the cries. When installing my sculptures I was told in the Museum that occasionally the lifts stop motionless and the cries are heard. People escaping from the fire reached that hill and died there. It was covered with their bodies. At the top of the hill a hospital was built for the still living victims of the explosion. The group of my figures was placed on one of the terraces near the museum. The whole city can be seen from there. People walk among my figures, leaving their traces on the gravel.[51]

By 1992, a petition is signed by more than 6000 Japanese citizens requesting Abakanowicz be commissioned for a permanent installation. She is offered a site at the Hiroshima City Museum of Contemporary Art. At first, she had the idea to build a hand-like monument, 640 metres high – the height at which the atomic bomb detonated, as if to catch it. Over time, in discussions with the mayor and other authorities, she came to understand that this idea was perceived as too aggressive. Finally, it was agreed the monument should be forty silent seated *Backs* in bronze. *Space of Becalmed Beings* is sited at the Hiroshima City Museum of Contemporary Art in 1993. A Butoh dance company headed by Akiko Motofuji (1928–2003), partner of Butoh founder Tatsumi Hijikata (1928–86), performs a work inspired by Abakanowicz's project in Hiroshima and sends her a recording. The artist suggests working with the group to choreograph a dance. It is performed in a warehouse in Japan in 1994; in 1995 at both a dance festival in Tokyo and the memorial ceremony of the fiftieth anniversary of the atomic explosion in Hiroshima; and at the 1995 opening of Abakanowicz's show at Centrum Sztuki Współczesnej Zamek Ujazdowski in Warsaw.

In 1993, shows *War Games* at The Institute for Contemporary Art, P.S. 1 Museum, New York (now MoMA PS1). The exhibition was curated by art historian Michael Brenson (b.1942), who first came to know the artist well in 1992, visiting her in Warsaw and writing an important article 'Survivor Art' for *The New York Times Magazine* (29 November 1992). They worked together throughout the decade and developed a deep personal friendship. The artist appreciated that his 'imagination seems to have roots in the remote cultures of Baltic countries as well as experiences growing [up] in Manhattan. Your words carry important meanings, unexpected associations.'[52]

In December 1993, she is awarded the Award for Distinction in Sculpture, by the SculptureCenter, New York.

After several years of close collaboration with the artist, including being together during the making of *Negev* in Jerusalem, Barbara Rose publishes the first monograph on Abakanowicz (*Magdalena Abakanowicz*, New York 1994).

In 1995, Abakanowicz opens at Centrum Rzeźby Polskiej, Orońsko, Poland, and there she creates the last of the *War Games* series: *Pasar*, *Runa* and *Ukon*, the latter of which remains in the museum's collection. In the same year, *Magdalena Abakanowicz: Bronze Sculpture*, Yorkshire Sculpture Park, Wakefield, England, features *Hand-like Trees*, a sculptural response to the artist's ambitions to bring about living architecture in the guise of a tree (p.172). The next year she shows *Hand-like Trees* for the first time in the US at Doris Freedman Plaza, New York (1996), organised by the Public Art Fund. This is followed by an installation on Riva degli Schiavoni for the 47th Venice Biennale (1997), and in *Human/Nature: Art and Landscape in Charleston and the Low Country* (1997) at the Spoleto Festival USA in Charleston, South Carolina.

In 1996, *Masterworks of Modern Sculpture: The Nasher Collection* opens at the California Palace of the Legion of Honor, Fine Arts Museums of San Francisco, featuring *Bronze Crowd* 1990–1. In 1997 the show travels as *A Century of Sculpture: The Nasher Collection* to the Guggenheim Museum, New York, where Abakanowicz participates in a symposium along with Mark di Suvero (b.1933), Martin Puryear (b.1941) and George Segal (1924–2000), organised and moderated by Brenson. Of this showing the artist wrote to Guggenheim Museum director Thomas Krens:

Seeing my work in the extraordinary context of this exhibition, I realize once again the difference of experiences which inspire art depending on political and economic systems. Everybody knows, for instance, that in Eastern Europe until the end of the 1980s artists' statements could become reason for political repression. This changed art into a weapon stimulating resistance. Many admired these heroic years but nobody realized the changes caused in people's mentality by the totalitarian system – the unpredictable reactions of the crowd.[53]

Later that year, she is included in the inaugural exhibition of the Guggenheim Museum, Bilbao, Spain: *The Guggenheim Museums and the Art of This Century*.

In 1997, the *War Game, Winged Trunk* 1989, enters MoMA's collection, a gift of the museum's board vice president, Agnes Gund, who had become a close friend.

With Gintaras Karosas (b.1968), artist and founder of Europos Parkas, Open-Air Museum of the Centre of Europe near Vilnius, Lithuania, she creates *Space of Unknown Growth* 1998 (pp.170–1). They share a history, recalling the Polish-Lithuanian Commonwealth (1569–1795), one of the largest states in Europe at the time, and establish a trust that allows Karosas to undertake the casting of these huge concrete ovoid forms.
Of their collaboration, the artist writes that 'here the imagination of man meets the wisdom of nature.'[54]

Receives in 1998 Poland's greatest honour, Order of Polonia Restituta at the rank of Commander's Cross with Star, having been awarded the Knight's Cross in 1980.

Abakanowicz on the Roof (1999) opens at the Metropolitan Museum of Art, New York.

In 1999, participates in a major outdoor two-person exhibition in the Jardins du Palais-Royal, Paris, with Beverly Pepper (1922–2020).

Shows selections from *Crowd IV* 1989–90 and *Infantes* 1992 in *To the Rescue: Eight Artists in An Archive* (1999) at the International Center of Photography, New York, before the show travels to two US venues.

I remember: it was the severe winter of 1942. The Germans occupied Poland. The war of Hitler with Russia continued. A transport of children from Poland to Germany, where they would be turned into Germans, was stopped by accident for a day and a night. The train was not heated. Hundreds of blond, blue-eyed children, in the unheated cattle cars, froze to death. When finally soldiers opened the doors, the bodies fell out stiff and hard like sculptures. I wasn't there. The person telling me about this event, built images in my childhood memory, clear, strong, and lasting. Today I had to face the terror attack in Chechnya, where hundreds of children were killed in their school on the day their school year should have begun. In Sudan, the extermination of hundreds of thousands dying of hunger and violence is another image of childhood in our time. We are aware that the human family on our planet isno longer divided between East and West, between those living under totalitarian and democratic systems. Two thirds of the world population suffers from hunger and poverty. Poverty has become a tourist attraction, something exotic, amusing, eagerly shown on certain television channels. [55]

Is bestowed the Order of Merit for Sciences and Arts in Germany, in 1999.

In 2000, the artist and her husband Jan establish a charitable foundation.

There is a generation of children of former gentry who after the war were thrown away from their estates, and then deprived of means of existence, social standing and their human rights. This generation lost for the rest of their lives the will to possess, to own something. Having nothing, you avoid a new condemnation by some new judges. Money? One can make out of them a foundation which could give scholarships to talented people or to help others deserving it. In this country only people of humble origin are striving to get big money and to become big owners. They were called 'red bourgeoisie' or 'red aristocracy'. Now they are becoming fashionable. Only intellect and imagination are values which can't be taken away by any revolution. [56]

2007-17

In 2000, named Officer of the Order of Merit of the Italian government, and receives the Leonardo da Vinci World Award of Arts from the World Cultural Council in Norway.

Unrecognized 2002 is dedicated in Park Cytadela, Poznań, Poland, a public project urged by former students.

Continuing her interest in man's inhumanity to man and disregard for the planet, first evidenced with *Hoofed Mammal Heads* 1989–90, *Mutants* 1992–2001 and *Birds* 1994–2009, she creates *Coexistence* 2002–10, her only figures with heads.

Now I am aware that people may have an inborn instinct for cruelty and the inexplicable pleasure that killing must give, a pleasure probably similar to sexual excitement, to orgasm. I suddenly thought in my imaginary world that my figures began to have heads, faces .... faces like masks growing on the body, out of the body ... The human trunk carries the unknown upon itself: a mug, snout, muzzle. [57]

From 2004 to 2010, summers in Villasimius, Sardinia, and is captivated by the landscape that evokes her *Embryology*, her mammoth *Skulls* and other interests in nature and art.

Any sculpture seems helpless when confronted with the powerful expression of weathered granite in Sardinia – unless the sculpture is saturated with bewitching human energy. [58]

In 2004, she is named Commander of the Order of Arts and Letters, France, having been conferred the status of Chevalier in 1983 and Officière in 1999.

On 1 May 2004, Poland joins the European Union.

In 2005, is awarded Poland's prestigious Gloria Artis Gold Medal for Merit in Culture by the Ministry of Culture and National Heritage and the Lifetime Achievement Award by the International Sculpture Center, Hamilton, New Jersey.

In 2006, completes *Agora* for Grant Park, Chicago, Illinois. Begun in 2003, this is the largest – and last – permanent public project executed by the artist: 106 headless figures, cast in iron and 2.7 metres tall.

Agora is a Greek word describing town meeting used for discussions of poetry and philosophy, for sharing of thoughts and performances ... This group confronts the viewer with himself, with solitude in multitude, but also with the certainty that we feel in a forest among monumental verticality ... We live in times which are extraordinary because of their various forms of aggression. We still remember Hitler and Stalin, Pol Pot, and other terrifying leaders. But today the new danger exists around us as if everyone were against everyone. Agora should become a symbol, a metaphor about this particular historical moment in which we need each other, in which we want to rely on each other more than ever. [59]

Is included in *WACK! Art and the Feminist Revolution* (2007), an exhibition which places her within the feminist art-historical canon, despite her being 'neither feminist nor an enthusiast of this movement.' [60] Originating at the Museum of Contemporary Art, Los Angeles, it travels to three venues in North America.

In 2007, the Fundacja Marty Magdaleny Abakanowicz Kosmowskiej i Jana Kosmowskiego is registered in Poland for the promotion, storage and conservation of works by Abakanowicz, as well as making them available to the public.

Skira publishes her autobiography: *Fate and Art*, Milan 2008.

Magdalena Abakanowicz: The Court of King Arthur (2008) opens at Palacio de Cristal, Museu Nacional Centro de Arte Reina Sofia, Madrid, and in the same year a one-person show at the Institute Valencià d'Art Modern in Valencia, Spain.

Undertakes a new site installation for the Centrum Sztuki Współczesnej Zamek

Ujazdowski, Warsaw, entitled *Magdalena Abakanowicz: Cistern* (2008).

In 2009, *Magdalena Abakanowicz: Space to Experience* opens at the Fondazione Arnaldo Pomodoro in Milan, Italy, one of the last exhibitions in which the artist plays an active role in creating the installation.

Embryology (pp.174, 176–7) is shown in *Touched* (2010), the Liverpool Biennial, England, UK.

Decorated by the Federal Republic of Germany with the Order of Merit of the Federal Republic of Germany, receiving one of the highest ranks of Knight Commander's Cross in 2010.

Abakanowicz dies of complications from Alzheimer's in Warsaw on 20 April 2017. She is buried in the Powązki Cemetery, the most famous and oldest in the city, where among the graves of distinguished figures are many cultural figures.

In 2018, a memorial in honour of Magdalena Abakanowicz is held at MoMA. 'The profound influence and permission of Magdalena and her work is for me, monumental. She was unafraid of scale, of history, of the enormity of human vulnerability, of emotional recognition in material form. Her legacy is gigantic.' (Ann Hamilton) [61]

In 2020, the University of the Arts in Poznań, where she taught for several decades, is renamed in honour of the artist to Magdalena Abakanowicz University of the Arts in Poznań.

CREDITS

Copyright

All works by Magdalena Abakanowicz are © Fundacja Marty Magdaleny Abakanowicz Kosmowskiej i Jana Kosmowskiego, Warsaw.

© Nairy Baghramian 185 bottom
© Daiga Grantiņa 185 top
© Tamara Henderson 184
© Estate of Marek Holzman back cover, 2
© Estate of Aleksander Kobzdej 40
© Estate of Jan Lebenstein 32
© Estate of Jerzy Rosołowicz 34 bottom
© Artur Starewicz/East News 8, 10–12, 16–17, 20–1, 24–5, 28–9, 86–7, 163, 166, 174
© Estate of Henryk Stażewski 34 top
© Vivian Suter. Courtesy the artist and Gladstone Gallery, New York and Brussels 183
© Estate of Jozef Szajna 84
© Estate of Stanisław Zamecznik 41

Photography

Unless otherwise stated, all images are © Fundacja Marty Magdaleny Abakanowicz Kosmowskiej i Jana Kosmowskiego, Warsaw.

© Abakanowicz Arts and Culture Charitable Foundation; Photo by Jan Nordahl 64, 74–5, 78
© Abakanowicz Arts and Culture Charitable Foundation; Photo by Norbert Piwowarczyk front cover, 4, 30, 39, 44–5, 54–63, 81, 89–93, 95–9, 101–5, 110–7, 122–3, 130–1, 136–43, 146–7, 151, 170–1, 182
Carl Ander / The Röhsska Museum 118–121
Installation photo from Adhesive Products, group exhibition: Lynda Benglis, Naira Baghramian, Olga Balema, Daiga Grantina, Sterling Ruby, Kaari Upson. Bergen Kunsthall, Bergen Assembly 2016. Photo: Thor Brødreskift 185 top
Photograph Wojciech Bruszewski, Lodz 72
Jarosław Brzozowski and Kazimierz Mucha / Wytwórnia Filmów Oświatowych sp. z o.o. 154–5, 158–9
Photo Lorenzo Capellini. Courtesy: Lorenzo Capellini 80
© Central Museum of Textiles in Łódź; Photo by Norbert Piwowarczyk 122–3
Cricoteka, Centre for the Documentation of the Art of Tadeusz Kantor, Kraków; photo © Jacquie Bablet 83
Collection Fondation Toms Pauli, Lausanne / Photograph by Bruno Voidey 36
Courtesy Tamara Henderson and Rodeo, London / Piraeus 182
Photograph Marek Holzman back cover, 2
Collection Bogdan Jakubowski, Paris 32
Photograph Jan Kosmowski 42
© Copyright by Piotr Ligier/NMW). Collection of the National Museum in Warsaw 40
Photo: Clare Lilley 172
Courtesy Marlborough Galleries, London and New York /Lance Brewer 167–9; /Pierre Le Hors 50–1; /Luke Walker 145
Photo by Walter Mori/Mondadori Portfolio via Getty Images 84
© 2020. Digital image, The Museum of Modern Art, New York/Scala, Florence 68
© Museum of Modern Art in Warsaw 41
© Muzeum Sztuki, Łódź 34 bottom
© Norbert Piwowarczyk 39, 43, 48–9, 52–3, 76–7, 132–3
REDCAT, Los Angeles. Photo: Brica Wilcox 184
Tore H. Røyneland / Henie Onstad Archive 178, 180–1
Artur Starewicz/East News 8, 10–12, 16–17, 20–1, 24–5, 28–9, 86–7, 166, 174
Photo Stedelijk Museum Amsterdam 69
Sterna Art Project and documenta14 183
Barbara Stopczyk 152, 156–7
© Harold Strak 106–9
© Tate, 2022 124–5, 134–5, 176–7, 185 bottom; /Andrew Dunkley 46–7; / Joe Humphrys 126–9
Toms Pauli Foundation, Lausanne Gift of Mr. & Mrs. Magnenat / Digitization Studio, Lausanne 160–2, 164–5
© Copyright by Krzysztof Wilczyński/ NMW. collection of the National Museum in Warsaw 34 top

NOTES

The Artist, The Person, pp.9–13

1. Letter from Magdalena Abakanowicz to Mary Jane Jacob, 1 May 1989. See *Magdalena Abakanowicz: Writings and Conversations*, ed. Mary Jane Jacob and Jenny Dally, Milan 2022, *pp.212–13*.
2. Letter from Abakanowicz to Agnes Gund, 18 November 1996. See Jacob and Dally 2022, *p.284*.
3. Abakanowicz, interview with Barbara Rose, 1988–91. See Jacob and Dally 2022, *p.189*.
4. This, and all other unattributed quotes from personal unpublished correspondence.
5. Jan Kosmowski in Lawrence Sabbath, 'The Weaving of Magic: Polish Woman Creates Electricity with Jute, Hemp, and Burlap', *Gazette Montreal*, 19 Feb. 1983, *p.B8*.
6. Betty Park, 'Magdalena Abakanowicz Speaks: The Renowned Polish Artist Discusses her Work and Life', *Fiberarts*, March/April 1983, *p.13*.
7. Ibid., *p.11*. See Jacob and Dally 2022, *pp.176–7*.
8. Magdalena Abakanowicz, 'Grain of Sand', in *Working Process e non Solo*, exh. cat., Collezione Gori, Fattoria di Celle 2002, *p.23*.
9. Letter from Abakanowicz to William S. Lieberman, Chairman of the Department of 20th Century Art, Metropolitan Museum of Art, New York, 24 November 1999.
10. Magdalena Abakanowicz, *Fate and Art*, 2nd edn, Milan 2020, *p.103*.
11. Letter from Abakanowicz to Joann Phillips, founding trustee of the Georgia O'Keeffe Museum. Undated, c.June 1997. See Jacob and Dally 2022, *p.287*.
12. Abakanowicz, interview with Barbara Rose, 1988–91. See Jacob and Dally 2022, *p.188*.
13. Sabbath 1983, *p.B8*.
14. Abakanowicz, interview with Barbara Rose, 1988–91. See Jacob and Dally 2022, *p.188*.
15. Letter from Abakanowicz to Mildred Constantine, 29 September 1999. See Jacob and Dally 2022, *p.88*.
16. Abakanowicz 2020, *p.137*.
17. Magdalena Abakanowicz, *Abakanowicz: Organic Structures*, exh. cat., Malmö Konsthall 1977, *p.36*.
18. Okakura Kakuzō, *The Book of Tea*, Vermont and Tokyo 1997, *p.52*.

Artist's Writings, pp.14–29

1. On Fiber: Presentation at *Fiberworks: Symposium on Contemporary Textile Art*, conference at Merritt College, Oakland, CA, 12–14 May 1978. First published in the booklet to accompany the event, Berkeley 1978, *p.10*. Also appears in Mary Jane Jacob and Jenny Dally (eds), *Magdalena Abakanowicz: Writings and Conversations*, Milan 2022, *pp.50–1*.
2. On Materiality: Statement dated 1969 in *Abakanowicz: Organic Structures*, exh. cat., Malmö Konsthall 1977, *p.36*.
3. On Making: 'Accomplishment', in *Abakanowicz: Organic Structures*, exh. cat., Malmö Konsthall, 1977, *p.37*.
4. On Space: From files at Norton Simon Museum, Pasadena. See Jacob and Dally 2022, *p.29*.
5. On *Abakans*: From interview conducted by Barbara Rose, 1988–91. See Jacob and Dally 2022, *p.191*.
6. On *Abakans*: Letter to Michael Brenson, 10 March 1994. See Jacob and Dally 2022, *pp.233–4*.
7. On Soft: 'Weich=Leben', in *Weich und Plastisch: Soft-Art*, exh. cat., Kunsthaus Zürich 1979, *pp.74–6*. English translation in *Magdalena Abakanowicz*, exh. cat., Museum of Contemporary Art, Chicago 1982, *pp.102–3*.
8. On History: Delivered on the occasion of receiving the Award for Distinction in Sculpture from the SculptureCenter in New York, 7 December 1993. See Jacob and Dally 2022, *p.251*.
9. On Poland: From an interview conducted by Barbara Rose, 1988–91. See Jacob and Dally 2022, *p.183*.

Knots: Abakanowicz and the Polish Art Scene in the 1960s, pp.31–41

1. The film was completed by Mucha after Brzozowski's death, which helps explain its double character, with the discrepancy between the dunes scenes, shot by Brzozowski, and others, by Mucha.
2. This and all following translations from Polish by the author.
3. See Magali Junet, 'Abakanowicz and Lausanne: The Path to Fame', in *Abakanowicz: Metamorphism*, ed. Marta Kowalewska, Łódź 2018, *pp.85–117*.
4. Abakanowicz did not partake in the widespread boycott of official cultural events after the imposition of Martial Law in Poland in December 1981 that coincided with her large monographic exhibition in Chicago in 1982, thus alienating many of her peers.
5. Joanna Inglot, *The Figurative Sculpture of Magdalena Abakanowicz: Bodies, Environments and Myths*, Berkeley, CA 2004.
6. On the influence of Abakanowicz's teachers and her peer weavers, see Marta Kowalewska, 'Sculpting Space', in *Abakanowicz: Metamorphism* 2018, *pp.9–56*.
7. The end of the post-Stalinist Thaw: Around 1960 the communist authorities decided to claim greater control of the cultural sector after half a decade of allowing relatively unrestrained artistic experimentation in the wake of political Thaw. These five years of political and cultural relaxation (roughly 1955–60) overlapped with Abakanowicz's entrance into the professional art sector after her 1954 graduation. Inglot 2004 reconstructs Abakanowicz's study years in Warsaw very well.
8. In addition to gouaches and oils, the exhibition also included paintings on cloth.
9. Tadeusz Kantor, 'Abstrakcja umarła niech żyje abstrakcja', *Życie Literackie*, no.50, insert *Plastyka* no.16, 1957.
10. Mieczysław Porębski, 'Iluzja. Przypadek. Struktura', *Przegląd Artystyczny*, no.1, 1957.
11. Ibid., *p.37*.
12. Piotr Piotrowski, 'The Thaw and Art informel' in *In the Shadow of Yalta: Art and the Avant-Garde in Eastern Europe, 1945–1989*, London 2011, *pp.61–104*.
13. Inglot 2004, *p.35*.
14. Ibid.
15. Stażewski theorised this principle in 1932: 'Źródłem formy jest kontrast', in *Komunikat Grupy* a.r. no.2, 1932. This short text, in a publication co-authored with Kobro and Strzemiński, is attributed to Stażewski.
16. Maria Kosińska, 'Po wielkim konkursie', *Glos tygodnia (Szczecin)*, 21 March 1965, in response

to the exhibition at Zachęta CBWA, *Exhibition of Gobelins by Magdalena Abakanowicz.*

17. Aleksy Czerwiński, 'Gobeliny-Obrazy', *Stolica*, 16 May 1965, *p.13*.
18. Janina Russocka, 'Abakany', *Zwierciadło*, no.14, 4 April 1965.
19. Elżbieta Żmudzka, 'Magdalena Abakanowicz', *Zwierciadło*, no.6, 9 Feb. 1964.
20. Many of these works later travelled from Zachęta CBWA to the 8th São Paulo Biennial, where Abakanowicz received the gold medal in the applied arts section.
21. Jacek Sempoliński, 'Wystawy i Problemy', *Przegląd Kulturalny*, 28 April 1960.
22. Żmudzka 1964.
23. Janusz Bogucki, [untitlted text] in *Magdalena Abakanowicz: Wystawa tkanin*, exh. cat., Galeria Współczesna KMPiK 'Ruch', Warsaw 1967, unpaginated.
24. Ignacy Witz, 'Abakanowicz, Truszyński, Zemła', *Życie Warszawy*, 19 March 1965.
25. Hanna Ptaszkowska, 'Gobeliny Magdaleny Abakanowicz', *Kultura*, 11 April 1965, *p.9*.
26. Ibid.
27. Aleksy Czerwiński, 'Gobeliny-Obrazy', *Stolica*, 16 May 1965, *p.13*.
28. Witz 1965.
29. Wiesław Borowski, [untitled text] in *Wystawa Gobelinów Magdaleny Abakanowicz*, exh. cat., Zachęta CBWA, ZPAP, Warsaw 1965, unpaginated.
30. Gerard Kwiatkowski, 'Jesteśmy optymistami', *Polska*, no.11, 1965; Marian Bogusz, 'I Biennale Form Przestrzennych', *Kultura*, no.32, 1965.
31. Magdalena Abakanowicz, *Fate and Art*, 2nd edn, Milan 2020, *p.49*.
32. Ibid. Abakanowicz recalled that the obligatory style of sculpture in Poland around 1965 was social realism; sculpture had to be figurative and worship communism. Whether that statement was a flaw of unreliable human memory or an intentional act of self-mythologisation, it has to be clarified that in 1965 social realist sculpture had been absent from both exhibition halls and official state commissions for a decade.
33. Inglot 2004, *p.57*.
34. Abakanowicz 2020, *p.42*.
35. Bogucki 1967.
36. Konrad Schiller, *Awangarda na Dzikim Zachodzie: o wystawach i sympozjach Złotego Grona w Zielonej Górze*, Zielona Góra and Warszaw 2015.
37. From the conversation with Stefania Zagudka, Warsaw, September 2021.
38. Marta Leśniakowska, 'Biopolityczne ciało w environmentach Stanisława Zamecznika', in *Nowoczesności: lata 50. i 60. – wzornictwo, estetyka, styl życia*, ed. Anna Kiełczewska and Maria Porajska-Hałka, Warsaw 2012, *p.50*.
39. Ibid., *p.42*.
40. Magdalena Abakanowicz, 'On Space' (1971), in *Magdalena Abakanowicz: Writings and Conversations*, ed. Mary Jane Jacob and Jenny Dally, Milan 2022, *p.29*
41. Magdalena Abakanowicz, in exh. cat., Pasadena Art Museum, 1971. The quote also appears in Jacob and Dally 2022, *p.30*.
42. See Ann Coxon's essay in this volume, *pp.65–77*.
43. Abakanowicz 2020, *p.42*.
44. On Abakanowicz and American feminists, see Agata Jakubowska, 'The "Abakans" and the Feminist Revolution', in *Regarding the Popular: Modernism, the Avant-Garde and High and Low Culture*, ed. Sascha Bru et al., Berlin and Boston 2011, *pp.253–65*. See also: https://doi.org/10.1515/9783110274691.253
45. Anna Markowska, 'Abakanowicz i " informel" raz jeszcze', in *Dwa Przełomy: Sztuka Polska po 1955 i 1989 roku*, Toruń 2012, *p.190*.
46. Ibid., *p.191*.

Every Tangle of Thread and Rope: Abakanowicz's Organic Environments, pp.65–77

1. Magdalena Abakanowicz, *The Fabric Forms of Magdalena Abakanowicz*, exh. cat., Pasadena Art Museum 1971, *p.15*.
2. Letter from Abakanowicz to Robert Brenn, 3 November 1972.
3. Magdalena Abakanowicz, *Fate and Art*, 2nd edn, Milan 2020, *p.46*.
4. This essay uses the US spelling of Fiber Art throughout to refer to the movement as it was termed in the US and Europe in the 1970s.
5. Louise Bourgeois, 'The Fabric of Construction', *Craft Horizons*, vol.29, no.2, March/April 1969, *p.34*.
6. *Deliberate Entanglements*, ed. Bernard Kester, exh. cat., UCLA Art Galleries 1971, *p.3*.
7. Jagoda Buić's sketch for an environment is illustrated in Mildred Constantine and Jack Lenor Larsen, *Beyond Craft: The Art Fabric*, New York 1972, *pp.127–8*.
8. Elissa Auther, 'Introduction', in *String Felt Thread: The Hierarchy of Art and Craft in American Art*, Minneapolis 2010, *p.xxii*.
9. Lucy Lippard, *Eccentric Abstraction*, exhibition booklet, Fischbach Gallery, New York 1966. It is interesting to note that Lippard retrospectively reversed this statement to accept more symbolic content in the 1970s when she was engaged in feminist critique.
10. Text for the exhibition *Organic Structures and Soft Forms* in Australia, 1976, in 'About the Rope', *Abakanowicz: Organic Structures*, exh. cat., Malmö Konsthall, 1977. Reprinted in Abakanowicz 2020, *p.60*.
11. The artist Faith Wilding (b.1943) has said, 'I did see Abakanowicz's work at the Pasadena Museum and it was an overwhelming experience which also spurred me to try to make something immersive, something I could walk into'. Email to Jenny Dally, 12 August 2019.
12. Abakanowicz, quoted in Constantine and Larsen 1972, *p.92*.
13. Statement for exhibition in Södertälje, Sweden, 1970, archive of Jasia Reichardt, London.
14. Letter from Abakanowicz to Robert Brenn, 3 November 1972.
15. Abakanowicz 2020, *p.59*.
16. Letter from Richard Demarco to Abakanowicz, 18 January 1974 (emphasis in original).
17. Abakanowicz 2020, *p.60*.
18. 'Introduction', in Claire Bishop, *Installation Art: A Critical History*, London 2005.
19. Magdalena Abakanowicz, *The Fabric Forms of Magdalena Abakanowicz*, exh. cat., Pasadena Art Museum 1971, *p.15*.
20. Letter from Abakanowicz to Christer Tannlund, 23 February 1976. Archive of Fundacja Marty Magdaleny Abakanowicz Kosmowskiej i Jana Kosmowskiego, Warsaw.
21. T'ai Smith, 'Tapestries in Space: An Alternative History of Site-Specificity', in *Fiber: Sculpture 1960–Present*, ed. Jenelle Porter, exh. cat., Institute of Contemporary Art, Boston 2014, *p.153*.
22. Arthur Danto, 'The Tapestry and the Loincloth', 1996, an unpublished essay commissioned by Mary Jane Jacob for The Fabric Workshop and Museum, Philadelphia, PA (an abridged version published as 'Reflections on Fabric and Meaning: The Tapestry and the Loincloth', in *New Material as New Media: The Fabric Workshop and Museum*, ed. Marion Boulton Stroud and Kelly Mitchell, Cambridge, MA 2002, *p.84*.)

Art as Spatial Dramaturgy: Polish and Italian Povera, pp.79–87

1. From manuscript *Teksty archiwalne: Rzeibienie przestrzeni*, 1975. Archive of the artist, Warsaw. Reprinted in Marta Kowalewska, 'Sculpting Space', in *Abakanowicz: Metamorphism*, ed. Marta Kowalewska, exh. cat., Centralne Muzeum Włókiennictwa in Łódź 2018, *pp.45, 49*.
2. 'To protest is to give importance to those things, situations, thoughts, against which one takes up a position. Protest is also the only possible active stance in the face of a threat, invasion; it is a defensive position. My life unfolded in such a way that in order to exist I had to accept this position. It was the constant act of confrontation, self-defense, which, although it could not be realized in the practical aspects of life, expressed itself in work.' Magdalena Abakanowicz quoted in Jasia Reichardt, 'Magdalena Abakanowicz', in *Magdalena Abakanowicz*, exh. cat., Museum of Contemporary Art, Chicago 1982, *p.148*. Abakanowicz's works are expressions of dissent even if, as she states, the limitations imposed by the regime were an intellectual stimulus: 'Somehow the conflicts within the regime stimulated our thinking, encouraging an analytical approach to existence in general, allowing us to observe the human being as such with his ambitions and desire that are never fulfilled and remain a longing.' Magdalena Abakanowicz, *Fate and* Art, 2nd edn, Milan 2020, *p.113*.
3. Jerzy Grotowski, *Per un teatro povero*, Rome 1970 (preface by Peter Brook, writings by Ludwik Flaszen, Eugenio Barba).
4. Silvia Parlagreco, 'L'assente presenza di Tadeusz Kantor', in *Tadeusz Kantor: Cricot 2*, Milan 2001, *p.39*.
5. *Kantor la mia opera, il mio viaggio – commento intimo*, Milan 1991 *p.24*. (Cited in *Tadeusz Kantor* 2001, *p.39*). Kantor formulated the idea of the 'poor object' as early as 1944.
6. Kantor, who had begun his career as a visual artist, spoke of a 'contradiction between reality and the concept of representation.' Tadeusz Kantor, *Tadeusz Kantor: Scritti*, ed. Silvia Parlagreco, trans. Ludmila Ryba, vol.1, Spoleto 2018, *p.432*.
7. 'Weich=Leben', in *Weich und Plastisch: Soft-Art*, exh. cat., Kunsthaus Zürich 1979, *pp.74–6*. English translation in *Magdalena Abakanowicz*, exh. cat., Museum of Contemporary Art, Chicago 1982, *p.102*.
8. Jerzy Grotowski, *Il teatr laboratorium di Jerzy Grotowski, 1959–1969*, ed. L. Flaszen, C. Pollastrelli and R. Molinari, 2nd edn, Florence 2007, *p.109*.
9. Ibid. In this sense the words of Eugenio Barba are also of interest: 'Jerzy Grotowski defines

theatre as a collective self-penetration. The theatre, if it wants to reawaken, to stimulate the inner life of the spectators, has to break down all resistance, to smash every mental cliché that protects against access into their subconscious. This theatre can be compared to a true anthropological expedition. It leaves civilized lands to venture into the heart of the virgin forest; it renounces the clearly defined values of reason to confront the darkness of the collective imagination. Because it is in this darkness that our culture, our language, our imagination have their roots ... At the Theatre-Laboratory, then, the spectators are forced to come to grips with their most secret, most hidden self. Brutally thrust into the world of myths, they have to simultaneously recognize and judge them, examining them in the light of their own experiences as 20th-century individuals. This face-off, this unmasking, is perceived by many as sacrilege. In truth, we are faced by a modern variant of the ancient catharsis or, to find a definition closer to us, of psychotherapy.' Eugenio Barba, 'Verso un teatro santo e sacrilego', in *Il teatr laboratorium* 2007, *p.90*.

10. In those same years an outstanding Italian artist, Maria Lai (1919–2013), drew stimuli from the same territory, the same legends, to weave dense, pregnant work that starts from thread and fabric to approach universal themes. Though we have no evidence that they met, the correspondence is nevertheless of interest.
11. Ron Grimes, 'The Theater of Sources', *The Drama Review: TDR*, vol.25, no.3, Autumn 1981, *pp.67–74*.
12. Magdalena Abakanowicz, 'About Headless Dances', in *Magdalena Abakanowicz: Coexistence*, exh. cat., Marlborough Gallery, New York 2003, *p.17*.
13. In the 1960s Grotowski's influence was already extending well beyond theatre and though his seminal text *Towards a Poor Theatre* (1968) was not published in Italian until 1970, his influence was evident as early as September 1967 when Celant organised an exhibition at Galleria La Bertesca in Genoa, under the title *Arte Povera e IM Spazio*. On 23 November that same year *Flash Art* published Celant's essay 'Appunti per una guerriglia' (Notes for a Guerilla) in which he spoke of 'poor research' aimed at recovering the identity between man and nature, man and his own actions. The artists mentioned are Michelangelo Pistoletto (b.1933), Alighiero Boetti (1940–94), Gilberto Zorio (b.1944), Luciano Fabro (1936–2007), Giovanni Anselmo (b.1934), Gianni Piacentino (b.1945), Piero Gilardi (b.1942), Emilio Prini (b.1943), Mario Merz (1925–2003), Jannis Kounellis (1936–2017), Giulio Paolini (b.1940) and Pino Pascali (1935–68). The source of the term 'povero' as Grotowski is explicitly stated. During the next year, Celant also curated an exhibition at Galleria de' Foscherari in Bologna (February 1968), and the important *Arte Povera + Azioni Povere* in Amalfi. His book *Arte Povera* came shortly thereafter in 1969.
14. As Abakanowicz herself points out, there is an enormous difference and clear separation between what was happening in the West in this period and what was happening in Poland. 'In 1968', for example, 'in Poland started a political crisis that began with students protest [sic.] against Communist repressions. It had nothing to do with the events in the West.' Letter from Abakanowicz to Michael Brenson, 20 June 1994.
15. After the Second World War – which saw Italy dominated by Fascism, then occupied by the Germans, on the edge of the civil war and finally freed by the Italian partisan movements together with the Allied forces – the country tried to find a political and economic balance within the postwar structure. The US Marshall Plan, or European Recovery Program, gave substantial economic and financial support to the process of social and industrial reconstruction, coming with it US influence on the country's postwar structure. Among the conditions to which the allocation of funds is linked is that of avoiding the establishment of a leftist government. American interference would mark profoundly the political debate of the following decade.
16. Parlagreco 2001, *p.39*.
17. Letter from Abakanowicz to Michael Brenson, 15 October 1993, in *Magdalena Abakanowicz: Writings and Conversations*, ed. Mary Jane Jacob and Jenny Dally, Milan 2022, *p.233*.
18. From Douglas Dreishpoon, 'Monumental Intimacy: An Interview with Magdalena Abakanowicz', *Arts Magazine 65*, no.4, December 1990, *pp.45–9*. Also appears in Jacob and Jenny Dally, Milan 2022, *pp.264–5*.

Crafting an Art Practice: The Postwar Polish Art Scene, pp.148–51

1. Secondary schools of fine art allowed students to obtain a graduate diploma and the title of professional visual artist, after passing the diploma exam.
2. These records are found in the Archive of the Academy of Fine Arts, Warsaw: diploma, Secondary School of Plastic Arts, Gdynia, dated 31 May 1949; enrollment notation in student record book of the State Higher School of Fine Arts in Sopot, dated 4 November 1949; and a handwritten document entitled 'Application to the Academy of Plastic Arts in Warsaw', dated 11 October 1950.
3. The application for certificate of completion of studies at the Department of Textiles and for beginning diploma work in the studio of Professor Anna Śledziewska, dated 8 October 1953, is in the Archive of Academy of Fine Arts, Warsaw. The document contains information about consent to the certificate of completion, dated 22 October 1953 and the diploma, dated 14 June 1954. See also Joanna Kania, 'Patchwork', in *Powinność i bunt: Akademia Sztuk Pięknych w Warszawie 1944–2004*, exh. cat., Zachęta Narodowa Galeria Sztuki, Warsaw 2004, *pp.290–4*.
4. See *Nowy przekład w kolorze – historia ZPAP 1911– 2011*, Warsaw 2010.
5. Jolanta Chrzanowska-Pieńkos and Andrzej Pieńkos, *Leksykon sztuki polskiej XX w.*, Poznań 1996, *p.266.*
6. ZPAP field offices existed in all the largest cities – voivodeship capitals – in Poland at that time. The division into sections was not identical in all cities. Starting in the 1970s, industrial design sections operated in some of the branches.
7. Marta Kowalewska, 'Doświadczenia z krosnem', *Art & Business*, no.3, 2007, *p.41*.
8. Starting in 1966, Abakanowicz was a member of this organisation. The Polish Society of Authors and Composers was known in Polish simply as ZAiKS.
9. One of the most important units responsible for the distribution of paid commissions for artists was the Studios of Plastic Arts established by the Minister of Art and Culture in 1949. Delegations and branches of PSP throughout the country associated artists from all disciplines of art.
10. Desa, coined from the words *Dzieła Sztuki* and *Antyki* (Works of Art and Antiques), was a state enterprise dealing in the trade of works of art and antiques, created on 3 April 1950 by ordinance of the Minister of Art and Culture together with the Ministry of Internal Trade. The showrooms of the enterprise operated all over the country and were treated equally with cultural institutions displaying art (including old and modern). In the 1970s, it had about sixty galleries and antique shops. At the end of the 1990s, it was privatised and divided into two companies with headquarters in Kraków and Warsaw. See Igor Bloch, 'W darze dla antyrewolucyjnej burżuazji. Historia Przedsiębiorstwa Państwowego Desa', *Szum*, no.20, Spring–Summer 2018, *pp.52–61.*
11. Ordinance of the Ministers of Foreign Trade and Finance, dated 4 January 1962. MP. 1962.9.31.
12. *Exhibition of Artworks by Magdalena Abakanowicz-Kosmowska*, Galeria Kordegarda, Warsaw, 1960; *Exhibition of Gobelins by Magdalena Abakanowicz,* Zachęta CBWA, Warsaw, 1965; *Magdalena Abakanowicz,* Zachęta CBWA, Warsaw, 1975. Zachęta CBWA was founded in 1949 at the Zachęta building in Warsaw. Under the institutional control of the Ministry of Art and Culture, Zachęta CBWA became the central state institution for the popularisation of art and the organisation of artistic life throughout the country. The institution operated under the name Zachęta CBWA until 1994, when it became Zachęta Państwowa Galeria Sztuki. See *Zachęta 1860–2000,* ed. Gabriela Świtek, Warsaw 2003.
13. Abakanowicz's membership documentation: Archive of the Main Board of ZPAP, Warsaw.
14. ŁAD was a cooperative of visual artists interested in the development of applied art in Poland founded in 1926. It harnessed the folk craft tradition to promote designs of everyday objects of high aesthetic quality in accordance with the needs of modern life and the characteristics of materials available in Poland. The ŁAD cooperative had shops with prototypes of offered objects such as unique textiles, furniture, ceramics and metal items. Activity was interrupted by the war, and was reactivated after 1945. From 1949, activity was subordinated to Cepelia. See Krystyna Zwolińska, Zasław Malicki, *Mały słownik terminów plastycznych,* 4th edn, Warsaw 1974, *p.163.*
15. Cepelia was the central association of handicrafts cooperatives which ran trade outlets, selling goods produced in affiliated cooperatives made or inspired by the works of Polish folk artists. It existed from 1949 to 1990. After the fall of communism, it was privatised. See Piotr Korduba, *Ludowość na sprzedaż,* Warsaw 2013.

16. *30th Anniversary of the Artist Cooperative of Plastic Arts 'ŁAD'*, Zachęta CBWA, Warsaw, 1956; *2nd State Exhibition of Interior Design*, Zachęta CBWA, Warsaw, 1957.
17. *Artists of Visual Arts from the Warsaw District of Association of Polish Artists and Designers 1945–1970. Biographical Dictionary*, Warsaw 1972, *p.15*.
18. The most important awards include: Minister of Culture's Award – First Degree, 1965; Level III Award of the Minister of Culture and Art for achievements in the field of artistic fabrics, 1965; Silver Cross of Merit, 1969; Diploma and Award of the Ministry of Foreign Affairs for outstanding achievements in promotion of Polish culture abroad, 1970; Minister of Culture's Award – Second Degree for original achievements in the field of artistic fabric, 1972; Golden Cross of Merit, 1974; Distinguished Cultural Activist, 1975; Knight's Cross of the Order of Polonia Restituta, 1980; Award of the Minister of Foreign Affairs, 1984.
19. Document at the Archive of the Main Board of ZPAP, Warsaw.
20. Elżbieta Żmudzka, 'Magdalena Abakanowicz', *Zwierciadło*, no.6, 9 Nov. 1964, *p.8*.

Abakany: The Essence of Time and Space, pp.152–9

1. Letter from Magdalena Abakanowicz to Barbara Strzelewska, a friend and former student, 1 November 1976. Archive of the artist, Warsaw.
2. Barbara Stopczyk, 'Jarosław Brzozowski 1911–1969', *KINO* 1970, no.52, *p.12*.
3. Ibid., *p.14*.
4. 'Little stabilisation' – the rule of Władysław Gomułka as the 1st Secretary of the PZPR (Polish communist party, ruling 1948–89), which followed the era of Stalinism. The liberalisation of social life, the withdrawal of the authorities from mass ideological indoctrination and amnesty for political prisoners were characteristic of this time. The economic situation improved, there was a demographic increase – Polish culture entered the period of its heyday.
5. Kazimierz Mucha, 'Forma przekazu czy twórcza interpretacja?', *Kamera 1969*, no.12, *p.3*.
6. Ibid.
7. Irena Huml, *Współczesna tkanina polska* (Contemporary Polish Textile), Warsaw 1989, *p.39*.
8. Conversation with Barbara Tryc-Dyksińska, in: *Twórczość Magdaleny Abakanowicz w aspekcie rozwoju uzdolnień plastycznych artystki* (The work of Magdalena Abakanowicz from the point of view of the development of her artistic talent), ANEKS, part III, *p.3*.
9. Magdalena Abakanowicz, *Teksty archiwalne. Kształt zawisły w przestrzeni* (Archive Texts: Shapes Suspended in Space), 1970. Typescript in the Archive of Fundacja Marty Magdaleny Abakanowicz Kosmowskiej i Jana Kosmowskiego, Warsaw.

Spaces Unguarded: Abakanowicz's Drawings, pp.160–5

1. At the end of the 1950s, unconnected with any weaving project, the artist was already executing collages that combined gouaches and torn/cut-out pieces of paper. Around 1963, she also designed models using bits of photographs of her tapestries as well as cut-out pieces of paper. The effect was quite surreal.
2. *Exhibition of Gobelins by Magdalena Abakanowicz*, Zachęta CBWA, Warsaw, 1965. A comparison of the titles and measurements of the tapestries mentioned in the list of exhibits has led us to believe that the small formats that can be seen on a photograph taken at the time are in fact drawings and not weavings. To view the picture, see *Abakanowicz: Metamorphism*, ed. Marta Kowalewska, exh. cat., Centralne Muzeum Włókiennictwa in Łódź 2018, *p.160*.
3. Galerie Alice Pauli, Lausanne, 1981 and 1982; Galerie Jeanne Bucher, Paris, 1982; Museum of Contemporary Art, Chicago et al., 1982–4.

Return to Paradise: Concerning Arboreal Architecture, pp.166–73

1. Magdalena Abakanowicz, *Fate and Art*, 2nd edn, Milan 2020, *p.9*.
2. Ibid., *p.13*.
3. Barbara Rose, *Magdalena Abakanowicz*, New York 1994, *p.7*.
4. Abakanowicz 2020, *p.148*.
5. Magdalena Abakanowicz, 'War Games', *Magdalena Abakanowicz: Recent Work*, exh. cat., Marlborough Gallery, New York 1989, *p.58*.
6. Magdalena Abakanowicz, 'Backs', *Konteksty: Cultural Anthropology, Ethnography, Art*, vol.60, no.3–4, 2006, *p.60*.
7. Letter from Magdalena Abakanowicz to Kuniko Lucy Kato, undated, c.1991.
8. Abakanowicz 2020, *p.158*.
9. Ibid.
10. Letter from Magdalena Abakanowicz to Kuniko Lucy Kato, undated, c.1991.
11. Ibid.
12. Michael Brenson, 'The Idea of Arboreal Architecture', *Konteksty: Cultural Anthropology, Ethnography, Art*, vol.60, no.3–4, 2006, *p.168*.
13. Magdalena Abakanowicz, *Space to Experience*, undated statement, c.1994.

Celebrating an Artist: Abakanowicz in Wrocław, pp.174–7

1. The world-famous architect was a lecturer from 1900 to 1913, and the director of the State Academy of Arts and Crafts in Wrocław during 1913–16.
2. Mariusz Hermansdorfer was an employee of the Muzeum Narodowe in Wrocław from 1964–6 and returned in 1972. He became its director in 1983, before retiring in 2013. The Four Domes Pavilion opened to the public on 25 June 2016.
3. 'I met Magda Abakanowicz in Brazil in 1979. I was once again organising the Polish section of the São Paulo Biennial. As it was the Biennial's fifteenth anniversary, work from artists who had won awards in previous years was on display alongside exhibitions of current work.' Mariusz Hermansdorfer, '6/2017: Magdalena Abakanowicz 1930–2017', *Ośrodek Kultury i Sztuki in Wrocław*, 22 June 2017: https://okis.pl/62017-magdalena-abakanowicz-1930-2017.
4. *Art at the Edge: Contemporary Art from Poland*, 1988 – a joint exhibition of works from the collection of the Muzeum Narodowe in Wrocław, which included Abakanowicz and which was later shown at the Museum of Modern Art in Oxford.
5. Exhibitions organised by Hermansdorfer of the museum's Abakanowicz holdings were staged in Krakow (1993); Székesfehérvár, Hungary (1993); Breda, the Netherlands (1994); Prague (1999), in addition to showings in our own museum in 1991 and 1999, the latter which travelled to Zachęta Państwowa Galeria Sztuki, Warsaw.
6. The title seems to indicate the period during which this work was made. In the preceding months she also created *Abakan Noir/Novembre–Décembre* 1971. Slightly larger at 340 x 200 x 200 than *Abakan January–February* (pp.136–9), it was shown in *Abakanowicz: Organic Structures and Human Forms* at Galerie Alice Pauli in Lausanne, Switzerland, in September 1975. Returned to the artist, to date this work has not been located, suggesting that perhaps, as with other pieces, it was reworked.
7. Around this time the artist's husband underwent heart operations.
8. Magdalena Abakanowicz, presentation at *Fiberworks: Symposium on Contemporary Textile Art*, Oakland 1978, *p.10*.
9. Hermansdorfer 2017.

Organic Structures: Abakanowicz in Norway, pp.178–81

1. This article is indebted to Runa Boger and her research on Magdalena Abakanowicz's impact on Norway through her two exhibitions.
2. Alf Bøe, 'Vår tids billedtepper' ('Today's tapestries'), *Bonytt 22*, Nov.–Dec. 1962, *pp.267–9*. (This, and all other translations of article titles are the author's own).
3. Mary Jane Jacob, 'Introduction', in *Magdalena Abakanowicz*, Chicago 1982, *p.13*.
4. The exhibition *Modern Polish Tapestry* in 1965 at Kunstindustrimuseet in Oslo was a result of this, in which Abakanowicz contributed two works, together with twenty-five other Polish artists.
5. 'Kunstneraksjonen' (the artists' campaign) in 1974 became a key contributor to this change: writers, sculptors, painters, composers, and other artists stood together to improve the conditions of artists in Norway. As a result of their efforts, textile artists united, and the organisation for artists working with textiles and fibre, Norwegian Textile Art, was created in 1977. Works in fibre were finally included in the artists' own ranks.
6. Following the show's success, several Norwegian institutions acquired works: Oslo kommunes kunstsamling bought *Argentine* 1967 and *Ovale d'Or* 1967. Universitetet i Oslo bought *Triptyque Noir* 1967. Kunstindustrimuseet was donated *100* by the artist.
7. Runa Boger, 'Magdalena Abakanowicz og Norge. Stilskaper eller frigjørende forbilde? En drøftelse av Abakanowicz' betydning for norsk tekstilkunst 1960–80. ('Magdalena Abakanowicz and Norway: Style creator or liberating role model? A discussion of Abakanowicz's significance for Norwegian textile art 1960–1980'), MA thesis, Oslo 2010, *p.49*.
8. Ibid., *p.47*.

9. Kirsti Hopstock, 'Effekter i grov strie' ('Effects in coarse straw'), *Morgenbladet*, 11 Nov. 1977.
10. Pål Hougen, 'Et jordskjelv i billedkunsten' ('An earthquake in the visual arts'), *Vi Ser på Kunst*, 23 Nov. 1977.
11. Installations by artists Britt Smelvær (b.1945), Karin Aurora Lindell (b.1955) and Kari Steihaug's (b.1962) are examples of this.

The Liveliness of Matter: Contemporary Dialogues, pp.182–5

1. Magdalena Abakanowicz, *Magdalena Abakanowicz: Organic Structures and Human Forms*, exh. cat., Whitechapel Gallery, London 1975, n.p.
2. Abakanowicz, from 'Magdalena Abakanowicz: The Human Condition in Fiber Forms', *International Sculpture* 4, no.2, April/May 1985, *pp.6–7, 24*. Also in Mary Jane Jacob and Jenny Dally (eds), *Magdalena Abakanowicz: Writings and Conversations*, Milan 2022, *p.179*.
3. Abakanowicz, *Polish Perspectives*, no.2, 1980, *p.62*.
4. Abakanowicz, from 'Rope Environments: Magdalena Abakanowicz discusses her work with Judith Bumpus', *Art and Artists*, vol.9, no.7, Oct. 1974, pp.37–41. Also in Jacob and Dally 2022, *p.61*.
5. Ibid., p.*154*
6. Works by Suter, Henderson, Grantiņa and Baghramian are recent acquisitions into Tate's collection.
7. For a discussion of this relationship in the context of contemporary art, see Jessica L. Horton and Janet Catherine Berlo, 'Beyond the Mirror: Indigenous Ecologies and "New Materialisms" in Contemporary Art', *Third Text*, vol.27, issue 1, Jan. 2013, *pp.17–28*; Eugenia Kisin, 'Durable Remains: Indigenous Materialisms in Duane Linklater's *From Our Hands*', *ARTMargins* 7.2: https://artmargins.com/durable-remains-indigenous-materialisms-in-duane-linklaters-from-our-hands-artmargins-print-7-2/, accessed 15 August 2020.
8. Vivian Suter, quoted in 'Vivian Suter: the rainforest-dwelling artist who paints with fish glue, dogs and mud': https://www.theguardian.com/artanddesign/2020/jan/07/vivian-suter-artist-interview-elisabeth-wild-guatemala-rainforest, accessed 7 January 2020.
9. Tamara Henderson in conversation with Rosanna McLaughlin, Studio International, August 2018: https://www.studiointernational.com/index.php/tamara-henderson-interview-you-could-say-the-maquettes-were-the-hypnotherapy-i-did-at-gatwick-airport, accessed 25 November 2019.
10. Recent examples of this include the 13th Gwangju Biennial *Minds Rising, Spirits Tuning* (Gwangju, 2020), the exhibitions *The Botanical Mind: Art, Mysticism and the Cosmic Tree* (Camden Art Centre, London, 2020), *Hilma af Klint: Paintings for the Future* (The Solomon R. Guggenheim Museum, 2018–19) and *Not Without My Ghosts: The Artist As Medium* (Drawing Room, London, 2020 and touring), as well as the Foundation for Spirituality and the Arts, which opened in 2021.
11. Abakanowicz, quoted in Barbara Rose, *Magdalena Abakanowicz*, New York 1994, *p.41*.

A Lifetime of Experiences: A Narrative Chronology, pp.186–96

1. Polskie Radio S. A., 20 March 1975. Translation by Marysia Lewandowska.
2. Magdalena Abakanowicz, *Fate and* Art, 2nd edn, Milan 2020, *p.9*.
3. Betty Park, 'Magdalena Abakanowicz Speaks: The Renowned Polish Artist Discusses her Work and Life', *Fiberarts*, March/April 1983, *p.14*. See Mary Jane Jacob and Jenny Dally (eds), *Magdalena Abakanowicz: Writings and Conversations*, Milan 2022, *p.177*.
4. Magdalena Abakanowicz, 'Portrait x 20', in *Magdalena Abakanowicz*, exh. cat., Museum of Contemporary Art, Chicago 1982, *p.26*. See Jacob and Dally 2022, *p.160*.
5. Magdalena Abakanowicz, interview with Barbara Rose, 1988–91. See Jacob and Dally 2022, *p.184*.
6. Abakanowicz 1982, *p.27*. See Jacob and Dally 2022, *p.162*.
7. Ibid, *p.28*. See Jacob and Dally 2022, *p.162*.
8. In 1957, the Academy reverts back to the name, the Academy of Fine Arts (*Akademia Sztuk Pięknych*).
9. 'Magdalena Abakanowicz: An Interview with Jeff Makin', *Quadrant*, vol.20, no.6, June 1976, *pp.52–3*. See Jacob and Dally 2022, *p.67*.
10. Letter from Abakanowicz to Michael Brenson, 26 August 1992.
11. Makin 1976, *p.53*. See Jacob and Dally 2022, *p.67*.
12. Jasia Reichardt, 'Magdalena Abakanowicz', in *Magdalena Abakanowicz*, exh. cat., Museum of Contemporary Art, Chicago 1982, *p.33*.
13. Abakanowicz 2020, *p.26*.
14. Ibid., *p.31*.
15. Ibid., *p.34*.
16. Ibid., *p.39*.
17. Douglas Dreishpoon, 'Monumental Intimacy: An Interview with Magdalena Abakanowicz', *Arts Magazine*, vol.65, no.4, Dec. 1990, *p.47*. See Jacob and Dally 2022, *p.266*.
18. Letter from Abakanowicz to Krystyna Kondratiuk, 27 March 1963. See Jacob and Dally 2022, *p.73*.
19. Elżbieta Żmudzka, 'How to name the woven paintings of Magdalena Abakanowicz? Maybe – Abakans? That sounds good. A bit traditional and at the same time emphasizing the authorship of a talented artist. We are not joking proposing this name,' in 'Magdalena Abakanowicz', *Zwierciadło*, no.6, 9 Nov. 1964, *p.8*. Later, in a letter dated 20 June 1994, the artist recalls to art critic and art historian Michael Brenson: 'The name Abakans was invented in the artist cafeteria in Warsaw after the opening of my exhibition [at Zachęta CBWA] in 1965 and before the São Paulo Biennale.'
20. Letter from Abakanowicz to Michael Brenson, 20 June 1994. Indeed, by 1965, art critic Janina Russocka wrote: 'The playful name "Abakans" became fixed, because these works of high artistic quality are actually uncommonly difficult to classify in any of the generally accepted concepts.' In 'Abakany', *Wiedza i Życie*, no.8, 1965, *p.354*.
21. Abakanowicz 2020, *p.64*.
22. In 1996 this school was renamed Akademia Sztuk Pięknych w Poznaniu (Academy of Fine Arts in Poznań), then in 2010 University of Fine Arts in Poznań (Uniwersytet Artystyczny w Poznaniu). In 2021, it was renamed again as University of Arts in Poznań (Uniwersytet Artystyczny im. Magdaleny Abakanowicz w Poznaniu).
23. Abakanowicz 2020, *p.101*.
24. Magdalena Abakanowicz, 'Magdalena Abakanowicz: Confession', *Sculpture*, vol.24, no.8, Oct. 2005, *p.34*.
25. 'Art is a Necessity: Ewa Izabela Nowak Talks to Prof. Magdalena Abakanowicz', in *Magdalena Abakanowicz: Retrospective*, exh. cat., Centrum Rzeźby Polskiej in Orońsko 2013, *p.7*. See Jacob and Dally 2022, *p.310*.
26. Starting in March 1968, *Wall Hangings* was a circulating show of the Museum of Modern Art, New York and travelled to eleven venues. The museum's press release notes that it was installed by Arthur Drexler, Director of the Department of Architecture and Design.
27. Abakanowicz 2020, *p.53*.
28. Fax from Magdalena Abakanowicz to Michael Brenson, 29 April 1996. See Jacob and Dally 2022, *p.237*.
29. Magdalena Abakanowicz, interview with Barbara Rose, 1988–91. See Jacob and Dally 2022, *p.184*.
30. 'Rope Environments: Magdalena Abakanowicz Discusses her Work with Judith Bumpus', *Art and Artists*, vol.9, no.7, Oct. 1974, *pp.40–1*. See Jacob and Dally 2022, *p.64*.
31. Ibid., *p.37*. See Jacob and Dally 2022, *p.60*.
32. Abakanowicz 2005, *p.37*.
33. Later she receives honorary doctorates from Rhode Island School of Design, Providence (1992), Władysław Strzemiński Academy of Fine Arts, Łódź, Poland (1998), Pratt Institute, New York, (2000), Massachusetts College of Art, Boston (2001), School of the Art Institute of Chicago (2002) and Academy of Fine Arts, Poznań, Poland (2002). She also becomes an honorary member of the Akademie der Künste, Berlin, Germany (1994), American Academy of Arts and Letters, New York (1996), and Sächsiche Akademie der Künste, Dresden, Germany (1998).
34. At the opening she meets Dr Patrick D. Wall, a professor in the Department of Anatomy and Embryology at University College London specialising in the physiology of sensory systems and researching the nature of pain. They correspond in whether *Seated Figures* 1974–6 are about life or death.
35. Abakanowicz 2020, *pp.104, 105*.
36. Jacob and Dally 2022, *pp.412–13*.
37. Ibid.
38. Abakanowicz 2020, *p.86*.
39. Ibid., *p.90*.
40. Magdalena Abakanowicz 'Backs', *Konteksty: Cultural Anthropology, Ethnography, Art*, vol.60, no.3–4, 2006, *p.60*. See Jacob and Dally 2022, *p.164*.
41. Abakanowicz, interview with Barbara Rose, 1988–91. See Jacob and Dally 2022, *p.193*.
42. Letter from Abakanowicz to Mary Jane Jacob, 16 June 1981. See Jacob and Dally 2022, *p.208*.
43. Abakanowicz, interview with Barbara Rose, 1988–91. See Jacob and Dally 2022, *p.202*.
44. Letter from Abakanowicz to Michael Brenson, 5 April 1994. See Jacob and Dally 2022, *p.235*.
45. Abakanowicz, interview with Barbara Rose, 1988–91. See Jacob and Dally 2022, *p.194*. (*Sarcophagi in Glass Houses* 1989, was

permanently sited in 1994 at Storm King Art Center in Mountainville, New York).

46. Ann Temkin, The Marie-Josée and Henry Kravis Chief Curator of Painting and Sculpture, Department of Painting and Sculpture at the Museum of Modern Art, in *Magdalena Abakanowicz: A Memorial Tribute*, booklet from an event at the Museum of Modern Art, New York, 27 February 2018, *p.5*.
47. Jacob and Dally 2022, *p.300*.
48. Abakanowicz 2020, *p.148*.
49. Abakanowicz, interview with Peter Boswell (associate curator, Walker Art Center), in *Magdalena Abakanowicz*, pamphlet, Walker Art Center 1992, unpag. See Jacob and Dally 2022, *p.249*.
50. Letter from Abakanowicz to Kuniko Lucy Kato, undated.
51. Magdalena Abakanowicz, 'Japan', *Konteksty: Cultural Anthropology, Ethnography, Art*, vol.60, no.3–4, 2006, *p.94*.
52. Letter from Abakanowicz to Michael Brenson, 11 December 1996.
53. Letter from Abakanowicz to Thomas Krens, 3 March 1997.
54. Guest book, Europos Parkas, Open-Air Museum of the Centre of Europe in Vilnius, Lithuania, 16 July 2005.
55. Magdalena Abakanowicz, 'Puellae, Bambini, Ragazzi', *Konteksty: Cultural Anthropology, Ethnography, Art*, vol.60, no.3–4, 2006, *p.130*. See Jacob and Dally 2022, *p.301*.
56. Letter from Abakanowicz to Barbara Rose, 14 December 1990. See Jacob and Dally 2022, *pp.223–4*.
57. Abakanowicz 2020, *p.192*.
58. Douglas Dreishpoon, 'Monumental Intimacy: An Interview with Magdalena Abakanowicz', *Arts Magazine*, vol.65, no.4, Dec. 1990, *p.49*. See Jacob and Dally 2022, *p.268*.
59. Unpublished text, 2005. See Jacob and Dally 2022, *p.303*.
60. Letter from Abakanowicz to Mary Jane Jacob, 14 October 1993. See Jacob and Dally 2022, *p.218*.
61. Email from Ann Hamilton to Mary Jane Jacob, 23 April 2017.

EXHIBITED WORKS

All works are by Magdalena Abakanowicz (1930–2017), unless otherwise stated. Works are chronologically organised; works with the same date are ordered alphabetically. Titles have been translated into English for the most part, with original Polish titles following in parentheses. Original French titles have not been translated. For some works, alternative titles are provided. Measurements are given in centimetres, height before width and depth. Page references to the works illustrated are given at the end of the entries.

***Jacquard project for* Polish Textiles (Tkanina polska) *book cover* 1952**
Graphite on graph paper 14.5 × 16
Private collection
p.150

***Green Composition (Kompozycja zielona)* 1956–7**
Fish
Gouache on cotton canvas 205 × 135
Fundacja Marty Magdaleny Abakanowicz Kosmowskiej i Jana Kosmowskiego
p.42

***Untitled* c.1958**
Screenprint and paint on cotton 136 × 78
Private collection
p.151

***Untitled* c.1958**
Screenprint on cotton 157 × 79.5
Private collection

***Untitled* c.1958**
Screenprint on cotton 131 × 81
Private collection

***Untitled* c.1958**
Screenprint and paint on cotton 139.5 × 88
Private collection

***Polish Textiles (Tkanina polska)* 1959**
Edited by Ksawery Piwocki (Warsaw, Arkady, 1959)
Fabric and print on paper 29.7 × 22 × 3
Collection of Cezary Lisowski, Design Archives Foundation

***Jacquard project for* Polish Textiles (Tkanina polska) c.1959**
Set of jacquard punched cards 80 cards, each 43 × 6
Private collection

Composition (*Kompozycja*) 1960
Fabric with White Plant (Tkanina z białą rośliną)
Gouache on linen 280 × 140
Central Museum of Textiles in Łódź
p.43

***Composition (Kompozycja)* 1960**
Oil paint on canvas 100.5 × 82
Fundacja Marty Magdaleny Fundacja Marty Magdaleny Abakanowicz Kosmowskiej i Jana Kosmowskiego
p.33

***Untitled* c.1960**
Oil paint on canvas 55.7 × 47
Private collection

***Textural Composition White (Kompozycja fakturowa biała)* 1961–2**
White ('Biały')
Sisal and cotton 164 × 106
ASOM Collection
p.44

***Sun (Słońce)* 1963**
Dark-blue and Black Textile (Tkanina granatowo-czarna)
La construction noire
Wool, cotton and artificial silk 152 × 211
Central Museum of Textiles in Łódź
pp.48–9

***Design for 'Tapisserie 21 brune'* 1963**
Ink and gouache on papers on paper 19 × 39.5
Private collection
pp.46–7

***Tapisserie 21 brune* 1963**
Brown Textile 21 (Tkanina 21 brązowa)
Wool 150 × 295
Fundacja Marty Magdaleny Abakanowicz Kosmowskiej i Jana Kosmowskiego
p.45

***Design for tapestry 'Teresa'* 1963**
Gouache on papers on paper 39 × 55
Central Museum of Textiles in Łódź. Gift of the Artistic Directors on behalf of Abakanowicz Arts and Culture Charitable Foundation
p.37

***Black and White (Czarno-biała)* 1965**
Hemp, horsehair, sisal and wool 118 × 294
Museum of the Central Pomerania in Słupsk
pp.54–5

***Desdemona* 1965**
Desdemona 29
Wool, fleece, sisal, cotton, artificial silk and horsehair 300 × 410
Central Museum of Textiles in Łódź
pp.52–3

***Helena* 1964–5**
Wool, cotton, sisal and horsehair 300 × 480
Marlborough Gallery, New York
pp.50–1

***Untitled* 1965**
Ink and gouache on papers on paper 50 × 70
Fondation Toms Pauli, Lausanne. Gift of Pierre and Marguerite Magnenat

***Untitled* 1965**
Ink and gouache on papers on paper 50 × 70.5
Fondation Toms Pauli, Lausanne. Gift of Pierre and Marguerite Magnenat

***Untitled* 1965**
Ink and gouache on papers on paper 50 × 69.5
Fondation Toms Pauli, Lausanne. Gift of Pierre and Marguerite Magnenat
p.160

***Assemblage noir* 1966**
Assemblage III
Oval (Owalna)
Sisal, wool, hemp and horsehair 300 × 220
Musée des beaux-arts, La Chaux-de-Fonds
pp.58–61

***Black (Czarna)* 1966**
Sisal, rope and horsehair 300 × 156
Marlborough Gallery, New York
pp.56–7

***Diptère* 1967**
Hemp, sisal and horsehair 270 × 260
ASOM Collection
pp.62–3

***Abakan étroit* 1967–8**
Abakan Madrid
Sisal and wool 320 × 100 × 100
Fondation Toms Pauli, Lausanne. Gift of the Association Pierre Pauli
pp.4, 89–93

***Abakan Open (Abakan otwarty)* 1967–8**
Abakan ouvert
Sisal 330 × 150 × 100
National Museum in Wrocław
p.101

***Abakan Orange* 1968**
Baroque Dress
Orange Garment
Sisal 360 × 360 × 45
Nationalmuseum, Stockholm
p.69

***Abakan Round (Abakan okrągły)* 1967–8**
Abakan rond
Sisal 340 × 150 × 100
National Museum in Wrocław
pp.95–9

***Abakan vert* 1967–8**
Sisal 260 × 60 × 30
Private collection, Warsaw
p.182

***Black Garment* 1968**
Sisal 350 × 250 × 250
Collection Stedelijk Museum Amsterdam
pp.106–9

***Brown Coat* 1968**
Abakan Brown (Abakan brązowy)
Sisal 300 × 180 × 60
Henie Onstad Collection
pp.104–5

***Abakan Brown* 1969**
Sisal 300 × 300 × 150
Röhsska museet, Göteborg
pp.118–21

***Abakan Red* 1969**
Sisal 405 × 382 × 400
Tate
pp.124–9

***Unnamed Abakan (Abakan bez nazwy)* 1969**
Sisal 255 × 65 × 30
Fundacja Marty Magdaleny Abakanowicz Kosmowskiej i Jana Kosmowskiego

***Abakan Yellow (Abakan żółty)* 1970**
Abakan Yellow with Ropes (Abakan żółty z linami)
Sisal and rope 380 × 380 × 70
National Museum in Poznań, MNP Rw 1839
pp.130–3

***Abakan Festival (Abakan Festiwal)* 1971**
Sisal 370 × 100 × 100
National Museum in Wrocław
pp.102–3

***Abakan Orange* 1971**
Sisal 401 × 290 × 370
Tate
pp.134–5

***Abakan – Situation Variable II* 1971**
Sisal and rope 400 × 250 × 100
Art collection of the city of Biel-Bienne, Switzerland
pp.110–13

***Untitled* 1971**
Ink on paper 50.5 × 73
Fondation Toms Pauli, Lausanne. Gift of Alice Pauli
p.165

***Untitled* 1971**
Ink on paper 53 × 70
Fondation Toms Pauli, Lausanne. Gift of Alice Pauli
p.164

***Abakan January–February (Abakan Styczeń – Luty)* 1972**
Sisal 330 × 325 × 55
National Museum in Wrocław
pp.136–9 (and front cover)

***Head* 1974**
Burlap and resin 90 × 64 × 60
Fondation Toms Pauli, Lausanne. Gift of Pierre and Marguerite Magnenat

***Set of Black Organic Forms (Zespół czarnych form organicznych)* 1974**
Rope, canvas and sisal
Dimensions variable
Muzeum Sztuki, Łódź
p.81

***Black Ball (Czarna kula)* 1975**
Ball
Sisal 140 × 110 × 100
Private collection, Warsaw
pp.146–7

***Hand* 1975**
Little Object
Sisal 12 × 21 × 16
Fondation Toms Pauli, Lausanne. Gift of Pierre and Marguerite Magnenat

***Black Garment VI (Ubranie Czarne VI)* 1976**
Sisal 330 × 220 × 100
Central Museum of Textiles in Łódź
pp.114–17

***Head* 1976**
Face
The Centre
Sisal 30 × 12 × 12
Henie Onstad Collection

***Tube (Tuba)* 1976**
Sisal and burlap 300 × 90 × 90
Fundacja Marty Magdaleny Abakanowicz Kosmowskiej i Jana Kosmowskiego

***Pregnant* 1970–80**
Sisal and horsehair 135.9 × 106.7
Harkey Family Collection, Dallas, Texas
p.145

***Winter* 1975–80**
Grey Green
Sisal 320 × 360
Grażyna Kulczyk Collection
pp.140–3

***Embryology* 1978–81**
Burlap, cotton gauze, hemp rope, nylon and sisal
Dimensions variable
Tate
pp.174, 176–7

***Embryology* 1981**
Ink and charcoal on paper 63.5 × 49
Fondation Toms Pauli, Lausanne. Gift of Pierre and Marguerite Magnenat
p.161

***Embryology* 1981**
Ink, charcoal and graphite on paper 48.5 × 63
Fondation Toms Pauli, Lausanne. Gift of Pierre and Marguerite Magnenat
p.165

***Embryology* 1981**
Ink on paper 49 × 63
Fondation Toms Pauli, Lausanne. Gift of Pierre and Marguerite Magnenat
p.162

***Embryology* 1981**
Ink on paper 63 × 49
Fondation Toms Pauli, Lausanne. Gift of Pierre and Marguerite Magnenat
p.161

***Abakan Brown IV (Abakan Brązowy IV)* 1969–84**
Sisal 290 × 300 × 30
Central Museum of Textiles in Łódź
pp.122–3

***Cocoon (Kokon)* 1987**
Animal horns and steel 14 × 30 × 13
Fundacja Marty Magdaleny Abakanowicz Kosmowskiej i Jana Kosmowskiego

***Anasta* 1989**
Wood and steel 159 × 600 × 210
Marlborough Gallery, New York
pp.168–9

***From the Cycle 'Anonymous Portraits II'* 1989**
Cotton, resin, sand and wood
69 × 18 × 18
Fundacja Marty Magdaleny Abakanowicz Kosmowskiej i Jana Kosmowskiego

***Head of Rhinoceros (Głowa nosorożca)* c.1990**
Burlap and animal horn 60 × 40 × 79
Fundacja Marty Magdaleny Abakanowicz Kosmowskiej i Jana Kosmowskiego

***From the Cycle 'Flies'* 1993**
Charcoal on paper 75 × 100
Fundacja Marty Magdaleny Abakanowicz Kosmowskiej i Jana Kosmowskiego

***Black Face* 1994**
Charcoal on paper 100 × 75
Fundacja Marty Magdaleny Abakanowicz Kosmowskiej i Jana Kosmowskiego

***From the Cycle 'Flies'* 1994**
Charcoal on paper 75 × 100
Fundacja Marty Magdaleny Abakanowicz Kosmowskiej i Jana Kosmowskiego

***From the Cycle 'Flies'* 1994**
Charcoal on paper 100 × 75
Fundacja Marty Magdaleny Abakanowicz Kosmowskiej i Jana Kosmowskiego

***Showcase with 'Object in Old Suit'* 1996**
Iron, glass, burlap and animal horns
94.6 × 76.2 × 46.4
Fundacja Marty Magdaleny Abakanowicz Kosmowskiej i Jana Kosmowskiego

***Showcase with 'Pink Faces'* 1996**
Iron, glass and polyester 93 × 76 × 46
Fundacja Marty Magdaleny Abakanowicz Kosmowskiej i Jana Kosmowskiego

***Showcase with 'Unknown Object'* 1996**
Iron, glass, feathers, animal horns and steel 93 × 75.9 × 46.1
Fundacja Marty Magdaleny Abakanowicz Kosmowskiej i Jana Kosmowskiego

***Showcase with Horns* 1997**
Iron, glass and animal horns
94 × 76 × 46
Fundacja Marty Magdaleny Abakanowicz Kosmowskiej i Jana Kosmowskiego

***From Cycle 'Flowers' – Vere Dignum Flower* 1999**
Ink and charcoal on paper 100 × 75
Fundacja Marty Magdaleny Abakanowicz Kosmowskiej i Jana Kosmowskiego

Additional Works

Jarosław Brzozowski and Kazimierz Mucha
***Abakans (Abakany)* 1970**
35 mm film transferred to digital, colour, sound, 13 min 5 sec
WFO (Wytwórnia Filmów Oświatowych) 1970
pp.152, 154–9

Unknown artist, Papua New Guinea, Middle Sepik, Blackwater region
***Didagur – Female Initiation Mask* 1970s**
Plant fibre, clay, cassowary feathers
76 × 60 × 89
The Andrzej Wawrzyniak Asia and Pacific Museum in Warsaw, Poland. Donated by Magdalena Abakanowicz in 1978

INDEX

Page references in *italics* indicate pages on which artworks appear; all works are by Abakanowicz unless otherwise stated.

First published 2022 by order of the Tate Trustees by
Tate Publishing, a division of Tate Enterprises Ltd,
Millbank, London SW1P 4RG

www.tate.org.uk/publishing

on the occasion of the exhibition

Magdalena Abakanowicz

Tate Modern, London
17 November 2022 – 21 May 2023

Fondation Toms Pauli at the Musée cantonal des
Beaux-Arts de Lausanne/Plateforme 10, Lausanne
23 June – 24 September 2023

Henie Onstad Art Centre, Høvikodden
26 October 2023 – 25 February 2024

Supported by

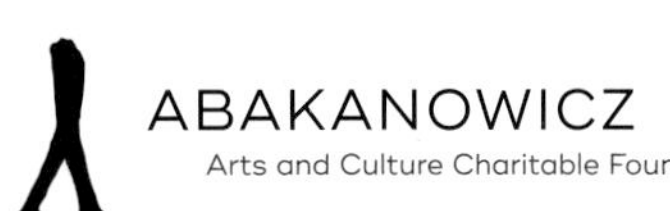

With additional support from the Magdalena Abakanowicz
Exhibition Supporters Circle:
The Polish Cultural Institute in London

Tate International Council, Tate Patrons and Tate Members

A catalogue record for this book is available from the British Library

ISBN 978-1-84976-673-9 (paperback)
ISBN 978-1-84976-836-8 (hardback)

Senior Editor: Emma Poulter
Production: Elizabeth Stanton and Bill Jones
Picture Researcher: Emma O'Neill
Art Direction: Astrid Stavro
Design: Sara Martin and Alessandro Molent
Colour reproduction by DL Imaging, London
Printed in Italy by Industria Grafica SIZ

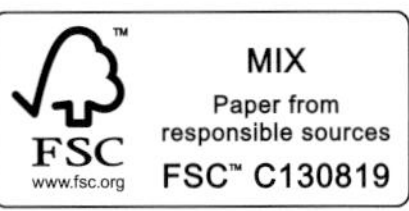

Measurements of artworks are given in centimetres,
height before width and depth

Front cover: Detail from *Abakan January-February* 1972 (see pp.136–9)
Back cover: Abakanowicz with *Abakans*, 1968
Frontispiece: Abakanowicz with *Black Garment* 1968 (see pp.106–9)
Page 4: Detail from *Abakan étroit* 1967–8 (see pp.89–93)

The contributors

Dina Akhmadeeva is Assistant Curator, International Art, Tate.

Iwona Dorota Bigos is Head of the Four Domes Pavilion, the contemporary art branch of the National Museum in Wrocław.

Ann Coxon is Curator, International Art, Tate.

Mary Jane Jacob is an independent curator and Professor, School of the Art Institute of Chicago.

Michał Jachuła is an art historian and Curator, Zachęta – National Gallery of Art in Warsaw.

Magali Junet is Curator, Fondation Toms Pauli at the Musée cantonal des Beaux-Arts de Lausanne/Plateforme 10.

Marta Kowalewska is an art historian and critic, and Chief Curator, Central Museum of Textiles in Łódź.

Claire Lilley is a curator and Director of Programme, Yorkshire Sculpture Park, Wakefield.

Magdalena Moskalewicz is an art historian and curator specialising in Eastern European art, and Assistant Professor, Adjunct, School of the Art Institute of Chicago.

Gabi Scardi is an art historian, contemporary art curator and writer.

Caroline Ugelstad is Chief Curator, Henie Onstad Art Centre.